MW00812664

Published by

 ANSIR PUBLISHING CORPORATION
Huntsville, Alabama, USA
Website URL: http://ansir.com
Email: info@ansir.com

Printed in USA
December, 2000
Copyright©2000 S. Seich

Original work, *Ansir for One, 14 rare conversations*,
Copyright ©1998 Ansir Communications Inc.
Author: S. Seich.
(Ansir Website) Co-developed by Seich & Clarke

ISBN: 1-929067-00-3

ANSIR COMMUNICATIONS INC.

What Test participants are saying....

"Hands down, this personality test beats any of the others I have come across. It is rare to find a test both so eloquent and so accurate that the results brought tears to my eyes because of the Truth it spoke."

Rick, Calif. USA, Visionary/Philosopher/Healer

"Accurate to the point of absurdity! It is like reading your autobiography, without remembering that you just wrote it. How someone other than myself can know me so well is almost a frightening prospect. This is incredible."

Ben, Ontario Canada, Visionary/Eccentrik/Idealist

"This test amazed me. I was expecting to be put into a broad personality category, instead I was told intimate details about myself, including examples of actions taken in situations. The Ansir test confirmed my self-proclaimed strong points, but also showed my faults. With this information I can work on improving myself."

S., Texas, USA, Realist/Kinsmen/Realist

"Fascinating. A must do and have for anyone interested in knowing honestly who they really are."

P., St. Maarten, Caribbean, Eccentrik/Sage/Visionary

"I was very impressed, it was like looking at a reflection of truths known but not spoken."

S. Johannesburg, South Africa Visionary/Visionary/Idealist

"A riveting, revealing ride! And this from the mind of a skeptic. Just imagine what a pleasant surprise it was to read my Profile. This test is accurate and I'm definitely impressed."

A., Nairobi, Kenya, Diligent/Healer/Sentinel

"The results of this dead-on personality profile are couched in a language that is so exquisitely crafted that even if nothing else came from this test—and a great deal *does*—it would be worth exploring just for the exquisite writing."

Moyra, NM, USA, Evokateur/Eccentrik/Visionary

...excerpts from "Ansir-in-Action" at www. ansir.com

Evokateur /Evokateur/ Philosopher—Profile Boss: Evokateur

Colleges everywhere wanted Julie, including M.I.T. Instead, she turned "tricks all day, every day for 3 months. Drugs kept me going, and I fed off the depravity." Her distrust of everything and everybody showed up the first time she took the Ansir test, and too many things didn't fit. "Then I sat there and said, 'Why are you lying?' This person who'd shown up in the test was the person I had been living all those years, but was somebody I'd made up to protect myself." She retested with a different attitude. Her test results this time were real. "You can put up all the false fronts you want, but do you really want to live your life like that? Ansir showed me there's no need to lie to yourself or anyone else about who you are." Julie got her degree and is pursuing a career in neuropsychiatry, profoundly grateful that life has given her a second chance.

Philosopher /Healer/ Empath—Profile Boss: Healer

"It really freed me to know that I don't have to convince people of my point-of-view, because sometimes they just aren't going to understand. The Healer working profile confirmed what I knew to be me but hadn't acknowledged or used to advantage. Working with only dead people and criminals in forensics wasn't going to be fulfilling." She made a career change and went into the field of epidemiology, where she brings her full intuitive power to the search for better means of treatment.

...excerpts cont'd Pg. 519

ANSIR STANDS FOR

A New Style In Relating

. . . and we really mean it!

Participants, Members, and professionals call this work "out-of-the-box." Well, if talking directly to people and listening and watching closely are out-of-the-box, we qualify. Every word you are about to read is based on thousands of conversations, between Ansir and everyday people. We confidently and honestly state that this work is of, for, and by everyday people, striving to make ends meet and hoping to find some joy and meaningful reward along the way.

We understand striving and hoping so well that we've dedicated our resources and time to finding answers to the most common and pressing personal questions—how to achieve success and happiness?

This book is but step one toward that goal. In *3 Sides of You*, we poke and probe humourously, take you apart from the inside out honestly, and put you back *more* together respectfully. We offer our findings more in the style of an interesting story, than a dry, serious study.

You're about to read truths about yourself and others that'll make you scratch your head in wonder at our knowing and/or daring. Many consider this a bold and brave undertaking. That's the only shade or shape truth comes in, we've found.

3 Sides of You is a complete revision of an earlier published work entitled, *Ansir for One, 14 rare conversations* (by Ansir Communications Inc., October 1998). We've grown, restructured, and learned a lot since then—mostly that participants wanted and were ready for more indepth explanation. In terms of approach and applicability, no work in existence compares to Ansir's.

Pg. ii

Frankly, no one was more surprised than author Seich, to discover that people not only understood but were hungry for more. You asked for more beef! Here it is. *3 Sides of You* is a sticks-to-your-ribs serving.

This completes level one research. Everything we've thus far learned about personality Styles is included in this stem-to-stern revision. Our focus now turns to level two, so get self-smart and join us, as we move from realization and understanding of Profiled potential, to its practical application in terms of individual fulfillment.

In level two we'll walk as you (as Ansir Profiled) in the real world and discover what happens when in company; when collaborating; when cuddling: and when clashing with other personality Styles. The underlying Ansir premise is this: personal success and happiness may be self-defined and measured, but are directly or indirectly dependent upon others.

Learn about self and others in *3 Sides of You*. The real time and life-serious fun continues in our NEXT work. Meanwhile, enjoy and learn from this eye-opening, self-freeing book. We promise two things. By the end of your read, you won't look at yourself or another in quite the same take-for-granted way as before. And you won't be bored while learning why.

Ansir offers there is nothing on this planet more complex and infinitely fascinating than the people who populate it. Like many who have experienced Ansir, you too may develop a new style of relating.

We don't want to change the world; we want you to. And here's a bookful of reasons that justifies our being confident you can.

TABLE OF CONTENTS

Section I of II
The Ansir Experience

Section II of II
About ANSIR

Everything

begins with the *3 Sides of You* test!

3 SIDES OF YOU TEST

Premise!

The test is founded on the ancient belief that humans are 3-sided beings. Philosophers and spiritualists have long espoused similar convictions. Plato's vision of Reason/Passion/Appetite is similar to the Bible's Mind/Body/Soul. At Ansir, we are most comfortable with the terms *Thinking/Working/Emoting*.

Thinking:
A discernible, predictable pattern of balancing and applying knowledge. How individuals process order, solve problems, and rationalize outcomes.

Working:
The conscious application of knowledge according to acquired skills and innate abilities of individuals.

Emoting:
An unconscious response pattern guided by unique intangibles, such as emotions, feelings, and nature.

As thousands have already learned and confirmed through Ansir, Self-understanding and Self-acceptance lead to greater Self-confidence, which can greatly enhance every facet of your life and living experience.

The 3 Sides of You!

Ansir's corporate test is a PAID online-only service

Ansir's consumer test is FREE and only available at the Website:
www.ansir.com

Profile results are returned upon completion of the test.

30 Minutes

That's all it takes for you to experience the only self-perception system created of, for, and by everyday people. The **3 Sides of You!** test measures self-perception. Our research offers invaluable insight into your dominant Style of thinking, working, and emoting.

We recommend:

When you take the test, it's best if you are alone and not likely to be disturbed or distracted. Take your time. Questions are personality-specific. This is not a "first thing that pops to mind" test. It requires thought and above all, self-honesty.

It's best to take the whole test at one sitting. You may retest as often as you'd like, or as often as needed to find your right Profile. Retesting to find your right Profile may not make sense to you now, but it will; once you realize that Ansir's Self-perception test is unlike any test you've taken before. The answers are yours, not ours.

About the Test!

There are 3-sections (realms), Thinking, Working, and Emoting. Each section has 56-questions. Participants rank Ansir's test, *3 Sides of You*, as one of the toughest but most accurate experiences on the Web.

Don't just take our word for it. Read the words of surprised others, then see for yourself if their view differs from yours.

"I have taken many personality tests and inventories online but this one has impressed me the most. It was not only accurate, it was frighteningly insightful."

—D. Ontario, Canada...Profile: Diligent/Healer/Empath...Profile Boss: Healer

"Absolutely, stupefyingly brilliant. I've taken the test four times in the last year; allowing sufficient time to pass between testings. Every result comes up the same. Unbelievably amazing."

—C., KY, USA...Profile: Visionary/Sage/Idealist...Profile Boss: Idealist

"Being a sociology major with a minor in psychology, I have taken a number of these tests. So far, this has been the one that has been the most accurate in its synopsis of my 'Self-perceived' personality."

—J., Louisiana, USA...Profile: Diligent/Visionary/Kinsmen...Profile Boss: Visionary

"I am amazed, I took the Myers-Briggs personality test, which told me a lot, however, this indeed is much more enlightening."

—K., Texas, USA...Profile: Empath/Extremist/Sentinel...Profile Boss: Sentinel

BONUS!

Ansir hosts a one-of-a-kind Community, where those who seek intelligent Chat, Discussion Boards, Peer-support, and creative outlet, gather. At Ansir you're not a stranger; you're Profile familiar.

OVERVIEW

Ansir's Profiling System!

3 Sides of You measures the Dominant Style of functioning in
3 major realms: Thinking /Working /Emoting

14 Ansir Personality Styles

2,744 possible Profile combinations

Core Functioning	Personality Style
Physicals...	Extremist & Realist
Instinctives...	Scintillator & Sentinel
Logicals...	Diligent & Sage
Practicals...	Eccentrik & Idealist
Emotionals...	Kinsmen & Empath
Intuitives...	Visionary & Evokateur
Spiritualists...	Healer & Philosopher

TEST RESULTS
An Ansir Profile
www.ansir.com

There are 2,744 Profile combinations possible in Ansir's Self-perception Profiling system. Finding your own right Profile is the hardest but most important step.

A sample Profile summary

Congratulations (*your own first name*)
You have completed the first and most difficult step toward greater self-understanding.

Your *3 Sides of You* Profile is:
Dominant Style of Thinking: (*automatically filled in from test results*)
Dominant Style of Working: (*automatically filled in from test results*)
Dominant Style of Emoting: (*automatically filled in from test results*)

Your summary also includes *Snapshots,* a listing of the most common characteristics for each of the 3-dominant Styles in your Profile. Ansir's *7-Profile Keys* provide full explanation.

UNLOCKING POTENTIAL

7 Profile Keys

7 VIEWS

Profile Understanding!

To get the most out of your Ansir experience, we offer 7 magnified views of your test results—your Profile. The views are presented as 7-Keys of understanding. In combination, the depth of understanding offered has proven to be personally helpful and powerful. *Everything* at *Ansir* begins with the test!

KEY 1: *Snapshots and Briefs*

Short descriptions of 3-dominant Profile Styles to help you determine if you've found your right Profile. If not, return to the test and adjust your answers for a better fit.

KEY 2: *Profile Boss*

You've found the dominant *3 Sides of You.* Who's in charge?

KEY 3: *Profile InDepth*

You've got your right Profile and met your Boss. Now it's time for in-depth exploration and enjoyment.

KEY 4: Life Purpose

Why are you *thusly* Profiled?

KEY 5: *Achilles' Heel*

What can get in the way of your success and happiness?

KEY 6: *Headhunter Shorthand*

Work attributes and occupation insight to help plan a more fulfilling career.

KEY 7: *Match/Mismatch (Style Sexuality is only available at the Website)*

What personality Styles are compatible with you?

Profile Snapshots

Concise overview of Ansir's 14-personality Styles

THE PHYSICALS

Characteristics Typical of this Personality Style

Thinking • They are risk-takers who plan with safety in mind but by the time testing begins, they've removed most safety nets.

• They are ultra-instinctive and able to predict behaviours or likely outcomes of man, animal, or machine.

Working • They are drawn to high-risk careers and dangerous recreational pastimes.

• They are highly intelligent and creative, and capable of 'smooth talking' like no other.

Emoting • They are often happiest and shine their brightest in stressful situations.

• Intimacy and romantic commitment may not last longer than a one-night stand.

THE PHYSICALS

Realist

Characteristics Typical of this Personality Style

Thinking • They are ever-ready to lend a helpful hand to friend or team.

    • They can fix what's broken, unlike any other.

Working • They are leaders who get the job done, no matter what.

    • They have intelligent hands.

Emoting • They are renowned for being quick-tempered.

    • Sex is often no more than pure expression of physical pleasure.

THE INSTINCTIVES

Characteristics Typical of this Personality Style

Thinking • They are the eternal optimists.

• They have an in-born knack for simplifying complicated tasks.

Working • They are easy-going, competent workers, whose potential for excellence and success often must be encouraged.

• They are natural leaders who emphasize team camaraderie.

Emoting • When confronted by anger, they head for the door.

• They can't sit still without fidgeting in discomfort.

THE INSTINCTIVES

Characteristics Typical of this Personality Style

Thinking • Loyalty and honour are favourite words and highest praise.

• They approach "new" with caution and suspicion.

Working • Generally, they are physically attractive but appear unapproachable.

• They are not afraid to speak up for themselves or for others when called for.

Emoting • No pain is greater for them than betrayal.

• They keep diaries or personal journals.

THE LOGICALS

Characteristics Typical of this Personality Style

Thinking • There's a right way and a wrong way of doing everything, and they know the most right way of all.

• They perform best when given their own realm of responsibility.

Working • They are reliable and dependable workers, who respect hierarchical order of command.

• Logical and perfectionistic, they check and re-check work, and resent being rushed.

Emoting • They are highly responsible providers for their families.

• They are pack rats who fill basements and attics with things that could be useful again, or that have value only to them.

THE LOGICALS

Characteristics Typical of this Personality Style

Thinking • They lose track of personal items and hardly notice clocks and calendars.

• They're often found to be extremely intelligent.

Working • They may be poor organizers of time and work, but few deliver projects as "well done."

• They are best at finding solution despite confusion or complication

Emoting • A great joy of theirs is exchanging ideas and exploring new perspectives with others.

• They readily assimilate with culture and philosophy, and are non-judgemental in their dealings with others.

http://www.ansir.com

THE PRACTICALS

Characteristics Typical of this Personality Style

Thinking • They may dress flamboyantly and act outrageously
but there's nothing flaky about them.

• They can mentally design and manipulate objects.

Working • Professionally, they seek cutting-edge industries or interests.

• They prefer working alone to teamwork.

Emoting • They are admirers and collectors of the *avante* and
eclectic—in art and friend.

• They prefer emotional intensity over familiarity, and
tend to change mind *and mate* often.

THE PRACTICALS

Idealist

Characteristics Typical of this Personality Style

Thinking • When these perfectionists reach solution, flow charts, schedules, and procedures mentally form and click into place.

• High stress for them is not being in control of all matters pertaining to them.

Working • They are the most competitive of all, and with their determined, quick-thinking they tend not to lose.

• These individuals are natural entrepreneurs...and dyed-in-the-wool workaholics.

Emoting • They like upper-class lifestyles, fast cars, and expensive gifts.

• They measure success by wealth and power.

THE EMOTIONALS

Characteristics Typical of this Personality Style

Thinking • Family is a common thread running through all they think and do.

• They are gifted negotiators.

Working • They prefer intrapreneurship to entrepreneurship.

• One word describes them best: responsible.

Emoting • They trust intellect over emotions.

• They have a tendency to become over-zealous about new concepts or ideas.

THE EMOTIONALS

Characteristics Typical of this Personality Style

Thinking • By proximity, they can tune into the emotional state of others.

• They are often unaware of their own intuitive power.

Working • These gentle individuals feel successful when they encourage others to be successful.

• They are natural-born teachers and instructors.

Emoting • Their emotions bubble over easily and unexpectedly.

• They may confuse being used with being needed.

THE INTUITIVES

Visionary

Characteristics Typical of this Personality Style

Thinking • When they solve problems, they focus on what's not been said or done.

• They have extremely strong egos.

Working • They're driven to do something significant with their lives.

• They want to be recognized and remembered for their achievements.

Emoting • Many are intimidated by the confidence they exude.

• They're impatient.

THE INTUITIVES

Characteristics Typical of this Personality Style

Thinking • They are the most creative individuals and often the oddest.

• They generally conduct their everyday living with seeming detachment.

Working • When focused, they're difficult to distract.

• Their creative genius is often unknown to others.

Emoting • To them the world in general is somewhat barbaric, and people, hurried and harsh.

• They're extraordinarily cautious about long-term commitments.

THE SPIRITUALISTS

Characteristics Typical of this Personality Style

Thinking • Avid, even voracious readers, they prefer non-fiction and biographies to fiction.

• They are keenly sensitive to noise and uncomfortable in messy environments.

Working • When they solve problems, they look at its effect and impact on the system as a whole.

• They have a natural talent for any field or endeavour where healing is involved.

Emoting • They have a personal and intimate relationship with a Higher Power.

• They tend to be highly protective of their privacy.

THE SPIRITUALISTS

Characteristics Typical of this Personality Style

Thinking • They question the need and reason for rules to the extent of being thought trouble-makers.

• Most of their higher or academic-level learning is done outside classrooms.

Working • As employees they refuse to tell others what to do and will not assume responsibility for any other's doing.

• They generally choose highly-specialized fields or industries and contract-out their services.

Emoting • Individual first and gender second is their order of priority and importance in choosing a mate.

• Dishonesty or deception are not practiced nor tolerated by them.

14 Ansir Personality Styles
2,744 Profile Combinations are possible

Core Functioning	Personality Style
Physicals...	Extremist & Realist
Instinctives...	Scintillator & Sentinel
Logicals...	Diligent & Sage
Practicals...	Eccentrik & Idealist
Emotionals...	Kinsmen & Empath
Intuitives...	Visionary & Evokateur
Spiritualists...	Healer & Philosopher

1 Profile Briefs

Dominant Style of Thinking

Profile Briefs™ are short, accurate descriptions of Ansir's 14-personality Styles. Initially they're helpful to new testers, in determining correctness of Profile. Thereafter, they're a quick and concise guide for identifying the personality Style of others you're interested in knowing better. From Profile Briefs, proceed to *Key 3: Profile InDepths* for greater insight and understanding.

http://www.ansir.com

THE PHYSICALS

Extremist

This is a head, not heart personality. Extremists are highly creative individuals, whose intellectual ability is often right off the measurement scale. Outsmarting death, the system, and others, is an adrenaline rush they not only seek but seem to need.

The master of hand for them is mind. When planning a new project or dangerous feat, their approach is logical and linear. They organize a solution system and meticulously follow through in step-by-step order and fashion. Their "tend" is to spend considerable time in the planning and organizing phases of projects. Analyzing all aspects down to the nittiest of grittys, they calculate problems and anticipate emergencies. Extremist thoroughness is necessary. Danger is a shadow-close companion of theirs.

The greatest gift of this personality is extraordinary physical sense and sensitivity. Their physical antennae and smarts can be so uncanny, so sophisticated, that when focused they assimilate with the object or subject of interest. This rare and cellular gift enables them to predict behaviours and outcomes under the most stressful of conditions.

THE PHYSICALS

Realists are goal-oriented and masterful orchestrators of plan and action…and usually won't tackle a project unless confident they have the necessary skills to succeed. If they say they can, they can and they do. These are confident and very proud individuals.

The physical world makes logical sense to them. Order and procedure lead to step-by-step progression, and action and consequence unfold predictably within the confines and limits of known. Realists have extraordinarily sophisticated internal-energy. Most think first, then determine a course of action. Realists feel, act, then think.

Realists have intelligent hands. For them, tools are but extensions of mind. Theirs, is a practical genius. They quickly become application experts but may have difficulty explaining the theory.

While others are still assessing and deciding, these individuals are usually up to their elbows busily doing and smartly acting—a natural, physical gift that ranks them nonpareil in emergency situations. Realists have the most powerful and efficient internal generator of all. However, such extraordinary energy can be balm or bane for them.

THE INSTINCTIVES

Scintillator

Scintillators live to please others, and until formal schooling begins, they do...and quite remarkably, too. They tend to smile earlier and more often than other infants. Most are easy to please, highly affectionate, and social-charmers by the age of two. They are bright, often the first to speak full sentences and they exhibit superior small-motor control.

Many child actors and models are of Scintillator Style because they tend to be more socially adept and outgoing than others. Engaging the body in any learning process cements knowledge for them. One of their natural talents is comedy. Scintillator minds virtually sizzle with comedic creativity and improvisational wonder. Many actors, performers, and artists of all status and stage are Scintillator to some degree.

Of all their talents, one of their strongest aptitudes is kinesthetic intelligence: a memory for movement and motion. Scintillators would sooner identify a suspect walking on the street or mingling in a crowd, than if standing in a police lineup. They are quick learners who can try something once and have the task mastered.

THE INSTINCTIVES

entinel

Sentinels read underlying meanings, veiled messages, subtleties of tone, texture, shade, and rhyme that reveal more than words explain. They hear before others, the bumps in the night, the knock under the hood, and the computer whistling when improperly shut down. Equally uncanny is their physical identification process which is intimate, accurate, and uncompromising.

Two curiously interesting characteristics of Sentinels are keen sense of smell and hearing. They may very well be the human bloodhounds whose nose-intelligence is highly prized in perfume and wine-making industries. Sentinels approach problem-solving by developing solution systems and logically, methodically, following through in step-by-step fashion. Sentinel, though more introverted than outgoing, is a very strong personality: sharp-minded, definite of opinion, and confident in action. Upholding and defending the concepts of just and fair seem biologically programmed into these individuals, who look after kin and own without fear or hesitation.

THE LOGICALS

Born competent and capable, Diligents harbour executive excellence and are the backbone of the business world. For these cerebral beings, reality conforms to the bounds and strictures of logic. Diligents play with ideas and make sport of problems.

When Diligent starts a project, they do so from the premise of a clearly defined problem and set objective. They then gather all relevant information, organize a system for its solution, roll up their sleeves, and with notebook in one hand and pen in the other, begin working Step One of their plan. Once all criteria have been met, checked, and rechecked again, they use that as foundation for processing Step Two. Detail and data are their barometer of progress. By criteria of fact do they measure success. This sequential, methodical, and meticulous approach is repeated at each level of development and through to completion. Throughout, they cannot and will not be rushed. They have developed and perfected their purely logical, note-taking approach for a reason. Diligent hates being wrong.

THE LOGICALS

Sage

Past events are so vividly imprinted on Sage, they recount them as freshly today as when they occurred. These individuals, with their gentle, unassuming manner, tend to be sociable and highly endeared.

Sages think randomly and often earn a reputation for being scattered and unorganized. For instance, solving a jigsaw puzzle is a linear mental process. Most start with a few core-fitting pieces then hunt, match, and build piece-by-piece, from core to completed puzzle. Sage, however, starts not at puzzle piece but at puzzle whole. Firmly holding a clear mental image of the puzzle, as if already solved, they move the scattered pieces to their proper place, matching location and arrangement with their completed mental image.

A passer-by may not immediately discern pattern of solution or stage of progress. Closer inspection, however, would reveal that though unorganized and though riddled by space and gap, viewed collectively the strewn tabletop bears an uncanny resemblance to the completed puzzle— only lacking in fit and snap.

THE PRACTICALS

Weird is a term Eccentrik becomes familiar with at an early age. For others, such labelling can be a tripping, burdensome cross to bear. For Eccentriks, weird is the wind beneath their creative wings and what lifts their pride beyond pedestrian concern.

There is something within them, some intrinsic fortitude that cannot bend as willow to wind. Eccentriks cannot and will not bend to accommodate. Once on their independent own, the Eccentrik butterfly emerges with a steely-determination to tailor life to fit them regardless of social norm or mores.

What is unique about the Eccentrik mind is its ability to internally rotate ideas. These are purely logical beings who approach problem-solving methodically and with step-by-step thoroughness. Always lurking in the back of Eccentrik minds is the question of whether or not their idea is workable—meaning producible. An idea that cannot be physically realized is a waste of their time.

THE PRACTICALS

An Idealist mind is a marvel of bedazzling complication and bedizzying speed. Few arrive at solution or deliver it faster than them. While their solutions may not be the only nor necessarily the best, their solutions have proven best enough and often enough to sail global economies.

Few experiences return them greater pleasure than creative problem-solving: their gifted-forté. They are the architects of dreams, the managers and overseers who shore-up and bank leading edges that others will later walk. Globally, historically, and evolutionarily, the movers and shakers among us are the ones who aren't easily nor readily pleased: the Idealists.

They usually only want (or *want for*) two things: money and managerial freedom. To have complete control over all aspects of a project is their dictionary-definition of satisfying. They love money and are generally very good at managing it. (*Any test participant who cannot balance a cheque book yet perceives Idealist as their Dominant Style of Thinking, please stop here and retest. The further and more that follows isn't you, either*).

THE EMOTIONALS

*K*insmen

High energy and organization are hallmarks of these busy individuals. Kinsmen enjoy a wide variety of interests, though for a vast majority music and fitness were found to figure prominently. Others, generally and genuinely "like" wide-smiling and warmly approachable Kinsmen. Most feel safe around them and for good reason. Kinsmen take care of others.

Like most logicals, when Kinsmen tackle a job or project, they start from the premise of a well-defined problem and a clear objective. However, in Kinsmen solution systems there is one personality-typical step that differentiates their approach from all others. At set intervals, Kinsmen makes allowance for consensus-taking. All privy and party to outcomes are invited to review their state of progress, to opine, and give their nod of approval before Kinsmen feels confident about proceeding .

Not fulfilling obligations, when and as promised, is demoralizing for conscientious Kinsmen. With their highly-evolved sense of responsibility and strong need to please, no other is as self-critical or as quick to don the mantle of blame, as them.

THE EMOTIONALS

Empath

From infancy, purely emotional Empaths intuit the world around them. They feel so intensely about everything that others can be confused by the depth and range of their expression—from uncontrollable laughter to inconsolable tears; sometimes both at once. Empaths respond quickly and personally to all and environment. For others it can be disconcerting, but for them, emotionality is the throne upon which their one-of-a-kind intellect sits.

When you know answers but can't explain how, cannibalistic self-doubt can gnaw and weaken confidence. Empaths often doubt their own emotion wisdom and try to be "logical" instead, which for these emotion-intellects is like swimming against nature.

Linear, step-by-step thinking must be taught to Empaths. In school, gold stars of former glory grades often turn into *good grief* by junior high. This is usually when their academic confidence plummets. Doubt can clip their potential's wings before they even attempt flight and before they test their unique intellectual superiority. These individuals often do not know they are born to do one thing better than any other—because of and based solely on, their birth gift.

THE INTUITIVES

Visionary

They tend to be ponderous thinkers and drop-of-a-hat dreamers, and don't mind passing time alone doing both. Able, and conscientious, they tend to inspire confidence in others. Enough so, to generally be thought likely to succeed. Historically, as evolutionarily, Visionarys are the most wealthy, powerful, and happy entrepreneurs on the planet. They've usually seen and smelled more of life's *kaka*, before passing the "Visionary Lesson," than most experience in a lifetime or more. Where most would buckle in ruin or run from the pressure, Visionary confronts head-on.

They're not only critical linear-thinkers who exceed solution and surpass expectation; they're intuitives. While Idealist can travel logic's path at lightning speed and find solution from step 1 through 10, in the same time, Visionary travels from step 1 through 40 and not only finds solution but returns with a mental blueprint, marketing strategy, and a coloured snapshot of the completed project. These individuals have potential to blaze and raze intellectually. What differentiates them from most is how they cope under pressure.

THE INTUITIVES

Evokateur

For them, being peculiar is more than nature, it is necessity. As north IS, as south IS, Evokateurs ARE the most unusual beings on the planet, bar none. These ones must be peculiar in order to fulfill their life purpose.

In everyday life, they generally choose spectator seats or assume sideline positions rather than join others in the fray, play, and decision-making. They prefer the rich fantasies and swirling tapestries of their own chimera to outerworld reality, and often conduct their living with a detached remoteness that's less than normal but more than aloof.

It's difficult for others to comprehend a world within a world, far less comprehend those who have one. Who among can imagine an internal reality that's more intimate, more satisfying, and more fulfilling than the reality we know as world and call home—but it is so, for Evokateurs.

There's a good reason for Evokateur oddness. It's the uniform most commonly worn by greatness.

THE SPIRITUALISTS

Three of the most common characteristics of Healer children and adults are: sensitivity to noise, aversion to mess and clutter, and a great need for privacy. For them there are no coincidences in life. Everything happens for a reason.

Most personality styles have unique and definite patterns of thinking. Idealists see patterns through time, Eccentriks mentally spin and sculpt, Diligents build step-by-step, and Visionarys see what is not here or there yet. To understand how Healers think, it's necessary to first understand that spiritualists are not step-by-step, logical thinkers. These individuals head straight for solution and leave both the proving and explaining to others.

In school, they tend to be consistent and conscientious but average students, until introduced to subjects that pique their curiosity. Their tendency then is to astonish with the range and flex of their sparked intellect.

One peculiarity of this personality is a common, even characteristic, fear of incarceration. Healers tend to behave well within the bounds of propriety and inside society limits. Needless to say, their personal and professional ethics supersede those of man and land.

THE SPIRITUALISTS

For no other personality can childhood and adulthood be such a trial-by-fire experience. Their sharp edges harden quickly to resist being blunted and dulled by external force or influence. Because of parent and peer pressure to conform, at an early age, these confidentOnes adopt a boxer's stance when dealing with others. With fists raised and determination coiled, they wage a war of independence against a one-size-fits-all world.

Philosophers seek in-depth explanation and drown-deep experience. There's no peace for the parent who teaches their Philosopher child how to tell time yet neglects to provide them a watch or clock for their own time keeping. Abrupt interruptions can be physically painful for them. Rousing them from sleep can be a rude-awakening for all.

14 Ansir Personality Styles
2,744 Profile Combinations are possible

Core Functioning	Personality Style
Physicals...	Extremist & Realist
Instinctives...	Scintillator & Sentinel
Logicals...	Diligent & Sage
Practicals...	Eccentrik & Idealist
Emotionals...	Kinsmen & Empath
Intuitives...	Visionary & Evokateur
Spiritualists...	Healer & Philosopher

1
Profile Briefs

Dominant Style of Working

THE PHYSICALS

Extremist

They are lords and masters of the physical world, for whom the term adventurer is most apropos. Extremists not only pushed the envelope through time, they ripped it open and stepped inside. Many never walked out again. But don't call them heroes; they wouldn't understand. Quick-thinking and quickest tongue are hallmarks of theirs. These ones could sell that proverbial ice to those proverbial Eskimos…for they've usually perfected the art of persuasion before age three.

In sales, they harbour star-potential. As though pre-programmed with agenda and over-packaged with confidence to meet it, these dynamos can't be deterred once mind and energy lock on a course of action. And, they're creative to the *nth degree*. Extremist can outrun, outwit, and out-last most others. Trial and tribulation aren't strangers to them; quitting is.

THE PHYSICALS

They're comfortable and capable in the physical world, their chief realm of functioning. Determined and tenacious doubt-removers, Realist breathes three-dimensional life into idea, concept, vision, and dream. There may be movers and shakers in the world, but Realists are the ones who position all that's moved and shaken—and who then develop, dispatch, and dispose of all after.

"What merit, what application, what authority, and when wanted?" is bottom-line Realist.

On-the-fly revisions are their particular specialty. They excel in public service fields where physical aptitude, stamina, and team coordination are emphasized. Somewhat egotistical, Realist thrives on recognition and outshining others. They like having control over their work matters and outcomes. What they do and how much they've done are their measures of personal value.

THE INSTINCTIVES

Scintillator

Dramatic and charismatic, these larger-than-life and natural leaders improve the workplace upon entry. One common oversight in business is taking them at face-value rather than looking beyond at potential. Without encouragement, Scintillators may only do enough to "get by." As natural for them as bend to elbow, Scintillators read energy levels of others and react propitiously. From tone of voice, flush of face, sweaty palms, or general countenance and deportment can they interpret the general state of others. But then, it was Scintillator who brought the science of body language to the world's attention.

Task-cutting and time-saving are their name's fame. If a shortcut is possible, turn the challenge over to a Scintillator. They'll find a way. Sometimes their creative laziness not only saves but pays dividends.

As agile of mind as body, these individuals tend to have an innate artistic bent as though born to entertain and create. Success for these individuals is a given, when they make career choices that work with their nature rather than against it. There is always much more to Scintillator than meets the eye.

THE INSTINCTIVES

Sentinel

Sentinels solve problems in linear order and meet deadlines conscientiously. They pay attention to details, so their conclusions are usually above reproach or dispute. They are team players who respect prescribed procedure, and are more comfortable when job objectives and expectations are clearly spelled out. Responsibly, Sentinels don't say they can or they will unless they're qualified and capable, not just of doing but of doing well.

Their keenest intellect is their sensory, gut-deep smarts—what accounts for their exceptionality and adds to their workplace value. For instance, in sales Sentinel ranks among the top achievers. With their unique sense-*ability* for reading between the lines, they're able to deliver what clients want more often than others. This cellular skill is an asset that Sentinel is often not aware of. Instead, many think they have a sensitive stomach for that's the cubby hole that houses their one-of-a-kind gift.

THE LOGICALS

Diligent knows how to work, likes to work, and knows how to get things done right the first time around. Their working style is methodical, logical, systematic, and perfectionistic. They are the workplace "pick of the litter" when the call is for dedication, loyalty, and thoroughness. They're worker bees with an impressive intellect and an unwavering dedication to the task, to the goal, and to the company's future.

Detail is their particular ease and expertise. Data measures progress and against the criteria of fact do they gauge success. They will not be rushed, take shortcuts, nor leave until the job meets their satisfaction. And they perform as precisely and reliably day in and day out...though not uncomplainingly.

Routine and predictability are reassuring to security-conscious, goal-oriented Diligent, who also tends to be an early riser. Throughout history, education and business have been modelled along Diligent principles of hard work, logic, discipline, honesty, a penny saved is a penny earned, God-fearing, and gold watch retirement. But old world dinosaurs they are not! As Tonto was to The Lone Ranger, Diligent is to movers and shakers.

THE LOGICALS

Sage

Sage likes challenges, the tougher the better. When they settle at their desk, they start where they last stopped, as if sleep or time had not intervened. Picking up threads from where last left-off is part of the mystery of their particular genius. From initial introduction, Sage *sees* projects as already completed. For them, each component or piece and part is equally important to the whole, so order of completion is irrelevant. They do "all" at once.

Sages are not necessarily team players or effective team leaders. They tend to do their best work alone and excel at finding alternatives to current policies and procedures. Organization of self, far less of team members, is often more than they can handle. However, as a team contributor, few prove as valuable or as generous with information. Regardless of the profession they pursue or the corporate role they play, Sage contributes intellectually and socially. They advance workplace success whilst promoting workplace camaraderie.

THE PRACTICALS

Eccentrik

Eccentrik usually decides well-in-advance who may or may not read their resumé. These individuals are success driven, goal-oriented, and astute business people. They participate on turf of their own choosing and keep time by their own watches.

As they live their lives on the tottering edge of eccentricity, personally, they seek cutting edges, professionally. Industries, fields, and ventures where success is yet to be proven, rules yet to be written, and environments without cookie-cutter-constraint are where these individualists excel. Eccentrik is not a pie-in-the-sky theorist, though pie-in-the-face is not beneath them. They are three-dimensional business realists for whom an idea without form, function, and marketability is an idea wasted. Theirs is a tactile, profit-oriented relationship with creativity and they tend to thrive on tight deadlines, often purposely mismanaging time to sweeten the challenge with a dollop of their own added pressure.

When Eccentrik's head lowers, remarkability's rise portents.

THE PRACTICALS

Idealist

Idealist strengths are leadership and management. Assuming responsibility for the whole of projects rather than for piecemeal contributions is bathrobe comfort for them. Innate perfectionistic tendencies combined with an unwavering focus on goals, has earned Idealists a reputation for being intense and bull-headed…as well as successful. They drive everyone hard but self hardest of all. To them, compromise is a dirty word.

Work is the main focus of their lives. These individuals immerse themselves for the long-haul and seem to have inexhaustible energy. It is not unusual for Idealist to be the first worker in each morning and the last one to leave at night. Extremely loyal to company and company cause, they tend to be long-term employees—provided recognition for their contributions is had, remuneration is generous, and the stairway to the glass dome remains open.

Many household-familiar names are of this working style.

THE EMOTIONALS

Kinsmen

Kinsmen are one of the most responsible human resource investments a company can make. Give a Kinsmen a problem, apprise them of objectives, and relax after that—for they rarely let others down. Another attribute of Kinsmen workers is their organizational skill. They gather, organize, and determine a plan with efficiency in mind. Perfectionistic and meticulous, their forté is for arranging and processing details within the context of larger pictures.

Risk-taking or innovative solutions may not be their strength but contributing to overall success is. Work is not the driving force in their lives, so working overtime or volunteering to work weekends should not be expected from them. While their need is fulfilled in the serving of others, their satisfaction is beyond the reach or glare of glass domes.

They usually prefer assistant over leadership roles. They may have the instinct but lack the interest for climbing corporate ladders or playing office politics. Teamwork, where collective efforts benefit the whole, is a concept Kinsmen understands at a cellular level. They tend to get along with everyone.

THE EMOTIONALS

Empath

Uniquely, Empath is not motivated by rewards of status, remuneration, or recognition. Instead, their inspiration comes from contributing to the overall success of group efforts or the success of individuals. They're the benevolent "King-makers," those unselfish magnanimousOnes who unearth potential in others and encourage greatness to bloom.

Empath may not seek leadership roles but many are seated close to top dog chairs in trusted advisor or support positions. They are trusted because of their highly-developed sense of committed team work. Empath works for and with people, harvesting self-fulfillment from the *now* of personal interactions. From companies they earn a paycheque; from people they earn self-confirmation.

With their seeming determination to avoid applause, accolade, and recognition, Empath is frequently found under umbrellas of untried-genius. Though umbrella'd anonymity is their choice and preference, such untried genius is both loss and waste for the corporation.

THE INTUITIVES

Visionary

They are the big-picture visionaries whose eyes are so firmly focused on future they hardly notice today's mud at their feet. Brainstorming and think-tanks are typical workplace innovations of theirs and reflective of their solution-curiosity and people-propensity. These individuals are intuitive intellects. Their approach to work and all is different.

Leadership is their natural role.

There is no such thing as disorganization, shoddy workmanship, or close-supervision with Visionary at the helm. They tend to be charismatic and quickly establish good rapport at all levels of interaction, from co-worker, to management, to industry. They are known to be tough, meaning, inflexible about poor job performance—their own or others'. One difference between them and other leaders is that Visionary encourages workers to independently explore better ways of doing that increase workplace productivity *and* pleasure.

THE INTUITIVES

Evokateur

Not even anonymity's generous umbrella can fully hide the truth about Evokateurs...they all harbour creative brilliance. They learn early in life that it's best to experiment silently and experience privately, as ample-confidence and sample-evidence will be needed to withstand logic's scrutiny, once brought to bear and to light. How readily they share their abstractions and creations with others, depends on whether their environment is one of encouragement or discouragement.

Their private Evokateur-world is more real to them than this one of ours, and satisfies most of their needs. Creativity is a cellular obsession for Evokateurs; they create anyway.

Many look for mundane-type jobs they can perform with one eye shut and mind half-alert...like assembly line work. Predictability and routine allows them to put brain and body on automatic pilot while they escape into their own world, where things are more interesting.

THE SPIRITUALISTS

Healer

These are the ones who change or broaden perspectives. The following excerpts are less specific than indicative of how conscientious Healers approach any job or task.

Healers find it odd that when people stub their toe they get angry, curse, and through hobbled grimace and gritted teeth ignore the pain. How much quicker the heal and more pleasant the day if that throbbing toe were held, its pain acknowledged, then comforted by sympathetic hands till pain eases and ends. After all, no matter the shoe, the speed, or the rocky path pointed, that toe never lets the body down. If small this change in thought does seem, apply that small principle to a larger scale, as Healers would, and note what differences result with change of belief.

When the body is sick or diseased, the prescribed policy is to view the disease with winner-loser hostility. Rather than stiffening resolve and muscle, and steadying nerve to control pain, rather than declaring all out war and focusing energy and resources on destroying the invader, flip perspectives instead. Focus light on body's plight, for it's every bit in need of caress as that stubbed toe once was. Accept the pain. Validate its existence. The body system may be confused as to which is friend and which is foe— the body for allowing disease to enter or disease for daring. Wars are always confusing. As peace follows surrender in war, heal and cure can follow surrender in body disease.

THE SPIRITUALISTS

Philosophers have an uncanny ability for being on-the-spot when leading edges are sharpened or discoveries unveiled. They seldom author the creation or event, however. Their knack is for pointing out what others may not see and explaining what new change has come.

They often clash with authority over *should* and *must* issues. Characteristically, they suffer an allergy to authority and uniforms, regardless of cut, colour, or cloth. Asking tough questions, such as why? and why not? tends to reduce their chances of succeeding hierarchically. Their reluctance to direct or boss others significantly reduces their value, managerially.

Philosophers tend to be most intelligent, most hard working, and most likely to refute or refuse any policy not in sync with their own. They often choose careers where they can freelance or contract their services. Wealth or material gain does not motivate them; affording choice does. Philosopher demands autonomy, personally and professionally. They tend to captain their own ships and are renowned workaholics. They may only do what they like, but they like doing it a lot, apparently.

14 Ansir Personality Styles
2,744 Profile Combinations are possible

<u>Core Functioning</u>	<u>Personality Style</u>
Physicals...	Extremist & Realist
Instinctives...	Scintillator & Sentinel
Logicals...	Diligent & Sage
Practicals...	Eccentrik & Idealist
Emotionals...	Kinsmen & Empath
Intuitives...	Visionary & Evokateur
Spiritualists...	Healer & Philosopher

1
Profile Briefs

Dominant Style of Emoting

THE PHYSICALS

Extremist

Early in life they seem to have decided that emotions and others would not play or share centre stage with them. Whether cellularly decided or externally influenced, Extremists are not emotionally vulnerable or available to others. They seem to have sworn an oath to "not love." By the time they leave home, they've likely developed their life pattern of uncompromising independence and dismissed the rules of society as being too restrictive for them. Extremists have a thrill-of-danger need that usually seeks satisfaction through physical challenges—breaking laws of nature or defying laws of science. Sometimes they seek needed thrill satisfaction through mental challenges—manipulating human nature and rearranging letters of law. An Extremist does not challenge laws of nature (physical or human), out of respect as most others do. The fuel that drives them is contempt.

THE PHYSICALS

Realist

They have supple, well-developed physiques and seem particularly comfortable in their skin. Their characteristic and identifiable walk is purposeful. Their posture is tall, their back straight, and there is a hint of noblesse mixed with vanity in their stride and strut. When physically fit, they epitomize and personify the miracle, perfection, and potent of the human form. They see the human body as both tool and joy. They revel in its practicality and marvel at its pleasure-ability. Realists are the most sexually assertive, experimental, and aggressive of all.

When provoked or frustrated, they tend to physically react rather than vocally express. Although these instinct-reactions can spawn extraordinary and even famous professional accomplishments—in sport competitions or emergency situations for instance —personally it can result in alienation and loneliness for these people-lovers.

THE INSTINCTIVES

Kinesthetic beings, they learn by physically interacting with the world. Their energy-intellect is so sonar-sophisticated and sensitive they can bodily feel the energy-mood of others or room. Before intellectual or emotional dimensions have time to analyze and prescribe action, their body has already responded instinctively. For them, as for all physical beings, body-instinct can be blessing or curse. Fidgeting is a tell-tale characteristic of this personality Style. Scintillators master early the art of converting physical assets into personal advantages, usually to charm their way out of trouble or to worm their way into another's affection. As children, they prefer the company of adults and older siblings who are often enchanted by their pint-sized antics and precocity. Scintillators like others to be happy, especially with them. Generally, these are the *Peter Pans* who look and often act younger than their chronological age, and who most dread growing old.

Why is this personality most likely to: be "daddy's girl" or "momma's boy" far into adulthood; be financially struggling at middle-age; have multiple marriages and divorces; have addictions to drugs or alcohol; and be the ones who abandon their children, physically, emotionally, and financially? Because Scintillators subscribe to physical rather than emotional satisfaction.

THE INSTINCTIVES

entinel

This is the most common emoting style of *3 Sides Of You* participants. Behind trademark reserve and alluring attractiveness is an individual who is hard to know and hard to love. Trust is the wall that divides. Whether Sentinel trust is an open or shut case, depends on how each has evolved and adjusted to three personality-typical determinants: language, loyalty, and new experiences. Characteristic of Sentinels is a "crane-calm" look of time-suspended stillness or fixed-concentration. None other portrays mind-at-work like them. Others are often surprised at the thoroughness and depth delivered when they reply.

No thought, no word, no action is more painful to these sensitive beings than "good-bye." So ingrained is their conviction that all good must come to an end, Sentinels may not risk "hello." To them, happily ever after only happens in fairy tales and forget that silver-lining crap! The only thing dark clouds bring is rain. If by nature, they are skeptical and by choice reticent, then one question begs answer. Is there a causal relationship between reticence and the fact that Sentinels suffer internal degenerative illnesses more often than others? Digestion diseases, like ulcers and colitis...and organ failure diseases, like heart and kidney are suffered by Sentinels at an earlier age, comparatively. What is eating Sentinel from the inside out?

THE LOGICALS

Diligent

Diligent often makes a conscious decision to avoid emotional expression and seems tight-lipped determined to remain that way. Emotional honesty is a challenge for most, but for Diligent it goes far beyond challenge's *mere*. For them, reality is a well-trodden narrow path between tried and true. Diligent builds their career, their life and love, one smart brick atop another. Their mortar is a mix of intellect and practicality, and of a kind intolerant of mistakes. Whether because of too high of expectations from parents, society, or selves, these strong silent ones must do everything right. And history has shown that success does not wander far from their name's fame and characteristic "rightness."

Occasionally Diligents encounter emotional situations that overflow their logical banks. Not used to the bombardment, unable to express the overwhelming flood of irrational sensations, they respond in startlingly explosive ways: from booming tirade and pounding fists, to venomous attacks, to tearing the place apart. Startling, because Diligents are the cool-headed rational ones among us. And while capable and competent intellectually, emotionally they are often as fragile and innocent as newborn infants. The mystery for loved ones and others is *why?*

THE LOGICALS

Through and through, Sage is a tribal-oriented being whose people approach and philosophy are one and the same. Each person is intrinsically and equally important to the whole human race, according to Sage. Highly social beings, they seek emotional support and intellectual stimulation in company with others. Their greatest pleasure is participating in the human aspects of life and they may very well be the most entertaining—if not the most interesting—citizens on earth. It is characteristic of this personality to theorize life, to speak in lofty terms of the state of the human condition rather than focusing on the individual or the specifics of issue. They keep an intellectual stick between them and others, because theory is safer than practice and commitment or personal inspection is not necessary or not called for.

In conversation, their attention tends to be rapt. Yours will not wilt or wander either, as their mind is fine and deep. In Sage, humour, pathos, and wisdom are well mixed and sweet. They greet others with hand and mind in all manner and matter, but don't expect to meet their heart. Sage attended its burial long, long ago.

THE PRACTICALS

Many Eccentriks know sooner and better than most that they are different. Rather than burrowing inside and hiding under heaps of self-doubt and self-hate, Eccentrik says, "Screw this," thrusts out their chin and takes control of their own ship's wheel. Exhilarating experiences, the blush of new and the rush of novel are what Eccentrik actively pursues in life. They personify individuality and do not aspire to being classified politically or otherwise by their ensemble, ensign or assembly. They know that while running with the herd may be safer it also means a life of eating trampled grass. A compromise they're not willing to make.

These individuals thrive on variety and are often more creative than small towns or small minds can tolerate. In cities or large centres their flamboyant style blends less noticeably in crowds and their creative curiosity finds broader intellectual and cultural markets for browsing and participating. The number-one emotional qualifier for them is the stimulation factor. Any and all experiences are eagerly met except one…intimacy. They may love, they may lust, they may share their body, mind, and being, but one thing they may not share freely is trust.

THE PRACTICALS

Idealist

While they have tremendous faith in their own abilities to produce and to lead, unconsciously Idealist fears that unless they take control all will be lost. Their fear may be justified. The world advances in every field of endeavour by march of improvement to time's measure. Perfection is crucial to progress. However fair or unfair, the blunt and brunt of responsibility is borne by those who see the highest potential in self and in others, and demand its fulfillment.

No matter what Idealist does, they tend to think, "…it could be better." They try harder than most, they feel more responsible than most, and they are harder on self than most too. They push impatiently toward perfection, even if beyond the scope or scent of realistic. Stopping and smelling the roses is unlikely for them. They'd be distracted by stray grass-clippings along the pathway and either overlook the roses altogether or view them through disappointment-tainted glasses. Perfect is a word they seem to have invented and feel personally responsible for promoting. They don't like things to remain the way they are, but want to improve everything they see and touch, including people. For them, external appearances reflect internal standards.

THE EMOTIONALS

insmen

Kinsmen are smart, sensitive, and gentle. To see them at their finest, to appreciate how brightly human stars can shine, join any charitable organization or participate in any public-aid program anywhere, anytime. Swelling the goodwill ranks is Kinsmen, who cares enough to apply money and elbow grease with equal ardor—for help and for benefit.

Others need to remind them how valuable they are, as they tend to forget. It may take convincing before they'll accept praise though. Humility is their customary way. From undertones, overtones, and intonations, they intuit the unspoken needs and underlying emotions of individuals or groups, whilst tracking mental precepts. They are natural arbitrators who excel in situations where logic and emotion conflict.

More often than any other, Kinsmen asks,"What is love?" Their own love reaches out to caress others and world with action, word, and wallet. They give all they think, all they have, and all the time they can spare, yet Kinsmen tends to think they're unworthy of love in return.

We are going to bite into the warm, chocolate-coated raisin that is the Kinsmen personality. Not with intent to harm but to understand why such gentle and generous beings suffer personality-typical bouts of emotional blues.

THE EMOTIONALS

Ranked among the most powerful, Empath is endowed with incredible gifts: emotion-acuity and intellect second-to-none. These innate skills and abilities are necessary as their purpose and message can alter man, world, and future, upon delivery.

They are purely emotional beings. Most don't realize how powerful they are, or how destructive they can be.

As children, when teased and/or taunted for being *sissy,* Empath begins to mask their feelings. When they begin to speak, they may mask their thoughts as well. Before they talked, they knew more or less what others were thinking and wanting, and often responded before words were spoken. When they learn to speak, they also learn what "good," "bad," and "worst" feels like. Good is when others like what they say; bad is when they don't; and worst is when others get angry. Why do they get this sure answer inside but when they act accordingly, get mixed and unexpected responses—from happy love to angry hate? It shakes their faith in their ability to understand, when loved and trusted others tell them with words what they feel is not right. They become reactionary chameleons, expert at fitting themselves into whatever mood-mold pleases, and thus beginning what will become an Empath trait, "tell them what they want to hear." Most Empaths have a lifelong love/hate relationship with spoken words, especially when pressured to reply quickly. These individuals can know the answer in 7-seconds but take 7-days to deliver it.

THE INTUITIVES

Visionary

Visionary tends to be noticed. Something more than attractiveness emanates; something tangible yet elusive draws others' attention. In social situations, they adopt an aloof persona out of innate shyness, often needing time to feel a certain level of comfort before removing their don't-approach masks. Once they do, the reason for reluctance becomes clear. Few are as passionate about people and life as Visionary.

Many are innervated in their charismatic presence though equally as many can be intimidated by the confidence they exude. If others are uncomfortable around Visionarys there's a reason. Interestingly, when two Visionary "strangers" meet, either a sense of déja vu is experienced or sexual sparks are ignited.

Intuition may be their gift but communication unwraps it. Visionary leads the world with words.

THE INTUITIVES

Evokateur does not live with us or as us in this world. They are born aware of other depths, dimensions, and realities. Others can find these purely emotional beings difficult to understand. Some find the concept of such emotionality interesting, some envy, but for most—nightmares are more welcome. Regardless, emotions rule Evokateur and that means one thing: ultra-creativity.

Evokateur-world, just behind Evokateur eyes, is as real for them as this one of ours. Relating to them is multi-frustrating for most, though multi-enlightening for some—those who understand and *experience* Evokateur discover that love has more layers than previously thought or known.

Others speak of Evokateur's extraordinary *oddness;* history speaks of their extraordinary accomplishments. However, extraordinary tends to travel odd paths; those on this or that side of normal. While they've many lessons to master, pleasing others is not one of them.

THE SPIRITUALISTS

Healer

Characteristically, Healers tend to be delicate and fragile seeming—but only seeming. Their fame and repute is more constitution of horse and steel-willed determination than frail or retiring. In fact, they are much more substantial in every regard than appearance indicates. If the voice of a Higher Power is foreign or frightening to you, then you are not a Healer. All Healers know their life-Partner intimately.

Their energy field ranges in size from vast to enormous making them extra-sensitive to crowding or closeness. Often they choose to live in rural settings and characteristically opt for minimalist decor over plush coziness. They often are light sleepers who don't need as much rest as others, and they usually don't need alarm clocks to awaken in the morning. Healers become disoriented by noise, especially argumentative voices and loud music. Messy environments make them feel physically uncomfortable. Gardening is a favourite pastime of theirs.

THE SPIRITUALISTS

If asked, they readily offer the shirt off their back. That act in and of itself is not unusual, but what differentiates Philosopher from others is that in their giving it's understood, they give but once and they'll neither button nor straighten collars afterwards. They walk with hand extended and arms open to help, but rather than giving, lifting and carrying, what Philosophers do is boost confidence. They expect others to pick themselves up, dust themselves off and get back in the race under their own steam and initiative.

An aura of confidence surrounds them and draws others like iron filings to magnet. A more inspirational and powerful being than Philosophers has yet to be born. They tend to be non-judgemental about sexual preferences or proclivities, and contemptuous of dictated propriety. What matters is the depth of fulfillment through emotional sharing, where innermost truth is offered and shared at soul-level with others, especially with their mate. Finding a compatible mate is the single greatest challenge for Philosopher.

2 Profile Boss

You've found the dominant *3 Sides Of You,*
but who's in charge here?

WHAT'S A
Profile Boss?

The single most valuable bit of information about your Profile.

Besides having a dominant style for each realm of functioning, each and every Profile has an overall boss—the Style that defines and decides life purpose.

Right now, and understandably, Boss means nothing to you, as you've yet to read your Profile *InDepths*. Ansir offers this beforehand and confidently, so put it on your back burner while reading: the quickest and most direct route to self-defined success and self-desired happiness is **knowing**, **respecting**, and **trusting** your Profile Boss.

Success and happiness are individually defined and measured. Every Profile has one Boss and two support experts (other dominant Styles), for fulfillment reasons that only make sense and only matter to the Profiled individual.

When reading your InDepths, read all 3-realms of functioning—Thinking/Working/Emoting—for each Profiled Style, to get a fuller 3-dimensional view and understanding of Self.

Boss is a sleeper...

Initially, it may seem too simplistic to be realistic or applicable.

If so, and until realization hits and your own confidence takes over, you may safely lean on Ansir's confidence regarding this most important Key. The shortest shortcut to your goal's achievement is self-understanding, meaning Boss trusting.

Boss knows best, knows why, and knows where to go; pulls innate talents and strengths of support experts together, then herds your collective *whole* toward fulfillment.

As self-understanding increases, Boss importance will too.

In the future you may question, "What's next?" or "How do I use my Profile information to best advantage and benefit?" Whenever your questions are success and/or happiness-related, the right and best answers are Boss-based.

PROFILED WHO AND WHY

Determining Boss

Ansir's *3 Sides Of You* test identifies Profiled "who." Boss identifies Profiled "why;" your reason for being, and reasons why you're so complex and complicated.

For most Styles, Boss is found in the emoting realm. For five Styles: Idealist, Visionary, Healer, Philosopher, and sometimes Evokateur, Boss is found in the working realm. **Never** is boss found in the thinking realm.

Locate your dominant working Style on the following pages and find your Profile Boss, according to the rules and exceptions provided. Once you've determined your Boss Style, keep it in mind as you proceed to Key 3, *Profile InDepths*.

What you're about to read is the core common that Ansir found, during thousands of conversations with others samely or similarly Profiled. Our Self-perception Profiling System identifies 2,744 unique Profile combinations, each with one Boss. When Profile Boss is NOT confident, Achilles' Heel steps in (Achilles' Heel is Key 5).

Most,

find fulfillment in the Emoting realm

IF dominant working Style is:

Extremist	or	Realist
Scintillator	or	Eccentrik
Sentinel	or	Diligent
Empath	or	Sage
Kinsmen	—	

THEN, Profile Boss is dominant emoting Style

Some,

find, fulfillment in the working realm

IF dominant working Style is Idealist, Profile Boss is Idealist
unless
dominant emoting Style is Visionary or Healer or Philosopher...
THEN, Profile Boss is dominant emoting Style

IF dominant working Style is Visionary, Profile Boss is Visionary
unless
dominant emoting Style is Healer or Philosopher....
THEN, Profile Boss is dominant emoting Style.

IF dominant working Style is Healer, Profile Boss is Healer
unless
dominant emoting Style is Philosopher...
THEN, Profile Boss is Philosopher.

IF dominant working Style is Philosopher,
THEN, Profile Boss is Philosopher.

SPECIAL CASE:

IF dominant working Style is Evokateur,
Profile Boss is dominant emoting Style
unless
dominant emoting Style is Visionary, Healer, or Philosopher...
THEN, Profile Boss is Evokateur.

3
Profile InDepth

You've found your right Profile? Met your Profile Boss? Then you're ready for in-depth insight and explanation. Profile Indepths can:

- help you better understand your strengths and weaknesses.
- help point you in the right direction for making the most of your strengths while not letting your weaknesses get the better of you.
- help you better understand how other people function, both on their own and in relation to you.
- help explain internal clashes or struggles that you might be feeling.
- provide insight into why you think and behave the way you do.
- *provide a swift kick in the arse if you're doubting yourself.*
- *teach you how to put the whammy on almost anyone.*

Katy, USA, Idealist/Eccentrik/Eccentrik

"Profile Briefs are the equivalent of a promo for a TV show. Profile InDepths are a TV show starring YOU...a program that takes you on a journey with a fascinating plot, emotional elements and insights that make you go Wow!"

Janet, USA, Visionary/Philosopher/Healer

KEY 3: PROFILE INDEPTHS
Dominant Style of Thinking

*Thinking: A discernible, predictable pattern of balancing and
applying knowledge. How individuals process order,
solve problems and rationalize outcomes.*

THE PHYSICALS

Extremist

His name is Pat and he is the youngest son in a family of four boys. His parents and three brothers are all upstanding, accomplished citizens and as pleasant as can be. By all accounts, Pat was the black sheep of the family. A hooligan on wheels and "a handful from breath one," his sleep-deprived parents admit. "Before he could walk, he could vault up and scoot along cupboards, piano and TV. Before we knew it, he was mountain climbing the barn and parachuting off the roof."

Pat defied discipline and pain equally. As a fearless competitor, he won most BMX races he entered: once with a broken nose after a spectacular pileup and once with a dislocated shoulder after a record air-borne flight, but bone-jarring landing. He unsettled the calm of the peaceful village by thumbing pomposity and propriety roundly and regularly. He set educated tongues awag in wonder and dismay at his refusal to discipline his abundant intellect. He didn't overstep bounds of legality. His, was high-spirited defiance and uncompromising independence. He scarred one companion and scared others away with his dare me then derring-do feats. By the time Pat hit high school, incorrigible but smart was his fame.

No ifs, ands, or doubts about it, he could be brilliant if and when he wanted. If the top math score was 98 percent, Pat's name accompanied the distinction...when in the mood to flex intellectually. He spent hours in the lab one semester, which warmed educator cockles until it was discovered his devotion was less to school science, than drug manufacturing. He worked part-time at his father's garage and always drove a car faster than the one he'd just wrecked. After dark, you could find Pat lolling about somewhere near the crowd, holding a beer, a joint, and a new out-of-town *chick*. He never attended school dances, never joined team sports and avoided close friendships; on principle, it seemed. It was rumoured he'd rebuilt a '48 Harley, but no one ever saw it or saw him ride it, and he'd neither confirm nor deny its existence.

When asked during his senior yearbook interview, "What are your after-grad plans?" he replied in typical Pat fashion, "Not sure." On Friday, the last day of school, he shocked many by attending the grad dance and joining an all-night party at the lake. Saturday morning he shocked all. Mounted on his homemade Hog, Pat drove slowly down the main street of town, turned off and onto the old highway, then headed full-throttle to join the posse of Hell's Angels.

This is a head, not heart, personality style. For them, matters of the heart seem not to matter at all. From an early age, Extremists display single-minded determination to go it alone, without permission, consideration or interference from others; not from parents or any other authority figure. Their seeming inability to care for or about others is much more than self-centred egotism. It's an inability to bond emotionally.

Whether cellularly predisposed or provoked by life experience, at one point in their earliest development Extremists experience such profound personal rejection that they disconnect from others emotionally. This self-protective decision is one they may not reverse for years, if ever. When they decide not to be available or vulnerable to others, they establish a relationship with the Grim Reaper—their life-long duelling partner. If their greatest glories and highest highs were not had challenging mortality, they would not be Extremist at all. These ones seek spectacular endings more than spectacular living.

Extremists are highly intelligent, creative beings. Their fulfillment is not had from contributing to a better world but from triumphing over physical reality. When planning a new project or dangerous feat, their approach is logical and linear. They organize a solution system and meticulously follow through in a clear and orderly step-by-step fashion. They tend to spend considerable time in the planning and organizing phases of projects. Analyzing all aspects down to the nittiest of grittys, they calculate problems and anticipate contingencies. Extremist thoroughness is necessary. Danger is a shadow-close companion of theirs.

While they may begin with built-in safety features, they systematically strip them away until the odds of going nose-to-nose with death are imminent. Only during the final stages of development do Extremists factor in Self. Project success takes precedence over personal safety. Respect for danger is apparent in their blueprints, but when finished, their plans leave little margin for human error and less for human frailty. Extremists are likely to experiment with drugs and use alcohol to excess, but the high they derive when challenging fear is their real addiction.

The greatest gift of this personality is extraordinary instinctiveness. Extremists anticipate intangibles beyond the ability of logical deduction alone. Their instincts are so uncannily sophisticated, that when focused, they assimilate with the object or subject of interest. This cellular gift enables them to predict behaviours and outcomes under the most stressful of conditions—natural or man-made.

One characteristic and global renown is their skill working with animals. In every field of animal history, handling, hunting or husbandry, Extremists are predominant and preeminent. These are the individuals who tame the lions, shoot the documentaries, and guide the hunting expeditions. Their discerning eye sees the colt's champion heart where most see shaggy coat and shabby lineage. They are the veterinarians, trainers, and handlers who understand what's wrong or right, by touch of hand or gauge of eye. The beast was big and scary until Extremist brought it back as food, transport, and companion. Space was a theory until Extremist took control of the stick. It was a practical and common butcher's glove until Extremist needed a shark-proof suit.

Animal mastery is but one example of their instinctive intelligence. Physical career choices, such as auto racer, test pilot, fire fighter, and war correspondent appeal to them. For challenging firsts—from space flight, to stunt work, to bungee jumping—if not the first challenger in line, Extremist would pursue and persist and most likely be first to conquer it.

Ego and exhilaration-driven, to experience the highest high, this personality may delve into the underbelly of life, where individual desire and tribal design conflict. Extremists are highly creative. Their intellectual ability is often off the measurement scale. Outsmarting death, the system, and others is an adrenaline rush they not only seek, but seem to need. The master of hand for them is mind. Fiercely independent, in thought and action, they alone determine whether their hands remain free or are cuffed. The most common personality in prison is Extremist. Ironically, this personality is rank and file common in law enforcement too.

No other style meets a mid-life crisis with more neurotic fear and reluctance than them. Their lives tend to be physically expressive and demand unflagging strength and stamina. Aging often becomes a livelihood issue and can cause them enormous insecurity; evoking an introspective journey they'd not previously entertained nor allowed. At this point, in their life, Extremist is most likely to settle down and train their sights and intellect on more pedestrian pursuits. Their focus and intensity, formerly applied to physical challenges, translates quite well in the business world. The challenges are different and there are opportunities to risk and feel the adrenaline rush they require—though less intense than *rushes* of past. Many turn in their adventurer Cards and take up mogulship in the second half of their lives.

Historically, as evolutionarily, Extremist is the explorer. The one who steps forward to test the merit of the scheme or strives to fulfill the dream by controlling where and how to place their confidence. The world was horizon-far and flat until Extremist sailed forth and returned with maps that spurred mind, sparked curiosity, and expanded global possibilities. Every new step of theirs is a footprint or footnote in history.

THE PHYSICALS

Realist

Anything Realist begins with honesty. History may have been otherwise written had Realists, like William F. Cody (Buffalo Bill), been the first whites that native Indians met on the shores and plains. Before Custer's last stand, Buffalo Bill warned, "To live in harmony with Indians, there is only one simple rule. Don't break your promises. Indians expect a man to keep his word. They can't understand how a man can lie as they'd just as soon cut off a leg as tell a lie." As scouts honour is to Buffalo Bill, honesty is to Realist.

Intellectually, they have potential to excel at any academic level they aspire to, but often don't know it. Due to their unique physical dimension, learning can be hindered in conventional classroom settings. Realists have extraordinarily sophisticated internal energy; they physically interpret and respond to world. Life is filtered through their body before being mentally and emotionally digested. Most think first, then determine a course of action. Realist feels, acts, then thinks.

They can quickly become the application experts, but may have difficulty explaining the theory. Theirs, is a practical genius. While others are still figuring things out, these individuals are usually up to their elbows and busily doing. Such instinctiveness ranks them nonpareil in emergency situations. Realists' primary intellect is body energy, and in that regard, they have the most powerful and efficient internal generator of all. However, such energy can be balm or bane for them.

The thorn of self-doubt lodges in youth.

In classroom settings, Realist tends to be the one yawning in the back row, and who is often accused of having a short attention span. While boredom may be blamed, the real culprit is pent-up energy. For Realist to learn effectively, excess energy must be diverted or released before mental processing can occur. Forced to sit still, and being confined to classroom desks, can be physically challenging and mentally fracturing for these individuals. Regardless of profession or career, whether they're a graduate or a school dropout, Realists commonly share a dislike for formal education. As long as they can do something to release their energy—chew gum, scribble or take notes—the classroom experience can be bearable and learning favourable. Without energy release, Realist is likely to fall asleep, cause a disturbance, or quit in frustration.

Teachers can be baffled by a Realist student, who fails the science test yet wins first prize at the science-fair. Class field trips, lab assignments, math games and word puzzles are examples of exercises that help these students learn. In fact, they tend to comprehend more when they rewrite their lessons or notes (physically repeat information) while studying. Action solidifies learning. They understand faster and more thoroughly by physical interaction than by memorization or deduction. For these students, having teachers who understand and respect their physical nature can make all the difference, in terms of academic achievement. Without such understanding and lacking an outlet for their burgeoning energy, these eager-to-learn and *proud* individuals may find school more confidence-destroying than educationally uplifting.

As students, they're often upbraided for their disruptive, restless behaviour. Their focus can waver as their internal energy ebbs and flows, which others too-frequently misinterpret as lack of intellect or interest. Realist ranks high among school dropouts. In frustration, most retire early from the education system. Self-pride is a major factor in their voluntary decision to quit, as is practicality. Situations that are hurtful to pride and then additionally lack concrete proof of progress, are situations that Realist will quickly, and often forever, turn their back on. School difficulties can have debilitating consequences for them. When they dropout, they may life-long *and erroneously* doubt their intellectual ability.

Unwilling to conform or unable to excel in the conventional education system, Realist may gravitate toward more tactile, technical fields of learning, which offer hands-on opportunity for them to acquire expertise and prove native excellence. They trust tangibles, three-dimensional realities, which reward and restore their confidence. Intangibles or concepts involving mental interpretation are processes they tend to mistrust, because of early classroom experiences. Fear of failure and ridicule prevents them from risking intellectually. Instead, they tend to place all faith in the physical world—their chief realm of functioning.

A hallmark characteristic of Realists is a curiosity about how things work.

They have a distinct propensity, if not an uncanny ability, to learn from hands-on demonstrations. Physical activity redirects their energy and frees their mind to focus clearly. Few can match the speed with which these individuals can take things apart and put them back together again. Without instruction, direction, or plan, but with object firmly in-hand, Realist can dismantle into components, decipher inner workings, mend, repair, and rebuild, like no other. If rocket science for others, it's but day camp to them. It could be said that Realists have intelligent hands. The majority of self-help books are authored by them, as are the majority of three-dimensional puzzles designed and solved by them. One book that Realist tends to conscientiously keep handy, but seldom is more than passingly familiar with, is a manual.

From earliest age, these little tykes can be found rummaging in kitchen drawers and tool boxes, where *real* play things are stored. Toys they most enjoy are those that require physical and mental dexterity, such as electronic games, chemistry kits, action figures, construction sets, paint-by-numbers and magic tricks. As teenagers, count on them to have their driver's license and their own car early, and be able to handle the financial responsibility as well as routine repair and maintenance, like changing oil and flat tires, et cetera.

Being independent is as style-typical, as logical thinking.

The physical world makes logical sense to them. Order and procedure lead to step-by-step progression, and action and consequence unfold predictably within the confines and limits of what's known. Cause and effect is where their particular genius excels. Realists are renowned for stepping in at any level of difficulty or dysfunction and making adjustments that fix or improve. Tools in their hand are but extensions of mind. They need only see a pattern, model or blueprint, to know how to proceed. Not surprisingly, these individuals thrive in the fields of medicine, engineering, architecture and agriculture. They predominate in the trade and labour industry, where evidence of Realist ingenuity abounds.

For them, it's the practical side of form, function and motion that's irresistible. They like knowing how things work—but so do other personality styles. What specifically differentiates Realists from others is how extraordinarily capable they are at fixing "things" that are broken. Whether the challenge is human body or mechanical workings, these individuals seem innately gifted for getting things up and running again. Realists acquire skill sufficient for doing in their sleep, metaphorically speaking. They seldom skim surfaces of anything that interests. These practical geniuses delve deeply into all that piques their curiosity.

With or without academic wings, these tenaciousOnes fly.

Self-reliant by nature, iron-willed Realists tend to succeed—with or without academic accreditation or approval. Scholastic battles, lost in youth, turn victorious when set to aspirations beyond school bells and doors. Any field of endeavour they aim mind, body, and determination toward, they have potential to excel. The intellectual thorn of self-doubt that can pierce and prickle in youth, can be an irritation that spurs them onto success in adulthood.

Whether their focus is livelihood or leisure, Realists participate enthusiastically and vigorously. They play hard, work harder, and shine brightest, when pitted against a worthy opponent or challenge. Their boundless energy fuels and fires their competitive drive. The adage "no pain, no gain," was likely first coined by them. If anything, the sweat of brow, the tautness of muscle, and the labour of breath, are invigorating to action-oriented Realist. Physical activity is an adrenaline release for their bottomless, perpetual energy. No other is as doggedly determined as them.

Realists are born leaders. They're goal-oriented and masterful orchestrators of plan, action, and results. Given a project, their approach is to plan their work, then work their plan. Abstractions are irritations they leave for others to explore, while they focus on the converting of concept into three-dimensional form. For Realists, body rules. Brain-backed brawn and bull-dog persistence are their name's claim and fame. By accomplishment, do they measure their own success. Upon their shoulders rests the laurel, "good old American know-how," for they're the competent and consistent performers who deliver as promised.

Lacking experience is not a deterrent, lacking training is.

Realists seldom tackle a project until they are personally confident they have the necessary skills to succeed. If they say they can, they can and do. These are very confident, very proud individuals. Having a clear understanding of rules, regulations, and expectations, from the outset, is important. They need assurance that the relationship or environment complements their action-first nature. These never-say-die individuals avoid risking failure by being fully prepared and fully apprised before proceeding. Once they commit to involvement and begin working, unsolicited advice from others is usually not welcomed and revisions to agreed upon plans may be met with more peeve than pleasure. Delays and interruptions are two conditions that are particularly trying for Realists. There is a reason why they hone their skills, learn the rules, and double-check plans, before beginning their work. Once they start, their number one goal is to finish the job.

Because they physically feel everything first, Realist takes criticism particularly hard. To them, the sting of criticism is equivalent to being publicly slapped and humiliated. When reprimanded, they become sullen or belligerent; when challenged, they may become volatile—which accounts for their hallmark repute for being quick-tempered. This is when the feel and act part of this personality becomes bane. Physical reactions are as natural for them, as sting is to nettle. Explosive responses are not only style-typical but Achilles' heel for Realists, who can spend a lifetime wavering between action and remorse.

The big sister, big brother personality

Not risk-takers per se, they'll risk their all when the safety of others is at stake. This logical, tenacious personality is seldom stumped or stymied. With uncanny ability, they can identify inherent need or danger in situations and muster *tout de suite* response in reply. Realists are practical mathematicians. Measures of distance, depth, weight and volume, seem to be intrinsically woven into their perceptual mindset. As pilots, of air and sea, their historical repute is famed and immortalized the world over.

Tribal-oriented by nature, Realists are like wolves in a pack: protective of kin and clan members. When others need, Realists are usually first in line with heart and hand extended to help. They are the guardians, the vigilantes, the rescuers and emergency experts; the deep-sea divers, the mountain climbers, the pilots, and the forest rangers. Physically "sharp" and kind natured, they prove exemplary in medical, rescue, and police situations. When the call is for action, savvy response, and coordinated effort, Realist leaders and leadership have evolutionarily led the pack and led the way.

Being misunderstood is highly stressful for these seemingly indomitable but ultra-sensitive individuals. Their communication style tends to range from refreshingly honest to blisteringly forthright, and they expect equal return of respect from others. They rely on the honesty of spoken word to gain understanding, rather than their having to interpret unspoken or wading through innuendo. When Realist thinks they're right, they're a hard sell to prove otherwise. Like a dog with a bone, the closer the concept to their belief, the harder they are to dissuade. The dictionary term *blunt* was likely born after Daniel Webster's brief but memorable acquaintance, with a Realist employee as his housekeeper.

For Realists, who feel everything deeply, passionate is a term most apropos. When they work, they're not averse to sweat or exhaustion. When they play it's no-holds-barred competition. When they laugh, it's belly-born and infectious. When they love, it's in celebration of just being. When met, they're sometimes found to be obdurate, obstreperous and even opportunistic. When encountered, they're remembered as having seemed or been honest. When known, always do they prove themselves to be reliable and real.

THE INSTINCTIVES

Scintillator

Bright, creative, and insatiably curious, they bring their proven brilliance to school—in part and plait of neatly brushed hair, in shiny shoes, and in beam of smiling faces. They line-up with the others, eager to learn, eager to please, but the first lessons Scintillators learn are: their bodies betray best intentions, and it's hard to please teacher. Fidgetiness—tapping fingers, swinging feet, squirming, scratching, itching—is not only hallmark for Scintillator, it's a cellular necessity. Classroom discipline too often and too firmly demands that they stop and still their nature. For Scintillators, much more than budding preschool brilliance can get nipped and tucked at school.

These individuals have trouble sitting still; physiologically they cannot. For Scintillators, life is filtered bodily before being intellectually and emotionally digested. Sitting idle and stiff, in classroom settings, can be physically, emotionally, and intellectually taxing. Their internal energy brews, boils, brims, and seeks physical release, usually in fidgeting...a tell-tale characteristic of Scintillator. In school, as toe twitches, neck itches, and seat wriggles, they get admonished by teacher to sit still, are rebuked for disturbing the class, and get accused of not paying attention.

Without vent of energy, paying attention is difficult for them. Their focus is distracted by internal pressure that builds, balloons, and escapes in itch, twitch and squirm. Fidgeting is the only release valve their body has, when confined or constrained. While it brings them relief, fidgeting annoys everyone else it seems, especially teachers. Keeping a lid on their internal cacophony without causing external discombobulation is a challenge for these high-energy beings, who can't keep still. Scintillator meets the impatience of others early and often, at home and at school.

Naturally athletic, they love sport competitions. It is not the prize, but the praise that follows winning that Scintillator most needs and strives hardest to attain. In school, however, what they often first meet is frowning disapproval. Little wonder, that ego-dependent Scintillator trips more often than others on those first two steps of education: spelling and reading. The ego-bruising they experience in early school days, can leave scars of academic self-doubt on these ultra-sensitive individuals.

Generally, Scintillator adults shy away from book learning, attending lectures, and recreational reading. Condensed study notes were likely an innovation of theirs. The less time it takes for them to get to the point, the better. Scintillator prefers home videos to movie theatres (unless a riveting action-film is featured), because it's difficult for them to sit still for long. They are the ones who nod off on the couch, watching television, even while viewing their favourites, like movies and sports.

Scintillator lives to please others. Until school they did, and often remarkably so. They tend to smile earlier and more often than other infants. Most are easy to please, highly affectionate, and social-charmers by the age of three. They are bright, often the first to speak full sentences, and exhibit superior small-motor control comparatively. Many child actors and models are Scintillator, who tends to be more socially adept and outgoing than most. However, in school, their boundless charm and exuberance is not met with their accustomed, preschool applause. Their physical bodies chafe at desk confinement and despite sincere effort, their brilliance gets buried under weighty demands for order and discipline. All Scintillator really needs is some physical activity, like gum chewing, to help divert their extraordinary energy so their minds can stay on track.

The Achilles' heel for these individuals is a dependence on others for self-definition. Whatever image of self they see mirrored in the opinion of others, Scintillator tends to accept as truth. Chameleons of the moment, these individuals aspire to meeting the expectations of others, first. When sensitive Scintillator gets reprimanded in school for fidgeting, it raises their doubt about the whole and all of them. They accept their low test score or wrong answer in class, as a pronouncement on their intellectual capability. They tend not to lean on past glories for consolation or confidence-starch, as others do. When the teacher gets irritated with their restlessness or frowns at their answers, Scintillator interprets it as having disappointed and commonly concludes they are "dumb."

Rather than redoubling their effort, asking for help, or offering an explanation in self-defense, they accept the given as proof and give up instead. Characteristically, Scintillators of all ages too-readily, too-often, and too-meekly accept whatever verdict others deliver as irrefutable and correct. Every Scintillator child needs a Goethe-type mentor or influence in their formative years; otherwise they may forever be looking for such.

"Treat a man as he is and he will remain as he is.
Treat a man as he can and should be, and he will become as he can and should be."—Goethe (1749-1832)

If Scintillator cannot win the gold star prizes, their sunny nature will find another way to please. Where once the budding genius sat in "damned if you fidget, damned if you don't" misery, now sits the doubt-encoded, self-defeated and self-demoted, class clown. It's not intellect they lack. It's energy-relief and self-belief they're missing. With their body at peace, Scintillators' innate genius and potential is revealed. Engaging the body in any learning process cements knowledge for them, whether jogging, playing games, or hands-on demonstrations. One of their natural talents is comedy. Scintillator minds virtually sizzle with comedic creativity and improvisational wonder. Many actors, stand-up comedians, and performing artists of all status and stage are of Scintillator style, to some significant degree.

Unconfident Scintillators

Lack of confidence can be a major issue for these individuals, who tend to give up, rather than plow through to the point of fatigue, failure, or success. They often set aspiration's flag at half mast, when flying it from the top of the pole is its rightful place. Scintillator students who encounter difficulties in school, often suffer adult doubts about their intellectual ability. Such defeatism prevents them from testing their own potential and power. The litmus test of their self-held defeatism is problem-solving.

An unconfident Scintillator suffers extreme stress when uncertain about what to do next. Their coping behaviours are usually: resorting to their old class clown routine, self-defacing humour, or giving up before their *self-thought* dumbness is proven and generally known by others. They often pursue careers that focus more on physical prowess or presence than cerebral contributions. Walking away when problems get tough, is as trademark Scintillator as fidgeting.

They can become drifters, moving frequently from one study...labour ...love...or location, to another. Scintillators often commit until interest cools or confrontation ensues, either of which is reason enough for them to move along. As eternal seekers of new pleasures and experiences, fulfillment for Scintillators can become a thread-bare possibility. By avoiding commitment, professionally and personally, they avoid both success and failure; seldom staying long enough for a clear determination to be made one way or the other.

Like rocks skiffing over water, Scintillator tends to skip across surfaces of life. They develop moderate skills in a variety of areas, seldom hitting their full stride or potential in any particular field or endeavour. Or even worse, putting all their effort-eggs in the first basket that returns them rewards of praise or applause.

"Those who say, I'll try anything once, often try nothing twice, three times, arriving late at the gate of dreams worth dying for."—Carl Sandburg

Driven by their need for instant gratification, Scintillator seeks new situations and relationships. The novelty of newness buys them another chance at success. In newness, there is non-judgemental acceptance, at least for as long as it takes for fresh of new to become familiar, then ultimately stale (failure). Persisting beyond failure—beyond familiarity and stale—are *tests* of worthiness, success, and acceptance; and examinations that Scintillator commonly avoids writing. They fear their test results may prove more disappointing to others than would their standard modus operandi of up and leaving. At least, with unresolved issues hanging in midair, there's a chance for reconciliation or appeasement later. A situation infinitely more agreeable to these people-dependents than the opposite of *never again*. For Scintillator, focus and discipline are the keys that unlock their creative potential.

Confident Scintillators

With uncanny ingenuity, Scintillators shine brightest when mental agility is practically expressed. Hands-on challenges afford immediate feedback and reward. Doing, releases energy tension and keeps their mind sharply focus. It's not surprising that many world renowned chefs are Scintillators. In cooking, product is derived from a physical blend of ingredients, taste, and temperature. The prize, a colourful display, appealing to eye and palate, is relatively instantaneous, as is praise, the reward.

Confident Scintillators are creative problem-solvers, who experience adrenaline rushes of excitement at new challenges. Their natural optimism keeps their head clear, so problems seldom impede or overwhelm. They prove ingenious at devising time-saving solutions. Any means or method that reduces tedium or labour is a solution embraced by them.

Products like: soap on a rope; Wite-out™ for typists; microwave popcorn; pull-tie garbage bags; back scratchers; plastic-tipped shoe laces; and home massages or workout equipment are Scintillator-typical innovations.

Their ability to simplify the complex not only applies to products, but to processes too. With wage cutbacks in the late '40s, after the Hollywood Cartoonist Union strike, Chuck Jones' cartoon-genius shone brighter. Some of his greatest achievements, such as the simplistic animation of *Road Runner and Coyote*™ became industry classics. His pared down character animations against minimalistic backgrounds exemplified Scintillator's innate labour and time-saving expertise.

One of their strongest aptitudes is kinesthetic intelligence; memory for movement and motion. Scintillator would sooner identify a suspect walking on the street or mingling in a crowd, than standing in a police lineup. They recall idiosyncrasies of behaviour and action, faster than vocal exchange. Being kinesthetically advantaged, they are deft of mind and hand. Digital art, such as special effects or animation, are areas where kinesthetic geniuses excel. They're quick learners and known to try something once to master the task. Three-dimensional puzzles or speed chess are mind/hand challenges that appeal.

Scintillator combines creativity with comedic wit, turning ordinary into extraordinary. Who would have thought it possible to make the cover of *Time Magazine* by writing about suburban American life, or that by combining foam, rubber, and felt, world celebrity would follow? Both Erma Bombeck and Jim Henson illustrated the depth and ingenuity of Scintillator creativity—a talent that blossoms, not from skimming but from delving deeply into each spot of life, regardless of place, placement or predicament. With their optimistic, light-hearted approach, Scintillators teach others it matters not if the glass be half-full or half-empty. For them, in every drop of life fulfillment's thirst can be quenched, if each but linger long enough to savour.

THE INSTINCTIVES

Sentinel

Keenest of observers, they are cognizant of underlying meanings, veiled messages, subtleties of tone, shade, and rhyme, that reveal more than words can explain. When they ask what's wrong, "nothing" replies won't satisfy. Before asking, they've sensed something amiss, something not right and seldom are wrong in their perceptions.

Confident Sentinels do not question their sensory dimension. They depend and decide based on the truth it delivers. Sentinels are additionally unique—their physical, mental, and emotional dimensions can function on relatively exclusive planes. Meaning, they are able to close off thoughts and feelings at want or will, and glean understanding exclusively through gut instinct.

Their physical bodies act like sophisticated tuning-forks. Divining reality and truth from the vibrations of the external world, Sentinels read impact and import with internal sensory receptors. Like surveillance cameras, these alert individuals record all that happens around them. As children, they are the finders of lost things and seem to keep track of where all family members are at any given place or time. It's not surprising that Sentinels rarely lose personal possessions, forget birthdays, or lovedOne events. Equally uncanny is their physical identification process, which is intimate, accurate, and uncompromising. If a group of children were given seemingly identical marbles, the Sentinel child would be most likely to pull their own out of a common pile. They would, from previous possession, have scrutinized closely and memorized the most minute markings that differentiate their marble from others.

The native language for Sentinels is literal, which they must convert into figurative for speaking. This may account for them being slower to speak than other children. However, this does not mean they are slow learners or even quiet. Sentinel toddlers tend to be non-stop, babbling brooks of *consonant* songing and *vowel* singing. It would seem their cooing and crooning is more purposeful than noise-making, for they tend to possess above average singing ability in later life. Many voice professionals, particularly singers of all musical range, scope and score, have Sentinel in their Profile.

Two curiously interesting characteristics of Sentinels are keen sense of smell and hearing. They may very well be the human bloodhounds, whose nose-intelligence is prized in perfume and wine industries. Aromatherapy is likely a Sentinel innovation. They also tend to hear, ahead of others, the bumps in the night, the knock under the hood, and the computer whistling when improperly shut down. Others may enjoy studying or reading, to the accompaniment of music, Sentinel finds it distracting.

Being literal, their thoughts lie flat on logical pages, unless imbued with three-dimensional life. Creative writing is not usually their forté, though an impressive number of nobel laureates attest otherwise. Learning to speak entails converting literal language into figurative expression, which can be a challenge for them in school. Generously sprinkling conversations and lessons with allegory, metaphor, and imagery, helps them learn.

Clichés, Aesop's Fables, jokes, and stories are favoured and most clearly remembered by Sentinels. They tend to be avid readers and may very well be the ones who made bedside lamps necessary. Generally speaking, Sentinels prefer non-fiction works—philosophy and psychology most particularly. They are also big fans of science fiction, where suspension of logic is accepted, and expected. Abstractions and surreal imaginings interest them, but three-dimensional proof is their everyday, real-life requirement.

The finite and clean efficiency of math appeals to Sentinels. Often, they personify the numeric system, giving 1-2-3's faces, gender, and personalities with specific behavioural traits. Some numbers are compatible with all, some with a few, and some are wholesale troublemakers. (Others may think 7 is lucky, but Sentinels offer that 7 behaves like a bully and is mean, because 7 ate nine). Mathematics, business, sciences, and physical arts, like architecture and sculpture are areas where Sentinel's literal sense-ability shines. When the book boasts "math is easy," or students claim "math is fun," chances are both author and instructor have Sentinel in their Profile.

Sight, sound, taste, touch, and vibrational surrounds are processed and understood bodily: first in gut...then mentally digested...then emotionally tagged before cataloguing. Expressing themselves through language is only a wee thorn in early development. The lifelong Achilles' heel for Sentinels is emotions. These individuals must be taught how to emotionally relate with others—along with lessons in diplomacy to blunt their truth-piercing arrows.

For Sentinels, emotions start out as a solid clump known as feelings. Through close parental guidance, while learning and experiencing, they sort through the muddled mix to locate which emotion most appropriately fits with information and situation. THAT LESSON is then labelled and stored as a complete experience in memory. Essentially, Sentinels must build a "sensory" reference library to match body and mental intelligence with appropriate emotional responses. When Sentinels trip, their most common stumbling block is emotions.

These individuals muscle-reflex to life with instinct awareness. Tightening of muscles occurs, raising internal alarm-hackles, long before intellect has registered cause for concern. Loosening of muscles is positive, meaning they're safe and can participate without guard or worry. Their order of functioning is sense first, think second, and emote last. Of all personalities, these individuals are the least emotionally impelled or compelled. Sentinel children do not lie in their early years. Code of honour, notwithstanding, they essentially do not anticipate or factor intangibles, such as another's feelings, into their thinking process. Candor comes naturally. Discretion may need to be taught.

Unfortunately, these individuals learn too well that discretion is the lesser form of valour. There tends to be only two varieties of Sentinels: those who are truthful and those who are not. And what Sentinels are least truthful about is their own emotions, their innermost wishes, desires, and needs. But here's the kicker, their dishonesty is never as damaging or destructive to others, as it is to their self.

The surest indicator of an emotionally dishonest Sentinel is their suffering of internal organ dysfunction or disease at a relatively young age. When "things" are not addressed, expelled, or vented, there's but one consequence: pent up frustration. Reticence—not heart disease, not addiction, not vital organ failure—is the number one killer of Sentinels. (Dominant Sentinel *thinkers* are advised to read Sentinel *emoting* as well). This is the only personality that needs to consult their emotional library before comprehending how they feel, and before sharing those feelings with others. That means, they may not have a point of reference or words to describe their deepest fears, passions, and needs, with others, so they bottle them up instead. Being dishonest is as foreign to Sentinel nature, as gossamer wings on donkeys.

Upholding and defending the concepts of just and fair, seem biologically programmed into these individuals. With a Sentinel child as a family member, siblings need not worry about being pestered by the schoolyard bully. They look after their "own" without fear or hesitation. Be it schoolyard, factory floor, boardroom, or picket line, these individuals step-up and step-in, when the scales of justice dip unfavourably for them or for their loved ones. They're less likely to turn the other cheek than confront head-on. Sentinels are proactive when it comes to issues that impinge or obstruct rights and freedoms. Not far from the tipping of tea into Harbour, was a Bostonian Sentinel outraged at the British tea tax. Whether unfairness is directed at them, or not, is inconsequential. If the scent is foul play, it's an irresistible reek that draws Sentinel's ire and fire. Pulsing in their blood are echoes of Voltaire, "I disapprove of what you say, but I will defend to the death your right to say it."

Sentinels are cellularly intolerant of heavy-handedness, regardless of the arm or authority attached. Parents will know their child is Sentinel, when they try to discipline one of their other offspring. The Sentinel will intervene on their sibling's behalf. Even if diaper attired, crawling, and communicating in a stream of incomprehensible babble at the time—their protection intention will be clear.

From birth, there's just something endearing and comforting about that streak of steel-protectiveness that runs through Sentinel core and spine. That steeliness does not seem to dissolve with age nor rust over time. When confident, they seem particularly immune to strains of emotional coercion or influence. It's noteworthy that a disproportionately high number of Sentinels are drawn to professions that protect and preserve, such as law, military, and eco-system concerns.

Often, Sentinel children experience extreme shyness in public and tend to keep within viewing/touching distance of Mom and Dad. The infant term, "making strange," may have been coined, because of them. With strangers, they are fish out of water, and can be entirely uncooperative and decidedly unaffectionate. These children cannot be convinced or encouraged to kiss visitors "hello" or "goodbye," unless they personally wish to; a precursor of the adult in the making. Sentinels cannot be ridiculed or cajoled into doing anything they're not comfortable with. This toddler refuses all but Mom's cooking or won't sleep anywhere but at home.

Predictability is very important to these sensory-intellects. As children, they most often need to be gently introduced to anything new. Rearrange the living room furniture, and together at the doorway, will sit the Sentinel child and the family cat staring, in mutual dismay at the outrage before them. At any age, these ultra-sensory beings are susceptible to audio-visual overload—be it stranger, nature, or noise. Their eyes, ears, and body picks up so much information that they require more time than others, to physically understand, mentally digest, and emotionally label it. New means change, and change means adjustment. In terms of adjustment, Sentinel needs to have control over its ebb, flow and gait. Otherwise, they may stop, step back, and step away, rather than await explanation.

They approach problem-solving by developing solution systems, then logically following through in step-by-step fashion. Sentinels tend to be meticulous about details and seldom err in judgement or procedure. As they resent changes to their world, they resent being caught unawares or unprepared. They're generally quite punctual and ready to begin work or play, upon arrival.

Chaos and cacophony are issues that cause Sentinel great emotional distress. Because they absorb undertones and subtleties, along with visual information, new situations that fluctuate before they have time to understand can bombard them with novel, unreferenced sensations. Bereft of comparative experience and unable to ingest and understand the information quickly enough, Sentinel would expectedly be emotionally overwhelmed. Their first response would be fear; their second, flight or fight!

Though more introverted than outgoing, Sentinel is a very strong personality: sharp-minded, definite of opinion, and confident in action. Taking them from the office for an impromptu night out on the town, will likely reveal their hallmark reserve and social shyness. Improvisation is not their strong suit. In their own spheres of comfort, they prove most competent, confident, and capable. If thrown into new situations, they often appear stone-faced and move with awkward, wooden unease, until they feel comfortable in their setting and safe with their companions.

Others may drink alcohol to relax, but Sentinel tends to become more tightly wound when they imbibe. More acutely aware of sounds or under-lying meanings in the careless words, slurs, and actions of tipsy others, their physical antennae can be set a-whirl, throwing these innately shy, reserved individuals off-balance. Their internal agitation may outwardly manifest in fluctuations of behaviour, from extreme friendliness, to extreme feistiness. Their resultant out-of-character behaviour is often as much a surprise to them as to others.

Their greatest challenge is trust.

Sentinel is the planet skeptic. They have no trouble finding four-leaf clovers, but they may first need to see a report on recent use of area pesti-cides, after which they'd inspect closer, to determine whether it was indeed a real plant and not a plastic fake someone had planted to make them look foolish. Being reckless or impetuous is not their repute nor claim. They do not necessarily focus on the negative, they just don't place much faith in "what you see, is what you get." Their finely tuned physical-sensibility often picks out the one jarring note from the chorus. Others may question, "What's in it for me?" Sentinel ever-expects a wolf will emerge from under sheep's clothing.

They'd rather be lonely than be betrayed; rather be wrong than be wronged, and they'd rather be thought a fool than be fooled, any day. Evo-lutionarily speaking, skepticism has held them in good stead, not risk. So they tend to stick with the sure thing, rationalizing that a "bird in the hand is worth two in the bush" Such characteristic, cautionary reluctance can prevent them from exploring their potential to its fullest.

Sentinel may warm up to life and others less quickly, and lack the charismatic glib that wins the popular vote, but beneath their imperturbable poise and hypnotic mystique beats the pulse of an exceptional and exceptionally loyal being. Once welcomed inside their private embrace, few exemplify the meaning of friend better than Sentinel—the one who surely inspired the phrase "still waters run deep."

THE LOGICALS

Diligent employees are the backbone of the business world. Their unique mental aptitude has contributed solution systems and inventions for accounting, processing, measuring and evaluating information—the consequence and requirement of industrial growth.

For these cerebral beings, reality conforms to the bounds and strictures of logic. Diligent plays with ideas: turning them about, sifting and sorting, and searching through their database of known possibilities. Possibilities are then pushed and prodded along the pathway toward solution. Some falter, some fail, some drop out; only viables press on. When one remains, it is a logic victor named solution, which ends round-one of the game. From there, physical testing begins. For Diligent, it is the mystery and challenge, within the process of solution-finding that interests and intrigues. What happens within is systematic thinking; a perfect marriage of logic and order.

When Diligent starts a project, they do so from the premise of clearly defined problem and set objective. They then gather all relevant information, organize a system for its solution, roll up their sleeves, and with notebook in one hand and pen in the other, begin working step one of their plan. Once all criteria has been met, checked and re-checked again, they use that as foundation and permission to move onto step two. Detail and data are their barometer of progress, and by criteria of fact do they measure success. This sequential, methodical, and meticulous approach, is repeated at each level of development, through to completion. Throughout, they cannot and will not be rushed. The phrase "slow and steady wins the race" was likely coined for, *or by,* Diligent.

These individuals are born competent and seemingly destined to execute; they harbour executive excellence. They characteristically do not defer decision-making responsibility to others, but are most comfortable and valuable when given a realm of their own to rule. Diligent is famous for taking care of things. That's what they do better than most, if not best.

Their systematic solution process serves two purposes: to provide a concise record of empirical data to model future success, and to provide support for their conclusions, should proof one day be needed. Diligent places all faith in, and depend exclusively on, their mental ability to fathom and function with perfect precision. The least likely personality to seek advice from a psychic or fortune-teller, is Diligent. When their decisions are questioned by others, these perfectionists suffer double-doubt syndrome. Is the error due to inattention during the process or due to wrong interpretation at conclusion? Each doubt must then be scrupulously investigated. To Diligent, it's check the checker time.

The order of investigation goes: step 1, 1a, 1b, 1c, 1d, 1e...et cetera, until fault is found or the step is found faultless. Each step that is re-confirmed, increases insecurity about their own deductive ability. It's difficult for others to understand the stress these individuals suffer, when called upon to defend their decisions and actions. They take such questioning personally and can seem obsessive about absolving themselves of blame. During re-investigation, they'll discover that either Shakespeare was right, "To err is human," or how wasteful the doubt-festering arrows of mere mortals can be. More oft' than not, 'tis Diligent who's proven right.

They've perfected their purely logical, note-taking approach for a reason.

Diligent hates being wrong about anything. They tend to keep on top of work-related matters, such as new innovations, industry trends, and whether there's a future for company and future for self, in association. Diligent uses their head. They look before they leap and apply their prodigious intellect to all aspects of life. Their greatest rewards often come through work, where their brand of smart is recognized and appreciated.

Diligent tends to be a technological junkie, to one degree or another, and as much today as evolutionarily. The computer is the brain child that passed their rigorous research and testing, before winning their nod of approval. Additionally, Diligent was among the first to recognize the efficiency of digital technology and first to apply it. The technical end of the computer industry is dominated by this personality, as is the technical side of radio, television, appliances, and telecommunications. Diligents swelled the ranks of early rocket scientists. Understanding how things work, fascinates and entertains their complex, logical minds. It is highly conceivable that when clocks were invented, Diligent was either beside the inventor or first in line to purchase the complicated time-piece sporting gears, springs, bells, or whistles. Once home, they likely commenced to taking it apart to understand how it worked, before putting it back together again. Diligent is a reluctant audience member for hands-on demonstrations. They much prefer having the object, the manual, privacy, and time, to tinker-learn on their own.

Regarded as most dependable people, Diligents build their professional and private lives upon firmly held principles of by-the-book correctness and above board ethics. They work devotedly and tirelessly—though not necessarily, uncomplainingly—and accomplish tasks with style-typical thoroughness and efficiency. Industry-wide, world-wide, Diligents perform much of the laboratory testing for other people's theories. Routine, that others find monotonous or boring, provides highly disciplined Diligent a sense of security and stability they find comforting. The process of testing or finding solutions, with all the learning opportunities along the way, is more satisfying to them than answers or outcomes. Decision-making by logical analysis, is a procedure they employ personally and professionally. Impulse buying, like impetuosity, is not their renown. Before showing up at the car dealer to purchase a vehicle, they've likely done exhaustive research, memorized the "lemon" list, know which model they want, and decided how much they'll pay. However, more time to test drive, mull, and haggle will be required, before they'll formalize an offer.

Creativity is one area that is particularly stressful.

Reality for them is tangible, measurable, and based on proven practice or premise. Creativity, which has no tried and true historical point of reference, is perceived as pure risk by them. Like flight without wings; it does not compute. Risk-taking goes against the grain of their cautious check and re-check nature, and they tend to adopt the role of devil's advocate throughout the process. Diligent, not known for being adventurous or experimental, can fall into patterns of staid conservatism and often requires convincing before trying a new idea or taking another approach. Once they've gained confidence and met with success, Diligent proves most capable of being able to assess and appreciate the potential in new ideas and processes. However, expect to hear frequent mutterings and grumblings, meaning, *"I'm from Missouri,* (the show me state), *so prove it."*

There is just something cellular in Diligents that cannot accept randomness and chaos, much less ignore it. Something compels them to discover what patterns of predictability exist and to find the logical order they know *must* lie somewhere within. As they take things apart to understand how they work, they push to find the breaking points of ideas, concepts, and plans. Others would be satisfied with the what and where of limits; not Diligent. Their perfectionistic nature kicks in and questions, "where within known and recommended limits is optimum performance and efficiency had?" By dogged-determination does Diligent unravel random and tame chaos, before moving onto the next step or new challenge.

It's likely that Diligent was the first to develop gambling systems. The mathematical challenge of demystifying chance and levelling odds is mentally irresistible, though gambling is an unlikely hobby or pastime of theirs. Gambling in theory is one thing; gambling for real, quite another. The fear of betting, risking, then losing the two things that matter most to them: money and reputation, are strong deterrents for *very* security-conscious, and proud, Diligent.

THE LOGICALS

Time lines tend to blur and blend together for this personality. Past events are so vividly imprinted on Sage, they recount them as freshly today as when they occurred. While seeming careless and confusing to others, for these individuals, time is but one piece of the intricacy and mix that constitutes the whole. The enchilada on their plate is intricately woven with Spanish language, Inquisitions, race annihilation, Flamenco, paella, Mayan temples, matadors, *For Whom The Bell Tolls*, pesos, 1492, classical guitar, Franco, and Agent 007. Intellectuals of the highest order, Sages view now and today as entwisted and inextricably rooted in timeless, borderless history.

Social interaction, synchronicity of people, purpose, and life celebration, are their historical perspective niche. From people, do Sages derive their greatest solace and enjoyment. These individuals tend to be highly sociable, and with their gentle, unassuming manner, are socially endeared. Their philosophy is reflected in their interactions with others, "there are infinite paths and infinite ways; and between the Big Bang and Eternity is where possibility plays."

No person, no thing, is definitively one way.

Sage tends to be less judgemental than most. A worthy lesson for all, in their live-as-live-may approach, which pays homage to the differences in culture, creed and race. The Ku Klux is an unlikely clan of theirs, nor is

Sage likely to have condemned Oscar Wilde, or captained slave cargo ships. They tend to see more reason to admire the many facets in the human diamond, than reasons for the burying, buffing, or blasting of kith and kin.

These individuals tend to build their lives around service industries and professions. Whether prime minister, scholar, foreman or dishwasher, their first love and satisfaction comes from the human part of daily interactions. Regardless of level of education, what role they play, or career path they choose, Sages tend to be intellectuals. Exchanging ideas, humour, and fact, is their hallmark fame and greatest personal reward.

Sage often earns the reputation for being scattered and unorganized. In a linear, logic-based world, they function with seemingly undisciplined randomness. Generally speaking, this logical world is intolerant of those who stray from step-by-step methodology.

For instance, solving a jigsaw puzzle is a linear mental process. Most start with a few, core fitting pieces, then hunt, match, and build piece-by-piece, from core to completed puzzle. Sage starts with the whole. Firmly holding a clear mental image of the puzzle, as if already finished, they move the scattered pieces to their proper place; matching location with their completed mental image. Passers-by may not readily discern the pattern of solution or stage of progress, however, closer inspection would reveal that though seemingly unorganized, and though riddled by space and gap, viewed collectively the strewn tabletop bears an uncanny resemblance to the completed puzzle—only lacking in fit and snap.

In linear-thinking, step-by-step order of processing builds toward solution. In Sage thinking, process is inherent in the whole. If each puzzle piece is equally representative of, and equally important to whole, then solution is possible from any point or part thereof. So, for this random thinker, the order of processing is irrelevant, because for every problem solution is inherent and inevitable.

Sage minds have potential to range far beyond genius limits. Unfortunately, genius tends to range beyond eyeglasses, car keys, clocks, and calendars too. The proverbial absent-minded professor was likely a Sage. These individuals tend to be intellectual institutions, ever-brimming with knowledge and wisdom. Most are self-taught, as they tend to agitate, not salivate, at Pavlovian school bell. Regimented learning is almost painful to Sage, whose interest needs time, to warm up to subjects. In school, just as their interest is sufficiently primed and ready for immersion, class ends; jarring, frustrating, and depriving them of intellectual exploration—their favourite pastime, (a Sage-common hobby).

No other is as comparatively capable of acquiring self-taught expertise, as Sage. Seemingly, by process of osmosis, through absorption of book, can and do they learn. Most are prodigious readers, who have potential to ingest and digest extraordinary volumes of material, like sets of encyclopedia, dictionaries from stem to stern, or every book in the local library.

By sifting, sorting, and extracting from the depths, they find what is wanted and when needed. And their genius can be endlessly distracted by interests that waft in front of their nose, irresistibly beckoning their curiosity to follow—a propensity that is both balm and bane for them, and cause of disdain by others. A stolen moment taken to investigate a curiosity pique can become a marathon of intellectual consumption, earning Sage a reputation for being fickle and irresponsible.

In the 21st Century, historical sages, tribal wise men, and public philosophers, are natures without niche and tend to be viewed as bumbling or incompetent. Assembly-line thinking, where human value is based on three-dimensional reality and measured by *graphable* productivity, requires a lowering of sights from far off clouds, to flat on feet ground. Sages tend to focus on forests, when toothpicks are what's required. An adjustment they tend to resist or ignore. Consequently, and routinely, they meet with general impatience and disappointment from others. If life's purpose is to inspire, not retire, the first step for Sage is to get back onto the treadmill and join in with others.

This personality is wisdom and compassion, and as rare now as evolutionarily. Sage has two important wisdom-wrapped messages to deliver: Part, particle, and participant are equally important to the whole. There are equally as many solutions for problems as people who solve them.

The greatest challenge for Sage is to adopt and intrinsically incorporate discipline, focus, and organization, into their daily life. Otherwise, the value of them and the benefit of their lessons may not be realized. Unless Sage assimilates and lowers their focus, the bell that tolls may very well toll for thee.

THE PRACTICALS

Weird is a term Eccentrik becomes familiar with, at an early age. For others, such labelling can be a tripping, burdensome cross to bear. For Eccentrik, weird is the wind beneath their creative wings and what lifts their pride beyond pedestrian concern. Complete conformity is not an option for these individuals.

They tend to be self-content and protective about being different. They have enough confidence in their intelligence and abilities, to withstand normally withering peer pressure. By the time they're ready to leave home, most Eccentriks have conformed—under the supervision of parents and school—as much as they're likely to ever do. Once on their own, the Eccentrik butterfly emerges with a steely-determination to tailor life to fit self, regardless of social norm or mores.

Their dress may be flamboyant, their work area may resemble a war zone, their inner circle of friends may be more a listing of Who's Not than Who's Who, but you'd be dead wrong to think there's anything flaky about them. Behind their mask and masquerade of zany outrageousness, is potential for world-class thinking. Eccentrik is a strong-minded and strong-willed personality. They thumb their nose at conventionality, at every turn and opportunity possible, but that's only the short end of their measuring stick. These individuals are astute business people, and serious contenders for glory and success.

What's unique about the Eccentrik mind is its ability to internally rotate ideas. They can maintain the whole of their three-dimensional vision and spin it, as others would a statue on a pedestal. By shifting their focus at want or will, they alter an object's shape internally. Like a sculptor, adding clay to this tangent, subtracting from that; magnifying this area, manipulating that part, and manoeuvring the whole, they mentally design before putting pen to paper. These are purely logical beings, who approach problem-solving methodically and with step-by-step thoroughness. Ever-lurking in the back of their mind is the question of whether or not their idea is workable, meaning, producible. An idea that cannot be physically realized is a waste of time, for them.

The Eccentrik gift for rearranging reality accounts for their predominance as designers and their prominence among inventors. In every realm of three-dimensional creativity—industrial, commercial, and gallery—their artistic presence and influence abounds. But, in the field of technical gadgetry is where Eccentrik creativity finds it's greatest whimsical and practical expression. Those everyday-use-items provide them endless opportunity, to play with product and purpose and create something new, improved or irresistibly unique. Transformers™, the toy that with a twist and a turn creates either a car or a robot, is a typical Eccentrik innovation. Inspired sufficiently, while listening to an idea, they'll construct a working-model using whatever's handy or available, before the thought's complete. Reinventing the wheel is a motivational challenge for them.

They do not fit readily nor easily into traditional corporate environments. Dictates, such as, "Wear suit and tie...Be here at nine," cause their freedom-fighting hackles to immediately rise. They'd be more likely to show up at ten and dressed in the mandatory suit, but sans tie, sans shirt, and sporting neon, hi-top sneakers. For Eccentriks, such self-sabotaging behaviour is more complex than the mere of challenging authority. It's an inborn, life-worn, knee-jerk reflex to prescription protocol, regardless of form or ilk. The pill of conformity lodges stubbornly in their throat. For

Pg. 118

this peacock personality, lock-step conformity threatens their individuality and infringes on their inalienable right to captain their own future.

Why?

Eccentriks are mind-ego functioning beings. At an early age, they realize they are different and respond in an unusual way. Despite their earnest contortions and eager hoop-jumping to please, despite parental pushing, prodding, and cheer, they still couldn't fit without causing blister or pain. There's something within Eccentrik, an intrinsic fortitude that can't play as willow to wind. They just cannot and will not bend to accommodate.

If being true to themselves disappoints others, "so be it!" they conclude, then walk away; undiluted within and undiminished in the only eyes that ultimately matter to them: their own. They focus on creating an identity where tap of self-definition does not drip or trickle in accordance with norm. Eccentrik keeps their spigot wide-open, allowing for the free flow of possibilities and perspectives, without check, choke or censure. One result of such open-mindedness is their renown for being creatively brilliant. One consequence? Their notoriety for being hard-nosed weird.

Because their belief grazes in lush, open-minded pastures, Eccentrik egos welcome a smorgasbord of experience, as opposed to the more narrowly defined standards of acceptability. Comparatively, their egos are thicker-skinned. They've built up layered resistance to the demands, disappointment, and derision, of a world less tolerant of those who list left or list right of *normal.*

Being unpredictable is their hallmark. Eccentriks re-invent themselves with regularity. Like mercury, they take the shape of their inspirations, contouring to fancy and wending with whim. They are guileless and unpretentious, and natural media darlings, who capture our attention, spark our interest, encourage us to laugh at ourselves, and show us how to find enjoyment in tote, task, and toil. Eccentriks do things, say things, and wear things others wouldn't or couldn't, for fear of ridicule or reprisal. Their outrageous actions and sensuous being affords others an opportunity to experience uninhibited and unabashed freedom, vicariously.

They may not know what they want, but Eccentrik knows what they don't want: to be run-of-the-mill. They disdain Lilliputian thinking that says, "eat all eggs this way." They approach others as they approach life; non-judgementally. Eccentrik will not white supremacists nor abortion clinic protester be. Such semi-god, demagogue practices bore and abhor them equally. The path they walk is broad but serpentine. They consciously and scrupulously avoid those that are straight and narrow.

High-energy individuals, always on the go, Eccentriks are roman candles that sizzle and pop with ahhhh...innervating others with their adrenaline rush and love for life.

The most common word in an Eccentrik's repertoire is "boring," which they use to rationalize a wide range of situations that used to be. Once the novelty of a job or relationship wears off, it becomes "boring," requiring they pack up their tent and move on. Rarely do they stay long enough for others to get to know them. Perhaps they fear that familiarity will find them more ordinary than extraordinary. Perhaps they fear disappointment, both ways from self.

Like Kansas summer tornadoes, they repeatedly touch down and lift off, not staying long enough to make a name for themselves or a commitment to others. Individuality, when used as a hammer, is bound to view the world as a collection of nails. Eccentriks teach others that genius does not come in one-size or one-colour, and that if life is dynamic, so too, should its participants be. These individuals live for experiences. Too often they deny themselves and others the opportunity of experiencing them—the vulnerable being behind the *weird* teacher, who applauds the novel and plucks pleasure from moments.

The challenge for Eccentrik is to learn that feeling boredom usually means, "you're just starting to get it." Hang in long enough and go deep enough, to discover the unique, evolutionary truth of self. Why is such a complicated and valuable individual here at this juncture in time? By going deeper, discover what leaving denies.

THE PRACTICALS

The mind of an Idealist is a marvel of bedazzling complication and bedizzying speed. Alacrity and acuity of thought processing are trademark Idealist. In terms of intellectual speed, they rank superior. Few arrive at a solution or deliver it faster, than them. While their solutions may not be the only ones nor necessarily the best, their solutions have proven best enough and often enough to sail global economies. It is not a coincidence that their brain child, the computer, thinks in like binary-fashion, as its Idealist inventor.

Few experiences return them greater pleasure than creative problem-solving: their gifted-forté. When they reach solution, Idealist sees patterns through time. Flow charts, schedules, and procedures, mentally form and click into place. While others are mentally digesting and discussing the merits of an idea, Idealist is mentally organizing and implementing. They're architects of dreams—the managers and overseers, who shore-up and bank leading edges. They may not be the visionaries who break new ground, but Idealist is usually on the field, when seeds of success get planted. Globally, historically, and evolutionarily, the mover and shaker among us is Idealist. And they've likely always been as they are now: the last to celebrate august events or auspicious occasions. Idealist is not easily nor readily pleased.

For others, membership has its privileges.
For Idealists, power decides who's privileged and who's not.

These individuals are the number-one purchasers of self-help books; the majority audience at motivational seminars; the ones attending night school; and the energy pulse at trade shows, on both sides of booths. Idealists make it their business to know all possible about whatever preoccupies their mind, sparks their interest, or fills the pages of their leather-bound notebooks. Usually, that's work: making money, winning recognition, and having more power at their disposal. They strive to become invaluable first; they then upwardly adjust their market price.

Value—how much things cost, how rare, how much does a dollar buy, and how much prestige goes with acquisition or position, are typical Idealist questions. If socially acceptable, the first question they'd ask is, "How much money did you earn last year?" That's how they measure their own value, in comparison to others.

Idealists think in terms of value and worth. When compensation equals their personally held valuation, or when they can dictate their own terms and write their own cheques, is when Idealists are satisfied on two, but not necessarily all levels. Firstly, their own high opinion of themselves is validated. Nothing pleases more or pridefully pops the buttons off Idealist shirts faster, than having answered the question, "What do you want?," and their getting it! Secondly, it gives them the opportunity to do their *style of schtick,* their own way.

To have complete control over all aspects of a project is dictionary-definition of Idealist satisfaction and intoxicating to them. A force to be reckoned with, is Idealist with an idea and the wherewithal to make it happen. Idealists love money and are very, generally, very good at managing it.

(Test participants, who cannot balance a cheque-book yet perceive their Idealist as their dominant Style of thinking, stop here and retest. The further and more that follows, isn't you either).

Besides acquiring the knowledge, and honing self and skills to the point of perfection, Idealists do one other thing that contributes to their long-standing record of success. They emulate it. They may adopt a successful other as a role-model, to learn from and, hopefully, surpass in terms of accomplishment, by making smarter moves and taking smarter risks. Their role-model may only be "famous" to them, but it's their record of success and their lifestyle that Idealist admires or envies. For these individuals, admire is a simile for envy.

As it's impossible to be a little bit pregnant, it's impossible for them to admire without some degree of envy. In keeping with their striving nature, the model Idealist chooses will be far beyond their current status quo, financially and socially, but within reach of their desires and dreams. Instead of being inspiration, their models are more akin to cattle-prod motivation. Forcing them to work faster and harder for success. But then, Idealists don't mind standing on tiptoe, to catch their reflection in elevated mirrors. When at eye-level, they tend to find more in their mirrored reflection to erase than embrace.

Idealists seem determined, to pit success against failure in winner-take-all competitions. Their drug of choice is mind-adrenaline. They choose situations that challenge their intellect, skill, timing, health, and even threaten their financial ruin. Their favourite games and tales involve risking to win. They'll likely only admit to having lost, if they're currently ahead of where they were, when defeated. Perceiving a sliver of chance to leap ahead of others, Idealist doesn't hesitate. They roll and risk.

Their world is populated by winners and losers. When bested by another, they may outwardly smile, but inwardly stew in self-disappointment bile. Idealist may quickly but not easily, walk away from defeat. They usually resolve to more creatively triumph next time around—whatever it takes. That path could wend unscrupulously. Idealists have a tendency to side with immediacy over wisdom, in heats of competition. These individuals never lose sight of goals, which can narrow their view to tunnel vision. They may be too-focused on winning, to hear the warning grumbles of conscience-discomfort. White collar crimes are the consequence of such focused ignore and/or ignorance.

To experience Idealists at play, join them in a game of Monopoly™. They're the ones who toss original rules and move the stakes to nail-biting heights. With them, each roll of dice portents ruin, passing *Go* is the mark of shrewd tenacity, and being *Jailed* a reprieve. It's unlikely that the term "gracious loser," was coined to describe an Idealist gamester. They play to win. They're renowned for being poor losers, but also renowned for paying their bets or debts. It's no mystery why gambling appeals to them, or why stress-related ailments, such as ulcers, migraines, and back problems, commonly plague them. They're the original stress-junkies.

Responsibility is Idealist's elixir, and the more, the better! They like being needed. It's a rare Idealist, who walks away from challenge or commitment (once anger has passed, that is). Whether by reputation, by title, or by legal right, all matters pertaining to dominion and domain become their business. Generally, affiliations and associations—from office, to friends, to family—are considered personally-reflective, thus subject to screening by Idealist's propriety filter. They are not reluctant to tell others what to think, do and say. All are entitled to their opinion. Not having control over key aspects of their life is high-stress for them.

By grit, by wit, by might, Idealists weave self into global tapestries. Proof, they can and do deliver better mouse traps, is their consistent historical distinction for being the second wealthiest and second most powerful personality style on the planet. Visionary is number one.

Interestingly, Idealists who are not receiving the recognition they feel their due, at work or home, tend to catch colds frequently. It seems to be an attention-getting ploy. Generally speaking, their health and constitution is rather robust. Additionally, getting these stoic individuals to miss a day of work is rarer than hens' teeth. Plowing through to successful completion, despite illness or adversity, is their nature and way. Spooning them some well-deserved attention-tonic seems to miraculously restore flagging health, as well as immensely boost their self-doubt immunity.

No free rides

Others and mate learn to place great faith in the ability and capability of Idealist. Trusted and loved ones tend to benefit materially and socially in their company. Be warned, though, any ride with Idealists is a taxi-ride, not a hitchhike. Fares will be charged and the tab usually reads "meet or exceed *my* expectations." Idealist expects all their investments of time, money, and affection, to improve and yield greater treasure or pleasure. Their Svengali-propensity may require others to compromise their independence, for the sake of the relationship. (One chief per Idealist tribe).

Trusting others to do things right is hard for these perfectionists. When reins and rights are turned over to them, Idealist's true gifts unwrap: creative problem-solving, organization, and delegation. When problems seem insurmountable, count on Idealist to deliver solutions and plans that work.

Why does Idealist's particular style of smart have so many thorns? Because they not only think, walk, and talk fast, many are nail-biters; a likely coping-behaviour from having to bottle their impatience with others, so often. While slower-thinking others mull, chew, and consider, Idealist is mentally tying the bow on the completed package. Additionally, having to listen to others discussing something they knew wouldn't work *ten minutes ago*, is sure to manifest as raw nerves and gnawed nails. Idealist has been labelled obstinate and uncooperative. When they take a stand, they can seem stone-deaf and resolute. In reality, they're receptive to ideas that sound better than their own, but quite deaf to ideas that ring failure to their ears. Failing anything can be crushingly humiliating for Idealists. They like a good challenge and prepare for one outcome: winning. Should a better solution than theirs be offered, they're quick to recognize and capitalize on it. It's not only the wind of their ideas that they use to fill global sails, but the most perfect wind they can muster.

Unless their innate critical aspect is tempered with greater acceptance and patience, Idealist may find themselves crossing that perfect finish-line, perfectly alone. While prickly pears can be a refreshing treat, the novelty and necessity of wearing gloves in their handling, wearies, wears thin, and wears others out quickly. Instead of expecting utopia to arrive full-blown, as Athena from the brow of Zeus, Idealists may benefit from learning to trust the irrefutable wisdom of time's lesson. Change unfolds, it does not unfurl.

Enjoyment of now is a right, a privilege, and an entitlement. As the world applauds what went right, they tend to focus on what went wrong. Idealist must occasionally bow to what is, and learn to enjoy the process as much as the change.

THE EMOTIONALS

Kinsmen

They require less sleep than others and seem determined to wear self and day out, with their full schedule of activities and appointments. High energy and organization are hallmarks of these busy individuals. Kinsmen enjoy a wide variety of interests, though music and physical fitness seem to figure prominently in their life. As instructors or coaches, especially sports-related, they have no equal.

Procrastination, their confidence barometer

When confident, they do not procrastinate but deal directly with problems or interruptions, before moving onto other interests and challenges. They'd not be able to maintain their energetic lifestyle or accomplish as much for themselves and others, if not masterly efficient and organized.

When unconfident, they may be the model of efficiency professionally but lackadaisical personally; to the extent of avoiding interactions and communications with family and friends. Others, generally and genuinely like Kinsmen, for they are wide-smiling and warmly approachable. Most feel safe around them, and for good reason. Kinsmen take care of others. That's their life purpose...and fulfillment.

Like most logicals, when Kinsmen tackle a job or project, they start from the premise of a well-defined problem and clear objective. They then gather all relevant information, encourage input, organize a system for solution, and begin work at step-one of their plan. Once all criteria has been met, checked and re-checked, they use that as foundation for step-two. However, in Kinsmen solution systems, there's one style-typical step that differentiates their approach from all others.

At set intervals, Kinsmen makes allowance for consensus-taking. All privy and party to outcomes are invited to review the state of progress and give their nod of approval, before work continues. Kinsmen knows how important individual endorsement is, to group success. By touching base with others, and reviewing progress, they not only shore up support for the project, but address emotional concerns or conflicts before they become obstacles and threaten the project's success. To others, the pace may seem plodding and redundant, but few can herd projects and deliver success as frequently, as efficiently, and with as little wear and tear on team members, as them. The more smoothly running the job or department, and the less stressed the staff and participants, the greater the likelihood that a Kinsmen is running the show. They're team players, so much so, their evolutionary name is pluraled.

One highly likely reason for their consensus-approach to problem-solving is, it absolves them of sole responsibility for unexpected or unfavourable outcomes. When they garner general approval from others, it reduces the likelihood of them letting others down or of being criticized. Not fulfilling obligations, when and as promised, is demoralizing for the conscientious Kinsmen.

Not meeting expectations equals personal failure

With their highly-evolved sense of responsibility and strong need to please, when things go wrong, Kinsmen tends to shoulder most of the blame. No other is more self-critical or quicker to don the mantle of blame, than them. Characteristically, they reach for emotional bats and administer a beating, long before fault is found or blame affixed. Even if found faultless, which is usually the case, its too late. They've already beaten themselves black and blue internally. Others don't realize how ultra-sensitive these individuals are, and how responsible they feel for all things associated with them. Their composed, outward appearance belies their internal anguish and fears. Professional actors could not hide, for one act, the emotional turmoil and truth Kinsmen hides daily.

They can recall occasions where others have disappointed them, but tend to forget the hurt that they felt. However, they relive in vivid detail, down to place, temperature, and time, the full measure and score of emotional suffering they felt, after having disappointed another. Kinsmen quickly forgive and forget the grievances others cause them, but they neither forget nor forgive themselves. In terms of excess baggage, Kinsmen hauls trainloads, generally.

Responsibility is a merciless task-master for them. It motivates, but demands they only produce and deliver, excellence. Despite outward poise, Kinsmen lacks self-confidence. This is usually a state of their own mind, as these individuals are largely regarded as capable and efficient. They may not make the same mistake twice, which is admirable, but their fear of doing so hobbles them to well-worn paths. Risk-taking is not their forté. They trust tried-and-true.

People-lovers and pleasers by nature, their greatest motivation is appreciation. As children, they are often models of compliance and helpfulness. They mind their parents, mind their school, mind their siblings, and mind their duties, equally responsibly. They often feel most rewarded when complimented for being grown-up. From earliest childhood, they seem to have an inordinate concern for, and an acute awareness, of the world around them. Watching television news or documentaries about the suffering of others is very disturbing, for these sensitive tykes. Oddly, horror shows are rated as their least favoured film genre, yet criminal biographies and crime novels rank high on preferred reading lists; along with romantic prose and poetry.

Kinsmen parents often consider their children to be the most valuable asset and contribution they can make to society. These individuals take their parental roles seriously and immerse themselves in all aspects of child-rearing, from school, to church, to community involvement. Though not charismatic, Kinsmen is highly sociable. They like to get out and participate in community life, and keep abreast of world events. While friend to many, and familiar to most, they may avoid close, intimate friendships outside their immediate family circle. The family unit is often their prime source of support and nurturance, which can put them in a position of front-line vulnerability. Without other options for companionship and emotional ballast, their mate tends to have a direct bearing on their state of happiness. It's uplifting when love and support are given; devastating and lonely, when withheld or denied.

The Kinsmen personality is divided. On one side is emotion (self-deemed irrationality) and on the other side, intellect (logic). Despite experiencing life first emotionally, they usually subscribe to pure mental processing. This intrinsic duality can cause them great stress internally and be cause for much confusion externally.

Others will know they're in the company of a Kinsmen, when their companion is one moment laughing, joking, as madcap as any in the crowd, but suddenly shifts gears to a more sombre note, without reason or warning. They can be warm and witty public speakers, with a knack for finding the emotional pulse of their audience, but in mid-thought and sentence, will switch tone and mood, as though stung by the get-serious "bee." Their characteristic about-face behaviour can leave others wondering where the personable one went.

Kinsmen are doers, who earn respect by the example of their living. In keeping with their highly evolved sense of responsibility and propriety—

as in *right*, *wrong*, and *should*, they tend to choose an upstanding, solid mate, who appreciates gold-plated citizenry and respects solid work ethics. It was most likely a Kinsmen who coined the phrase, "As you make your bed, so shall you lie," for they plan each step carefully, before planting their foot or taking a stride. If not so logical-practical and so selflessly accommodating, they would not be Kinsmen at all.

A love/hate relationship with risk

A critical demanding environment, or individual, can severely wear and tear on Kinsmen, though they seem irresistably drawn toward such adversity. Their intellectual side likes control and stability, but their emotional side desires caprice and uncertainty. They are attracted to bad boys and bad girls, who thumb their noses at conventionality. But their logical *should* and *please* side cringes and dismisses such flights of insanity.

Few are as comparatively intelligent; few are as emotionally gifted; yet none ignores half their power—their emotional creativity—as routinely and regularly as Kinsmen do. They tend to react and respond in pre-scribed, approved ways, when leading with their own emotional truth and expressing their own creativity is the only should, that *should* be followed. The internal battle waged between Kinsmen's intellect and Kinsmen's emotions can rage unceasingly and cause much insecurity. Their tend is to trust knowledge and opinion over feelings, which prevents them from trying new, and sometimes needed, experiences.

They often need to be forced by circumstance or challenge, to explore their creative potential. Their paths of logical preference—right, wrong, and should—tend to be quite narrow and deeply-rutted. Having an irascible boss, a hard to please mate, or a seemingly impossible problem, can initially intimidate, but can also force their "best" to rise, from their safe, conformity fox-hole. Only if emotionally hot pokered, does Kinsmen take chances. Though world-class intellects, these individuals respect what's already been proven and is widely known. Their tend is to have enough knowledge tucked inside their capacious minds, to regurgitate impressively and apply admirably—but they ignore their greater genius and power: emotions, *aka* self-truth and self-held convictions. Kinsmen seem to need regular doses of emotion-shaking, roller coaster rides, in their lives. As vehicles need tune-ups and cats need to stretch, Kinsmen needs intense emotional workouts, to balance their intellect with emotion, and keep all systems running smoothly. We recommend that Kinsmen *thinkers* read Kinsmen *emoting*, too.

They're flexible enough to please most, and smart enough to overcome or walk away, when the relationship proves hopeless. However, it's easier for others to take advantage of their hardworking, pleasing-propensity, than to take advantage of their wallet. Kinsmen is very security-conscious. They analyze, re-check the facts, then take a poll before leaping. Risk-taking is not in their nature. Unlike Diligents, who don't risk for fear of being found foolish, Kinsmen doesn't risk for fear of letting others down.

Kinsmen focus on long-term benefit; an attitude reflected in their consumer spending habits and investment decisions. They purchase with quality in mind, choosing durable over fashionable, as in well-established neighbourhoods and sturdy furnishings for home. If the old car was reliable, they're likely to trade it in for a newer version of the same model (and often, even the same colour).

Community activities and charitable concerns tend to be time investments of theirs. Astute in the ways of finance and cautious with a dollar, Kinsmen uses money as a tool, to acquire the better things in life for their family and their self, and in that order. They're often wise investors and generous in the provision of security and comfort for their family; whatever realm that definition includes—home, community, or world.

Kinsmen keeps ego, *and self,* out of all interactions and decisions, by adopting common views, by deferring to others, and by voicing pre-scribed and approved opinions. Agreement, acceptance, and conformity, are very important to them. One challenge of theirs is to follow their own emotional truth, whether it opposes logic or conflicts with others. Their characteristic "maintain harmony at all costs" nature, so welcomed and appreciated by others, often smothers Kinsmen's greatest power: their individuality. Analysts, therapists, and counselors, are familiar with the self-denial and martyr propensity of these logical, sentient beings, who shut off and shut their own truth away.

THE EMOTIONALS

The collective of all acquired knowledge, from books, opinions, and accumulated life experiences, is called belief. Ego interacts with the world according to, and in strict accordance with, each individual's belief. Most depend on knowledge to function, but not emotionals, like Empath.

Empaths walk against the prevailing wind, in terms of thinking style.

They funnel all of life through their emotional "thought" filter, which empties directly into their emotional "expression" beaker. There, truth tests are conducted and appropriate feeling/thinking instructions are attached, before being relayed back and acted upon by emotions. Emotions package truth and deliver it to mind; and at that point, things can go very wrong for Empath.

Knowledge is redundant for Empath. For them, all that's evolutionarily known, from time's beginning to *now* is on tap in soul, expressed through intuition, and acted upon by emotions. Every bit and bite, every synaptic skip, scratch, or squiggle of knowledge, is stored in soul. Why the redundancy and why the need for the duplication of belief?

Emotion-intelligence is emotion-born. Mind intelligence is book, opinion, and experience acquired. Emotions are never the same twice, thus creativity, perceptions, and solution possibilities, are infinite in range and scope. Belief, on the other hand, is concrete-constant and can be retrieved and regurgitated in the exact form as originally experienced and stored. Emotion is far more efficient and much quicker than belief, but its arrow-straight path to solution can confound others and conflict with a logic-bound, prove-it-first world. Their ego has been bashed and bruised so often, they tend to unnecessarily complicate things. Like salmon swimming against the current, Empath swims against their nature. They doubt and deny their emotions, and try to be logical instead.

In this conversation, Visionary is talking directly to Empath. Few understand Empath as well as Visionary; though few are as intolerant of Empath's denial of self and shirk of responsibility, as them either. Others may not understand all within these pages, or within this personality style, but Visionarys and Empaths will. The gap between the two is as wide and broad, as non-trust can stretch. Understanding closes gaps rather quickly, and that's the reason for this style-to-style conversation.

When you know answers, but cannot explain how, cannibalistic self-doubt can prey on confidence; unless ego is strong enough to ward it off. From infancy, purely emotional Empath "senses" the world around them. They feel so intensely about everything, others can be confused by the depth and range of their responses—from uncontrollable laughter, to inconsolable tears; sometimes both at once. For others it can be disconcerting, but emotion IS this personality style.

All their lives they'll experience intense, unpredictable, and inexplicable feelings. Moody, others may call them, for Empath responds quickly to their environment. They laugh readily, at drop of amusement's hat, and as readily cry when shown kindness or faced with anger—whether they're bearer or recipient. Too often, they're told to "buck up...stop blubbering," which, for these sentient beings, is like denying the cat its whiskers. Emotions are at seat of Empath power, and the throne upon which their fine intellect sits.

To compare emotion–intellect and logic,
let's play the child's game of "Concentration."

For the game, a deck of cards is dealt face-down on the table. The objective is to match cards in paired sets. Each player, in-turn, randomly selects two cards and turns them face-upwards. If the cards pair-match, the player takes possession of the cards by removing them from the table. The player continues, until they fail to make a match. Unmatched cards are flipped over, and next player takes a turn. The game ends when all cards are matched. The one with the most matched pairs is the winner.

Most players use logical thinking; Empath uses intuition. Others would match by memorizing card positions or by chance of luck. Empath would match cards by emotionally sensing: then, more frequently pairing, than those depending on logic and luck. Depending on their degree of self-trust, if Empath were the first player, others may not get a chance to play at all. Confident Empath can potentially clear the table. Emotion-intellect is a power that Empath is often unaware of, or deeply mistrusts. Such ignorance or fear can have them riding in back seats through life, when front seats are their more rightful place. If such omniscient-like potential exists, why the self-doubt?

With bright smiling faces and eyes set on gold stars, early school experiences show Empath to be a very bright student. Striving to please, they reveled in earning praise and reward. Delight changed to distress, when math became more complex and science more complicated. With diminishing self-confidence, Empath realized their core functioning differed from others'. Emotion-intelligence, in higher learning, can have betraying consequences. With heartfelt eagerness, Empaths proudly offered answers as before, but suddenly, answers weren't enough. They had to be explained and proven, as well.

To understand their heart and confidence-shaking confusion, imagine a decision-making tree. The trunk represents the problem, branches represent solution paths possible, and one of the innumerable branch tips contains the right solution. Empath senses or feels the correct "solution" branch tip, but proof demands a step-by-step explanation. Struggling to provide the proof that pleases and wins, Empath grasps trunk, branches, and branch tips all at once. Juggling the entire tree, they're afraid of letting go of any part that may eliminate their chances of proving the solution later. With so many branches and branch tips available, Empath understandably gets bogged down in details. Essentially, they understand the problem and know it's solution, but get confused and lost on the proof-path between them. Others may perceive them as slow decision-makers; explaining is what causes their delay. Empath may take seven seconds to *feel-find* answers, but need seven days more to first convince themselves it's a good or right answer, and to formulate an explanation that logicals will understand and can accept.

Linear-thinking, a process light years behind emotion-intellect, must be taught to Empaths. Gold stars of former glory grades, often turn into good *grief* by junior high. This is usually when their academic fame wilts and their self-esteem withers noticeably. (One of the first signs of an unconfident Empath is weight gain). They first question intuition...then intellect...then themselves. When self-doubt comes into play, Empath is easier to bruise than a banana. Self-doubt can clip their wings of confidence, before they even attempt flight and test, for themselves, the advantages and superiority of emotion-intellect.

Overcoming self-doubt is a two-step process for Empaths. Place trust in your emotional wisdom; it is truth and self-truth is always and most, right for you. Take control and regain self-confidence, by learning "logical's" language, and their manner of being and doing. The rules of the world, (in past, now, and future) are determined by majority vote. Guess what? Logicals rule! As an emotion-intellect, Empath is a minority. To excel, they must become familiar, then proficient, with the prevailing order and rules; and proficient in the skills that are understood and practiced by the linear, logical *thinking* majority. Skills, such as: memorization, organization, and hierarchical problem-solving, are not only daily, but success essentials. Empath generally chooses EITHER/OR assimilation.

EITHER...They are spurred into gritted action and bury themselves in studied concentration, to learn how to deliver the proof others need. By functioning in Jeopardy Game™ fashion, using innate emotion-intellect, they learn to trace a path backwards, from the branch tip of solution, to the trunk-of-tree problem. Once done, they can immediately chop, haul, and torch, what's unnecessary. As confidence grows, the clutch and hold-all fear lessens. It becomes easier to pare away, then trash and burn the irrelevant. Trusting emotion-intellect to find the correct solution, and then applying more simple logic, to follow the path back to the problem's beginning (the proof that logicals require), can make all the difference in terms of confidence. Notice the difference in problem solving, between logicals (knowledge-intellects) and Empath. Logicals start from the problem and hunt for solution. Empath, (emotion-intellects) starts at solution, then retraces the steps backward to problem. Which approach do you think is more efficient and advantageous short-term, long-term, personally, and professionally? Empath is distinctly advantaged. Agree?

OR...Empath can be rendered immobile by academic self-doubt, and may make the mistake of turning their back on academic pursuits. Regardless, even those who avoided the grindstone are respectfully common on lists of nobel laureates, artists of music, painting or theatre, and are particularly predominant among teachers (educators). So, even if academia is not the preferred route, making the honour roll in life is seemingly inevitable—once Empath overcomes self-doubt. Then, creativity, that doubt's been smothered and choked, is free to fly as far as dream, desire, and determination, dares and desires. Learning to trust self implicitly, and not being intimidated by demands to prove or explain, can be a lifelong challenge for these individuals.

Mentioned above, is one of Empaths greatest talents: an in-born ability to teach. Their purpose seems providential—to teach others "to love one another." The world is a better, smarter, and happier place, when Empath mounts the lectern. Their characteristic people-patience is one factor, but it's their emotion-intelligence that tips the ability scale in their favour. From fifty paces, from look of group, from glint in individual eye, can they sense prevailing conditions, and modulate their tone, tempo, and content, to match and meet. When a student raves about an exciting lecturer, chances are, Empath heads that classroom. Generally speaking, this is not an assertive nor charismatic style. Yet, when Empaths teach, they come alive. They tend to be dynamic, even mesmerizing speakers, and have little trouble holding the group's attention. It would be rare for Empath to be caught unprepared, for their scheduled lecture or lesson. These individuals are conscientious, responsible, and reliable.

Empaths tend to be happy souls; providing their *reward needs* are met. (Their needs are few, and of the type money can't buy). They may not be the comedic performers at centre stage, but they're an appreciative and easily-pleased audience. One of their most endearing qualities is their willingness to laugh at themselves. Being mocked or good-naturedly teased, is high amusement for them. This is the personality style of infinite emotion-variety and depth. When their fancy is tickled sufficiently, these are the ones who can and do "wet their pants" laughing. No other laughs with such unbridled joy, as Empath. And actually, poking fun at them is not hard to do; Empath is nothing, if not interesting. Take their innate need to help others, for instance. Making others feel good, makes them feel *gooder*. Tell an Empath you've a problem that stumps, and before eye's blink, they'll blizzard possibilities. Tell an Empath you're feeling a bit down on yourself, and before next sigh's escape, they'll provide reasons to admire self anew. Tell an Empath you can't understand, and they'll snug time and mind with yours, to enlighten.

Others grow accustomed to their helpfulness, and their self-effacing manner of deflecting praise or appreciation. It's Empath who says, "Ahh! no problem," as they scoop up a friend's soiled laundry, to drop at the cleaners on their way home. But its their martyr propensity that others tend to rib and tease most. It's a typically, selfless Empath, who picks out the driest slices of roast beef at dinner, willingly takes the broken popsicle, or gives up their seat on the bus, et cetera. If within their power, Empath will choose the least and give up the most, because they would rather see others pleased, than themselves. And despite protests from others, will even insist that their *"preference"* is for less over more. It's Empath, who senses something wrong with *so-and-so*, and on follow-up, learns of *so-and-so's* timely need of them. Their name won't be listed among fair-weather friends, for Empath is there for others, come rain or shine.

Note: Without having focused on, or investigated, it was realized after our Empath conversations began, that ESP is a common Empath tool. We invite all Empaths to participate in their own ESP exercise. It may help instill confidence in ways that our words cannot—how different emotion-intelligence is, and how uniquely gifted you are. Whenever you get those 'feeling' waves, define them, identify whom is involved, then jot all down in a special journal. Keep your own record of what is felt and what results, as proof.

Empaths are the champs at snappy comebacks. Entering into light-hearted banter or debate with them, is an intellectual challenge for others...and treat for all. When Empaths are feeling confident and happy, few are as quick-witted or humourous, as them. They do have one odd-seeming behaviour characteristic: when hurt by others, Empath shuts their doors, turns off the phones, and in private, treats their self. They're not comfortable indulging their sweet tooth, watching that risque film, or sleeping in till noon, when others are around.

These emotional beings tend to keep their pain and their pleasures secret. Most will have a special "treat" stashed in a drawer in their desk, briefcase, or night table. Gaining weight easily is also characteristic. Many can become so self-conscious about their weight, they nibble in public and gorge in private. Some of the very best cooks are Empaths, who seem to have a highly developed sense of taste. This personality is least likely to smoke cigarettes or drink milk regularly. Milk can be tainted by other food odours in the fridge, and tastes off to them, unless it's ice cold.

Generally, Empaths don't like being alone. When ill, most others like to recuperate in private. If left alone when they're sick, Empaths often get sicker and take longer to recover. No other is as crazy about newborns, infants, and small children, as them. Actually, the helpless of any species— flora or fauna—respond noticeably well, to Empath affection and ministering. Anything they plant in earth: house plants, gardens, fields, vineyards, and orchards, flourishes under their care.

Sadly, Empaths are seldom aware of their emotional gift. It is common for them to underutilize their talents and undervalue self. They prematurely throw in their towel, before realizing that, for them, rationalizing is like exploring dark caves blindfolded. Empath's emotional-dimension is so sophisticated, so far beyond logic's comprehension, they'd have to walk backwards, a lifetime or two, just to break even. It's still a logic run and ruled world. Empaths are emotionals, and would be well-advised to learn the logical language. Thereafter, speak your own native tongue: emotions. Trust no other, no book, no source of information/inspiration that does not align with your own emotional truth. By feel, is truth known. That's your gift: trust it, use it. Success for these individuals comes by way of emotions, not mind.

Emotions are the who and what of Empath.

THE INTUITIVES

Visionary is the overnight success. The one who makes it big after years of struggle and disillusionment. They tend to start out pretty good: do well in school; are athletic; often attractive; seem well-liked by peers; and comparatively, quite content people. They tend to be reflective thinkers and drop-of-a-hat dreamers, who enjoy passing time doing both. Able and conscientious, they tend to inspire confidence in others; enough so to earn honourable mention on a number of likely-to-succeed lists. When Visionary graduates youth, they tend to meet success early, in *early* adulthood. Not long after that, things tend to go kinda wrong, kinda quickly for them. An internal rebellion arises and they begin questioning, long before middle-age, "Is that all there is?"

None are as surprised as Visionary, to learn that education is more often a degree of self-alienation than ticket to self-fulfillment. Creativity and individuality get bruised, get ignored, or get lonely, out there. The higher the rung and the more dollars involved, the less meaningful it all seems to become. The treadmill of youth that once ran so smoothly, now jerks along mindlessly. Their natural drive and curiosity are replaced by apathy. Disillusionment and dissatisfaction mount, until one day the hollowness inside them erupts, into a roaring crescendo of deafening, threatening, self-doubt. Without invitation or shove, they leap off the treadmill. Stepping on every sidewalk crack along the way, Visionary heads home, where, in profound soberness, they take stock of their self and their life.

What they learn, during this Visionary-common experience, decides whether they'll begin living as born and meant, or continue much as before; by dictate of circumstance.

Historically, as evolutionarily, they're the wealthiest and most creatively powerful style. When confident, you'll not find them avoiding problems with substance abuse, shoving issues under the carpet, or blaming others for their lacks and losses. Before their characteristic leap and retreat, Visionary has usually slogged through more than their fair share of *kaka*. Because they're intuitive—emotionally awake and aware—what they experience externally is taken inside, filtered for practical value, then filed for their later use. As open and visible as they seem to be, (expression and action), that's only part of all they're processing internally. Being emotionally awake and aware, is what differentiates Visionary from most others.

Once they leave the treadmill, they rarely return.

Visionary is born with a burning need to do something significant with their life; something meaningful and people-bettering. Others can imagine what ringing in the ears is like, but only Visionary knows what an internal clock sounds and feels like. From birth to death, *tick-tock* is their pulse-close, persistent companion. It won't be ignored, can't be drowned out by noise, and through thick and thin, it beats strong and steady. For Visionary, time is always running; always winding down. Its measured passing fuels their drive, as much to find fulfillment as find peace (happiness). Why they, alone, have and hear this tick-tock is unknown. Though it seems that their success, happiness, and nature are tied into it.

Those who work Visionary are not common. So how come the few are so uncommonly successful? What do they discover that day, that accounts for their historical distinction? What lesson do they learn that others don't or won't?

Pg. 144

Visionarys are critical linear-thinkers, as well as intuitives. While Idealist travels logic's path at lightning speed, from step 1 to 10, and finds solution, in the same time, Visionary travels 1 to 40, and not only finds solution but returns with a mental blueprint, marketing strategy, and coloured snapshots of the completed project. These individuals have potential to blaze and raze intellectually. When they solve problems, they don different perspective glasses; those with a 360-degree view. Able to see beyond logical boundaries, they focus on what's been overlooked, been dismissed, or not been tried at all. Visionary starts at logic, then moves beyond it's did it, done it limits. Their solutions can seem quixotic, and initially, are often rejected for being impractical.

Others tend to focus on parts. Visionarys focus on the whole, with two assumptions. Assumption 1: *If they can envision, then doing MUST be possible.* Assumption 2: *Essential parts and pieces will assemble, and arrange appropriately within the larger context, when wanted and as needed.* These individuals won't give up. To them, obstacles mean that alternatives have yet to be found and tried. Those 360-degree perspective glasses are the secret behind Visionary creativity, but it's their unwavering confidence in outcomes, based on two firm assumptions, that proves their power and leads to uncommon success.

Hardship and misery may precede the learning, but Visionary is one of the few who learns and masters the lesson: logic has limits, while intuitive-intelligence is boundless and bountiful.

A Visionary life is as rift with problems and grief, as any other. Most suffer childhood abuse and violence. Many suffer personal and financial setbacks, from death of key loved ones, to bad luck, to bad health. Some battle behavioural and substance addictions. What mainly differentiates this personality style from others is how they cope with stress.

Visionarys tend to have extremely large and strong egos, which helps them handle the world or escape it when necessary. Uniquely, intuitives have the ability to consciously retreat to innermost sanctums, when emotional protection, guidance, or nurturance is needed. They're seldom stumped for long, and don't suffer from loneliness or boredom, like others do. Escaping inward offers them creative privacy, where they can play with ideas or sort through concerns. Most importantly, beyond the solutions, solace, and comfort had within, what Visionary introspection does, is forge a direct link between their emotions and mind (logic). The result is an intuitive connection that, when used, becomes the pipeline through which their own success and happiness are carried. Visionary starts at logic, like most others; but that's just the beginning for them, not the end. These individuals, like their decisions, are emotion forged and shaped.

Visionary leapt off the treadmill and went home to find self-truth. While they've long known that emotions are a most trustworthy and comforting guide, they only trusted emotions in private. Often it takes years of hardship, before Visionary applies intuition in everyday life. By definition, Visionary is an intuitive intellect, meaning, emotions decide and confirm their decisions. Others may wonder what all this intuitive-intellect and emotional-smarts is about. To illustrate the difference, between logicals and intuitives, let's take one common issue—doubt, and explore it from their perspective. Visionary learns lessons faster than most, and THAT'S their only advantage.

Intuition versus intelligence, both versus doubt.

Intelligence defines individual belief—the sum of knowledge gained from books, opinions, and experiences. Ego is identity's representative that interacts with the world, according to, and in strict accordance with, belief. Intuition is the vault of all experiences. All that has evolutionarily been, from soul's beginning to now, is on tap and accessed through emotions. Forging a link between mind and emotions is intuitive-intelligence, which is belief-expanding and ego-starching. For Visionary, ego represents more than individual belief. It represents emotional truth too. It can take years before Visionary realizes, trusts, or uses their intuitive advantage, and natural power.

Doubt cannot obtain more than a temporary hold, on a confident Visionary. When others doubt, they generally consider it a harbinger of trouble. Most respond characteristically. For instance, when Diligent doubts, they check and re-check their steps and information, until confident enough to move on; Kinsmen looks to others, for general agreement and procedural approval; Sentinel is relieved, for they've been expecting trouble to show up. All, but confident intuitives, respond as oyster to sand when doubt visits. When oysters cannot dislodge the grain-of-sand intruder, they build a wall of resistance around it, until eventually, it becomes an intrinsic part of their being. A hard, impenetrable pearl that, while not of their own choosing, is of their own making. And though not obviously or readily apparent to others, the doubt pearl accompanies them and influences their every decision, action and relationship in life. Not so, for confident Visionary!

When sand bits of doubt visit, they're removed before lodging takes place. Should logic fail to eliminate doubt, Visionary turns the matter over to emotions, and lets their truth surgeon remove it. The sooner doubt is removed, the better. Visionary is impatient. Their tick-tock purpose clock never stops or lets up. Where others won't go, without a firm nod from logic, Visionary boldly steps forth when intuition nods, though logic protest loudly. Doubt can and does take many prisoners, some for life; but it does not warden confident intuitives, like Visionary.

These individuals don't suffer doubt long enough for pearling to occur. They don't need to. For them, intuitive-intelligence ensures that the very best decision has been made. After that, it's a matter of adjusting the course to meet their vision, and overseeing the processing of details.

Visionarys don't accept can't-be-done excuses or rationalizations. If they can visualize it, they know doing it is possible.

Four things are individually guaranteed to evoke Visionary impatience; and if found in combination, their wrath. Incompetence. Apathy. Reluctance. Reticence. No relationship will long-survive if any of the above exist or persist. All are deemed a waste of time by them. Time is Visionary's most precious commodity. They don't condone its waste, by self or others. Nothing will end relations faster with Visionary, than reticence. These are intuitives of a very tall order. When disparity exists, between what they intuit and what's being presented, others may meet a 360-degree perspective investigation. Visionary proves ultra-determined and ultra-creative, in devising ways to learn what they gotta-hafta know.

These charismatic beings love people. The tribal need to belong courses loudly through their veins and visions. Characteristically, and in one form or another, their earliest and most frequently asked questions is, "What purpose, this human?" They intrinsically feel a need to do something significant, "but what?" niggles and bothers endlessly. However long it takes, however many libraries of opinion they swallow, or trails they traipse, pursuit of purpose can have Visionary chewing up life in a virtual feeding frenzy, searching for reasons to justify their being. They go through careers, through friends and experiences, like an August prairie grassfire—and all to the accompaniment of an internal tick-tock marking time's passage.

An impatience to do everything better and faster, fuels their drive to contribute significantly. Visionary is highly competitive. Most achieve greater excellence when pitted against an opponent, whether real or imagined. As children, many conjure up their own motivation, by imagining themselves in a race against phantom competitors, while completing mundane chores and tasks. Visionary immerses their self in all, and usually meets rapid success. They tend to leave as rapidly too—once they've learned all they can or wish, or when they're not challenged and boredom sets in. This personality can easily be workaholic, but with difficulty, worker bee. They tend to view details as drone and routine as drab. Eventually they realize that somewhere between driving need and mirrored actuality, marked disparity exists. One day, Visionary quits the race, retreats from others, and burrows inside to steep and review.

The Visionary Lesson

When they emerge, it is often with re-ordered priorities and an oath, bound and tied in determination, to not allow any opinion to precede their own, and to do nothing, from thereon, that does not *feel right* to them. That's when Visionary becomes. Stepping out from the common fray, they firmly fix sights on the whole of innermost dreams, leaving the handling of pieces and parts to others. That which helped them cope in trying times, some reminiscent of Biblical Job, is their key to self-fulfillment. These individuals harmonize intuitive and intellectual dimensions, and the power unleashed by that combination is evidenced by their historical success. Belief cannot range further or travel beyond, that which is known. Emotional intelligence is unlimited. Intuitively, we already know more than we have learned, studied, or been taught. Visionary drinks deeply at intuitive-wells. Mind-intellect can only project a known distance. Intuition is not bound by logic or time, so it's beam can bounce from known to infinity. And that's the Visionary lesson.

These individuals tend to be the most boldly risk-taking of all. When Visionary stops rationalizing, stops trying to fit into logic-built molds and starts trusting intuition instead, they tap into unfathomable good luck. Timing...in, trying...in, doing...in, life, is the second secret of Visionary success. Their *now* is one tick-tock faster than others'. Intellect and ego become a formidable combination, when the intuitive bee settles in a Visionary bonnet. Changing *is* to *was*, by replacement with *next*, is their name's fame and claim. Their birth responsibility is betterment, of others and world. Their tend is to do both frequently.

Visionarys are charismatic.

If directly asked, however, most would agree that charisma is their default birth setting, and proves one thing—the Creator's favourite form of humour is irony. Visionary has a "presence thing" that others initially sense as intimidating. It's an energy born of confidence, that pulses and vibrates, yet belies the often shy individual. This irony is no secret to them. Rather than rail at the unfairness, they overcome their *presence* anomaly, by moving beyond shyness and approaching others first. Otherwise, they may spend much time alone. For Visionary, who loves and needs people, being unapproachable is unacceptable, and in terms of their own fulfillment, counter-productive. Instead, they take a deep breath of showtime bravado and involve themselves in what tends to be their passion, pleasure, and purpose: people. Visionary relates readily and easily with almost any other. However, when wanted or when advantageous, they can and will lean on their default intimidation, to control others and situations, personally and/or professionally

Communication is their key realm of functioning.

In the realms of interpretation, elucidation, oration, creation, or entertainment; as in law, science, leadership, humanities, or arts: Visionary leads the field with words. In conversation, will others most readily recognize Visionary. They like words and tend to be highly skilled in using them, to evoke imagery and excite emotions. Words kernel truth to Visionary, who says, "people will tell you all you need to know if you but listen closely enough." They often hear unspoken as clearly as spoken. Only Healer and Philosopher can penetrate the truth of another more quickly than Visionary.

Characteristically, when they're are at a loss for a bit of information, instead of fumbling and stammering mentally about they'll say, "it'll come," and they continue without. At some future point, mid-stride or mid-sentence, and without fanfare or introduction they'll insert the missing bit and proceed. What they do is plug the question into their intuitive dimension, then walk away. When the answer perks, they offer it up as received, without stop of word, work, or thought. Trusting intuition to supply the answer is natural for them. Your companion is likely Visionary, if they query a point made moments, to months earlier, and now seeks it's further edification. Neither thick as board nor troublesome, it's just that their intuition had previously registered a gap in logic and decided it was time to fill in the blank. When interested, Visionary persists or pesters, until clear understanding is had.

These individuals can watch television and read a book at the same time, and follow both plots with ease. Visionarys love music. It tends to play constantly in the background of their life. They can shut out noise and interruption when focused, or when they choose to not be disturbed. Also, they rarely clutter their minds with referenced information, such as phone numbers, addresses, birthdays, et cetera. Names and faces, they can't seem to forget. If pressed, they'd likely be able to rattle off the names and seating order of their first grade classmates. Visionary doesn't memorize what they can readily look-up. They don't rely on to-do lists or appointment books, yet rarely miss a beat in the day, far less a meeting.

If a Visionary hurts your feelings, it was intended.

These individuals both feel and think as they speak, and often think clearest when challenged or pressured. Leather breath—putting their foot in their mouth—is not a Visionary trait, though razor-barbed rebuttal is. As others speak, they intuitively follow along, conjuring pictorial images of the conversation. Like flowing movie frames, one follows the other in logical order and sequence. When information is missing, confusing, or false, a blank frame displays in their logic-film; disrupting the flow, which they note and later will query. Visionary intuits more than others realize, and more than they let on. They don't assume or presume. They expect word confirmation. Reticence is a common thorn of frustration for them.

When their intuitive antennae detect inconsistency, between the form and feel of another, they tend to push for explanation. They can be totally unabashed about asking questions, regardless of how simple or inane their query doth seem to others. Some want to know, some like to know, some prefer not knowing; but Visionary must. If cats, they would have long been extinct, due to curiosity. Questioning, risking, and boldness tinged with impatience, are trademarks of theirs.

Visionary's innerworld is rich with imagery. For them, ideas are things that have form, grow wing, and take flight. They usually dream in colour and expect more from sleep than restful respite. Sleep is an opportunity for problem-solving. Upon retiring, they review outstanding issues or unsolved problems, essentially setting the matter on their back-burner to simmer while sleeping. Visionary usually has a story or two to relate, about ideas or solutions that came to them in dreams.

Most, from the earliest age, have the ability to alter dream content in progress, much as they alter reality in wakefulness. Inner sanctums are visited for insight, escape, or nurturance, as readily when awake as when asleep. If odd-seeming, remember, these are visionaries of the tallest, most practical order. Their purpose is to see what is not realized, or not yet available. Accessing intuition through emotions is their gift. Trusting it implicitly and acting upon it—above all else and other—is why *visionaries* are Visionary. Though all have equal potential and opportunity to learn the same truth lesson, these ones most often do.

Their *why* is to improve the world in a manner that benefits others. Each step and stop taken is their own responsibility. No tool, other than self is supplied. No matter how brilliant the mind or how sound the knowledge, logic, alone, cannot accomplish such an onerous task. When backed by intuitive wisdom, even from the ashes of ridiculous, possibility Phoenix's can rise. Focusing on the most personally rewarding vision, then trusting that details will fall into place, as and when needed, is how they achieve their success. Consciously accessing intuition's power is Visionary's style and way.

THE INTUITIVES

Evokateur

Between birth and death they'll know many names, from earliest unusual, to talented/gifted, to odd, to weird (which too-many think they earn), to remarkable, and even rare genius—the moniker most apropos. Rare, though a term used to describe others, was likely coined for Evokateurs. It could very well be held in wait and reserve for those present, who may not yet have realized the who and why of their being, so have yet to become. Read on, if what it takes is truth in word and fact of deed. This conversation is in tune and tone of Healers and Philosophers, who know Evokateurs best.

For Evokateurs does the axiom, "unfulfilled genius is so common it is almost a parable" most aptly apply. Yet there is no such thing as an unconfident Evokateur. These individuals are not plagued by self-doubt; their ravage and savage is reluctance. Evokateurs generally meet ridicule and rejection before they meet acceptance. For them, being peculiar is more than nature, it's necessity.

As north IS, as south IS, Evokateurs ARE the most unusual beings on the planet, bar none! No amount of complaining, fussing, exertion, effort, or influence on the part of others, can long-term alter that. These ones must be peculiar, in order to fulfill their life purpose. Too many, too often, get in the way of them doing so. Evokateurs are confident about their own ability and value; it's others who doubt. Why? Because Evokateurs don't want to be in this world; they know one that's better. Their own!

In everyday life, they prefer spectator seats or sideline positions, over joining others in the fray, play, and decision-making. They prefer the rich fantasies and swirling tapestries of their own chimera to outerworld reality, and often conduct their living with a detachment that's less than normal yet more than aloof. Within Evokateur, between mathematic formulation, artistic creation, and fantastic imagery, does the pendulum of precocity swing widest and swoosh loudest. They're the authors, artists, and composers of universal metamorphosis.

From Evokateur's love-gilded, gift-guided chalks, brushes, and pens, does creative genius flow most freely and most frequently. Lewis Carroll, from the same fabric that won him mathematical acclaim as Professor Dodgson, created an imaginary world without benefit of input, influence, or blueprint. He introduced a literary style that did not exist before him.

It's difficult for others to comprehend a world within a world, far less understand those who have one. Who among can imagine an internal world more intimate, more satisfying, and more fulfilling, than this real world outside; but it is so, for Evokateurs.

As Alice fell down the rabbit-hole and woke in Wonderland, we need only blink to enter Evokateurland, where wonders never cease. Besides expanding the mind, this journey may awaken patience and acceptance in others. Both are generally lacking and sorely needed by these individuals.

Others may not ever understand Evokateurs, which is understandable. Their tendency is to only touch on normal, not stay. Fulfillment for them is not found on narrow path'd normalcy, and though infrequent, their visits may not be easy for others to live with, work with, or love. There's a very good reason for Evokateur oddness. It's the uniform worn most commonly by greatness.

Any time Evokateur shows up in the Ansir Profile (and rings of truth), ultra-creativity shows up too. For any rare individual who functions as

Evokateur in all 3-realms (thinking /working /emoting), fame is practically guaranteed. In the working realm, there is mention of such historical fame; those of like-peculiarity wearing like-uniform.

Evokateurs see patterns where reality is fluid, flowing, and ever-changing. Energy awareness and reality transformations occur beyond bounds of logic, beyond notions of space and time, and beyond the logical world outside. They are not linear-thinkers. They're intuitives, who nest in the vaults of their own evolutionary wisdom. They may be peculiar to others, but to time, they are Masters of creativity.

Belief is the sum of information acquired from books, opinions, and experiences, which is stored in mind as knowledge. Belief is the mill that grinds the grist called logic. When enough logic is strung together, it becomes a line of reason for rationals to follow. Ego is belief's representative that interacts with others—according to, and in strict accordance with, belief. Additionally, eager-to-please *ego*, filters and excludes incoming information that does not fit or match belief's criteria. Evokateurs have no ego, so they have no doorman screening incoming possibilities. They place little faith in belief, as with knowledge comes rules, which to them are more restrictive than necessary.

Put a rule on the table and watch Evokateur butter bread with it. They know full-well what rules are, but their nature is to question, not bovinely swallow and regurgitate. (Fortunately, they tend to have a cellular code of ethics that makes it inconceivable, that they'd be other than love-inclined and improvement-tended. No human or global destruction was, is, or will be invented by Evokateurs. If things turn out that way, the fault lies not with its inventor's intention, but with its interpretation and application by others). In Evokateur-world there are no rules; anything goes. Possibilities are urged to roam and range with infinite freedom, speed, and grace. Logic is for explaining, not for creating.

He died in 1920, at 32 years of age, yet his notebook scribblings are still being pored over, by today's mathematicians—attempting to prove his answers. From auspicious beginnings, and in such a short time, this self-taught, mathematical whiz-kid, Srinivasa "Ramanujan" Aiyangar, was more often right than wrong; despite lacking the education to qualify his genius or quantify his intuited insights and discoveries. In a maze, intuition could find solution on its own, but it's handy having logic along to record progress and map the path's way. For Evokateur, finding solution tends to be less of a problem than bringing it back; which parallels their inner-world eagerness and outer-world reluctance.

Intuition knows, logic proves, then bundles and labels as plausible. Rather than relying on knowledge, Evokateur uses their outside eyes to see what is, while their inside eyes seek why and what more. When *more* is found, their keen interest takes over. Evokateur withdraws externally, to more intensely experience and more fully explore, internally.

Other intuitives filter life through their intuitive-dimension, and from the gleanings, take what they need for practical, world application—like Visionary, for instance. Evokateur doesn't filter at all. Instead they walk directly into intuitive vaults, where their soul's every experience, from Big Bang to now, awaits. They make a nest at smack-dab centre, burrow in, and play with possibilities. They don't look for practical and applicable solutions; they look for understanding. As they see it, both solutions and goals are inherent to understanding. To focus on goal or solution, is to miss much beyond it, that could be more valuable.

Evokateur "play" means explore—suspend logic and follow discoveries—rather than start with set problem or goal and see what discoveries will fit. They create with intuition; most *construct* with it. Evokateur knows by feel—not by logic, which, of infinite possibilities, are truest and rightest. Emotion is their light, reason, and medium. Logic explains what they discover.

Their Achilles' heel is rejection, so most only dare and create while "inside," and private. Evokateurs come in all shape and manner of packaging, and are found in all walks of life. Try as they might and would like, they, generally, have difficulty fitting into the normal mold. They're common by population, (Ansir's Profile demographics), as it's relatively easy to function without sharing or exposing truth of self. But they're rare when it comes to *Profile Boss*. If it feels right, these intuitives work toward fulfilling that truth, even if they cannot afford it.

Whether costs are money or people-related, Evokateurs pay for their love.

What they love is creating new perspectives, then fashioning new eyeglasses, for others to better see different points of view and alternatives to this reality. Eccentriks play three-dimensional spin-and-sculpt, in mind, but need physical form and proof to be satisfied. Not Evokateurs. They take concept, and whilst spinning and sculpting they run it through form, formula, facet, and paces of life, to see how it would or could fly. For them, actualization is not necessary. They internally live abstractions and theories, as vividly and intensely as others three-dimensionally. For Evokateurs, satisfaction is only had in Evokateur-world, where there's no need to explain, no judgements to fend, and no mess for them to clean-up after experiencing ends.

Ridicule, rejection, and being misunderstood, are the three most common reasons why Evokateurs keep their creativity a secret from others. Their approach and observations are often so far-advanced or so far-fetched, they can confuse or irritate others; sometimes unintentionally. Unless they are involved in discussions or activities that specifically interest them...or in company equally interested and interesting, Evokateurs tend to be ignored or go unnoticed.

When interested, they can be as enthusiastic and irrepressible as children, for they are purely emotional and extraordinarily passionate individuals. Evokateurs tend to have a great sense of humour. While they shun and shy at being the centre of attention, or being put on public display, they can be charming and entertaining in less formal settings. Due to innate bashfulness, they are often accused of being anti-social. However, social situations are highly stimulating for these individuals, whether they actively participate or not.

Evokateurs never stop creating.

As sticky fly paws indiscriminately trek, collect, and track through all on the table, Evokateurs trek through sights and sounds of external life. They may not spend much time in this world, but while here, they're ultra-alert to impressions and thoughts that may strike a creative chord within them. From the ordinary and everyday mundane, they extrapolate wonder and marvel.

The outside world provides raw material for their inspiration sponge and creative forge. They pick and choose from world offerings of nature, relations, and noise, the bits and morsels that feed their inner-world imaginings. All they seem to need from this world are the most base and basic necessities, like food, love, shelter and encouragement. Given some or all, their inner-world expands, from Evokateur-world to Evokateur-heaven. When they hit their stride, their foot can impact with enough force to quake and vibrate for centuries.

How to identify an Evokateur?

By their eyes...for iris is but lip into abyss of soul.

Evokateur eyes can shine, sparkle, and twinkle unlike any others'; they're different up-close. No matter what shape their face, manner of bearing, or station in life, no eyes are as soul-revealing as theirs. No other sees visions like those that lurk behind blink of theirs either...from crash, hiss, and thunder, in storms unknown, to horrors unfathomable. To see paradise or hell and experience every passion between, study the works of Evokateurs past and present. Earth shakes and heavens move, when these ones bring their world to ours.

When occupied, they're unaware of anything, but that which has drawn their attention. As children, Evokateurs may create imaginary friends rather than play with real others. They often exhibit an ability for making up intricate stories or plays and acting them out. These little tykes occupy themselves with whatever is on-hand, and more content than most, to play on their own. They seem born with creative bent and flair, and inexhaustible energy. Evokateur children ask innumerable questions, and accept it better than most, when others are unable to satisfy their inquisitiveness. If off-put or ignored, they stop asking and start looking for answers, themselves.

Albert Einstein, when five and sick in bed, was given a pocket compass by his father. Albert asked why the needle always pointed in the same direction. His father was unable to answer. Albert didn't pester or persist with his father, but determined instead, to read and find out on his own. One of his earliest school reports was on compasses.

These children tend not to forget the questions they asked, but went unanswered. It may take years, but their dogged-determination to understand will be satisfied, one way or another. Most study, gain experience, and acquire expertise through their own initiative. When the plague shut his school down, student Isaac Newton took advantage of the imposed holiday and while at home, laid the groundwork for contributions that later brought him immortal fame. Self-sufficiency and great need for privacy are hallmarks of this style.

Evokateur-world is completely satisfying, so they've no ego-need to make self or their work known. Fame and money are not carrot or karat enough to entice them. They may seem obsessed to others, with their characteristic compulsion to *work-work-work*, but its not the devil that rides Evokateur; its emotion that fills, drives, and makes.

Emotions are creative, and Evokateurs are pure emotion. As with Empath and their powerful emotional-dimension, if the creative-dimension of an Evokateur were suddenly dumped into almost any other, the shock would be so immense and intense, imminent institutionalization is presumed. In fact, Evokateur is no stranger to institutions that provide care to those deemed incapable, incompetent, or unfit. These individuals stand out, which can be more bane than bliss.

Where most see peculiar, when they see Evokateur, time, history and evolution see genius at work. Usually in the realm of work is their remarkability made known, and where you'll meet Evokateurs past and present, doing what comes most naturally: expressing their emotionality at what others call work.

THE SPIRITUALISTS

Healer

Few are as gifted or as physiologically complicated, as Healers. None are more reluctant to be, than them.

Two personalities have the birth gifts and power to alter the future quality of life for all planet beings: one is Healer. Need is great, and time has come, for these powerful individuals to step forward and brazen a bolder presence. Perhaps by walking in confident Healer shoes and through insight of what confident is and what confidence does, we can scale the walls and slay the dragons that prevent unconfident Healer, from joining their confident kin. Perhaps through illustration of global necessity, we can encourage them to embrace their responsibilities and pursue self-fulfillment as birth intended.

Characteristically, Healers tend to be delicate of feature and fragile seeming. However, their fame and repute is more constitution of horse and steel-willed determination than frail or retiring. In fact, they are much more substantial, in every regard, than they appear. Three common characteristics of Healer are: sensitivity to noise, aversion to mess and clutter, and great need for privacy.

Incessant noises, like television, music or loud voices, will soon have these sensitives seeking sanctuary behind closed doors. Interestingly, Healer is either an avid fan of television and motion pictures, or an avid avoider of such. Avoiders cited a propensity for getting too emotionally involved in the human dramas, as their reason. "As painful as being drawn and quartered at times," said one. Interestingly, watching Olympic Games on TV can be a wrenching experience for these sentient beings, who feel the heartbreak of defeat as keenly as the athletes.

Innately artistic, Healer seems particularly talented at interior design. Their style, at work and at home, could be described as austere or minimalist, with an almost trademark preference for natural over man-made materials. One reason for their design renown, may be their acute sensitivity to the world around them; another could be their ultra-creative bent. Healer has the largest energy field of all planet beings. It can be so powerful that others may feel drained or overwhelmed in their presence. Visionary emanates a powerful presence, but comparatively, Healer pulsates—which may account for their being so photogenic. Though that also may purely be due to their innate attractiveness; often described as an ethereal type of beauty that shines from within.

Such extraordinarily large energy must require extra-large elbow room, for Healer needs lots of space. Cluttered and crowded rooms or plush-coziness, rubs abrasively and irritatingly against their senses—like sandpaper on skin. Their common preference for natural environments is understandable. Organic materials, such as wood and plants, breathe, offering their energy force greater physical and auric comfort. Being dressed in synthetic fabrics can have them feeling headachy or claustrophobic, and uncharacteristically irritable in short order.

Needy and protective of privacy

If the voice of a Higher Power is foreign or frightening to you, you are not of Healer style *in any realm of functioning*. We strongly recommend you retake Ansir's Self-perception test. All Healers know their life Partner intimately. They do not look through stained-glass windows, behind burning bushes, or between the covers of leather-bound books, for self or life affirmation. In fact, it rather saddens them to see others look beyond self for guidance. They look no further than their own breath and hand, to find their who and why. Healer communicates directly, often, and in private with their Higher Power. And, whether turned inward or outward, their eyes see evidence of a Higher Power everywhere, especially in people. The world makes sense to them in ways others can't understand. There are depths and levels of consciousness that spiritualists are aware of that logic cannot measure and, therefore, cannot accept. For instance, Healer never feels alone; not even in times of doubt, joy or fear. They have a sense of being part of a team. A comforting, counselling awareness that's ever available for guidance or companionship. For them, there are no coincidences in life. Everything happens for a reason.

The "row" and "hoe" of Healer is changing belief.

As a surgeon removes cataracts from clouded eyes, Healer removes doubt from clouded views. Most particularly, those that perceive self as powerless and Higher Power as a powerful mirage in the far-off, blurried distance. Healers are often thrust into authority roles, as a consequence of their personal experiences or professional achievements. Contrary to their intentions and nature, they may find they've acquired an audience of admirers or followers, seeking their wisdom.

The hoe they apply is highly selective, aimed with discretionary eye, and wielded with light touch. It weeds out disbelief by furrowing a link between individual and Higher Power, allowing a freer flow of communication. Then, with job done, Healer steps aside and steps away. They do not claim to "heal," or convince and sell. Their objective is to remove the weeds of doubt that obscure truth and choke betterment.

She was the pre-eminent physician of her day, as well as an artist, a musician, a poet, a scholar and writer. Through her own initiative, and by placing all trust in her spiritual guide, she became the healer-of-choice to Pope, King, and pauper alike. She knew things science of her day could not justify. She heard and saw things others did not. She also knew the penalty for arousing public suspicion and skepticism, so kept silent about her spiritual beliefs. Her deeds and reputation eventually placed her beyond reproach and above question. In typical Healer fashion she talked with the Higher Power—a communion as suspect in her time as in ours. Had she been born in another place and time, she may very well have been a defendant in a heresy trial presided over by Sir Francis Bacon, and met a witch's fiery demise. Her name is Hildegaard Von Bingen, a self-taught, 12th-century nun.

Those rare Healers who accept their spiritual gifts and powers, reveal remarkable intellect and ability. For Healer, it's less a matter of acquiring knowledge than a challenge accessing their own. They've evolved through all personalities, except Philosopher. Their palette is replete with infinite colours and rich hues of their evolutionary experiences, which are stored in soul's library and accessed through emotions. Remembering who they are, through private introspection, is how Healer learns their purpose and harnesses the power to fulfill it.

In fertile Healer soil, genius flourishes, but seldom reveals, except through application—at work. By their doing, usually in some one-on-one capacity, Healers fulfill their unique life purpose: to heal others. While for many, the term *heal* means practicing medicine. In terms of this style, heal means an active involvement in some people-benefitting service or practice. Having evolved to the spiritual state, these individuals have no need for an ego.

Ego is how each individual represents their belief, (accumulated knowledge), to the external world. Confident Healer relates intuitively. They don't need a buffer zone or a go-between to edit or filter their truth; that they receive and deliver directly.

Unconfident Healers deny or fear their spiritual dimension, and they usually develop an ego to relate in-like and in-kind with others. As weights in a saddle handicap racehorse speed, egos handicap Healer's nature. Their awkward ego-addition brings them unique challenges and returns consequences that can range from humorous to humiliating. This conversation is with confident Healers. Their unconfident kin will either hear the ring of truth's bell or not. Everything in life is choice, including denial of self and avoidance of responsibility.

Changing belief

Healer thinking is not logical, it's holistic. They intrinsically feel the interconnectiveness between earth, beings, and life. Most personality styles have unique and definite patterns of thinking...Idealist sees patterns through time; Eccentrik mentally spins and sculpts; Diligent builds step-by-step; and Visionary sees what isn't. To understand how Healers think, it's necessary to first realize that spiritualists are not step-by-step, logical thinkers. These individuals head straight for solution and leave both proving and explaining to others. Healers are Spiritualists, meaning intuitives *plus*. Their solutions embrace wholes of concepts; going beyond the pieces and parts that touch solution, to all aspects, directly or indirectly affected by solutions.

When they access intuitive wisdom, they're not limited to the plod or narrow of mental processing. Their creativity is unlimited and lightning quick, comparatively. In school, they tend to be consistent and conscientious, but average students, until introduced to subjects that pique their curiosity. Their tend then is to astonish with the range and flex of their sparked intellect. Boredom is the most common complaint heard from Healer students. For them, formal education is mostly a review of what's already known and doesn't hold their interest. When they get to the parts they like, these pundits can fly.

From an early age, they seem to know what path to follow. If any Healer is not aware of their own purpose, or not sure which way fulfillment lies, it's because they deny innermost counsel—their own truth. Healer and the Higher Power communicate directly and the message is clear: heal. Regardless of endeavour, whether global or human, as in science, medicine, arts, entertainment, literature or music; Healers are here to awaken and uplift the human condition. Most pursue higher education; less for the educational aspect than for the permission, granted by legal degree, to practice their chosen field. Healers assure others of their qualifications through certificate proof. Since they are insatiably curious about that which interests, they tend to acquire substantial proof over time. Removing doubt is their specialty, and the first doubts removed are those concerning their qualifications. Healers are usually impeccably qualified, academically and legally.

One peculiarity of this personality is a common, even characteristic, fear of incarceration. Healers tend to behave well within proprietary bounds and societary limits. Of all styles, they're least likely to require close supervision or discipline, even when children. Receiving a spoken or written I. O. U. from them is equivalent to receiving a certified cheque from others. Healers tend to bone up on the laws and social norms of foreign countries, before boarding the plane for a visit. Needless to say, their personal and professional ethics supersede laws of land and man.

The weeds their unique hoe culls are those that stunt growth by blocking truth. Like those weeds of alienation that cause others to feel as alone, as that proverbial tree that falls unnoticed and unheard...like weeds of short-sighted greed that, like Popeye's™ Wimpey, will gladly pay a rain forest, for a hamburger today. Or those weeds of irresponsibility that adamantly defend man's right to speak, whilst poisoning his food, water and air.

To find a Healer look close to earth.

Healers are well-grounded individuals. As Hildegaard Von Bingen learned from talks with the Higher Power, and from her herbal research and use, all that man needs to thrive and survive is provided on earth. It was likely a Healer who wryly observed, "we dig our graves with our teeth," for no other has been more instrumental in stirring global-consciousness and promoting system-thinking, than them.

It's a Healer, who understands that overpopulation will not be controlled, unless economic success and social status no longer depend on the number of offspring. Change belief, and the desire for large families will decrease, as will population. It's a Healer, who forces an examination of lifestyle, past, present and future, when the symptom is gallbladder pain. Change belief, and pain will be reduced and cause eliminated, often without surgery. For them, healing of man and earth is an inside job. Once belief is changed and each is reconnected to their own self-renewing, self-maintaining, and self-transcending power, each will understand that life is created and they, Co-Creators.

Life for Healers is a living, feeling system of interconnections and interrelations that evolve from, revolve around, and sustain and support one another. When an ill-wind blows, it not only sickens land and sea but all upon and within, as well. Healers are the original environmentalists, as they were the original nutritionists, naturalists, pacifists and activists; who walked under all manner of banners for all-people causes.

Healers have performed many roles throughout time, but always have they changed beliefs, as spiritualists. Not long ago, environmentalist was a dirty word: one that earned political contempt and evoked corporate as well as public derision, for its bleeding-heart sentimentality. Now, environmentalist is a badge of honour that garners more global respect than any army's uniform. Motives and intentions of environmentalists are clear; their covenant and business are one and the same: life. Global perspective changing is spiritualist-typical, and most typically Healer's.

With such enormous innate power to harness and direct, and such responsibility to shoulder, it's understandable why Healers are reluctant to be. One thing confident Healers have learned that unconfidents may find encouraging: evolution allows time for ability to evolve sufficient for flight, but not always time enough for courage to arrive with it. The difference between those who find self-fulfillment and those who don't? Some trust their wings will work, when they jump off the limb that frightening first time.

Though well-armed with skills and gifts, to fulfill their self-chosen life purpose, unconfident Healers lack one thing, courage. That, they must find on their own.

THE SPIRITUALISTS

Philosopher

Profiles having Philosopher as the dominant Style of functioning for Thinking /Working or /Emoting, will read the full, 3-realm InDepth. Philosopher is a powerful Style and exerts much influence on decisions and actions of any Profiled individual. The influence is one of encouragement, which manifests as greater confidence and self-determination.

Life Purpose

T'ween Healers and Philosophers, lines of demarcation blend and blur. Much as yin to yang and kith to kin, where one leaves off the other begins.

On the crest of evolutionary waves that gap here and there, cerebral giants surf. Masters and transgressors, they ride the flow of destiny guided by infinite wisdom and eternal truth's knowledge. They are Philosophers and they're tethered to the board of humanity, by an unyielding thong of love-responsibility. Their eyes pierce fog-banked inanity; their ears prickle at imperious disdain; they bristle, roar and challenge at man's enchain. On tides of metamorphosis they taxi, dismantling treadmills along the way. To empower, by unshackling from bonds of blind obeisance, is Philosopher's purpose and their soul's, *sole* reason for being.

Philosophers are not common.

They're difficult to recognize and generally not that available. For this conversation it's necessary to know two things in advance: they are Healers *plus*, and unconfident Philosophers usually emote in Sentinel style, which is an 180-degree turnabout from their truth and light years from their spiritual nature and power. Why so unPhilosopher? Sentinel instinctively looks for reasons not to accept and trust people, whereas Philosopher sees souls. What reason then to not trust? It's understandable for Sentinel to approach others with caution and suspicion but unnecessary for the highest level spiritualist, like Philosopher. Any *3 Sides Of You* participant, whose Profile includes Philosopher and Sentinel Styles, is strongly recommended to either re-take the test to confirm or to take self by the scruff of the neck and ask, "why the skepticism?"

Philosophers are the kids, the newest personality addition.

According to the scientific theory of evolution, the tactic of neoteny guarantees that it is youth, pre-adults, who accept the inevitable and advance openly and readily forward. When it's time to leave the water and evolutionarily lung-up, lunging will happen whether gill or tradition likes it or not. Youth embraces inevitability first.

Philosophers are personality equivalents to the colour white. As white is the inclusion of all colour, Philosophers are the inclusion of all personality styles. "Been there, did it, done it" is their cellular recall. Like Healers, they're here to awaken others. Healers awaken truth—the who of each. Philosophers awaken power—the why of being. Their presence is not to guru or lead (unless others prove unable) but to help others prepare to meet the next inevitable step confidently.

Full-blown, as Athena from the brow of Zeus, are Philosophers seemingly sprung. No child is more challenging to raise and no adult more inspiring than this sophic, soul*full* one. Parent, individual, or organization cannot veer confident Philosophers from their self-charted, self-determined course. Unconfident Philosophers, just like unconfident Healers, can be any personality that intimidation convinces them to settle on, or that criticism leads them to be.

Perhaps by meeting confident Philosophers here, those less confident will find the strength to reclaim self again. It's never too late. Time has neither beginning nor end and does not expire, as mortality with last breath. Time and change have a chicken-and-egg relationship. They chase each other so closely its hard to tell which is behind and which is ahead. Sometimes change thinks it's ahead, only to find itself spitting out the dust kicked up by time's passing. Philosopher's concern is not of change being late but of it not coming at all.

On both sides of the parent–Philosopher child experience, difficulty abounds.

Childhood can be tough. So tough that many Philosophers either avoid their own power till later in life or avoid straight through to the end. They can be any personality or professional they choose; for they're past-life familiar with the thinking, working and emoting challenges of all. The only one they've not been is Philosopher. Most won't fulfill their covenant this time around either.

Appealing rationally is key for any successful relationship with them. If Philosopher accepts the underlying purpose and principle they accede willingly. Neither non-conformist nor rebel, per se, they just don't bow to authority or policy that conflicts with their own soul's wisdom. Once that nature-need is satisfied, Philosophers are most pleasant beings. None can compare to the rare individual who dwells non-judgementally within; but when will-o'-the-wisp is the norm and respect the expected, no other is less compliant or more irreverent than them. If being aware of the importance of self is childish, then Philosophers epitomize childishness. Harmonious relations can seem contractual, in that guidelines must be clearly spelled out and an all-party agreement reached before they'll proceed. Emptying of sleeves, fulfilling the tenets, and honouring the pact are essential. Philosophers demand equal accountability from others as they, themselves, deliver.

Not emotionally effusive nor notably affectionate, Philosopher children are insatiably curious, and *Johnny-one-note* persistent in garnering fullest explanation for their understanding. They seem surprised and get impatient, when others can't answer their penetrating and often complex queries. Neither surface skimmers nor shallow swimmers, Philosophers seek in-depth explanation and drown-deep experience. There's no peace for a parent who teaches their Philosopher child how to tell time yet neglects to provide them a watch or clock for their own time keeping. What good is knowledge if not used? What point is life if not lived? These may be questions for others but are characteristics for Philosophers.

They have fascinating inner lives, where audio-visual richness flourishes and flows unceasingly. Unlike Evokateurs, who, too, have fascinating innerworlds, Philosophers are outwardly focused and directed, and eager to experience all that reality offers. Whether celebrating, suffering or fluxing somewhere between; these tribal-focused individuals want, and even need to be immersed in the everyday win-lose, flail, fun, and fight aspects of life. They're the little ones who refuse to be put to bed, when company visits. The first to notice a new neighbourhood kid, cat, or car; and the outspoken one who announces that "Gran's breath smells like Uncle Bob's feet." Count on them to make self and opinion generally known.

Their characteristic propensity for intense concentration, which manifests in broad and rapid gain of expertise, is exhibited early and often with a disconcerting boldness. Little escapes their notice or question and less their personal investigation; which can turn nurturing and parenting them into a hair-raising, hair-graying ordeal. Philosophers are difficult to distract when focused, and need the predictability of order and routine to ground them. Structure frees them to explore deeply without the jar and jolt of unexpected breaks. For instance, Philosopher can go without sleep readily enough, but when they sleep it's the sleep of the dead. Those who know them tend to give their sleeping form wide tip-toe berth. Rousing them can be a rude-awakening for all. Abrupt interruptions can be physically painful for them.

They have a precocious bent for grasping abstract concepts, such as time, distance and space. Parents are often amazed at the genius displayed by their Philosopher offspring, who seem to excel at all that draws their interest. These little tykes confidently step out to greet new others as they do to meet new challenges. All exhibit an early aptitude, in one regard or another, though precocity never had a more recalcitrant vessel. Unlike most precocious children—such as Evokateur, *Wolfgang Amadeus Mozart*—Philosopher children will not perform on cue. They're not motivated by applause or praise, and generally will do nothing for the mere of pleasing another. With the severing of their umbilical cord, Philosophers take a firm hold of their own freedom's reins. Usually, they can't be coerced, manipulated, intimidated, licked, stamped, stapled or folded when their druther differs.

Guilt neither roosts nor nests in their nature.

Many Philosophers describe childhood and adulthood as being a trial-by-fire experience. Their sharp edges harden quickly, to resist being blunted and dulled by external force and influence. Because of parent and peer pressure to conform, at an early age these seemingly over-confident or cockyOnes adopt a boxer's stance for dealings with others. With toe, they draw their line of defense and battle all who dare to cross or oppose them. With fists raised and determination coiled, they wage their own war of independence against a, *do what you're told* and *one-size-fits-all* world. They keep their guard up and keep their distance, until they learn the lesson of Rupert's Drops: power is not in form but in nature.

Self-realization in Rupert's Tail

In glassmaking, there is a phenomena that occurs when a small glob of molten glass is rapidly cooled. The result is a solid, tadpole-shaped object, with a bulbous head that tapers to a delicate curved tail. Despite their fragile look, Rupert's Drops seem indestructible. Direct sledgehammer blows glance off ineffectually. They were first introduced as toys, in the 17th century to the court of King James I, by his grandson, Prince Rupert of Bavaria. The real beauty of Rupert's Drops is not in their appearance or strength, but in their nature. While seemingly indestructible, one clip or snip of delicate tail's tip explodes the Rupert's Drop into a powdery handful of harmless dust. It is the nature of Rupert's Drops, born of the rapid cooling of surface over warm interior that accounts for their phenomena—an explosive disintegration of form back to particle beginning. And so it is with Philosopher.

They're born full-blown but spend much of their childhood and youth, by forcing others to understand and accept them. Their function is to be more droplet of water, not ocean, for they've did-and-done all before. Nature is discovered in the tails of Rupert's Drops; in souls for Philosophers. Accepting that others may not ever approve or understand them, *because they can't,* is the snip of realization that explodes and disintegrates Philosopher defensiveness.

From the dust of former needs and habits, self-awareness stirs and true power awakens. Realization, of who and why they are takes shape and has a name. Philosopher: spiritualist of the tallest order and responsibility.

Others, like glass, mature by the process of annealing. They take form under more evenly tempered conditions and require a slower, more steady pace for development. Through step-by-step guidance and experience, others bloom, grow, and ripen to self-realization: not Philosopher. They come with self-realization snugged into conscience. When they draw their lines of defiance and pen their lists of demands, they not only deny others access to them but limit themselves in terms of their person and purpose. Erasing the line that divides them from others, frees them to be as born and meant.

Philosopher power only reveals when they stop expecting and stop demanding confirmation of, and for self. Once they accept that validation cannot be had externally, they lower their fists. Where once shrillness was heard and desperation felt, there is quiet calmness instead. They hear but one voice and feel the fullness of their so-long felt, but misunderstood and misused strength. Only from soul, through guidance of intuition and by way of emotions, will they receive all they need to be Philosopher and meet their responsibilities. Their fulfillment is experiencing, for they've already passed all possible life lessons. They're not here to serve self, but to help others *BE* their own selves fully.

They're often the most difficult of students to teach. The education system is logic-based, where each grade level builds upon the preceding, in foundation to rooftop progression. In school, classes are scheduled to break and courses to change every few hours. Such disruptions are mentally jarring and emotionally stressful for these cerebral giants; who need more time to warm up and unwind, than school clocks and rules allow. Such portioned toe-dipping leaves Philosophers with more questions than answers. Like Sage, Philosopher often learns more on their own than in classrooms. Alternate schools that offer a more open and flexible learning environment, are more compatible with Philosopher's style of learning, than standard education systems.

Sage, Empath, and Visionary—their needed teachers and mentors.

Intuitives understand logicals but logicals can have difficulty understanding intuitives, especially headstrong Philosophers. They may be mulish and disdainful of rules, but few are as sensitive or easily discouraged, as young, unconfident Philosopher; and is why so many compromise and conform rather than become. The random/matrix/holistic thinkers among us, need guidance and encouragement from like-others in formative years. Logic cannot fully satisfy intuitive curiosity. Facts are not enough. Intuitives need depth to understand and spiritualists are highest-level intuitives. The depth of their required understanding goes as far down as to where *all* began.

What logicals don't understand about intuitive learning is...

...intuitives mentally see and emotionally feel information. To understand, they must combine the two dimensions. Information needs to be explained clearly and thoroughly enough, for them to create a see-able, feel-able, and therefore sensible picture, before understanding occurs. Logicals gain understanding from words; intuitives from emotion-images. Factual logic may answer the main question but not address the questions that flow and follow...like what preceded this, where does that go, and why and when does it end? If a picture says 1000 words, expect intuitives to have as many questions? Intuitives, except Philosopher, compromise their natural and most efficient way of learning, by adjusting to normal (logical) teaching methods. Because Philosopher nature will not compromise or accept anything at face value, grade school can be difficult—as much for them as for their logical teachers.

Logic can be more demoralizing than enlightening, for intuitive-intellects like them. Logicals often have difficulty understanding intuitives' illogical problem-solving approach and their off-the-beaten-path inquisitiveness. For instance, logical Sherlock Holmes piled brick upon logical brick to arrive at an answer with elementary ease. Intuitive Inspector Hercule Poirot tended to know the answer first and, by working backwards, pieced together enough logical bricks to support (logically explain) his intuited-solution. *(Note: TV's Detective Columbo works Sage).*

Knowing is not enough; logically proving is necessary. Philosophers can handle themselves quite well, once acceptance of self and limitations of others are known; but they can experience grief and ultra-frustration as students, in a "learn what's needed to pass the grade" education system and a "prove-it first" world.

Philosophers tend to be voracious readers. As kids, they're usually far advanced of their peers, in terms of reading and comprehension. Anything that interests can spark a frenzy of focused study and investigation, until their curiosity is satisfied or their interest wanes. Like Healer, their greatest challenge is not to gain education, but to reacquaint themselves with their own soul's wisdom and apply those experiences wisely and responsibly. Philosophers trust their god-spark truth, to guide them well and right in manner and decisions. These individuals aren't torn by self-doubt. Intuition reveals their *who* and *why* and that's all the guidance they need to proceed confidently.

Beginnings

Without solid accreditation or reputation, Philosopher may always be perceived as a loose cannon. Being different and often labelled delinquent, they'll be dismissed or overlooked unless they earn recognition by working inside, rather than outside the system. Most—particularly working

Philosopher, steps in line with others and in same robotic-fashion, climbs the necessary steps to higher education. Their decision is less motivated by a desire for learning than for the respectability that comes with a degree.

Those who do not gain verification and authorization, by higher education, tend to lead lives that deny them opportunities to exercise their potential. They usually excel in less-structured study environments, like college and university. That's when the congenial genius their parents once knew, returns, resurfaces and takes flight. Others tend to listen to those with impeccable accreditation, especially those whose name is followed by Ph. D. August academic weight lends credence to their words; a state and condition particularly important for this style. In order for Philosopher to fulfill their life purpose, they must speak and be heard.

Who would have listened...

...had he not held a doctorate in philosophy and had he not in the '40s and '50s garnered respect for his achievements in the field of psychology? In the '60s this Philosopher began to speak from the centre of a cultural revolution. He encouraged all to, "Think For Yourself, Question Authority." He advocated all exercise their inalienable right to independent thought and action. He offered others opportunity for mind exploration and heightened sensory awareness. Settling for a puny percentage of potential—mind alone—was unacceptable to him, given that the means and way for more were available. He did not invent the revolution, the time, nor the place of its unfolding. That was a genetic, evolutionary inevitability, but he recognized it and brought it to the world's attention.

The youth were ripe and listened, the rest were outraged. It earned him establishment disdain, professional discredit, and legal persecution, which has ever-been Philosopher's fate. With intellectual thumb on evolution's pulse, he felt the fetal stirrings of a developing Information Age. He embraced it with characteristic Philosopher excitement, envisioning mind-expanding possibilities and future benefits. While his contemporaries, entertained thoughts of rocking chairs and reminisced of good ol' Woodstock days, he explored leading-edge technology. He knew, from front-line '60s experiences the immoral outrage and mortal consequence, when institutions felt threatened by individuality. Back then he'd said, "Think For Yourself. Proceed with caution, as proper use of the brain is not endorsed by federal governments nor huge corporations involved in serious financial profit from a brainwashed and enslaved population. Mild discomfort may occur, as confusing independent thought challenges popular views of the world."

Characteristic of Philosophers, he did not trust authority, particularly when money and individual freedom mixed. Philosopher's suspicion-of-authority-roots are gnarled and deep and may entwine with temple and moneychanger days. He anticipated a twenty-first century struggle between individuality and multi-national combines, which control the planet without regard for populations. The internet provided a portal of hope through which a well-aimed wrench could one day be thrown, if or when needed. To him, the internet was a global forum where individuals could meet and interact as never before. Little wonder this cerebral giant was excited. Individuality could be accessed and expressed freely; collectively and globally.

With the same intellectual enthusiasm he welcomed life experiences, he welcomed death in '96. It is not difficult to imagine him—soul-intact—settling into a new place or phase; a genetic, evolutionary inevitability. He had no regrets nor did others who knew him. He lived harder, faster and fuller than most and left the world greater than whence he came. A Philosopher and transgressor, he was an irrepressible, remarkable and powerful individual. His name? Timothy Leary, Ph. D.

Puppet or puppeteer

By knotting tighter the threads of human individuality, do Philosophers ensure the human pattern is neither faded of importance nor unravelled from the weave. When humans are devalued is when Philosophers change roles, from participant to leader. Awakening the power of truth within is Healer's purpose. Philosophers go one step further. They strongly encourage others to live truthfully. That means doing everything with enough conviction and commitment, that the stamp and proof of self indelibly remains. There are no coincidences or isolated incidents for them. Everything personal and professional ripples planet consequences. They don't put professional distance between self and responsibility nor condone such teflon-remiss in others. According to Philosopher, the closer responsibility stays to self the greater the care taken and given.

As each is a self-scripted star in their own life story, each also has the power and freedom to pen their demise. Living according to individual truth considerably reduces the possibility of self-defeat becoming a pattern moment-to-moment, year-to-year, and life-to-life. The age of responsibility is the age of maturity. Until then, evolution of self is like the stage in metamorphosis known as larvae. More than egg, less than butterfly, looks like a worm, feeds off anything within touch, taste, or sight, and leaves dung heaps behind for others to clean-up. For some, self is directly tied to the opinions of others, as larvae to twig and leaf. For some, self is hidden by self-induced, self-stunting fears, thus remaining at the safe larvae stage rather than risking imago. Every other can tell each what to think, say, and do, but no other can dictate nor predict *how* each will feel. And while such is surely proof of how significant emotions are, its not significant enough for Philosopher.

Nettles

Philosopher purpose is to awaken the power of individuality, sufficient for others to willingly move beyond the safe, unproductive bounds of thinking and expressing, to the riskier "pudding" aspects of doing (fulfilling life purpose). But there's a catch. As that famous moral monkey "think no...hear no...say no..." depicts, Philosopher will not directly influence others. At most they enlighten or encourage. Without telling, showing or forcing, and without use of show-stopping miracles like feeding the multitudes or raising the dead, Philosopher penetrates without interfering with the superior ability of each to know—by feel—what's best and most right for them.

Not only must *what to do* and *why to do* be self-determined, but *how* and *when* too. Individual feelings are the only motivator and motivation that inflames and sustains drive, and returns rewards that are meaningful and therefore, more confidence-building than money or applause.

They love socializing with friends but may not socialize with the general populace readily or often. They don't collect friends; friends tend to collect them for their wisdom, wit, and great sense of humour; for their bold honesty, contempt for authority and refreshing perspectives. Others know Philosopher by name or by fame. Philosopher knows others by grain of their soul's truth. The difference between what they know of another and how another relates, frustrates them greatly and brings out their prickliness. Others may not notice their entrance, yet feel the sting of their nettle before they exit.

Philosopher honesty can ring rude in ears unattuned though sweet in ears familiar. They never lie (it physically weakens or sickens), but may not know what degree of truth each is willing to handle at each now of time. It can be as uncomfortable being around them, as being around a precocious, outspoken child. Generally speaking, their purpose does not allow them the luxury of one-on-one contact like Healer. Philosopher usually stands further back and influences or interacts from a distance. They surf atop tides of change, to see what's coming and prepare others for its inevitability. It's not the few they notify; their focus is on the average and many. Those they offend unintentionally, are those who acknowledge the need for change but choose to ignore it. Those they offend intentionally, are those with a propensity to shoot messengers bearing news that threatens their status quo.

Anger is the most common first-response tool and one that all, regardless of age, are familiar with and adept of use. Anger is an all-purpose, equal-opportunity, logic-blanket, under which emotional truth of remorse, fear, love and hurt get hidden. Philosophers are anger experts, who can avoid its smother or rip off its cover as needed. Logic respects and promotes *shoulds* and *musts*, and *rights* and *wrongs*, but truth doesn't. And neither does Philosopher.

Like them, truth respects self only. TheseOnes explode logic leaving holes and gaps big enough for individual truth to walk through. Anger is but one tool from an infinite array found in their tool-belt. Like Visionary, if they hurt your feelings it was intended. Visionary wants to understand others for their own sake's benefit and advantage. Philosopher already understands others. Their purpose is to have each understand for their own sake and benefit. After that, whether to invest in change or load the messenger shooting pistol is each's decision and responsibility. It cannot be an easy task, uniting mind and body with soul, without judgement or malice like Philosophers do.

Anathema, to them, is adulation of any form or kind—be it devotee, fan club, society, group, or organization; where individuality lauds, applauds, and lingers in the shadow of another. Each and every soul is unique in terms of gifts, talents, and experiences. Trying to tailor one to fit into the mold of another is more than denial of self. To Philosopher, it's soul death. What fulfilling, far less significant, life can come of that?

Philosophers have an uncanny ability for being on-the-spot when leading edges are sharpened or discoveries unveiled. They seldom author the work or event themselves. Their knack is for pointing out what others may not see and explaining what new changes have come—or are coming. Philosopher often sees the naked truth where others see the Emperor's new clothes.

They tend to view mind-expansion as a personal and interpersonal journey to multi-layered reality and intellectual enlightenment. Philosopher encourages others to travel innermost sanctums, to remember and reconnect with their own wisdom. If energy can neither be created nor destroyed, and bacteria does not spontaneously sprout life in petri dishes, they view it as self-defeating and soul-demeaning to think of birth as life's beginning, and death as its end. Each soul encompasses evolutionary history, where experiences from Big Bang to present are indelibly scribed and etched. Life is a game that guarantees win-win; each has one and gets to make of it whatever they can, want, or will. There are no forfeitures, no loss of turn, no rejections and no revoking of privileges. And no soul here is less than essential.

From thinking and saying to doing

General discontent and disillusion grew louder, found a voice, became a movement, then a cultural-revolution in the '60s. It was first expressed by youth whose intelligence-fired dragon snorted pervasive and pernicious discontent. In unison they questioned the materialistic dream that failed to deliver enduring satisfaction or personal fulfillment as promised. It was unacceptable that human potential should be cookie-cutter trimmed to fit outdated molds; that success equalled material gain and that rewards were based on conformity, not creativity, not individuality. Before things quieted down, some barriers had been dismantled and some new in-roads paved, but the greatest long-term hatch came from the conscious-awareness egg that was laid during those hippie-cool, bell-bottom'd days.

Alternatives were needed to appease the growing, global discontent of youth that questioned existing reality and leadership motives. Conscious-awareness said "make love," while existing reality bombed, napalmed, off-loaded banned products to the third-world citizens, and agent orange'd its own. Conscious-awareness said "make peace," while existing reality threatened global annihilation with mortiferously sophisticated technology. Conscious-awareness said "save the pygmies, save the whales, save the trees," while existing reality polluted from ocean floor to outer space and ravaged native, culture, resource, and all habitat between.

The alarm had sounded, the awareness flag was raised and pursuit of alternatives became the order-of-the-day. Finding alternatives to existing reality was the objective. A new age of consciousness, the Green Movement emerged, where individuals were held to be equally valuable to, and responsible for, the welfare of planet and specie. Humans were raised, from the factory floor to their rightful place as the first and most responsible link in the great chain of being...and their rightful role as protector of life and respecter of the Higher Power's creations.

Same 'o, same 'o, stops here.

These purely intuitive and spiritual kids are future leaders. They're here now, to help others prepare for a different world, as this one with evolutionary predictability and inevitability, shifts. Philosopher leaders will think, speak, and act, differently than leaders before. They won't repackage and offer same 'o, same 'o, nor will they depend on charismatic salesmanship to sell their digestibility. Their focus, as leader, will not wander then from where it is now. Their eyes are riveted on dismantling corporate power, combine thinking, and collective anything, that honours profit more than planet and being. Their function is to inspire individual responsibility first, because only from there does responsibility for else and other follow. Where most leaders walk toward their audience, mount platform, and face-to-face persuade, Philosophers walk as one among and face the same way.

As rolling stones gather no moss, Philosopher gathers no followers. They carry no hammers, distribute no leaflets, and avoid pulpit, podium, public office and lectern, unless they must. If asked, they answer; if interested, they explore; if invited, they decide go or stay; and if required they pass, unless they require. Philosophers have matured beyond ego-need for recognition; beyond feeling better by comparison to worse; beyond pleasure by hurting; beyond obligating by helping; beyond mere of pleasing; and beyond valuing any practice or person that does not honour life first. Philosopher, like Kinsmen, lead by manner of their living example. Anything less is irresponsible; anything more is meddle and unnecessary.

Philosopher knows that consciousness is a personal journey, that when travelled far and deep enough arrives at truth. Souls take care of each other. The thread of self is inextricably woven and inter-connected to all manner and matter of life. Every breathing thing is intimately significant and intrinsically essential, and only Co-Creator humans have the power and freedom of choice to create or destroy.

Grease, not cog

They consider themselves more as grease than cog, and often clash with authority over should and must issues. Characteristically, they suffer an allergy to authority and uniforms, regardless of the cut and colour of cloth. Asking tough questions, such as why and why not, tends to reduce their chances of succeeding hierarchically. Their reluctance to direct or boss others significantly reduces their value, managerially. They tend to be most intelligent, most hard-working, and most likely to refute any policy not in sync with their own. Entirely self-determined and self-directed, Philosopher is adamant about staying that way. Always and only, do they follow their own soul's path and way.

Since they only do that which they choose and approve, they are generally known for being open-minded and confident...and successful. They often choose careers where they can contract out their specialized services. There are two reasons why Philosophers prefer entrepreneurism over employeeism. One is freedom, the other is suspicion.

The beacon that guides spiritualist is internally generated and driven. They prefer the freedom of entrepreneurship to schedule their own work and time. Regarding money, they tend to be suspicious of its inherent manipulation aspect. When they take control of particulars, such as hours of work and terms of compensation, it reduces dependency and the likelihood of abuse. It's not barter and exchange they're suspicious of—exchequer motives is what raises their antennae. Employer/employee relations have historically been less than equitable.

Wealth or material gain doesn't motivate them; affording choice does. Philosopher demands autonomy personally and professionally. Trust is not the determinant, authorship and ownership of responsibility is. Personal accountability is a major issue for them. They deliver it themselves in word and deed, and encourage the same in return from others in relations and relationships. They tend to captain their own ships and are renowned workaholics. They may only do that which they like but like doing it a lot, apparently.

They're usually well-educated, and while capable of pursuing any career and succeeding, they predominately function in two areas: reason—as in philosophy, psychiatry or psychology; or information—as in technological sciences like planning, programming, and design. In both, is the matrix thinking of Philosopher an advantage. They tend to dig deeply and discover through depth and breadth of exploration, the inter-relations and interconnectedness of pieces and parts to whole. If seeming diverse, the common element underlying these two people-focused fields is communication.

Evolutionarily speaking, information has evolved from oral, to papyrus, to paper, to Guttenburg press, to mass production, to instant computerization. Man also evolved, from muscle-flex of Bronze Age, to hand coordination of Industrial Age, to mind-projection of Information Age. What is particularly interesting about the Information Age is that never before has such a perfect vehicle existed for theseOnes to oversee and interact with the average and many, than afforded by the Internet.

It's noteworthy that Philosopher has been on the Net for years, because wherever they're found, big businesses that require their style of watch-dogging are usually heel-nipping close. Remember, Philosopher surfs evolutionary waves. Where they are, is a more accurate predictor than *Granny Clampett's* weather beetle, that changes affecting the average and many are coming. Their being on-the-spot at this unprecedented technological and information-rich juncture is significant.

Graduates of every test and trial, Philosopher is master of the highest degree in the class of spiritualist. They can be the kindest, but are also the toughest. If asked, they readily offer the shirt off their back. That act in and of itself is not unusual. What differentiates Philosopher from others is that, in their giving, it's understood they give but once and they'll not button nor straighten collars afterwards. They walk with hand extended and arms open to help, but rather than lifting and carrying, what Philosopher does is boost confidence. They expect others to pick themselves up, dust themselves off and get back in the race, by their own steam's initiative. They *know* how powerful each is; their objective is to awaken that realization in others and encourage them to use their power bravely and responsibly. A more inspirational and powerful being, than Philosopher, has yet to be born. No human is more loving or more able, in finding the marvel and spotlighting the magnificent, than them. However, no human is less likely to wipe noses, listen to whingeing and whining or long-tolerate a doubting Thomas. They love too-much to.

An aura of non-threatening confidence and genuine warmth surrounds them. Others find them easy to talk to and easy to like. Sexual attraction, for them, tends not to be a gender-specific. As Philosophers communicate with souls, they mate with souls—whether male or female packaged. They tend to be non-judgemental about sexual preferences or proclivities, and contemptuous of dictated propriety. What matters is the depth of fulfillment through emotional sharing, where innermost truth is willingly offered and openly shared with their mate.

In youth they may have been promiscuous. In adulthood, lovers are friends and companion, with whom emotional commitment is shared, and where love unrestricted and uninhibited is reciprocated. Entirely intuitive, creative beings, they embrace the whole and depth of intimacy. Sexual relations are deeply spiritual, deeply pleasurable experiences. Like Evokateur and Healer, Philosopher has a rich inner life, of fluid imagery and sensory wonderment. They choose outer-world living, but during sex, they return to innermost sanctums. In union with the emotional essence of their mate, they follow passion's wake in the submit and submerge of surrender's embrace. A fusion of time, space, and sensation, the flow of carnal energy blurs and blends, as lust courses freely between, within, and beyond them from reality's crisp edge to surreal's tottering limbo. For them, sex is the greatest physical-emotional experience of all. Philosopher needs a mate who can ground their out-of-body experience, when inner and outer awareness unites.

They seem to have an anti-establishment gene that causes their rebel hackle to rise at meet with authority. That powerful aura, that draws and comforts the average and many, threatens authority with the damage potential of a diamond drill-bit. Philosophers do not seem to need any-one or anything. Those, who would possess them or cause them harm, cannot find a vulnerability to pierce or attack, or a toehold from which to launch an advantage.

"We can't solve problems by using the same kind of thinking we used when we created them." —Evokateur, Albert Einstein

What most raises Philosopher ire is authority's insistence on running the world with logic. Like cud is regurgitated grass for cows, logic is regurgitated opinion for humans. Whenever and wherever cows belch or dispose, they enrich air and fertilize earth. Whenever and wherever logic burps or disposes, it can and does destroy life. If the situation were reversed, cows would have long-been eradicated for posterity's sake, but logic is not eradicated though posterity be at stake. Instead of looking to visionaries and dreamers, whose eyes see beyond known, authority persists in thumbing worn logic-pages and recycling ineffective solutions.

Genius and creativity are not reserved for the few or the remarkable. Some are not born exceptional, ALL are. Birds of flight all have wings, cats of prey all have claws; why would a Higher Power play *Advantage-Disadvantage Roulette* with Co-Creators? Genius is not measured by ability to recall or recant knowledge, but by how far creativity advances current knowledge, or by shade and degree of variance from principle.

A degree of creative variance can result in significant differences. For instance, but for one or two evolutionary degrees, chimpanzees would be human. How creative are chimpanzees? They can recall knowledge in human-like fashion but cannot communicate, dream, laugh or use thumbs like humans. Often is it stated or lamented that each utilizes but twenty-percent of mind's potential. Perhaps the missing eighty is stored elsewhere. Why not in soul? After all, that's the one-hundred-percent of each that exceeds death.

Lemmings

Generally, it is thought that acquired knowledge is the basis upon which life decisions are made. A non-fizzle, lemming end, for those born with power and creativity equal to that of Creator, thinks Philosopher. Speech, dream, laughter, and flexible thumb divide human from beast. According to Philosopher, self-doubt divides each from their greatest birth power—soul wisdom. Individuality, from infancy to adulthood, tends to land heavily on authority toes, and from infancy through adult-hood is strongly discouraged. Individuality upsets carefully laid logical plans, where time-efficiency and cost-effectiveness take precedence over human concerns. Individuality asks "why?" long after logic has answered. Least satisfied of all with pat logical answers is Philosopher, who tends to ask the tough questions logic can't or won't answer. They don't give in, give up, or give way. That's why authority has evolutionarily felt threat-ened by them. They personify and exercise authority's greatest fear— con-fident, creative individuality.

For long–term intimate relations, few Styles are confident enough.

Generally, these are attractive individuals, whose intuitive-intellect can snug with any person, profession or situation, when wanted. Like Healer, whomever theseOnes are with is the only one that exists for that shared moment and time. Every person, every soul they encounter is presumed self-significant. In their presence others tend to feel comfortable and safe, for these are extraordinarily, accepting individuals. Hallmark gentleness and magnetic confidence account for their attractiveness. Few leave this life having acquired more admirers and friends or having experienced more love and "thanks" than Philosopher. They may depart, after having loved many and experienced much, but one experience they may not know is intimate love.

> *"Don't tell me you're honest, be honest.*
> *Don't tell me you're loving, love.*
> *Don't anticipate me but give me your truth for mine to know.*
> *Be you. I'll be me. Let our combined best lead to betterment and*
> *fulfillment of us and each."*

When relations proceed on that basis, that individual is Philosopher to some significant degree. Why is it so hard for Philosopher to find a soul-fulfilling mate? Because they see more in others than others see in self...or live. More rare than a devoted student for teachers, is Philosopher finding a mate who can understand and love them equally.

Visionary's famed impatience with reticent others, causes many to feel uncomfortable around them. The reticent or dishonest feel uncomfortable around Philosopher. They can accept and understand anything about another, except dishonesty or reluctance. Those in their close-proximity or intimate embrace know what safe is and what love is, and how simple both can be. Truth is simple and simplifying. Few are brave enough to emotionally and honestly go where Philosophers live. TheseOnes are born at the "do love" stage. Many are still working their way through the think and repeat chapters. Most are further along though likely struggling with the *feel* and *speak* sections of the "How to live and love" book.

Loving them is easy. All it requires is bold honesty and naked vulnerability. Their level of functioning is intuitive-intelligence, so while a mate can find intimate fulfillment with them, that state is seldom reciprocated. Philosopher generally is not known for complaining about bills, details, or relationship responsibilities, as much as the reluctance of their mate to risk and explore their own truth and potential. Finding a compatible mate is the single greatest challenge for Philosopher. Their Achilles' heel is not ranging far enough to find the rightOne. They may have many relationships, but may not marry.

As white is the absorption of all colour, Philosopher is the sum of all personality styles. They are...the risk-taking Extremist; the friend-in-need Realist; fun-loving Scintillator; non-conformist Eccentrik; loyal Sentinel; methodical Diligent; diplomatic Sage; perfectionistic Idealist; kindly Kinsmen; emotion-smart Empath; big picture Visionary; creative Evokateur; and perspective-changing Healer...rolled into one.

These *kids*, which in terms of personality styles Philosophers are, seem to be making their presence more generally known. They are last resort leaders who step forward before final flushing occurs. Their appearance and number at this time is significant. How significant depends on whether they choose to live as unconfident others or as confident Philosopher. Unconfidents will spin their wheels and though successful, spin out their lives seeking fulfillment. If lucky and before life's end, they'll learn the lesson of Rupert's Drops: their soul was born full and filled. Confidents will spin a web of encouragement where all they meet and touch will be inspired to seek their own fulfillment, rather than stepping in line and processing time as most do.

No other spots, rides, and tames, evolutionary waves like them.

What crest do you now ride, Philosopher? What do you see? Others may not understand your style of being, but will understand your reason for being. Your purpose is to one day speak and be heard. Are you speaking loudly enough now, for others to hear what you have and must say? Your playing small and staying mute serves no purpose at all.

KEY 3: PROFILE INDEPTHS

Dominant Style of Working

Working: The conscious application of knowledge according to acquired skills and innate abilities of individuals.

THE PHYSICALS

For them is the term adventurer most apropos. Extremists not only pushed the envelope through time, they ripped it open and stepped inside. Many never walked out again.

Warning signs, danger postings, and red alerts, are markers that indicate where safety ends and danger begins. While cautionary for others, markers stand on *this side* of where these ones have been and gone. Be it on land, air, space, or sea, Extremists chance first, chance faster, chance farther, plant the flag, and write the rule book along the way. But don't call them heroes, they wouldn't understand. They don't do *diddly* because of, or for others. They do because no other did or dared, and they're confident they can.

Extremists do what they like and tend to do it better than most. Generally, they are highly intelligent, physically fit, and hell-bent on overcoming physical adversity. What they're not, is long-term disciplined or long-term focused. These individuals live in the now, in the whorling excitement of moments. A rare find would be an Extremist junior executive. The physical vigour and vitality of youth, and youthful adulthood is spent pursuing adrenaline-pumping challenges. To them, the greater the danger and the higher death's probability, the more irresistible the project becomes. Boardroom skirmishes, take-over bids, cut-throat tactics, or inside trading, pale in comparison to what draws and drives them.

Expediency is everything.

Quick thinking and quickest tongue are Extremist hallmarks. These ones could sell ice to those proverbial Eskimos. Getting what they want, in the shortest time, with the greatest personal reward possible is more than motivation to them. It's goal and expectation. Extremists don't ponder the meaning of life or wrestle "who am I?" issues. Their conflicts are man versus man or man versus environment—not man versus self. They know who they are and bodily apply their knowing.

Extremists are lords and masters of the physical world—their chief realm of functioning. They deal with tangibles and concretes, and leave navel contemplations to others. As though pre-programmed with agenda and over-packaged with confidence, these dynamos usually can't be deterred once mind and energy lock on a course of action. And they're creative to the *nth* degree. Extremists can outrun, outwit, and outlast most others. Trial and tribulation are not strangers to them; quitting is!

They'll catch the trophy fish; others clean it.

The art and science of persuasion is one they've usually perfected by the age of three. In sales, they harbour star-potential. Extremists are innately charming and charismatic and can be irresistible when *so* motivated. While they like the challenge of closing the deal and perfecting the plan, they tend to be impatient with follow-up and after-deed processing. Management would be wise to give Extremists freer reign. Take advantage of their extraordinary creativity and people convincing skills but provide organizational support to enhance their producer strength and offset their processor weakness.

If ever a lone wolf was, it was of Extremist style. Their commitment and loyalty are more project than team motivated, and more completion-of-project than corporate-future concerned. These individuals are freewheeling, independent spirits, who seem only to be passing through, on their way to the next more exciting adventure. Extremists have no qualms about packing it in on a moment's notice and heading for new challenges—regardless of current remuneration or responsibility. As they avoid making personal commitments, they avoid investing their time and talent if credit is corporally shared rather than individually given. Their ego doesn't like sharing limelights.

Extremists are the jack-of-all-trades, whose bag of tricks sags under the weight of acquired skill and experience. When their interest is piqued or if emergency demanded, they have ingenuity potential for one-take success. By demonstration, by explanation, or by reading of book, Extremists can acquire the knowledge necessary to get things done. It's not unusual for these individuals to play many roles and master many tasks in their lifetime. Earning the income to afford their expensive gear and equipment and support their action-oriented lifestyle is their motivation, not gold watch retirement.

These individuals generally avoid managerial roles. Leadership—being responsible for others—is not the strong suit of a lone wolf. However, Extremists are often exceptional strategists and planners and can be invaluable project leaders if given support and authority to run their own show. They are logical, linear thinkers who scrutinize every detail and aspect of a project. When interested, few can design a plan of action more successfully. Their thoroughness is exemplary but what makes them unique is how they deal with pressure.

Extremists metamorphose

They seem to have evolved with a sixth sense about the nature of physicality. Uniquely, they have the ability to instinctively trace and track physical logic, be it electronic circuitry, or blood circulation, man-made machine or animal behaviour. Extremists ably incorporate and design around intangibles that cannot be accurately measured by logic or instrument. This inexplicable communion enables them to adjust on the fly, and may explain why Extremists succeed where most fail. They walk away unscathed and victorious from situations that most wouldn't, many didn't, and they shouldn't have, either. By instinctively sensing fatigue, pending failure, or stress in advance of all hell breaking loose, they remain proactive and aggressively in control, rather than reactive and scrambling for recovery. In terms of physical reply or response, no other can avert disaster as effectively as them.

If firefighting, they think as fire; if mountain climbing, they think as rock; and if selling, they think as buyer. For instance, whether in big game or domestic training, Extremists excel in animal hunting, handling, and husbandry because of their instinctive gift and edge. They seem to become one with prey and/or pet and can uncannily predict animal response and behaviour. Their affinity with and love of animals, birthed anti-cruelty laws in the entertainment industry, in sports, and in communities worldwide. An Extremist may sooner part company with humans than their pets.

In every field of physical endeavour, an Extremist has been on the spot when new ground was broken. No other walks the razor's edge with as much sure-footed confidence. They've tested all sky craft, all earth craft, all water craft, as well as all equipment that went under, over, and into the hemisphere. They've met and faced beast, aboriginal, warrior, chief, and king; in adventure, exploration and in war of all kind or cause. When a frontier is ready for exploring or a perimeter needs pushing out, Extremist is the lone *Joan* or *Johnny,* at helm of thrust and at centre of spotlight.

THE PHYSICALS

Realist

Their eyes are bright, their clothes clean-pressed, and their skin glows with the sheen of good health. They make the first pot of coffee, read the newspaper, update correspondence, prepare notes for the meeting and are on their second wind before others show up for work. Their team arrives on time; cognizant of their unyielding hard line on tardiness and their tendency to smartly upbraid or dismiss offenders. Others knock before popping in to wish them "good morning," unsure their cheery greet will be as cheerily met and returned. Realist is moody. Having twice met them at their worst, others more wisely approach them gingerly. The sun is up, Realist is on board and getting work done is their day-long objective.

They are comfortable and capable in the physical world, their chief realm of functioning. Whether building, repairing, searching, or rescuing, they're the rallying force for friend in need and the front-line of difference for deed. Determined and tenacious doubt-removers, Realists breathe three-dimensional life into ideas and visions. There may well be movers and shakers in the world, but it's Realist whose positions it for moving and shaking—and whom then develops, dispatches, and disposes it later. They're practical individuals who tend to view abstractions as distractions. "What merit, what application, what authority, and when wanted?" is bottom-line Realist.

Team leadership, their strong suit

They like action, not theory, preferring to build and test concepts using tangible construct rather than theoretical formulation. Self-confident and capable, they are natural leaders who interpret plans, organize action and get results. Though innately charming and sociable; they tend to drive themselves, and others, hard to meet goals and fulfill objectives. When it comes to work, their personal and personnel expectations are high. Their style is uncompromising dedication to duty and task at hand.

Realists are natural, three-dimensional analysts, able to accurately measure weight, height, distance, and depth by sight and touch alone. Dexterous of body and instinctively advantaged, Realists can spot the dangers as readily as the deficits in project, blue-print, or plan. On-the-fly adjustments and response revisions are their particular specialty. Natural leaders who never lose sight of the goal; Realists can be counted on to get things done. In their hurried enthusiasm, they may improvise shortcuts or skip steps in the process, and fail to meet their own high standards of excellence. Correcting mistakes or repeating procedures is lesson enough for these individuals. They don't repeat mistakes or err in judgement twice. One issue Realists don't over-rush is safety—particularly with the well-being of others at stake. First-aid and emergency backup plans are firmly in place when Realists orchestrate team efforts. Steel-toed footwear, safety harnesses, legislated work standards, bullet-proof vests, implosion demolition, and metallic butcher gloves are examples of Realist contributions; reflective of their worker bee and worker welfare conscientiousness.

They take care of people, while taking care of things.

Realists are the big sister and big brother personality. Responsibility for others seems intrinsically woven into their physical make-up and life-approach. Underlying their characteristically strong physique and natural athletic prowess is a brave nature and responsible soul. One that investigates the bumps in the night, confronts the bully, builds the tree house, puts out the fire and hides the matches, finds lost mittens, rescues kittens, removes the rusty nail, disinfects then dresses wounds. Realists excel in public service fields where physical aptitude, stamina, and team coordination are emphasized.

Many medical, emergency, and professional tradespeople are of this personality style; as were many of the Molly Maguires, Thomas Edison's round-the-clock team, architect extraordinaire Frank Lloyd Wright, and birth control advocate, Margaret Sanger. What attracts Realists to public service, besides their friend-to-need heart, is their own need for well-defined work practices and parameters. Realists are logical, practical workers. Their greatest gift and most valuable tools are their intelligent hands. While others are fine-tuning plans and concerting efforts, Realists are already doing. Their physical body comprehends and reacts seemingly unconsciously. In emergency situations, few can respond as physically smart and mentally sharp as them. Structured environments, where parameters of acceptability are well-defined and procedures are well-documented, appeal to independent Realist. They generally need to know, in advance, where outermost limits lie. Since they're action-oriented, they like knowing the bounds within which their own efforts and energy can or may fly.

The last to bow in defeat.

Their physical ability and mental agility shines all the brighter, the greater the challenge. If given the proverbial immovable object, Realists become the irresistible force. With them, something is bound to give. In their professional dealings they're forthright and direct and tend to push for clear understanding before proceeding. Only when satisfied with all aspects of job expectations and their *required* autonomy, will Realist leave the table and start working. For them, having a clearly defined objective is important, because while Realist delegates and takes direction well, they take criticism poorly. When challenged or criticized they can become confrontational and defensive. Additionally, they can be headstrong and obstinate in persisting with their own on-the-job solutions, rather than consulting with others when problems crop-up.

Realists are methodical, orderly problem-solvers and somewhat egotistical individuals. Their brand of ego likes competition and thrives on recognition and the outshining of others. These individuals welcome responsibility. They like being in control of situations and usually prosper most when self-employed. As employees they step-in-line with prevailing order and policy and tend to keep their focus narrowed on task at hand. They tend not to compete for promotion but do strive for personal recognition. Their competitiveness may be reserved for interests and activities outside the workplace. Their practical, dutiful nature places them high in demand as dependable employees. However, fame and success may elude until they strike out on their own. They do best financially, when they compete to earn.

Realists generally pursue careers where proof of their professional contribution is tangible, meaning visible and touchable. What they do and how much they've done is how they measure personal value. They are the builders of skylines and the fixers of man and machine. They are also the ones who don't trust others to compensate them fairly. Hourly wages, pay scales, and salary negotiations are monetary reward systems that Realist likely introduced, to replace historically exploitative compensation practices. Quality of life and respect of worker rights, are battles led and hardest fought by them.

They don't fuss and tinker nor bluster, blather, and balk. They take a look, take a breath and get stuff done. If they say they can, Realist does— no matter what.

THE INSTINCTIVES

Scintillator

If ever a natural born schmoozer was, they must've been Scintillator. Dramatic and charismatic, these larger-than-life individuals improve the workplace upon entry. While easy to recognize a Scintillator, it's easier to overlook the power and potential buried beneath their pleasantness. To identify these individuals, look for those of physical attractiveness with readiest smile and laugh; those whom clients ask for by name; those sparkplug motivators on the happiest, most productive teams; those who shortcut production problems with seeming ease; those who teach best by demonstration; those who boost company morale by attending every company affair and contributing to overall fun; and those who frequently visit the coffee pot or candy machine.

Scintillators, with their powerful energy field and sunny dispositions, are infectiously uplifting. One common oversight in business is taking them at face-value, rather than looking beyond at their potential. Scintillators are dependents who commonly harbour greatness inside self-doubt, but who bloom readily and quickly when placed under lights of encouragement. Svengalis or King Makers could not find more capable or malleable clay to mold than them. The corporate world would be wise to invest time and training in Scintillator mines, if highest return on human capital is desired. Without encouragement Scintillators may only do enough to get by or get through.

As natural for them as bend to elbow, Scintillators read energy levels of others and react propitiously. From tone of voice, flush of face, sweaty palms, or countenance and deportment can they interpret the general state of being of others. Scintillators know from forty paces whether its a good time to ask for a raise or whether a co-worker needs assistance, a pep talk or avoiding. But then it was Scintillator who brought the science of body language to world attention.

Others sell by focusing on expertise or benefit; Scintillators sell by way of personal charm. Their focus is less on product or profit than on client. These individuals have very large egos, but it's not the stroke of money or prestige that fuels their drive. What motivates them is acceptance and their goals are recognition and respect. In sales, being first choice of clients is more satisfying to them than being Top Seller at the office. They tend not to stray far from that people-first philosophy, regardless of workplace role or responsibility.

Scintillators influence with their winsome ways and person-ability. People-pleasers through and through, they're masterful at using their magnetic vitality to win the favour and support of clients and co-workers. They cajole, humour, and by physical manner or agency generate an environment of positive energy feedback. Others feel good being around them. It's not surprising that in every field of the entertainment industry, from advertising, to sports, to centre stage, Scintillators predominate. They exude physical vitality and attractiveness and seem preternaturally skilled at projecting a larger than life appeal.

It's likely because of Scintillator that the need for personal managers evolved. Detail and rainy-day planning are not their forté. These individuals live in the now and bore quickly with routine, mundane, or accountability. They're often chronically lax about documentation and follow-up. Off-setting their weaknesses, by providing them support in areas where they lack organizational aptitude, increases their contribution and value substantially by freeing them to do what they do best: perform. In the workplace their renown is for making the big gestures, like closing the sale, completing the project, streamlining productivity, and motivating others. They are more comfortable being goal torch and support than goal setter.

These individuals have a natural affinity with people and possess extraordinary leadership ability. Their stamp and style of leadership highlights camaraderie and teamwork. Their easy-going, even casual nature is a boon to collective efforts where diverse skills, talents, and temperament must marry for group efforts. Scintillators are strong proponents of organized labour and reputed supporters of team concepts. They like knowing upfront what their legal rights and benefits are—as leader or worker—for a reason.

Scintillators do not like contention or confrontation yet are irrepressibly curious and creative. While they don't mind playing with the lion's tail (bending and testing rules), they're careful to avoid lion's jaws by not bending too far and upsetting.

They're as loyal to the corporation as the corporation is loyal to them—no more, no less. Office politicking, posturing and elbowing for position are not games that interest. Work is not their be-all, end-all, and they seldom suffer workaholism in-like with other leader styles. Monetary incentives, such as overtime pay, they tend to view more as infringement on their time than as bonus. Climbing the organizational ladder is a long-haul commitment that generally does not appeal either. They may need to be convinced and generously compensated before assuming the greater responsibility of so-called promotions. Money, position, or prestige are not the corporate carrots that attract them. Acceptance and respect from those they work with, and for, matter most.

Scintillator proves particularly valuable in high-stress work situations. When the clock is ticking, the budget restrictive, and a winning campaign due by morning, having a Scintillator on the team can keep morale high and creativity flowing. Their sophisticated, internal antennae unconsciously gauges the energy level of others and environment. Energy-intellect, their innate gift, is valuable in the workplace. While advantageous in sales, energy-intellect proves superior in human capital management.

With comedic wit and infectious optimism, Scintillator breaks through tension barriers that impede progress and dull creativity. Once tension is released, focus centres and ideas flow. They were first to recognize and address the debilitating effects of stress on the psyche and the physical well-being of workers. Coffee breaks, flex hours, ergonomics and fit-body/fit-mind awareness are Scintillator contributions to the workplace.

As managers, they generally consider the effects of overtime on staff members ahead of corporate goals or deadlines. Some management styles endorse an open-door policy; Scintillator removes the door altogether. Because their personal best tends to only flourish in work environments where camaraderie is prevalent, often their first priority as leader is to encourage that sort of work environment for others. They invest time in getting to know their associates well enough to offset individual weaknesses with group strengths. When an extra helping hand is called for, they're more likely to pitch-in themselves than to delegate. Harnessing, harmonizing, and herding the whole toward collective success may be a rare leadership skill, but it is Scintillator-typical.

When these managers make career or corporate changes, it's not unusual for former associates and clients to follow them up the ladder or out the door. However, getting them to manage may take convincing. Scintillator tends to view work as a necessary evil. These individuals suffer most from Monday workday blues and are least likely to volunteer for overtime. It's highly probable that *Happy Hour, Hump Day,* and *T.G.I.F.* (Thank God It's Friday) were introduced by Scintillator, to celebrate the passing of the work week. Their philosophy may be "work to live," but few managers can inspire team success as efficiently or effectively as them.

By assessing the steps that comprise the whole of a problem, Scintillators are ingenious in devising unique and innovative solutions. Task-cutting and time-saving are their name's fame. These fidgeters and squirmers look for any means to alleviate tension and boredom.

They'll find a way

If a shortcut is possible, turn the challenge over to a Scintillator. Their *creative laziness* not only could save but could pay dividends. It was surely a Scintillator who, frustrated at having to retype the entire correspondence because of a wrong keystroke, decided instead to bury the mistake under a dab of white paint and over type the correction. Thus, the typist's best friend, Wite-out™ was born. It became an overnight success for its inventor, as industry welcomed the time and cost savings afforded by such a simple solution. Any means, method, or innovation that reduces tedium and labour is a solution welcomed by Scintillator.

As mentally agile of mind as of body, these individuals tend to have an innate artistic bent—as if born to entertain and create. Actors, stand-up comedians, and performing artists are usually Scintillator to some small or significant degree. Their minds spark and fire with comic genius and improvisational wonder. None more exemplary than Jim Henson, who mated puppet with marionette and gave birth to wide-mouthed animations imbued with endearing, human qualities. Henson introduced the world to a new art form, as well as to a stable of imaginative characters including a femme-fatale pig and a pontificating frog that appealed to child and adult alike.

Whether construction, production, food preparation, or competitive sport, Scintillators are like highly-charged machines in perpetual motion. Physical activity opens their mind to greatest learning potential. They think best when doing. These individuals excel as athletes and renowned health practitioners—particularly in the physical or nutritional fields.

Scintillators are the professional ball players who chew gum/tobacco to better focus on performance. They're the physical therapists who manipulate body energy with gifted expertise. Kinesthetic beings, they learn by physically interacting with the world. When interested, they tend to be exceptionally quick-learners and need only attempt a task once to have it mastered. Few can match their ability to communicate and teach by hands-on-demonstration. In fact, this is the personality that takes it apart and puts it together again, without instruction (and when kids, often without permission). Like Realists, Scintillators have intelligent hands.

Greatest obstacle to career success

Scintillators tend to avoid risk-taking and are hesitant about making long-term professional commitments. As previously stated, King Makers could not find more capable, malleable clay than them. The dependent-nature of Scintillator prevents them from testing their own mettle. Too often they play mountain: expecting the world to come to them rather than striding boldly forth themselves. Scintillator requires regular doses of positive feedback before their self-confidence kicks in sufficient to flight-testing their greatest gift, creativity. Depending on others is not a personal weakness for them, it's a personality style characteristic. They often consider themselves a poor judge of their own value. Instead, they look for self-confirmation and permission to believe in themselves according to the opinion-yardstick of others. For Scintillator, it's not the winning of prizes that motivates them; it's the praise following winning that inspires.

Their success is a given, when they make career choices that work with nature rather than against. A supportive and encouraging environment can coax out their reluctant ingenuity, tucked behind the attractive affability. There's always much more to Scintillator than meets the eye.

It is necessary they be as discriminating when choosing work environment, as when choosing careers. Otherwise, they tend to become jacks-of-all-trades but masters of none. While they experience variety, they seldom find personal satisfaction or self-fulfillment. Fears of: trying and failing self, and of risking then disappointing others are the two most common reasons why Scintillator gives up or submits, when the going gets rough. (We strongly recommend that Scintillator workers read Scintillator thinking and emoting realms, too).

Their challenges are self-trust, responsibility and discipline. The Higher Power provides birds all they need for nest-building, but does not build their nests for them. Scintillator tends to expect ready-built nests.

THE INSTINCTIVES

Sentinel

Rarely are Sentinels late for work. They perform efficiently, professionally and seldom make or repeat mistakes. Conscientious about meeting objectives, they voluntarily offer to stay late if needed. Their appearance is neat and their presentations impeccable, though their desk and work areas can range from messy to eyesore. In every work concern and regard, Sentinel seems able—as in cap*able*, depend*able*, and respon*sible*, but there's something that management finds perplexing about them. Something disturbs.

Perhaps it's that characteristic independent streak of theirs, the one that does not willingly nor easily bend to corporate will. Maybe it's their impenetrable, unreadable reserve that needs to be invited to opine, then delivers insight and depth unexpected. It could even be their protective and outspoken propensity, that with raised hackle and fury defends others, regardless of rule or ramification. It might even be their simmering intensity that does not abide fools. Or their ambition, that if focused and aimed, promises to disrupt or unseat. Sentinel, if sometimes perplexing and disturbing, is always a valuable addition to any corporation, endeavour, or industry.

Head, not heart

They're world-class thinkers who logically and methodically solve problems in linear order and fashion. They pay particular attention to details and their conclusions are usually above reproach. But it's their innate talent that accounts for their exceptionality. Their keenest intellect is not mind; it's their sensory, gut-deep smarts they most trust and most often subscribe to. Sentinel can more accurately read and predict intent and/or intention from intangibles, such as tone, and undertone than from word or action. They see and hear more than others, a talent evidenced by the predominance of Sentinels in the investigative and interpretive professions. This cellular skill is a valuable asset that Sentinels, themselves, are often not aware of. Instead, many think they have a sensitive stomach, for that's the cubby-hole housing their unique truth barometer.

In corporate sales, Sentinels rank among top achievers. With their unique sense ability for reading between lines, they're able to deliver what clients really want, more often than others. Of course, it works both ways. They'd be the ones most likely to hear the false note or spot the flaw in the company's annual belt-tightening speech and depend on them to challenge directly. While normally reticent and reserved, they tend to be headstrong and intractable when they embrace a cause or seek restitution for real or perceived injury. However, do not expect an emotional tirade. Sentinel doesn't bring emotion to the table and they discourage others from bringing and using it too.

While not emotionally impulsive or impelled, these strong, silent types are passionate about all they hold dear and true. They seem to have an inborn sense of fair play which they apply equally to cause as to country and cousin. Upholding the principle that every man be free and entitled to fair treatment and representation, seems intrinsically woven into their psyche, as evidenced by the disproportionately high number of Sentinels in all realms of the legal profession. In home, community, and the world at-large, the strongest proponents and public defenders of man, nature, and beast is Sentinel. They expose wrongs and enforce rights.

They are acutely aware of authority and power in all relations and relationships, and are not easily nor often intimidated. "Autonomy or show me the door" could be their motto. This does not imply that Sentinel is a loose cannon on corporate decks by any means. They're very much team players. They like prescribed procedure and are most comfortable when fully informed of employer and job expectations. Conscientious and responsible, Sentinels do not say they can or will, unless qualified and capable of not only of doing, but of doing well. Being placed in a work environment of prevailing distrust or close supervision is a stifling, untenable situation for these competent, freedom fighters.

Self-doubt—their nemesis

When feeling insecure about their role or importance, they tend to push until their fear is unquestionably confirmed or alleviated. Typically, Sentinel insecurity manifests as the blaming of others for the doubts they, themselves, are experiencing. They may also be overly critical of associates or of management in order to make themselves shine comparatively. They may challenge authority directly and precipitate a parting of ways. Sentinels need performance feedback. For them, negative feedback is better than none at all. When unconfident or unsure, they can disrupt team efforts and dampen office morale. It would *behoove* employers to recognize the early, so-characteristic signs of Sentinel insecurity and review their current policy of human capital management. There's greater corporate loss in having Sentinel leave, than in accommodating their few self-security requirements.

Given freer reign and more respect, Sentinels prove to be productive contributors and cooperative associates. They thrive in environments where rules and objectives are spelled out, where progress/employee evaluations are standard procedure, and where deadlines are realistic. Sentinels are often highly disciplined, intelligent beings. When confident of their work future and if left to their own devices, they can be trusted to bring the winner's cup home regularly.

The physical-sensory dimension of Sentinel is preternaturally sophisticated. They're natural diagnosticians, spatial engineers, and environmental wizards. Visually they seem able to measure distance, calculate area and space; by touch they ably and accurately gauge volume and weight; and by "mental" glance at what exists, they can uncannily assess what more is needed or possible. Vibrational attunement is Sentinel's gift; and they're renowned for locating buried cables, underground minerals and choosing archaeological sites. As scientists, strategists, archaeologists, diviners, sharpshooters, or carnival weight-guessers, they are physiologically predisposed for three-dimensional excellence.

Sentinels expect and plan for the unexpected. Few situations cause them greater stress than being caught off-guard. In fact, they're the ones who most often have night dreams about being caught unprepared; for examinations, speeches, or performances. While conscious, they conscientiously plan their work and work their plan. Unexpected problems can *initially* overwhelm and have them looking for justification to explain or reaching for blame rather than focusing on remedy.

They often must first understand what occurred, what caused it, and what the standard procedures are, before initiating a course-of-action. Creativity and snap decisions are not their forté. Generally speaking, when overwhelmed Sentinel's instinctive response is fright, then, like high-spirited thoroughbreds, flight. Indeed, this is one personality who probably should not be thrown a surprise birthday party. They may be in Timbuktu before cake candles can flicker.

Management may not be their strong suit.

Their strengths are consistency and reliability, rather than creativity. As managers, they can be overly conscientious and may run themselves and others ragged trying to meet deadlines and objectives. They assume management roles in much the same way they approach personal relationships, tentatively. Sentinel tends to initially be reserved and aloof. As familiarity with their role and responsibility develops, as their level of confidence in their team's ability grows, and most particularly, when confident they have the support of associates; they can be gregarious even charismatic leaders, for they're already capable.

Sentinel managers may be perfectionistic and demanding but are generous with recognition and reward for their team members. They are not at-arms-length administrators. They like to know what's going on and are not averse to rolling up their sleeves and pitching in to help. They're very protective of worker rights and benefits, and will, as a matter of course, vigorously defend their team or corporation should such be warranted.

They tend to be of two mindsets: those who enjoy socializing with coworkers, and those who do not. Professionally, as personally, they're selective about close friendships. When they attend work-related functions and gatherings, they tend to stick close to their inner circle of associates rather than mingle freely with others.

Generally, Sentinels are ambitious and savvy about office politicking. They can be fiercely competitive and when push comes to shove, assertive. Inferior work and disloyalty are the two infractions that most often lead to banishment from Sentinel-managed teams. They tend to avoid personal familiarity with associates, relying more on their record of performance as measure and basis for reward and promotion. Since they don't form close emotional attachments, they have no compunction about dismissing team members who perform below standard or prove disloyal. While poor work performance may initially be met with encouragement and ultimately with warning, disloyalty is met with an immediate and irrevocable amputation of relations.

These individuals are not easy to get to know and sometimes are hard to like, but if the corporate effort is made few can match Sentinel's productivity and reliability. No other personality style equals their loyalty.

THE LOGICALS

Diligent

Large desk and chair are the focal point of the room. If given a choice, their desk is wooden. Paperwork is not strewn but neatly squared and butted inside the desk-blotter's borders. Pens, pencils and practical paraphernalia are gathered and grouped. Steaming mug, set on corporate coaster, is within hand's reach, nestled between a gold-framed family photo and cordless phone. The computer is the one *PC's R'Us* magazine touted in this morning's read. That mysterious box on desktop's left is a sleek, modern calculator. File cabinets are clearly labelled and uncluttered. The bookshelf is full and the spines read easily and in topical order.

The chair is old leather, soft, cracked, and worn; its fit tailored for one body's domain, one body's form. Heavy springs pleasingly protest each heave or swivel at rise or seat. The look is order, the odour is business and the room temperature reads Diligent at work. Work can be the environment where they feel most at home; and they've a tendency to bury the who, if not whole of self there.

Work, their dominant realm of functioning

Diligents know how to work, like work, and they know how to get things done right the first time around. Their working style is logical, systematic, and perfectionistic. They're not risk-takers nor graduates of the fly-by-the-seat-of your-pants school, but they usually do have one toe of theirs on the inside of winner circles. Diligents are consistent, persistent performers. They may not razzle and dazzle with quickness of wit or boldness of action, but others worry less and worry less often when they're on the job.

These individuals interact with all aspects of life intellectually. Physical reality is but an extension of their mind's ability to process information into tangible form. They think first, think second, weigh it some, chew a bit more, then make a decision. With each decision, highest ethics are reflected and personal commitment is given. Detail is their particular ease and expertise, data measures progress and against the criteria of fact do they gauge success. They won't be rushed, take shortcuts, or leave until the job is completed to their satisfaction. And they perform as precisely and reliably day in and day out. Routine and predictability are reassuring to security-conscious, goal-oriented Diligents. They may insist on being fully informed of relevant information, overall objectives, and outcome expectations before they tackle a job, but once all is gathered, leave them alone. They function at one pace—their own.

If not in their office, don't expect to find Diligent socializing at the water cooler, unless it's an opportunity to mix business with pleasure. Social chit-chat and light-banter camaraderie are neither their forté or style. Nothing pleases intellectual Diligent more than waxing philosophical or swapping hypotheticals. They're the ones held in rapt attention during the budget and forecast segments of the annual banquet, but stifling yawns behind polite social smiles at midnight. There is an aura of elegance about these individuals, mixed with a rustle of starched formality.

Generally, Diligent is early to bed, and early to rise. In Aesop's fable, *The Ant And The Grasshopper*, Diligent would be the "work while the sun shines ant." Throughout history, education and business have been modelled along Diligent *ant* principles of hard work, logic, discipline, honesty, a penny saved is a penny earned, God-fearing, and gold watch retirement.

But old world dinosaurs, they're not! They tend to walk one step behind leaders. In one hand they carry a safety net, in the other a backup plan-should the leader stumble or fail. As Tonto was to Lone Ranger, Diligent is to movers and shakers.

They usually occupy responsible positions, such as management or administration. Not intimidated by power, Diligents settle comfortably into almost any business role or environment. They're valuable team players and respecters of hierarchical authority, but seem to miss attending the political innings that matter most. While keenly aware of title, prestige, and benefits, they are seldom self-assertive or self-promoting. Their tend is to rely more on their record of performance than political acumen, to advance up the rungs of corporate ladders. Besides, they're often too busy focusing on the doing to play office politics.

While invention and innovation are foreign to their cautious nature, one of their stronger suits is the proving or disproving of other people's theories. Their objectivity is pure, their testing process exacting, and their conclusions usually above reproach. Don't rush them or push them to hurry results; Diligents do it their way, logically and sequentially. Since they tend to deliver home-runs regularly, give them what they need: time.

Haste makes waste.

Forcing them to speed up usually has the opposite effect. While to them it appears they are working faster, they're really just working more. To compensate for the rush, they build extra checkpoints into the process to catch errors they expect to result from forced haste. When a Diligent says, "it works," head for the bank. Their innate perfectionism and sense of responsibility precludes them giving the go-ahead without substantial reasoning and proof to back their conclusion.

Some leaders are charismatic, inspiring others by sheer force of personality. Some are visionaries who inspire others by the scope and breadth of ideas. Diligent leadership is more of the inspiration-by-perspiration variety. They build faith in others by stacking sound decisions, one atop the other, until notice of value by sheer contribution is neon-noticeable. They may not enjoy or encourage close camaraderie with associates, but they're respected leaders who can be counted on to deliver as promised. As they resist being rushed in their work or decision-making, they resist being swayed by emotional pleas in their dealings with others. They have a good head on their shoulders, so appealing to intellect is not only the wiser but the recommended approach. Diligent managers may run their teams and departments with less help than usual, and though hard-pressed to keep up with the workflow their staff is usually more generously compensated than office counterparts, too.

Economic efficiency describes their management style. Dickens' *Scrooge* was Diligent, and though his miserly ways are a-typical, his one-right-way-pickiness are not. They expect a great deal from their team and run their departments with military-like efficiency, and they reward and arbitrate fairly. Diligent bosses encourage staff to actively participate in workplace business. They poll for opinion and input and encourage open discussion or debate—in fact, they enjoy it. While staunch supporters of collective thinking, Diligents do reserve the right to draw their own conclusions and make final decisions, without compunction to take a consensus beforehand or provide an explanation after.

Efficiency experts

For them, there's a right way and a wrong way of doing everything and they seem to have an uncanny knack of knowing which way is *rightest* of all. Beating within Diligent breasts is a caped efficiency expert, willing to spring into action or mount the soapbox at invitation or provocation. In matters of procedure, all are welcome or subject to Diligent's opinion. Going by the book of tried-and-true is their nature and few can economize time, motion, and resources, like them. Associates may grate in irritation at their insistent step-by-step procedures, but their way, even if not the best, will at the least prove proficient.

Achievement and success for Diligent comes by way of logic and persistence; two personal attributes they look for and prize highly in others. Historically, some of the most exacting careers have been performed by Diligent. As cartographers, assessors, accountants, researchers, engineers, tool-and-die makers, jewellers, and programmers...et cetera, exactitude is their reputation. When consistency, and uncompromising attention to detail are necessary, or when the most from the least is essential, set the challenge before a Diligent and trust their best to rise to the challenge.

Creativity and risk-taking are not Diligent strengths. Their talent is in finding the most effective solution within the parameters of known and maximizing results and return on investments. Application, more than invention, is their strength. They may not have been the engineer whose chocolate bar melted in breast pocket while testing microwaves, but they were probably among the first to sip microwaved coffee. Diligents have evolutionarily been elbow-close to breakthroughs and discoveries. In their workplace, they usually have the latest tools and equipment and keep abreast of industry news and trends. When workers brag of having the newest version or the latest technological innovation somewhere nearby is a Diligent with purchasing authority.

They may talk in slower even tones, as they have quite a vault of information to sift through before offering their best, considered opinion. They may walk with measured stride but rarely are late. Their dress may be banker conservative but there's nothing buggy whipish about Diligent thinking. The computer industry owes them a vote of thanks for not only giving early testing a big checkmark, but for being the most enthusiastic purchasers and *implementers* of up-to-date products. Corporally and privately, Diligents were the important first paying customers and optimistic supporters through doors that later, when opened, revolutionized global industry and business practices.

When the call is for dedication and thoroughness, Diligent is one of the best human capital investments a corporation can make. They're worker bees with a prodigious intellect and devotion to the task, the goal, and to the company's future. No successful corporation earned that distinction without Diligent onboard.

THE LOGICALS

Sage

They usually are late, sometimes dishevelled; they have active lives, active minds, and numerous outside interests. But always do they sport a smile reflective of an innately cheery disposition. They greet everyone by first name and never miss complimenting others on their achievements. They get their own coffee and head for their desk—the one off to the side heaving under the weight of stacked files, folders, unread memos, wilting plant and a watch they'd left and forgotten last night. Draped across the back of their chair is yesterday's suit jacket. Underneath that, a nondescript cardigan that seems to have been there forever.

They likely stayed till late last evening; they usually do at the start and end of a project. They've earned the right to pick and choose from all jobs available. You'd think they'd pick an easy one now and again but they don't. They like new challenges. The tougher the better it seems. When they settle at their desks, they start right in as if sleep or time had not intervened. Picking up threads from where last left off is part of the mystery of Sage genius. When interested, they are dog-with-a-bone focused.

The first visitor to their desk is the supervisor, wanting but not expecting an update on the project's progress. Others fill in daily reports but expecting that from a Sage is a more frustrating affair than asking and making own notes. Record-keeping or consistent report-writing is not a strong suit of theirs. Even after being apprised, however, nail-biting by others may not be over. Sage doesn't complete tasks in logical, linear fashion. They can't. Their thinking process at best is random; at worst, scattered. Sage largely ignores step-by-step procedures as though beneath their contempt or beyond their comprehension.

These individuals, from initial introduction, look at each project as though already completed. For them, each component, piece and part is equally important to the whole, so order of completion is irrelevant. They work on all at once. As the audience holds its breath while the plate-spinner keeps all in motion, others hold their breath when Sage is conducting the show. Until the end, when things seem to magically come together, confidence quakes visibly in the wings.

These individuals tend to be intellectual institutions, ever-brimming with knowledge, information and wisdom. Most are self-taught and acquire near-expertise by reading the book, as readily as others by instruction and experience. Rare geniuses, totally unstructured in thought, Sages approach problems from any or many directions. Their wide-ranging intellect has potential for finding infinitely creative and practical solutions.

Fluctuating between Plato and Pluto, they can turn think tanks into three-pill headaches. They can mentally step-in and step-out, turn things upside down and inside out with a dexterity that others, in frustration and confusion, may discard as fool's gold when ingot's the more likely and accurate case. Theories, ideas, and concepts are their expertise and realm of greatest contribution. They prove well-practiced and generously capable of creatively advancing any cause or conversation.

It was Sage who came back from lunch with the other workers that day, to find that the churn had been carelessly left on and the fresh batch of soap was now floating in spoiled ruination atop the bubbling vat. Sage assessed the situation with the others, and opposed the group's decision to trash the mess. Instead, Sage recommended they process the light-as-air batch and see what resulted. When done, it was they who again questioned whether floating soap was not an advantage for bathing. And thus, the first batch of "floats in the tub" bar soap was born, not aborted. They are not limited by linear or logical thinking. One Sage lesson: there are equally as many solutions for problems as people who solve them.

Though ostracized for their unorthodox thinking and work style, their unconventionality is their strength. Sages thrive and excel in situations where problems are unknown and outcomes unpredictable. As associates, they inspire and contribute through intellectual creativity. Lacking innate organizational ability and the discipline (or interest) to follow rules and procedures, Sages are not known to be effective leaders or efficient administrators. These individuals are seldom ego-driven or status-conscious, so political elbowing for prestige and position is not a game they'd likely play. This is a head personality style—the idea people who take what is and creatively find a better way, identify weak links, or find a novel application. Unlike Visionary, Sage deals with concrete realities of here and now rather than future. Sage may have added spokes and tread to the wheel—but they did not invent it.

Loyal employees

Because they are so unassuming and undemanding, employers may overlook them for promotion or fair wage compensation. Sage may not notice for a while as they tend to keep their nose pretty close to the grindstone. However, should they look up and realize the slight or oversight, they resign and depart quietly rather than confront and make a fuss. They seldom have difficulty being appreciated or more equitably compensated elsewhere. They tend to develop a wide network of loyal friends and professional acquaintances among their wide social circle. Sage is one employee that management would be well advised to be scrupulously fair with, as they may not *squeak up* for themselves, though deserving.

Sages are not usually team players. They tend to do their best work alone. Organization of self, far less of others, can be a challenge for them.

However, as team contributor few prove as equally valuable. When Sage discovers a more efficient procedure or learns of a production improvement they like to share their insights with others. Their contributions to team and goal success are most often intellectual generosity. As employees, they may not synchronize well with the daily work clock but are renown for turning in excellent work—especially when allowed to have autonomy over both time and procedure. These individuals are not pragmatic of mind, so regimentation and overly-structured environments can stifle their ingenuity. Given an objective and left to their own devices, they usually surpass expectation. However, it may be wise to allow some leeway on deadline. While Sage excellence can be counted on, its delivery may take longer than scheduled.

Sage individuals are gentle natured, corporate morale-boosters. Cooperative and easy-going, they tend to get along with everyone. One of their greatest pleasures is socializing—the exchanging of ideas in personal interactions. Their encyclopaedic minds and their all-embracing approach to human life make for interesting discussions. Sages are renowned conversationalists. They prefer intellectual stimulation and eagerly assimilate with most groups and cultures. They're innately humourous, able to laugh at themselves and readily find humour in the human foibles and frailties of everyday life. Diplomats and ambassadors at heart, regardless of what profession they pursue or role they play, they are socially astute and promote an environ of camaraderie. Of Sage (men and women) it was surely written, *"It is almost a definition of a gentleman to say that he is one who never inflicts pain." —Cardinal Newman.*

One of the bravest human resource investments could be a Sage. It may initially seem that the proverbial absent-minded professor has come on board but given patience and free rein, it could be Thomas Edison that showed up instead.

THE PRACTICALS

Eccentrik

What would you get if you combined an emotional vagabond, a dyed-in-the-wool non-conformist and a genius? An outspoken employee garbed in the latest fringe fashion...hoot couture they'd call it, who insults the company president on principle and cares not one whit; who keeps the office in stitches with their barbed wit and comedic brilliance; and who could, given the right inspiration and the VP's corner office, (and a midi studio), come up with an idea that could place your company on the stock exchange by noon tomorrow. That's an Eccentrik. But would you hire them?

If traditional is the prevailing odour in your workplace, you'll likely never meet far less interview an Eccentrik. These individuals know what they don't want: following dictates of any kind. Be it dress code, traditional business practice, or regular paycheques, it reeks anti-Eccentrik to them. Also, they usually decide well in advance who may or may not read their résumé. Eccentrik has been different from birth. They know it and rejoice because of the difference. While other personalities conform to comply, Eccentrik has unshakeable faith in their world-class mind. By the time they leave home, they've conformed as much as they will. But, if you think a rebel without a cause dwells within, you've another think coming.

These individuals are success driven, goal-oriented, and astute business people. They participate on turf of their own choosing and keep time by their own watches. As they live their personal lives on the tottering edge of eccentricity, they seek cutting edges professionally. Industries, fields, and ventures where success is yet to be proven, rules yet to be written, and environments without cookie-cutter-constraint; are where these individualists excel.

Their heads may be shrouded in clouds of genius but their feet are firmly planted on terra firma. These are not pie-in-the-sky theorists, though pie-in-the-face is not beneath them. They are three-dimensional practical. An idea without form, function, and marketability is an idea wasted. Theirs is a tactile, profit-oriented relationship with creativity.

In its infancy and heyday, Silicon Valley crawled with Eccentriks. They birthed the prototypes that launched everything from speedier chip to orbiting satellite. When NASA began they were the pioneers whose elbows rubbed against theorist and drawing board alike. Advertising, fashion, publishing, the avante of any industry seethes with Eccentrik energy. But of all industries, none have they impacted more than the whimsical, practical world of gadgets.

Whether new or improved, small appliances and handy-dandy gadgetry fascinates. A roll-call of this industry's inventors would read as a "Who's Who" of Eccentriks. This depicts the remarkability of them in fact and in deed, but key to the success of this personality is freedom. Their potential only flies when wings are not trimmed or clipped in any way. When they graduate childhood, it is with steely determination to avoid lock-step conformity. Subsequently, many Eccentriks fall through professional cracks due to corporate impatience.

An Eccentrik inspired is a polestar-wonder. Their minds are uniquely sophisticated. Eccentrik sculpts three-dimensional objects inside their head. As others work clay—adding, shaping, removing excess, Eccentriks manipulate form and shape mentally. They do not need to externally sketch and draw; they create internally. More importantly, their creative genius is such that when an idea intrigues or inspires they can throw together a rough prototype or construct a working model from whatever material is on-hand. No matter which side of the table they sit on— whether as buyer or seller—few can perceive the physical potential or spot the weakness of an idea as quickly as they can. Others need eyes to see how things work; Eccentrik needs only think to see and know.

Their desks are quite neat, though shelves may sway under the burden of half-baked/half-burnt ideas, while *dones* lay neatly stacked on shelf or floor. Their work area may be a showcase of outrageous cartoons, 3-D puzzles, and favourite toys. To the world they may look hopelessly disorganized (and could be at home) but when it comes to work, Eccentrik is anything but. Surrounding themselves with eclectic clutter and acting zany are part and parcel of their off-the-wall genius. Just shut their door before office tours begin.

When Eccentrik is at their desk, they're working. When focused they're utterly absorbed. They may not show up till ten and be first out the door at five, but worry not. When Eccentrik's head lowers, remarkability's rise portents. These individuals thrive on tight deadlines, often purposely mismanaging time to set up their own challenge. Stretching management's nerve to breaking adds a extra dollop of rare to their pressured pleasure. As tension of water traps bubble to surface, Eccentrik equates tautness in chest and shortness of breath with elixir of life.

Bonus-incentive remuneration is a financial motivation that Eccentrik finds particularly appealing. They like the intellectual challenge of "reaping by earning" but what they most like is having the wherewithal to afford their expensive and usually lavish after-hour activities. Eccentrik often spends as much as they earn. Offering bonus incentives kills two birds with one stone: it boosts their productivity and boosts the economy. Regardless of monetary incentive though, Eccentrik will up and walk if not sufficiently challenged by the work, or if their efforts aren't appreciated. They tend to be short-stint career hoppers, citing boredom as the bane of their existence. In actuality, lack of exploration is the most likely and more frequent culprit.

Eccentriks tend to deke themselves out of abundance and recognition, for as long as it takes them to learn that the path to true freedom is depth, not breadth of experience. Financial difficulties are common when Eccentrik flits from flower to flower, rather than delving and drinking deeply of *inner's* most vigorous nectar. Feeling boredom usually means "you're just starting to get it." Leaving not only delays failure, it postpones success.

A handful and a god-send, Eccentrik roundly and routinely pooh-pahs conventionality. Their comedic streak may entertain and exasperate; their ability amaze. They are more team contributors than team players. Show them the general direction others are heading and they'll meet at first juncture, bulging with creative solutions, and a frisbee for play after business is tended.

Because they choose their own work environments carefully, they're usually professionally compatible with associates and tend to get along well with most everyone. Eccentrik may not socialize with associates; they tend to separate their personal life and the office. They love people and tend not to be judgemental, prejudiced, or discriminating in any human regard. They are, however, decidedly allergic to stuffed shirts, starched views, and brown noses. Though social by nature, Eccentrik usually works alone. Their thinking is original, they solve problems internally and they neither explain, apologize, nor defend their *differentness.* If not for that spit-in-your-eye difference in thinking and attitude, they wouldn't be Eccentrik at all.

These individuals are goal and results oriented. As long as the goal is achieved rather quickly, applause is loud and rewards lucratively, they are happy employees. Oddly enough, though they personally stick their necks out in all manner, season, and reason, Eccentrik is not known for risk-taking, professionally. Perhaps it's because their gift is for internally rearranging physical objects, not abstractions. Success and satisfaction for them usually comes through the concrete realization of their imaginative re-arrangements.

These ones readily become obsessed or scattered by compelling, competing interests that pique their curiosity and vie for their easily distracted attention. Many Eccentriks develop reputations for being unreliable, changing jobs and careers often. Like Kansas summer tornadoes they repeatedly touch down and lift off, not staying long enough to make a name by earning acclaim for their self. Boredom shoulders most of the blame for their inconsistency, but the real culprit is lack: lack of depth, lack of focus, and lack of self-discipline. Management would be wise to give freer rein and greater encouragement to Eccentrik employees. When some Kansas summer storms touch down, they alter landscapes and history as well.

Eccentrik is here to show us there are infinite paths in life and every single one warrants investigation. The workplace just happens to be the classroom where those Eccentrik lessons are observed and learned. Giving that proverbial typewriter to an Eccentrik chimp could very likely produce a laureate novel. That's precisely the type of challenge on which they thrive. The Internet is where Eccentrik has most recently been gathering and meeting. With them, expect a global warming.

THE PRACTICALS

Idealists are the natural planners and administrators for whom power is a snug, tailored fit. The innate gift and ability of these movers and shakers is generating ideas, planning strategies, and charting future courses. If unable to move the mountain they wear it down by mind-backed, money-backed abrasion. Idealist's quicksilver thinking, risk-taking bent, and pernicious dissatisfaction with the way things are; is the wind that drives and fulfills them. Their mind functions with such speed that most are left scratching their heads in wonder and dread: in wonder of intellect; in dread of how to please.

Uniquely, Idealist sees patterns through time. By mentally pushing an idea to the point of failure, they can predict feasible outcomes with uncanny reliability and consistency. While others are still discussing concept possibilities, Idealist is planning how to turn concept into profit.

Their strength is management. Assuming responsibility for the whole of projects rather than for piecemeal contributions, is bathrobe comfortable to them. Innate perfectionistic tendencies combined with an unwavering focus on goals, has earned Idealist the reputation for being intense and bull-headed, as well as successful.

They drive everyone hard, but self hardest of all. Their standards tend to be set unrealistically high, where even exceptional falls short of acceptable and only perfect will do. Their watches seem to be set one stroke faster than realistic, causing them to read time-elapsed as plod rather than progress. Frustration is the stone they whet both their tongue and wit on. When things go wrong, Idealist fluctuates between being difficult and being impossible. If being peeved and showing it were an Olympic event, Idealist would *own the gold* for their characteristic display of ill-temper when upset and their propensity to blame others. Conversely, when all is right in their world and they do stop to play or pay visit, their sharp minds prove masterfully entertaining. Quick thinking it is their fame. Few rise victorious from battles-of-wit with them.

Not having control over what they deem important and relevant can be very stressful for Idealist. Their perfectionistic strivings complement team efforts but may undermine teamwork. Success is likely and least trying when Idealist leads with ideas, delegates responsibility, then oversees progress. Hands-on processing and laborious detail are excruciating for fussy Idealist. Their strengths are strategy and management, which does not imply they're better delegators than workers. Such is not the case with these workaholics. Their motto is, "Achieve success. Do whatever it takes," meaning, they contribute in whatever way they can and that's necessary. Idealist often views others as lazy. Compared to them, most are.

When they turn their attention to task-at-hand the expected result is exceeded expectations. Idealists get stressed not having control over all aspects of their work, from beginning to end. More often than not, while their part is done punctually and perfectly, confusion and delay are usually found elsewhere on the line. If not invited, they invite their own nose, to sniff out the problem and help things get rolling again. Nothing is more irritating to Idealist than incompetence in individual or in management. This personality cannot compromise and is likely to upbraid associates for inattention to detail or poor work ethics—which may further the team's objective but strain team relations

To identify an Idealist worker

During workflow disruptions they're the ones who fidget and pace impatiently, or found huddled around the problem but don't belong there. Idealists don't stand in groups socializing or bury their head in a book during down-time at work—unless such delays are common, in which case, they've likely washed their hands of the incompetent lot. Management would be wise to observe the behaviour of workers during workflow disruptions. The one who gets visibly stressed and gets actively involved in problem-solving is likely Idealist. This personality harbours potential for managerial excellence. Their historical record reads success.

Idealists are renowned risk-takers. Their self-confidence has earned them distinction as one of the best at beating the odds. Computerization would not have occurred as quickly or at all, had Idealist not chanced walking the tightrope whilst pushing concept ahead. When decisions stall at draw, Idealist more often chooses *Go*, than *Stay*. Kerneled in risk, they see springboard opportunity for leaping ahead. Whether problem-solving, investing, selling ideas or running a race, Idealist strives for first place. They like competition, the gaining of upper-hands, and they can be unscrupulous in their relish to win. Idealist is not discriminating in how they earn their money nor are they squeamish about stepping on another's toes. Crossing the finish-line first is ego all-important. Demanding perfection, at each step, is their way of insuring glory at goal's end.

Idealist's potential is most often sparked in environments where skilled support can bring plans to fruition. Skilled and competent are key. Idealists tend to get choleric in the company of those whose ambition and aspiration is settled at mediocrity. They neither take criticism well nor tolerate it often; and are wholly intolerant of insubordination. A successful production team would theoretically include an Idealist leader and a Diligent worker. While the crisply-efficient Idealist will shortly be gnashing teeth and rending garments in frustration with check and re-check Diligent, the quality of outcome would justify the grief and aggravation that's inherent in their 'styled' combination. Few are fastidious enough to please Idealist.

It's their organizational nature that spawned a stationery plethora of notebooks, appointment schedulers, fridge-magnet reminders, corporate progress-boards, gold star reward charts in school, and list-making paraphernalia of all size, shape and colour. They're champion list-makers. No other charts, measures, and tracks progress, like Idealist. Whenever a book of show-and-tell is published, such as: "Ten steps to..."; "The most important reasons why...."; or when, "best of-worst of..." lists are drawn up, author and majority reader are likely one and the same: Idealist.

Both career-aggressive and self-promoting, Idealists are instinctively astute in the ways of politicking. While they share ideas and pull their own weight, they expect to share the spotlight when credit-applause begins. Work is the main focus of their lives. These individuals immerse themselves for the long-haul and seem to have inexhaustible energy. Generally, they need less sleep than others. It's not unusual for Idealist to be the first person to show up for work in the morning and the last to leave at night. They're extremely loyal to the company and the company's cause, and tend to be long-term employees—provided recognition for their contributions is had, remuneration is generous, and the stairway to the glass dome stays open.

Careers that offer unstructured and unlimited earning potential appeal greatly to them. Money and recognition are their motivation. They tend to measure the value of self and others against the yardstick of wealth. To them, self-worth is money and money is power. If the scales were to be tipped either in favour of money or power, Idealist would choose money. If it's *"no tickee-no laundry"* for others; it's *"no money-no power"* for them.

Born entrepreneurs

Idealist commonly reaches a point in their career where striking out on their own is less a decision than a necessity. As self-confidence grows with serial success and listed achievement, their ego's need for bigger challenges and bigger rewards grows, too. Idealist rather quickly outgrows low-ceilinged employment situations and are too ambitious to queue up for seniority lines, where the payoff is years and miles down the road.

Their life-purpose is to improve things and their mental energy doesn't allow them to sit long enough for complacency to take root. They're number one list-makers for a reason: they've much to do before day's or life's end. Deciding to strike out on their own is a hard decision for these security-conscious, failure-fearing individuals. However, few ducks take to water as naturally, as Idealist to entrepreneurship. Intelligence, perfectionism, and competitiveness are a combination that wins investor and client confidence alike. Also, when self-fulfillment is measured by wealth, as it is for Idealist, by motivation alone do odds rise in favour of their success.

Networking is an in-born skill. They generally keep within short reach, a short-list of trusted professionals they can depend on to do things right, and who respect/accept their need to be personally involved in all common aspects of association. They seem to know *Who's Who* in all fields and they cultivate long-term work relations and friendships with those they professionally trust. Unlike most, Idealist tends to be conversant in all areas of their business' operations, from client to distribution. As managers, they can be hard-nosed demanding about productivity and fussy about workmanship. Efficiency and perfection are their hallmarks. To them, compromise is a dirty word. When it comes to work, Idealist earns and wins respect quicker than they win congeniality awards. One possible explanation is "Nice guys finish last," as coined by Idealist, Leo Durocher.

It's been said, "They're the ones with a little churl in the smack-dab middle of their forehead. When business is good, they are very, very happy. When business is bad, none more horrid." Business, for them, is whatever occupies their mind and fills their time. When things are bad, Idealist makes a decision: give up or get creative. History doesn't record them as quitters. For them, success is less speculation, than assumption.

As full members of the workaholics club, Idealists build their private and social lives as extensions to their work. Holidays with family can involve work in different cities or attending a seminar in a foreign country, or New Year's Eve aboard a client's yacht. While Idealists routinely take risks at work or gamble for recreation, they tend not to jeopardize their family's security, though everything else be up for grabs.

Generally, they're sophisticated individuals who socialize with decorum and reserve. They subscribe to publications, clubs and groups that complement or are advantageous to their career pursuits. While Idealist likes the applause and recognition at work, socially they prefer being on the sidelines, rather than at centre stage. They're basically loners who discourage incursions into their private life. They maintain open, professional relations with associates but tend to keep a cool distance, personally. After years of working in close-proximity, Idealist may not have met an associate's family but would likely be able to rattle off with precision, particulars of that associate's family, (from past mention)—like names, ages, special interests, along with every professional strength and weakness of their associate, (as per their keen observation and keener opinion).

It is not essential for their self-fulfillment that the greater good be served. It's the mental challenge inherent in whatever they undertake and their innate pursuit of recognition and monetary reward that motivates them. Each Idealist arrives with their own *To Do* list in hand. From each checkmarked completion of theirs, may benefit for all be derived.

THE EMOTIONALS

Kinsmen

These individuals are inherently, innately and sincerely *good*. They see good in others, they do good for others and others feel good in their company. They remind us of what is ultimately important in life and why each has others in the world.

Don't look for them to be perched atop soapboxes. These intelligent, unprepossessing individuals are not driven by ego, avarice, or applause. Their style is more of the show than tell variety; their living is their teaching. Kinsmen are known by their deeds and they do a lot! When helpful Kinsmen find fulfillment, there's less lack in the world generally and more happiness specifically—for those fortunate enough to know them as mate, parent, or friend. Family is the theme that repeats throughout all they do. The world is but an extension of that deeply-rooted conviction.

Kinsmen are a wise, short or long-term investment for any company to make. Set the problem or challenge before Kinsmen, apprise them of needs and objectives and relax after that. These ones don't let others down. As trustworthy and reliable as they are, the workplace is not where Kinsmen fulfillment is found. Working overtime or volunteering to work weekends should not be expected of them. Their greatest joys and rewards are found beyond the reach and glare of glass domes.

Kinsmen fulfill purpose and self in the world outside of work. They tend not to be self-promoting or career aggressive, and usually prefer assistant over leadership roles. They may have the instinct, but lack the interest, for climbing corporate ladders or office politicking. Kinsmen tend more toward intrapreneurship—contracting to provide in-house services to an existing corporation, than entrepreneurship. They can wear many hats, adjust their pace to match any other's but tend to be more dependent than independent and less innovative than creative. Teamwork, where the collective effort benefits the whole, is a concept that Kinsmen understand at a cellular level. Any team or team effort is improved by their addition.

One hallmark characteristic is their general consensus approach to problem-solving. Highly intelligent and structured in their thinking, personally and professionally they organize projects into systems and follow through with step-by-step thoroughness. At set intervals, they seek general consensus on results to date, gaining approval from all concerned before continuing. This ensures that all problems are addressed, opinions represented, and adjustments made prior to the project's completion. Being conscientious, they earn respect from others by doing it right the first time around. Meeting or exceeding expectations is important to them, as anything less is high-stress. Others may wonder why such intelligent, competent individuals are so cautious. The blame is criticism—Kinsmen's Achilles' heel.

Not meeting the expectations of others is viewed as personal failure by them. They are unlikely to hide behind excuses or defend themselves when disagreements arise. They're more likely to shoulder the blame and get busy straightening things out quietly and efficiently than protest or complain. Count on conscientious Kinsmen to not make the same mistake twice.

If a Kinsmen has difficulty relating to an associate, then that person must truly be trying. These individuals tend to get along well with everyone. However, should being wrong through no-fault-of-their-own persist, they may still shoulder but eventually, even their famed patience wears thin and runs out. When Kinsmen have had their fill, frustration boils over in one of two typical ways. They'll either internalize their grievances and step up their check and re-check procedures to the point of near-paranoia, or they'll vent outwardly and emphatically—from short tempered nastiness, to abruptly leaving for unscheduled holidays. Being unfairly dealt with can emotionally overwhelm these fair minded beings.

An attribute of Kinsmen workers is their organizational skill. Going off half-cocked or coming to the table unprepared are not traits of theirs. They gather, organize, and determine a plan with efficiency in mind. Perfectionistic and meticulous, their forté is for arranging and processing details within the context of larger pictures. Risk-taking or innovative solutions may not be their strength; contributing to overall success is.

Of all and many abilities, the one most ascribed to Kinsmen is their unflappable, enduring patience. Many judges, magistrates, and religious leaders are of Kinsmen style. Situations that call for calm, collected reasoning, such as arbitration or contract negotiation are areas where these astute individuals excel. Their rational influence can soon restore order, when conflict and passion collide. They have a great talent for being able to incorporate the emotional and intellectual needs of others, into win-win solutions for all. Since they are not strongly ego-driven, Kinsmen tend not to complicate issues by interjecting their own views and opinions. Instead, they focus on finding the middle ground in situations, where general agreement and acceptance are found.

Security conscious Kinsmen are not conspicuous consumers nor do they subscribe to vows of poverty, either. Financial security is very important to them. Consequently, they are loyal, hardworking employees and astute money managers. One lesson from the model of their living is, abundance is not greed; husbanding and hoarding are. Kinsmen invest in the world, in fact, in deed and out-of-pocket. So, while motivation and life purpose may not be found in the workplace, the means to their fulfillment is—and that obligation they meet capably and responsibly.

Kinsmen like to socialize with work associates and often pitch in to help organize company get-togethers and celebrations. If any truth exists in the adage, "to ensure the job gets done, give it to a busy person," that busyOne would be Kinsmen. Their innate sense of family is reflected in their work relations. When they commit their time and talents, they commit broadly to contributing to corporate success. Generally, they are sociable, sophisticated individuals, who readily assimilate into any work environment and strive to excel. They decline being the centre of attention, though their hands are usually the first behind-the-scenes planning and preparing.

As leaders, they tend to have an open door policy of accessibility and cooperation. Staff dare not go in empty-handed or empty-headed, however. Kinsmen are strongly goal oriented and perfectionistic. As they hold high standards of performance for themselves, they expect high-level competence from team members. They are patient bosses who usually develop a close relationship with staff and office associates. One of their strong suits, career-wise, is coaching...an ability to recognize and guide potential to excellence. Kinsmen influence has produced many stars, from top corporate executives, to entertainment greats, to athletic All-Stars. They are most capable and comfortable in assistant chairs.

As managers or workers, Kinsmen are valuable assets to any industry or field. Sitting atop corporate ladders is not where Kinsmen find fulfillment. That, they find in the world of people, not in the world of business.

A better right-hand associate cannot be had. Management would be wise and lucky, to identify Kinsmen already on staff and ensure these individuals are positioned so their exemplary skills for negotiation, organization, and project or people management can be exercised to all's benefit and profit.

Why lucky? Based on Ansir's research to-date, Kinsmen is the rarest working style.

THE EMOTIONALS

Empath

Empaths can be one of the very best human resource investments any company or corporation can make—depending on whether appreciation is had or not.

There is something most unique about Empaths. They generally are not motivated by rewards of status, remuneration or recognition. Instead, their inspiration comes from contributing to the overall success of collective or individual efforts. They tend to be exceptional workers, whose greatest value is in their teaching example. Empaths are innately, evolutionarily, and without doubt, the most extraordinary teachers on the planet. It is more than a natural skill. In electricity, load determines the source. They've a most particular skill and genius. Empath's *load* is a cellular covenant to teach others how to love—self, and one another.

Confident Empaths are the benevolent King-makers, those unselfish, magnanimousOnes who unearth potential in others and encourage greatness to bloom. They are emotion-intellectuals of the tallest order and don't need proximity to fathom the emotional state of another. They often know by sight and feel alone. That ability, in combination with their sincere love of people, enables them to hear unexpressed self-doubt and to relate at a level of intimacy that dispels fear and boosts confidence. One of the industry contributions that Empaths have spearheaded is in-house training. Without exception, the battle to constantly upgrade worker skills

Pg. 244

and knowledge has been hardest fought by them. Whenever an ugly-duckling new employee turns into a top-notch swan, the hiring decision was likely an emotional's and most likely an Empath's.

For them, potential perceived is more important than what is spoken, written, or apparent. They may not be risk-takers when it comes to decision-making, but they'll risk all when their emotions nod go-ahead on people. Their hunches, generally, are an exacting science. Unfortunately, because they are seldom politically ambitious or self-promoting, Empaths can be overlooked in the workplace. They tend to be very capable individuals who, too-often, are pegged into doing roles when their greatest value is facilitating excellence. It is up to management to recognize Empaths as more than the conscientious workers they characteristically are. These gentle ones don't blow their own horn—though they could and maybe should, now and then. But then, they wouldn't be Empaths.

They may not seek leadership roles in business but many are seated close to "top dog" chairs, in trusted advisory or supportive positions. Empaths are trusted because of their highly developed sense of commitment to team work. Doing it for the Gipper motivates them, whether Gipper be boss, office effort, company goal, or profit.

By appreciation received from others, do Empaths measure their own value and extract personal reward. Receiving a "thanks" in the form of a monetary bonus or interoffice memo is too arm's length impersonal for them. Empaths work for and with people, harvesting self-fulfillment from the now of personal interactions. From companies they earn a paycheck; from people, self-confirmation. As loyal as they are, however, their own high, personal standards preclude blind obeisance. It is a rare Empath who can be bribed or coerced into doing anything that is not honourable or ethical or that compromises their own sense of propriety.

Their creative problem-solving can prove profitable in decision-making. Have them participate in strategy sessions or think-tanks to notice the difference between their suggestions (when they do speak up) and those of others. Often their suggestions are dismissed as too people-focused rather than profit-oriented, or too novel to implement. Their solutions may be presented in a halting or confused manner, but often contain a creative breadth and depth that logical thinkers need time to consider before realizing inherent import and practicality.

And...that is the single greatest challenge for Empaths: to trust their emotion-intellect enough to clearly speak out and more confidently explain or defend their view when questioned or opposed. Out-of-the-box creativity is not their strong suit; supporting, bracing, and nudging others' ideas forward, is.

Business does not yet respect emotionality, often viewing such as an individual weakness or as a sure sign of an irrational...if not addled mind. More and more, creativity is a business necessity as problems become increasingly sophisticated and globally inter-twined. If ever an opportunity existed where the meek could inherit the earth, it is in the realm of corporate creativity. Emotional Empaths function much like Visionarys, Evokateurs, Healers and Philosophers, who are collectively and individually extraordinarily creative beings. They're all emotion-intellects, not rational thinkers. Historically, business has viewed emotion much as oil does vinegar, refusing to mix unless shaken or forced.

Recently, a paradigm shift has shaken things up and forced change. Corporate focus is shifting from provision of product, to provision of service. Meaning business success will depend less on a corporation's ability to meet needs of a target market, than ability to meet the emotional needs of diverse clients. That's something demographics can't now measure nor polls predict. Empaths (ranked historically among business *meeks*) are born people-emotion smart.

Emotion-intellect is often beyond the comprehension and patience of logical thinkers. Most get impatient with Empath's random process of deduction and their confusing decision "declarations" that take ten times longer for them to explain than took them to arrive at. Even confident Empaths battle self-doubt. Their renown for accurately reading and interpreting emotions, earns them distinction as advisers and consultants.

In business dealings and negotiation, their natural gift can be invaluable. When honesty and good intentions show up, Empaths can sense and acknowledge. Conversely, count on them to find the hidden card up another's sleeve or detect the ulterior in motives. On their own they may not do much with this information, but in a team environment (where others assume responsibility for actions), their insights prove beneficial and advantageous.

Why then, with such gifts of creativity and emotion, do Empaths settle for assistant-type roles when leadership seems more fitting? First of all, Empaths are not ego-driven. At work, they don't seek applause or need recognition. Their goals are not self-serving. In business, where squeaky wheels tend to get the grease, they may not be invited to opine or participate in discussions where and when *Brownie points* get earned; so they won't and don't. Yet some of the most successful partnerships in entertainment, in business, in science and art occur when one of the partners is Empath: Banting and Best, Watson and Crick, Elton and Bernie, Laurel and Hardy, George and Gracie, to name but a few. They often need the support of another more forceful personality style with whom to create and work; One smart enough and confident enough to recognize and encourage their ego-less creativity.

Another reason why Empaths avoid leadership roles is how they deal with conflict. They often don't want the responsibility for disciplining or opposing another. They avoid confrontation, particularly anger, and may even be thought as push-overs by others. Empaths are pleasers and are more than willing to cooperate and help out...but Empath's "mama didn't raise no fool."

This personality style just doesn't have the same ego-protection needs as most others. While they readily perceive the deceit and deception behind plans or intentions, they tend to draw their own conclusions without need for explanation or demand for apology. Compromising self is not a big deal, if doing so pleases and does not harm them or hurt others. In fact, Empaths tend to view dishonesty more as valuable insight, than insult. Their accommodating nature may seem gullible or naive, but Empath's truth feeling and seeing eyes are wide open. They control the degree and extent of their involvement.

Whether a member of the collective or one in partnership, Empaths make valuable contributions to corporate success. Management would be wise to look for Empath talent untapped and untried on staff. These individuals harbour potential behind gentle manner and ready helpfulness. The key that unlocks their potential at work, as in every realm or relation, is appreciation. Not money. Not power.

Empaths make the best of situations.

Characteristically, bright-eyed and bushy-tailed (some, not first thing in the morning), their cheery disposition can be infectious and inspiring. Empaths bring a sense of family to the workplace, by getting involved organizing birthdays celebrations, office parties or holiday events. Social beings from birth, Empaths are ever-ready to exchange information that assists, helps, or pleases others. They seem to be magnets for the sad and sorry tale, as well as filter for late-breaking news, jokes, and gossip. In fact, but telegraph, telephone, or tell-an-Empath to make known. Their first love is people, including all the triflings, trumpetings, and triumphing that comes with them.

Most are highly skilled socially. Few can put others at ease or keep conversations flowing with as much style and ease as Empaths. Theirs, is a warm, welcoming, non-threatening presence. These ambassadors of fellowship love co-workers first and job second. That's not to imply they're irresponsible layabouts; nothing could be further from truth. Empath's hallmark is for being dedicated and reliable. They are the dependable souls who show up on time, perform diligently and dutifully stay for over-time, volunteer their weekends if needed and attend company functions.

As stated above, Empaths prefer associate/assistant roles over leadership. In partnership and in membership they tend to excel. And though proven capable and confident in their ability to fathom the emo-tional truth of others, Empaths characteristically have trouble identifying and expressing their own feelings. Self-doubt is an Empath issue, and important for employers to know. They bite back their suggestions for fear of being ridiculed. They go with the flow of general opinion and often need a nod of approval before offering up their ideas for improvement to procedure and plan. Their creative input could be profitable.

It is not unusual for an Empath to come up with an answer in seven minutes, yet deliberate seven days before disclosing or discussing with others. What they do in the interim is put together the proof or work up an explanation to substantiate their offerings. They, themselves, often don't know from whence idea or solution came. By the time most Empaths reach adulthood, they've been ridiculed aplenty for not being able to explain what they just somehow know. So they learn to be silent or be sure. In business, their noise could be the sound missed and needed. These individuals tend to be less assertive and will generally acquiesce, or cave-in, or say nothing. Their nature is to build bridges of understanding, even if that means going against their own better judgement.

With their seeming determination to avoid recognition, Empaths are frequently found under umbrellas of untried genius. The reason is usual-ly lack of self-confidence, except in one area—teaching. On the planet, no other has as much innate ability to teach as them. Regardless of the task, the subject, or the student, these individuals have a cellular gift for communicating understanding. The greatest advice to any business interest is recognize which employees are Empath and immediately place them in positions where their teaching skills can be used to advantage and benefit.

Most Empaths prove capable at any task they turn hand and mind to, because they're not logical thinkers. Efficient and quick, they've usually stripped away procedural nonsense that others doggedly follow. Consequently, they develop efficiency expertise and shortcuts that prove invaluable when incorporated into the production process.

The difference between an ordinary and an extraordinary Empath employee can be directly measured by the amount of appreciation each is accorded. Extraordinary Empaths are appreciated; ordinary's don't know if they are. Most personalities are motivated by rewards of recognition or remuneration; Empaths settle for fair and discount the rest. Encouragement, support, and an occasional "well done" can open the confidence throttle on their willing and capable, but timid genius.

It is an Empath that states, "I knew, but didn't say." Their meeker voice of reason is often drowned out by the ego-drive and din of others. "I told you so," after the fact, is also a common saying of theirs. While others may push to the front of the crowd to be heard, Empaths are often just as pleased to be counted as one among.

Perhaps kerneled in the words of Nelson Mandela's inaugural speech is a wisdom that will encourage Empaths to trust their greatest gift, emotion-intellect, to give voice to the creative individual within, and to contribute as born and meant.

Our deepest fear is not that we are inadequate.
Our deepest fear is that we are powerful beyond measure.
It is our light, not our darkness, that most frightens us.
We ask ourselves,
"Who am I to be brilliant, gorgeous, talented, and fabulous?"
Actually, who are you not to be? You are a child of God.
Your playing small doesn't serve the world.
There's nothing enlightened about shrinking so that other people won't feel insecure around you.

Originally from, "Our Deepest Fear," A Return To Love, by Marianne Williamson.

THE INTUITIVES

We will be talking about, and to confident Visionarys. There is a great difference in how confident and unconfident Visionarys work. Unconfident Visionarys work exactly like confident Idealists. They take jobs and probably do exceedingly well. Work is the favourite realm of functioning for Visionarys and Idealists. Knowing what they were born to do and pursuing it, is when Visionarys become. They were shouldered the responsibility for making a dent and a difference, in the lives of others, and world, because they can, when they work true to self.

Born to do, and lead the way for others

Blazing intellect and impassioned determination are their vehicles to fortune and fame. Historically, the wealthiest and most powerful personality style on the planet, Visionarys are seemingly born card carrying members of the workaholics club. Yet, even among that select group, theirs is often the most serious affliction. These individuals love work and they immerse themselves wholly in all undertakings. They are the big picture visionaries whose eyes are so firmly focused on future they hardly notice today's mud at their feet. Brainstorming and think tanks are typical workplace innovations of theirs, and reflective of their intellectual curiosity and people propensity.

Creativity seldom rests.

These individuals are intuitive-intellects, a fact that adds an interesting blip to their complexity and boosts their advantage. Plugging a problem into their intuitive dimension, Visionarys trust that resolution will brew and perk untended, while they function unperturbed externally. Intuitive-intellect means their approach to all and life is different. Visionarys don't care about colouring inside logic-lines and don't worry about straying beyond the defines of reason. Their most trusted guide is intuition (emotions), their guide for problem-solving, decision-making, and personal relations. In the same time that intellectual sizzlers find solution from step 1 through 10, Visionarys have potential to travel 1 to 40 and not only find solution, but return with plans, strategies, and schedules fleshed in feasibility. Details take care of themselves, when sight locks on the whole of even the most illogical dreams. Few are as preternaturally gifted to author new realities as Visionarys.

Likely, the concept of teamwork was first practiced by them. Not only do they love people, they have a knack for unearthing and encouraging the best in each to bloom. But the reason may be less magnanimous than practical, for they're lazy in the most productive sense. Creativity and leadership are their strengths. They conceive the ideas, formulate the strategies and administer progress, but they need capable others to process details and help turn concept into reality.

Two Visionary interpersonal characteristics are: curiosity and intuitiveness. Their curiosity is near-insatiable. Everything fascinates and little escapes their probe and scrutiny. In terms of intuitiveness, Visionarys never leave home without it. These are the ones who attend or chair meetings and by intuiting mood and mindset of participants, know when to hold and when to play their cards. They feel in advance, whether successful conclusions can or will be had and focus on removing doubts before they become obstacles. Whether sports, strategy, senate, or sales, Visionarys have an uncanny ability to anticipate the mood of others and determine the degree of cooperation or opposition in person or room. Overcoming adversity and opposition are specialties of theirs. They see 360-degrees of possibility for everything, but only one way to evoke change: emotionally. Logic can sell the explainable. Only emotions can sell the inexplicable—what Visionarys tend to offer.

When it comes to taking chances, Visionarys lead the world. But then, they do have that ace up their sleeve: intuition. Others may consider them extraordinarily bold risk-takers. Their own opinion differs somewhat. When emotion gives the nod, Visionarys see it as considerably riskier to ignore their truth in favour of logic...and less rewarding. Logic can exist without intuition, but intuition always and already contains the full score and measure of logic. Logic is not diminished or erased by intuition. It's enhanced exponentially.

Visionarys are most capable negotiators. Under pressure, when flames grow hotter and odds rise against, the calmer and more creative they tend to become. As Eccentriks mentally spin and alter three-dimensional reality, Visionarys spin perspectives with roulette-wheel ease. There are no one-way solutions for them, but infinite possibilities from which to choose best. Creativity-on-tap is the advantage intuitives have over logicals. One ranges 360-degrees; the other follows straight and narrow.

They are characteristically direct and forthright, which can be comforting for some but unsettling for many. One objective is uppermost in all their personal and professional dealings: understanding. Visionarys must feel and accept the rightness of situations, before deciding or acting—and must feel the truth of others, before doing either. When there is a conflict between their internal reading and external reality, Visionarys side with emotions, always. After that, it is a matter of confirming their intuited impressions through verbal investigation—or interrogation, as it may seem to others. They place the onus on others to prove them wrong rather than doubt self first.

Visionarys can be outstanding public performers and electric speakers. They fathom audience personality with their emotional antenna and adjust tone, tempo, and rhythm accordingly; maximizing both effectiveness and efficiency. They have skill and intellect sufficient for mass manipulation, but Visionarys sheath deed in honour—ever cognizant of their birth covenant to serve the greater good.

Large egos needed

Their life purpose dictates they overcome and prevail, despite opposition. Visionarys do not have the luxury of time. They're here now to make a betterment difference. It is not enough for them to envision alternate realities, not enough to theorize and ponder abstractly—they must think, express, and do. That means their egos must be strong enough to break with old rules; ignore ostracism to outrage, and ride roughshod over the naysayers and bottom-lines that get in their way. Whether in business, politics, arts, or academia, Visionarys often butt heads with status quo. Intuitives, like them, frequently experience frustration in a logic-run and ruled world. Logicals tend to view their visions as distortions of normal and Visionarys as peddlers of snake oil.

The indomitableOnes

These are the unsinkable human corks, who bob no matter how swift or deep the negativity or how strong the current against them. They're the ones whose crowns are removed by ignorance and who suffer public humiliation, but soon earn a standing ovation for outstanding achievement, anyway. Even if no other can or will, Visionarys have faith in themselves and keep going. They do strive for approval and do thrive on applause and recognition, but they can and do go without, if they meet neither friend nor supporter on their self-chosen path to fulfillment. Visionarys get there anyway.

These individuals are generous in dispensing appreciation and credit to others, though their own name may be slightly larger and more boldly displayed on marquee. Being extremely competitive, they tend to shine brighter, the greater the challenge. Pressure hones their skill and heightens enjoyment. When they throw their hat into the ring of office politics, Visionarys seek creative freedom opportuned by position, more than titled prestige. They usually avoid corporate power games aimed at squelching or killing the competition. They get more creative, the greater the challenge or opposition. They earn industry respect through innovation and timing, rather than by shark and vulture tactics. It is a rare Visionary who does not aspire to having their life achievements etched on headstone or scratched into history. Consequently, they conduct their living so that dignity and honour surround their name. Being swayed by insincere stroking or being manipulated by others is not only unlikely, it's unVisionary. For them, dishonesty and deception ring Big Ben loud and sound a death knell on trust relations.

To live, as in George Orwell's novel, *1984*, is an ultimate nightmare. They respect hierarchical structure, order of command, and though impatiently, due process. But they've little respect or tolerance for clone-propensities, prescribed protocol, or stone-tablet procedures. Not line-dancers, Visionarys refuse stepping in tune or time with any line, unless they agree in whole and principle. Neither non-conformist nor rebel per se, they are strongly individual. They have a keen sense of propriety and are innately sociable, and can handshake and schmooze with the best of them. However, they are scathingly intolerant of Pavlov dogs, should such canine inclinations be found manifest in corporation or corpuscle.

If management expects to hear an echo of their own opinion, avoid Visionarys. They echo no other. Visionarys only become, after having successfully conquered self-doubt; usually in adulthood. From that point on, they cannot be persuaded to adopt any opinion that contradicts their own—nor will they likely participate in any endeavour they do not intuitively embrace and endorse. Visionarys do not engineer bombs, sell armaments, or chop rain forests. Their visionary gift and life purpose is to architect improvement for others, not profit through demise. Their standards exceed laws of land and man. Visionarys are intuitives, therefore, their ethics are cellularly guided and governed. Their responsibility is to do something significant in their lifetime. When the world is bettered by invention, innovation, entertainment, or leadership guide, in those human-bettered vapours is proof of Veni, Vedi, Vici...Visionary has been, seen and conquered.

As leaders, they have no equal. As managers, only confident Idealists match their exceptionality. Regardless of what role they play in their big or small world or hat they wear—CEO, student, performing artist, or punch card 508—Visionary workers perform much the same.

At work

They're fussiness and conscientiousness incorporated. Efficient, demanding, bossy, hardworking, curious, witty, glib, and generally, they're on *this side* of nice. They learn fast and in most that they do, they do noticeably and comparatively well. They're curious about all facets of the business and the reach of operations, and take a keen interest in co-workers. They quickly establish friendships and even quicker, earn respect. They keep their professional life separate from personal and tend not to socialize outside the workplace. They're generous with ideas and direct in word and action–not rude, just real. They work tirelessly and have usually devised a system for doing, that only someone who loves what they do and wants to do more would come up with. They tend to get paid more but even co-workers agree...they earn it. Despite the fact that Visionarys are renown for changing jobs and careers often, they don't have trouble getting favourable references from former employers or securing positions elsewhere. The ones least likely to be fired or earn retirement watches are Visionarys. That's the general skinny on Visionary employees. Management would be wise to recognize Visionarys currently on staff. They're born to lead, not follow.

Leadership, their most natural role.

There's no such thing as disorganization, shoddy workmanship, or close-supervision with Visionary leaders. They delegate well and handle problems of project, personnel, and process efficiently. They tend to be charismatic and often have a good rapport at all levels of interaction, from co-worker, to management, to industry. They are known to be tough...meaning inflexible about poor job performance. They can handle a variety of tasks simultaneously without losing track, losing their temper, or buckling under stress. The most noticeable differences between these leaders and others is that Visionarys encourage, even insist their staff explore better ways to increase productivity, as well as ways to increase pleasures of working. Whether that entails in-house day care facilities, flex-hours, music, exercise facilities, or catering services...if it improves productivity, profitability, and results in an environment where workers are happier, it'll most likely be instituted by them. They are the original workaholics and are very conscious of feeling at home at work.

Regardless of field or job, whether the opportunity be business, art, or science, Visionarys can go anywhere and experience success....if they love what they do. They often form a tight team or network of associates they can trust to get things done their way, meaning flawlessly and promptly. The team qualifiers are: personal ambition, taking direction well, and meeting objectives independently. Visionarys are not baby sitters. They resent being distracted from their own work by details that should have been discussed upfront, by problems that should have been addressed upon arrival, or by those who cannot deliver as promised. Incompetence, dishonesty, apathy, or any combination thereof, are cause for dismissal from Visionary-led teams.

They are very good teachers. Thorough and comfortable with authority and responsibility, they use wit and allegory to bring their points home. But don't fall asleep in their class. Not only do Visionarys work toward and expect full comprehension by lessons end, they tend to measure their own ability by student performance. Pupils don't fail the course; Visionary teachers do.

If generous in commending and rewarding when pleased, they're equally contrary when not. These individuals are hard-driving perfectionists, who expect excellence and superior performance from self and others. Details may not be their cup of tea, but when *the proverbial* hits the fan, Visionarys handle adversity with aplomb. When trouble visits, they tend toward clear-thinking serene rather than whose-to-blame mean. They are unlikely to wear themselves out by jumping to conclusions when things go wrong. They think fast and best under pressure. They are, however, uncompromising sticklers when it comes to accountability. If your work partner, associate, or boss is Visionary, apprise them of problems quickly. Otherwise, expect brusque and blunt should time be wasted or responsibility off-loaded.

What makes Visionary leaders so highly respected and admired, is their manner of separating issue from person. Generally, they don't browbeat another for making mistakes. They address the process, the lack of knowledge, or the inattention that caused it. Others may feel as though hit by a sledge-hammer when they meet the vent of their frustration (Visionarys undress like no other), but it's issue that fists are applied to, not flesh. Anyway, such heavy-handedness would be counter-productive. They find and encourage the best in others, if for no reason other than it benefits them short and long-term. When others are confident and competent, Visionarys are closer to getting what they want done without need of worry or their direct involvement. These impatientOnes resent having to tell others where and how to place their feet, and would sooner end the relationship than assume the responsibility of having to do so.

They like competition and relish the challenge of testing themselves against a worthy opponent. If bested, they tend to be more impressed than displeased. Of course, they don't lose often. Intuitive-intellects make for stiff competition. Victors should prepare to meet an ultra-competitive and creative blitzkrieg from them, next time around. Unscrupulous they are not. If crossed or betrayed they are tempest in teapot, and usually sever relations forever.

That which pushes them to excel and experience as much as possible is reason-rooted in birth covenant. Whether Visionarys are consciously aware of their evolutionary responsibility or not, seems to have little bearing on performance or unfolding of being. Most change careers often; excel in most all they try; exhibit extraordinary creativity in problem-solving; exude high energy; emanate self-confidence; interact easily with others; and communicate exceptionally well. Born to orate and elucidate, as if fashioned from same leader mold, Visionarys change worlds, change hearts, and change minds with words.

The anti-establishment movement of the 60s swarmed and seethed with Visionary influence and focused outrage. They removed the concept of blind obeisance, redefined conscientious-objector, exposed corruption in government and challenged political and justice systems alike. They then donned suits, ties, and running shoes, rolled up their sleeves and revolutionized human rights, legal rights, environmental husbandry, arts, humanities, scientific innovation, medical invention, and ultimately spawned the Information Age. Conscious-awareness and intuitive-intelligence are but beak and wing of this bird.

Responsibility is genetically woven into their makeup. When they say they can—they do. But remember, for these individuals their first priority is finding and fulfilling their own life purpose. They have something significant to personally do. Until they find their own niche, they harvest from a wide swath of experiences. Immersing themselves fully in numerous fields and opportunities, they seek alignment of external deed with internal need. If not intuitively right, regardless of success, regardless of consequence or plea, Visionarys move on and resume niche-hunting again. These gifted and charismatic individuals tend not to captain other people's ships long. Most pursue entrepreneurship, where they have the creative and risk-taking freedom they need, to build the visions that burn within; those that may not be realized in a logic run workplace.

Whether client, corporation, community, or country is in need of the most creative solution or far-sighted plan, the first and best choice is Visionary. None are as preternaturally advantaged and personally motivated to author new realities as these intuitive leaders.

THE INTUITIVES

Evokateur

Some seek fame through work and for various reasons: some for rewards of power or wealth—some for both—some for sheer exhilaration; some for recognition; some for the betterment of others and some for betterment of all. Evokateurs shun fame but fame may not shun them. Rare ingenuity and rare originality, are the two most common reasons why fame is more familiar than stranger to Evokateur workers. Through their work are Evokateur persons known; by their work are Evokateur souls known.

They may first be thought peculiar, but for "Working" Evokateurs, extraordinary could be their second distinction. This personality pulls mind and body completely out of the thinking, working, and loving realms of life. To find answers, to find reasons, to find alternatives, to find selves, Evokateurs go home to intuition where infinite wisdom is found and truth felt and known. Home for them is emotions. Intuition at work must equal infinite creativity, for no other is as potentially creative. Evokateurs can have difficulty explaining their work to others. Not for lack of ability to communicate—they tend to be highly articulate but for lack of understanding "capability" on the part of others.

Most create in private, choosing to hide their creative gift rather than risking ridicule by sharing. However, not even anonymity's generous umbrella can fully hide their truth.

Evokateurs harbour brilliance. This conversation is with, for, and about Evokateurs; who flex their difference and stick their chin out and hold it high, no matter how many swipes and punches non-comprehension throws. Working Evokateurs are the ones who let the fruits of their love— their work and labour stand as their testimony.

Galilei Galileo (1564-1642), was the foremost mathematician and philosopher of his day. Galileo re-ordered solar logic by supporting the controversial Copernican theory, which placed the sun at the centre of the universe with Earth orbiting around.

Absent-minded, Sir Isaac Newton (1642-1727), was born the same day Galileo and Michelangelo died. Considered one of the greatest scientists that ever lived, Newton proved the Copernican theory, discovered universal gravitation, developed the theory of colour, and developed the branch of mathematics known as calculus...et cetera. While still in his twenties, Newton was elected to the Lucasian Chair (the Lucasian Professorship of Mathematics is the most famous academic chair in the world). He was also the first scientist to be knighted.

In 1862, a stammering Charles Lutwidge Dodgson (1832-1898), master mathematician, lecturer, and scholar, took lunch along the banks of the Godstowe with the dean's three daughters; one named Alice. Three years later, as Lewis Carroll, he invited the world to keep Alice company at a Tea Party in Wonderland, where Mad Hatter, Cheshire Cat, and surreal nonsense ruled.

Paul Cezanne (1839-1906), startled the world with his bold stroke and brash brush that fathered modern art. Instead of painting being a passive view of the world, Cezanne's creations moved beyond the canvas. They interacted with the world.

One of the most famous artists of the 20th century, Pablo Picasso (1882-1973), introduced the most revolutionary modern art of all time,

Cubism. A God's-eye view of reality, where every aspect of the whole subject is seen simultaneously in a single dimension.

Glenn Gould (1932-1982), a pianist extraordinaire, who at Three was considered exceptional; at Twelve, brilliant; at Twenty, a genius as profound as Scarlatti, Beethoven, Chopin and Liszt; and who at Thirty was retired and recluse.

Dr. Albert Einstein (1879-1955), physicist and Nobel laureate is perhaps the most well-known scientist of the twentieth century. Einstein is best known as the creator of the special and general theories of relativity, and for his hypothesis concerning the particle nature of light.

Dr. Stephen Hawking (1942-), world-renowned theoretical physicist and cosmologist, was born 300 years to the day, after Galileo's death. His research centred on Black Holes and from the late '60s onward he's been in the forefront of Black Hole research. Following in the footsteps of Sir Isaac Newton, Professor Hawking now holds the Lucasian Chair that has only seated the world's most influential in science and technology. His view is that science is for everybody and should be understandable by everyone. To that end, through lectures and books, his tend has been to make it so.

Evokateurs are the abstract theorists, brave artists, masterly writers, gifted musicians, and great composers among us. The ones who go places that logic will not travel till proven. Explaining is logic's job; creating...intuition's. Evokateurs learn early in life it is best to experiment privately and experience silently in their world, as ample-confidence and sample-evidence will be needed to withstand logic's scrutiny in ours, once brought to light and bear.

How readily they share their abstractions and creations with others depends on whether their environment is one that encourages or discourages. These individuals tend to walk that hypothetical fine line; if today a genius, but yesterday a fool. Evokateur-world, more real to them than this one of ours, satisfies them—except for validation of creativity and reciprocation of love.

For them, validation is like receiving a nod of permission to work more, and work more freely. Love reciprocated means having a for-better-or-worse ally. And while the relationship can be their perspiration's-inspiration, seldom is it motivation's fan or fuel. Creativity is a cellular obsession for Evokateurs. They create anyway.

If them...

...would you not like to come back *here,* and fall into the lap of those glad to see you; those who inspire and share their views and discoveries as openly as they discuss their difficulties? Evokateurs don't do diddly-squat within manipulation distance of money, or within clutch and grasp of those who'd control their tongue, time, ethics, or creativity. Most die poor. Many are bent and busted long-before. Some die mysteriously and some all alone, especially working-Evokateurs.

But whether rich or poor; bent, busted, or broke, former working-Evokateurs are much with us today. Their work tends to outlive them and is more accessible and more appreciated now than then. Today, everything originally theirs is ransom'ly or museum'ly treasured. In their day, seldom so. Working-Evokateurs need others because many are incapable of financially supporting themselves. Meeting adult obligations is less important to them than work of their own...whether understanding, appreciation, or compensation is had or not.

Their drive is not ego, money, or applause, but expression of self. Some have others who stand beside them with moral and money support, like Theo van Gogh for his big brother Vincent, who otherwise may have met the common Evokateur fate of being ignored and forgotten. Work is how these ones communicate best and preferably with others. Through their work, Evokateurs show and share their love.

'Work' needs new definition...

...for theirs is a characteristic preoccupation with it. When Evokateurs love what they are doing, rare can and does result—which is reason enough for business and industry to actively seek their employ. Be warned, however. To Evokateurs mundane is pain/bane and bore. It was rumoured that Dr. Albert Einstein only owned one suit, a brown one. Actually he had many suits, though all of same cut, colour, and cloth. Details of what to wear, what colours, what shoes, were too trivial for him to waste time on. Removing mundane freed him to work more. That's what validation does for Evokateurs. It inspires them to love harder and work more. When Evokateurs do what they love, all else tends to fade in importance, particularly the petty and picayune of life, like food, housing, and clothes.

To satisfy those basic life necessities, Evokateurs generally look for mundane-type jobs they can perform with one eye shut and mind half-alert, like assembly line work. The drone-like predictability of routine tasks allows them to put brain and body on auto-pilot while they escape into Evokateur-world, where all is more interesting. Associates may think them highly focused and diligent, as they are hard to distract when concentrating. Evokateurs are masters at the physical art of looking interested. When in company or in conversation with others, they may nod and respond appropriately, though mentally be miles away and lost in own reveries.

Alternate realities are their speciality. Being able to blast logic with enough emotional force to change logic's direction is their purpose for being. As science-fiction writers, they are peerless. Evokateur lessons don't entail thinking, they've got that down pat. Instead, they change outer-world reality by means of inner-world imaginings. Evokateur-world is an audio-visual, logic-exploding, emotion-exploring experience. In every field of creative excellence, the cream at the top is thickly-clotted with Evokateurs.

Their impression of the outside world is one of drab harshness, like an ant farm with beepers, compared to their inner landscapes. Dr. Albert Einstein stated, "One of the strongest motives that lead men to art and science is escape from everyday life with its painful crudity and hopeless dreariness, from the fetters of one's own ever-shifting desires. A finely tempered nature longs to escape from the personal life into the world of objective perception and thought."

They'd druther live in a world of their own choice and making.

Evokateur-world is rich beyond any earthly reward. Why leave, other than must, an infinitely diverse sanctuary where solar systems realign—as in Galileo's; where reality splinters into dynamic components and breathes life—as in Picasso's; where energy not only creates and destroys, but rests as well—as in Einstein's; where an invisible force called gravity is the weave and reason for planet and life—as in Newton's; and where stars implode and time ends—as in Hawking's?

Unlike others, Evokateurs are content with conceptualization. Others desire a three-dimensional construct of their ideas. Evokateurs are satisfied with abstraction. Conceptualization satisfies their creative need; theoretical testing satisfies their curiosity, so actualization is redundant. Dr. Albert Einstein did not need a physical demonstration to prove that an atomic clock travelling at high speed in a jet plane, ticks more slowly than its stationary counterpart. Internally creating and mathematically testing his special and general theories of relativity, $E=MC^2$ was proof enough.

Recognition is not a hankering of theirs. When Sir Isaac Newton sent a brief exposition of his theory of colours to the Royal Society in London, his work met skepticism and criticism. He immediately withdrew his paper and pursued other interests. Thirty-two years passed before he resubmitted "Opticks," which explained his colour theory in greater detail and was then accepted. As their discoveries are self-wrought and begot, so too, their awards. Though applause and accolade ring as sweet in Evokateur ears as any other, those are not the sticks that prompt or propel. Like Professor Charles Lutwidge Dodgson—who life-long denied association with his pseudonym, Lewis Carroll—Evokateur Nobel Prize winners consider the obligations that go with fame, more intrusive than rewarding.

Rare indeed...an Evokateur CEO

An almost characteristic non-concern of theirs is improving bottom-line profitability or developing profit strategies. They tend to leave that to logic and others. They're more likely to provide new product concepts and new perspectives for investigating, or adding a twist of unique to ordinary and proposing new roads to take. While they don't mind re-inventing the wheel, a challenge they'd prefer is replacing it.

There are infinite work outlets for Evokateur creativity, though choices seem commonly threaded. From satellite design to laboratory, from concert hall to art gallery, from hallowed hall to broadway stage, or from science fiction to space odyssey, what Evokateurs bring to this world is their inner, one-of-a-kind own. Most of us ponder such issues as time, space, matter...and reasons for being and life. Most also leave answering and explaining to somebody else. Historically those "somebodys" have been Evokateurs. Their renown is for tackling universal issues.

Betterment or improvement is a consequence of their contribution, not the objective; replacing old or nudging it further along, is. Evokateurs give logic new sight with fresher focus built-in. These highest level visionaries usually travel beyond the bounds of known and beyond the limits of permission. They are not known as respecters of business mandate or protocol, which is why Evokateur CEOs are rare.

Pg. 268

Because logic must be thoroughly convinced before changing its mind, the onus is on Evokateurs to provide palatable pudding for proof-testing. Often can they be found strolling halls of academia, where their fame echoes in the air and hangs on the walls. Evokateur creativity is often beyond the ready grasp of common thought, requiring they be equally creative in devising methods of expression sufficient for explaining the depth and breadth of their ideas. That's how the branch of mathematics known as calculus was born. Sir Isaac Newton was formulating the three laws of motion, but prevailing Greek geometry proved inadequate for his purposes. Though forced to share the credit for inventing calculus, Newton used his "new math" to develop the law of universal gravitation.

"If I have seen further than other men, it is because I stood on the shoulders of giants."—Sir Isaac Newton

There is a sense of continuity with Evokateurs. They seemingly pass the torch from one to the other, and with each passing goes inherited responsibility for improving on the immortal work and fame of those who went before. With each successive contribution, possibilities compound and multiply. What Evokateurs do stands taller than their person. As Newton stood on the shoulders of Galileo and all the *greats* between, Einstein picked up the torch from those who went before and carried it far enough for Hawking to forge ahead with. Cezanne passed modern art to Matisse and Picasso, as the torch was passed from Handel to Mozart, to Beethoven, to Chopin, to Liszt...et cetera.

Space and time seem to fascinate Evokateurs. They are the number one purchasers of telescopes and celestial material of all matter and kind. These peculiar individuals look up at skies with others, but see more than moons, stars, and dippers. They look for order in weave, and for home. To them, from stars we come and to stars we go. In-between there is life with infinite mysteries to solve, with reasons to explore, and experiences to live.

Evokateur-world is sensory rich and replete.

Beethoven did not need ears to hear music. He had a full scale orchestra at beck-and-call within. He played, practiced, and knew each note and sound intimately, internally, long-before written, and performed. For Evokateurs, each step towards actualization diminishes the original's quality and impact. The process of translating emotion into thought dilutes the most. Then converting thought into forms others can appreciate or understand strips complexity further and dulls vibrancy.

Be it in science, music, art, or literature, Evokateurs begin with inner-world intensity but after translation, end up with lukewarm representation, comparatively. What they see and hear inside cannot be duplicated externally. The tools and materials available are inadequate. Little wonder these individuals are reluctant to share. Even when they control every step of the sharing process, it can be like dreaming in colour but waking to monotone. If that were not enough to dissuade, they must also contend with the curse of creativity: rejection for being too-different. Of all, Evokateur's most often are unappreciated in their own lifetime.

They are more than non-conformists, they're entirely non-conforming (the former protests; the latter doesn't bother to acknowledge). Generally, they won't be told what to do. These fiercely-independent individuals assiduously avoid commitments that infringe, impinge, or threaten their autonomy. Whatever time they are willing to share with others, and for however long their willingness lasts, is as long as they tend to commit to others and situations.

Together, working-Evokateurs can be clannish and cliquish. They understand each other, often greatly admire one another and support one another. As for liking each other—highly unlikely. Evokateurs, who place little faith in the opinions of others, tend to place all-faith in their own and discount or disregard the rest. It would seem they prefer their own "sort," just as they prefer their own ideas. Remembering they are *gone* a good deal of the time, it makes perfect sense why they'd gravitate to specialized company, and companionship upon return. But it doesn't explain why, personally, they can find ready counsel and comfort with one another, yet professionally, they can't find much to admire or recommend in each other's work.

Their temperament is characteristically split between gentle/unassuming and irritable/irascible. The inability of others to see beyond normal and narrow, is the most common cause of Evokateur irritation and withdrawal. As children, they get used to perimeter participation. They stay within viewing and hearing distance of others and tend to only participate when they want or if forced. As adults, their involvements are strictly by choice. They will not and cannot be forced. When provoked, as when inspired, they disappear into their private sanctums where they'd much rather be, anyway.

Work non-cease

Most of their creativity is done in private. Usually what others see is but tip of their creative iceberg. Evokateurs are risk-takers, who stretch the boundaries of human logic through intuition-backed intellect—which is bound to bring them into direct conflict with prevailing order, *aka* logic.

Galilei Galileo was the foremost mathematician and philosopher of his day. Galileo re-ordered solar logic and challenged authority with his support of the Copernican theory. Additionally, he invented a pendulum clock; laid the groundwork for thermometer development; formulated the laws of relationship between space traversed and time interval in free-fall, and the motion of projectiles; improved the telescope for celestial viewing; discovered Jupiter's satellite moons; invented the military compass; patented a machine to raise water levels; invented the microscope; developed a system for determining longitudes at sea; and re-designed magnets. Then, Galileo's creative expression was rudely interrupted. He was found guilty of heresy and placed under house-arrest for life by the Catholic Church. An Evokateur's workplace is usually a cornucopia of imaginative expression. More than evidence of their hardworking propensity may be found; could be "future in progress" there, too.

"The only real valuable thing is intuition." —*Dr. Albert Einstein*

Evokateurs are the ones who leave giant footprints that map and guide mankind's journey and progress. In every field and profession, these pure intuitives meet challenges and set new courses. The lesson learned by the model of their success and contributions is, we already know more than we have learned, studied, or been taught. By tapping into the evolutionary pool of infinite wisdom, soul-close within, will infinite possibility for self-fulfillment be realized.

Intuition is creativity and each human's birthright and gift. Evokateurs have proved that, beyond a shadow of doubt, in times past as they will in times present and future. When Evokateurs leave, more doors are left open for others than were open for them.

THE SPIRITUALISTS

Healer

Healers NEVER show up for work unless perspectives—in their chosen field of interest or industry—are in need or are in dire need of changing.

Few are as gifted or as physiologically complicated, as Healers. None are more reluctant to be than them. Healers are born with rare ability but often don't know it. Consequently, no one benefits.

If "none so blind as they who will not see," none can more capably illuminate some other way, than Healers. This personality comes bearing powerful gifts intended to serve one purpose: changing belief. With their holistic perspective, conscientious nature, and intuitive-intellect, Healers have potential to succeed in any career of their choice. But where they characteristically excel is in any field or endeavour that serves the greater good, like music, art, literature, entertainment, and most particularly, the science of medicine. When Healers focus on matters of health and enlightenment, the word "superior" needs redefining. Professionally they qualify like everyone else, with license, certificate, and degree. But it is soon realized by others that their skill and ability goes beyond the normal glean of books or experiences.

Know more than what is seen, heard, and taught?

Healers are spiritualists. On the uppermost rung of intelligence ladders, Healers and Philosophers sit side-by-side. Intuitive-intellects, like them, are not tethered to logic and opinion. Healers have lived all but one personality and do not rely on the knowledge they've gained in this life alone. They consult their own vaults of wisdom, where every experience from *Big Bang* to now is recorded in soul and accessed through emotions. These individuals arrive knowing more than possible from word or book. Their greatest gift is their conscious evolutionary memory, which recalls all they've done and lived. That's what intuition is: an infinitely generous database of all that was, from which all that can be flows. We needn't bother to explain that these individuals are ultra-creative; but will anyway. To illustrate the creative advantage of intuition over logic to help explain why Healer skills and abilities exceed knowledge alone, let's consider music.

Logic is represented by the pure foundation notes, A, B, C, D, E, F, G. Creativity bent logic this way and that and discovered notes beyond the foundation: sharps and flats. By splitting the pure, creativity exponentially increased music's potential and possibility. Over time, once their measure had been gained, once their definition had been worked out and agreement reached, logic incorporated sharps and flats into known, thus expanding music's foundation.

As musicians, logicals have potential for technical perfection. They would sit at the keyboard armed with a background of vast musical knowledge from which to build music. Logical creativity is contained within the bounds of known rules and notes. Their challenge is to find new musical interpretations, mixes, and twists, and does not range beyond proven limits of upper and lower. They convert old music into new sounds.

Intuitives bring an equally vast knowledge with them, but their challenge is different: *to marry what's known, with what's felt.* Intuitives follow emotions, not rules, not notes. Inside logic's music base they search for sound combinations, distortions, and subtleties that most accurately reflect how they feel. They take known and using emotions as guide, find sounds that ring as true without as within. They convert sounds of music into musical experiences.

Logicals can be talented, are often disciplined and determined, and are commonly listed among the great of renowned musicians. Where they are not listed is among the great composers. That distinction belongs only to intuitives who, like Healers, go beyond what is deemed logically possible. Intuitives know one thing logicals do not. Infinite possibility and ultra-creativity live in one place, intuition. And the only bus that goes there is emotions. Logic, no matter how broad or wide, follows a straight line. Intuition neatly tucks the logic narrow into its brace and continues on its merry own...360-degrees around and beyond it.

A funnel-type of relationship exists between logical and intuitive creativity.

Imagine a typical funnel shape, then label the spout logic. Keep in mind the spout's trajectory travels beyond the spout—from tip to infinity. In the case of logic, the path of creativity is infinitely long and straight but narrow in terms of all possible. Label the funnel's triangular-shaped bowl, intuition. Again, the trajectory of the bowl stretches from lip to infinity, and while long, creativity's path gets broader the further it goes. If the two paths were superimposed, logic's entirety would easily fit into intuition. But the whole of intuition, even if stuffed, couldn't fit into logic...and that pretty accurately illustrates the relationship between logic and intuition in everyday life.

In order for intuitives to be understood and accepted by logicals, their creativity must be refined and narrowed enough, to fit into logic's spout. The funnel bowl represents the process of filtering and fine-tuning, that intuitive-intellect must first go through, in order to be accepted by logic.

The onus is always on intuitives to tailor themselves to meet logical approval. Logic, by definition, cannot stretch beyond upper and lower limits of known.

Logicals never meet intuitives on their own turf. They can't go there, far less understand and accept them there too. In the real world, Healers meet logic and gain approval at spout, so to speak, when they qualify by license, certificate or degree. But that is not all they bring to whatever field or career they choose. Once the *requireds* and *compulsorys* are passed, they bring their *bowlful* of accumulated experiences to bear in their work. These individuals cannot disregard the infinitely broader, wider base of their known. Past life experiences are the source of their power and creativity. To repeat, the greatest challenge for Healers is accessing the wisdom of their past life experiences; those stored in soul and accessed through emotions.

When Healers subscribe to their own truth and counsel,
wisdom vaults open and potential flies.

Though most ignore or deny, one characteristic all Healers share is a personal relationship with the Creator. The reason why Healers see the holistic order of things and place such importance on system-thinking, is because of their intimate relationship with the Creator. It is not surprising, based on evolutionary experience and divine awareness that these spiritual beings view life, not as a sum of diverse parts and pieces, but as a living system of interconnections, interdependent relations, and relationships. Like a pebble tossed on water, tweaking, tampering, or removing one aspect, ripples consequence through all.

Holistic Healers do not solve problems, they address issues. It does not matter what career or job they choose, when Healers trust their inner truth and assume responsibility for their gifts, they are professionally, as personally...as evolutionarily, exceptional beings. Otherwise, they tend not to function as Healers but parody the behaviour of respected others. A practice as common as mud for unconfident Healers. The confident of this style have power and potential to rule worlds. Their purpose, however, is to ensure planet and specie survive despite rulers, leaders, and lawmakers. They do that by changing belief, from stubbed toe to conscious-awareness.

Why Healers avoid assembly line work.

Healers find it odd...

When people stub their toe, they get angry, curse, and through hobbled grimace and gritted teeth, ignore the pain. How much quicker the heal and more pleasant the day, if that poor throbbing toe were held and it's pain acknowledged instead. Then comforted by warm, sympathetic hands till pain eases and ends. After all, no matter the shoe, the speed, or the rocky path pointed, the toe never lets body down. If small this change in thought does seem, apply that small principle to a larger scale, as Healers would, and note what differences result with change of belief.

When the body is sick or diseased, the prescribed policy is to view the disease with winner-loser hostility. Rather than stiffening resolve and muscle and steadying nerve to control pain, rather than declaring all-out war and focusing energy and resources on destroying the invader, flip perspectives instead. Focus light on body's plight, for it's every bit in need of caress as that stubbed toe once was. Accept the pain, validate its existence. The body system may be confused as to which is friend and which is foe. The body for allowing disease to enter or disease for daring to enter? Wars are always confusing. As peace can follow surrender in war, heal and cure can follow surrender in body disease.

In Aesop's fable, *The North Wind* could not, by force of cold or might of gale, remove the man's coat. But the Sun, by focus of warm smile, won the challenge with the man's willing surrender of his overcoat. The body is a living, responsive system. As toe cannot go but where body dictates, disease cannot reside without body's awareness. Healing is an inside job. If caress quickens stubbed toe's relief, would not a collective cellular-caress quicken cures if thoughts focused on healing, rather than war?

Applying the simple principle further, farther, wider; Healers question how far from acceptance and cooperation ever is healing. Both come inextricably bound and wound when love visits. When children stub their toe, they cry out in acknowledgement of pain. With love in heart and hand, adults comfort and massage their sore wee toe and kiss and cuddle to ease pain. Healers wonder if we do not view each other as stubbed toes too-often, and too-readily in life. It seems avoidance is easier than care, anger is faster than understanding, complaint is quicker than compliment, and ignoring common, if not prevalent. When others hurt, they are generally left to fend for themselves, as stubbed toe often must do. When our children hurt, we hurt too. What's the difference? Other than pedigree and proximity, nothing.

Move the concept out further yet and apply.

Consider how different human interactions and behaviour would be, if all believed, as Healers, that every person born is a reflection of Creator, and that every person seen and met, is seen and met for reason. They cannot separate parts from whole, one from others or thoughts from actions. To them, but one blood circulates, through Higher Power, through one, through each, through all, then back again in perpetuity. That is why Healers do not make good assembly line workers. When they work, their vision does not rest on part or piece but seeks deepest understanding and its broadest application.

As the pre-eminent physician of her day, she attended Pope, King, and pauper alike. In typical Healer fashion, she talked to God—a communion equally frowned upon by science as religion. "Destiny is carried inside each of us like a seed," she claimed. If encouraged to grow, that seed awakens the soul from its ancient sleep, to guide each to purpose and fulfillment. She held the view that man is Co-Creator of the Universe, with divine power and freedom of choice to create life or to destroy it. From her wealth of self-acquired herbal knowledge and remedy use are many modern day pharmacopoeia derived. Long before Sir William Harvey described blood circulation, she understood and incorporated that mystery in her work. Her art is said to invoke a sense of universal harmony. Her writings, at a time when few women were literate, are of scholarly significance. Her music, still available, is said to stimulate neuropeptides, generating a sense of peace and well-being on the part of the listener. Had she been born another place and time, she may have been convicted of heresy and met a fiery stake demise due to public fear and skepticism. Her name is Hildegaard Von Bingen; a self-taught, 12th-century nun, who at the age of eight was tithed to the church.

At work

To reiterate: they have potential to succeed in any career or role they choose, but where Healers characteristically excel is in any field of endeavour that serves the greater good, like music, art, literature, science...and most especially, medicine. Like Healer *workers*, Dr. Joseph Lister and Louis Pasteur, these individuals are bold supporters and outspoken proponents of prevention over intervention. And it matters not whether the issue is body health, animal husbandry or tea making. Conscious-awareness is their approach; human betterment their aim. For instance, replacing a heart valve is band-aid solution and a problem that promises repeat; unless surrender to pain's truth and change of belief is embraced by the patient. Pain today, will likely stop with treatment. Tomorrow's comfort depends on health-system awareness where individuals assume cell and self responsibility.

For Healers, humans are energy beings, in like and link with universe and cosmos. Thoughts are purely creative energy that often must be formally expressed with language and action, before affect or effect can be determined. Healers know emotions do not need word or action in order to understand thoughts. At thought's inception, cellular communication occurs and its import and impact is instantly known and transmitted throughout the body system...long before logic forms words or takes action. It is not pain they erase nor habits they break, but thoughts, belief, that Healers change.

Intuition is their guide; emotions are their diagnostic tools. Healers chameleon another's energy. With lightning's speed and in lightning's nature, they follow energy's bodily course and flow. Diagnosing by intuitively feeling, they become one with other(s). That assimilation skill is the core and gift that defines Healers, and the unique that distinguishes them as spiritualists from all others. They are exceptional workers and listeners, but exemplary diagnosticians and practitioners.

Professionally and personally, they approach life holistically. As acupuncture relieves a headache, by stimulation of pressure points elsewhere, Healers meet logic, but intuitively connect to truth—which, too, is often found elsewhere than in words or actions. Pain and cause are seldom covered by one and same bandage. And while much of the above seems to be body/health related, the same principles are applied by Healers, regardless of topic, object, or undertaking. Whatever Healers are involved in, they apply the same conscientious care to core of task and extend it to the farthest reach of their responsible shoulder. What they do is less important than the benefits or changed perspectives that follow. Their concerns tend to be focused on people-betterment, in some small or significant way.

Truth can hide behind words in language expression, but thought deception is not possible in energy communication. Evolutionarily, Healers are the degree'd masters of energy language. Belief is the sum of an individual's knowledge. Ego is belief's representative that interacts with the world in strict accordance with individual belief. If we cannot be less than, nor more than we think; Healers change belief from external dependence to internal mastery. Instead of looking outward for intervention and cure, Healers turn others' focus inward and summon the most powerful help possible, self-truth.

Healers, like Hildegaard Von Bingen, awaken the soul from its ancient sleep and introduce that infinitely creative and powerful God-spark to its landlord of this life's duration. No external truth truer, no external power greater, than that which resides and presides within. Healing is an inside job, where understanding and acceptance can return miracles every bit as spectacular, as the parting of the Red Sea for Moses. But then, as Hildegaard proposed, each human is born with Co-Creator power built-in.

Not surprisingly, the majority of medical professionals, health care providers, and wellness practitioners are Healers. For this style, both person and purpose tend to be found and fulfilled under one and same bandage: in the service of others (regardless of career chosen). Healers are here to teach others that changing thought content and intent, changes energy's message and focus.

Gaining cellular cooperation, by aligning logic with innermost truth, is when healing from symptom, to source, to system occurs. When united and focused, the resulting energy vibration can alter physical matter and change reality. When applied in Healer fashion, this simple but powerful premise can effect change, whether applied to cell, self, care, cause, or world. For them, it is all but a matter of changing belief. None are better at that, than Healers.

As life is our own creation, so too our demise. If each could understand, accept, and trust the infinite power of their own God-spark within, each and all would live more consciously, more kindly, more bravely, and more lovingly...as do they, the phenomenals called Healers.

THE SPIRITUALISTS

See Pages 170 - 194 for Thinking/Working/Emoting *InDepths*

KEY 3: PROFILE INDEPTHS
Dominant Style of Emoting

*Emoting: An unconscious response pattern guided by unique
intangibles such as emotions, feelings, and nature.*

THE PHYSICALS

Life Purpose

Extremists are the evolutionary adventurers. Their purpose is not to integrate into society but to explore outer rims and walk edges of untried possibility in the three-dimensional world. They elbow self and soul to the front of the line, so theirs can be first hand or foot in every corner or field of endeavour.

Intimacy & Emotion

Extremists do it their own way and they go it alone; no other has a vote or say. These individuals may not need the companionship of others and may not heed social norm and mores. Their life is their own business and they conduct it according to own want or will. While physically and mentally vibrant, Extremists tend to be pain-dulled and heart dead. It seems they never bonded with anyone, not even with their primary caregivers. Early in life they seem to have decided that emotions and others would not play or share centre stage with them. Whether cellularly decided or externally influenced, Extremists are not emotionally vulnerable or available to others. They seem to have sworn an oath to "not love." Of all, they are least likely to make a commitment to others or assume responsibility for others either. Their message in all interactions, from work to mating, seems to be "Just passing through. Don't count on me."

From infancy, Extremists walk a tightrope over the valley of death, without balance bar or safety net. Their internal rheostat seems stuck on the highest adrenaline setting, which satisfies a hunger only they have and can understand. At the point where stimulation overload occurs for others, is where interest kicks in for them. As moths are drawn to the flame, Extremists are drawn to the beckoning crook of Grim Reaper's finger.

Serious games with mortality

If not tried before and death a possibility, count on Extremists to be first in line with their arm raised in fisted defiance and dare. With blueprint in hand and determination in jaw, they rush challenge's gate. They come alive the more formidable the obstacle and the less their likelihood of walking away. Fear's chill is their thrill. To them, the adrenaline pump fuels, feeds, and fulfills more than accomplishment. They don't care if the camera records or the crowd applauds, or if their name is chiselled in history or stone. What they seek and what they need are the sensations buried deep inside fear; else and other is secondary.

Few can or will understand Extremists. To most they are logical thinkers with an illogical purpose. Nothing in history, that portended or promised danger, missed their meet or defied their conquest. Where safety ends and danger begins, is where Extremists play their cat and mouse games with death.

They don't allow others to love them, particularly in the first half of their lives. Some maintain their emotional distance and detachment from others, till death do them part. Most find that by middle-age, as physical prowess declines, desires for love and intimacy increase and needs for security rise. Until they volunteer for such commitments, Extremists do not make reliable marriage partners. Words like monogamy, responsibility, and reliability are not common in their youthful vocabulary. They generally prefer loneliness to regular family life and salaried living.

As mates and parents, they tend to be of the absentee variety. Extremists are already fully committed...to a way of life where self-determined priorities take precedence over the wants and needs of others. Their personal rewards come from physical exertion; their fulfillment from subduing the environment and pursuing the elusive and impossible.

When planning a project they emphasize project success over personal safety. Others, such as mates, they may not factor at all. One reason why Extremists avoid commitment and close relationships is because they choose a lifestyle where death could be one dice roll away. They willingly, if not eagerly take chances but are reluctant to have dependent others lose as well—should the dice roll unfavourably. If they did not take life-threatening chances, if they did not place all faith in their own ability to succeed by going it alone, they would not be Extremist. By the time they leave home, they've likely developed their life pattern of uncompromising independence and dismissed the rules of society as being too restrictive.

Laws are made to be broken.

Laws of nature they seem to defy, especially during times of great peril and emergency. Laws of man they circumvent when deemed most expedient by them. Extremists have potential to be unscrupulous manipulators. Generally, they are physically attractive, confident in manner, glib of tongue, and smart. Few can, as artfully or skillfully, deceive as an Extremist, with deception in mind and plan in hand.

Of their many talents and gifts, the most outstanding is an ability to assimilate—they become one with their adversary. When focused, Extremists penetrate to the core and pulse of logic. In man, as in animal, they find the right combination of tone, word, and action to set the stage for utter trust-me persuasion. If a shorter, faster, easier way exists, Extremists will find it. That's their nature. Their thrill-of-danger need usually seeks satisfaction through physical challenges—breaking laws of nature or rewriting laws of science. Sometimes they seek thrill satisfaction through mental challenges—manipulating human nature and rearranging letters of law for man and land. Extremists don't approach any law with respect. Their approach is decided and their challenge is driven by contempt, only!

With their disregard for conformity and safety, they may be attracted to the underbelly of life. For them, the underworld where reality is re-interpreted, re-invented, or suspended altogether, can be irresistibly inviting. Negative consequences are not a deterrent. Extremists are long-used to thumbing their nose at right, wrong, shouldn't, and can't. Many tend to see themselves as a law unto themselves. If the challenge appeals and they think they can conquer, Extremists tend to try—legal or not. Whether successful or not, they're usually prepared to celebrate or suffer the consequences. For these ultra-alert individuals, being caught unawares is unlikely. Extremists can be brilliant planners, organizers, and strategists, and most creative when left to their own devices. A common personality in prison is Extremist, but they're also as commonly found in high-risk public-service occupations. Swelling the ranks of professions, such as firefighter, peace-officer, national security...et cetera, are quick-thinking, instinctive Extremists.

Seduction is their middle name.

As life mates, a poorer choice could not be made. As lovers, the best possible. For a good time call a hedonistic Extremist, but don't expect them to be tamed, be trained, or even to stay long! "One night stands" may be the length and measure of their commitment's duration. These individuals live life in the now. For them, sexual relations are more about sensory sport and play than about shared intimacy.

Mates tend to find them particularly attractive. Extremists ooze self-confidence and are often as body proud as peacocks. Because they function with precision and discipline, in the physical world, they tend to have exemplary physiques, supple and ever-primed for their next adventurous meet. Their athletic performance and ability is superior. Sexually, they're tireless! Creative and enthusiastic, they generally are more experienced in matters of sex, romance, and risque than others. However, others could more successfully till the ocean than expect a return of their love and loyalty. Enjoy their pleasurable company as can, and as may, for Extremists move on, once the novelty of new love has worn off or it threatens to be habit-forming. Variety is the spice of their sexual life. Intimacy and commitment just get in fun's way.

Emotional introspection and sharing innermost feelings with others is not usual for these individuals. Extremists are not any more plagued by self-doubt than by indecision. They rather stringently avoid the company and companionship of those who spend more time on why, than on when and how. Theirs is a most unreadable face. Extremists keep their emotions unto themselves. What others see is what they intended. When the inside story differs, no one's the wiser but them.

Two situations are very stressful for Extremists: confinement and aging. They rarely get bored; they usually don't stay in place long enough for boredom to enter, far less settle. Personal or professional situations that call for constancy of person, performance, or behaviour, only raise rebellion in them. Like caged animals, they bolt at first opportunity, regardless of how their leaving affects others. Often, Extremists choose careers that require youthful strength and specialized, athletic abilities. Because they depend on physical prowess, aging is one hardship they can't out-run, out-manoeuvre, or out-smart. For them, self-identity, self-esteem, and even earning capacity get tightly wound, wrapped, and knotted into age. For most, mid-life can be a crisis; for Extremist it can be an unravelling.

They rage, fume, and howl at the silver-haired moon of injustice, but eventually their indomitable nature does what it does best. It adjusts and takes control.

If an Extremist decides to settle down, it usually occurs at the crossroad where maturity meets and accepts mortality. They adjust their mental view and re-direct the flow of their boundless energy. Some, with newly-aroused visions of white picket fences settle into committed relationships. These individuals can be exceptionally successful business performers, once they focus their intellect on corporal challenges and set their determination on success. Many become shrewd business heads, who build financial empires in their elder years with the same logical drive and daring they once used to manipulate the world physically.

They elbow self and soul to the front of the line when the challenge is danger, but are conspicuously absent when the call goes out for emotional honesty and/or commitment. And that is unfortunate. For all their fame for bravery and ground-breaking achievement, *of all* it is most often the lone wolf Extremist who celebrates alone.

THE PHYSICALS

Life Purpose

These are the builders throughout each tunnel of time. Whether their hand held sickle, quadrant, scalpel, or shovel, they forged respect of worker and shaped human rights. They organized unions, pulled children out of mines, demanded education, defined safety and decent living, birthed public health, then fought dignity battles for freedom and vote. Realists are, evolutionarily, the passionate lovers and fighters among us. Their purpose is to give three-dimensional structure and substance to life, and they've done it with bold spirit and bodily might.

Intimacy & Emotion

Sexy, sensuous, and somatic

They have supple, well-developed physiques and seem particularly comfortable in their skin. Their characteristic and identifiable walk is purposeful; their posture tall, back straight and there's a hint of noblesse mixed with vanity in their stride and strut. Fluid, controlled in motion and exuding self-confidence, Realists move like the natural athletes they are. When physically fit, they epitomize and personify the miracle, perfection and potent of the human form; when unfit, few prove as disciplined or able to shape up as them. Their body seemingly responds to their want and will. For Realists, the human body is both tool and joy. They revel in its practicality and marvel at its beauty and pleasure capacity.

Realists love to test their own prowess and endurance in exertions of work, recreation, and pleasure. The last ones to approve of golf carts on golf courses, were Realists. For them, exertion, even exhaustion, is intrinsic with sport and fun. Competitive body-building is usually not a sport for them, though regular visits to the fitness club are style-typical. Their membership and attendance is more for body health and maintenance than for aesthetic appeal—though sex appeal is important. Realists are the most sexually assertive, experimental, and aggressive of all. Compared to others, they are least concerned with dictates of fashion or stereotyping of beauty. To them all human bodies are beautiful. But then, these are highly confident beings—fully clothed or butt naked.

The eternal, proverbial "Red Hot Lovers"

Realists live life physically. They understand their world by touch, taste, sound and smell, and they express their emotions through carnal recreation. For them, sex is one of life's greatest pleasures. They are renown for being highly skilled, enthusiastic lovers. Irresistible, irrepressible, and generous, they seldom lack for partners nor are they patient with mates of lukewarm libido.

In physical intimacies, they relish the challenge of the quest, the art of seduction, and erotic explorations. From atop passion's wake, they ride the rhythmic flow of physical sensations. With each yielding pulse and beckoning vibration, they welcome ecstacy's meet and energy's release. Sexual role-playing games—bondage, domination—were likely first practiced by them. For most, sex is primarily an emotional experience. For this personality, sex is life affirmation and self-fulfillment, (an understanding that's equivalent to "Relationship Success 101" for their mate).

Realists have difficulty comprehending puritanical attitudes or accepting the social strictures placed on sexual behaviour. Personal commitment, tenderness, or love, are viewed as being outside the domain, and outside their definition, of sexual relations. It's highly likely that Swinger Clubs and other private institutions that pander to personal pleasures are Realist innovations. For them, sex is a purely physical expression of lust; more about animal-instinct and human health than emotionality. "What's love got to do with it?" is a Realist question.

It's a plain, drab cookie without the sweet of chocolate and the crunch of nuts...and life would certainly be blander without the decadent, chewy Realist. They work and play hard; they help others readily; they seduce quicker; they stand on guard, stand in line; they mend the fence, pilot the plane and clear the path for others; but they may not walk there, themselves. They may be here, there and everywhere, but like to stay one arm's length from *hug*.

In social situations they stay outside the perimeter of personal involvement, until comfortable in their environment and confident of being accepted before they'll participate directly. In all other situations Realists make themselves at home, by pitching in and earning acceptance through "doing." While physically and sexually expressive, Realists avoid emotional intimacy. They willingly offer the sweat of their brow, the shirt off their back, their laughter, good humour, and wit, but when it comes to close relations they turn away from intimacy's bonding embrace. Others may interpret this reluctance as lack of care or fear of commitment; neither is true. What they fear most is trusting others. Passionate and capable of scaling the fullest range of experiences, Realists too-often deny the existence of heartfelt emotions and avoid sharing and explaining innermost truth with others.

Achilles' heel

The unique complexity of their physical dimension can be both blessing and curse...the latter most especially in close relations and relationships. Realists are physiologically predisposed to feel first, think second and emote last. When provoked or frustrated they tend to physically react rather than vocalize. These individuals process all information physically, through their body, before intellectually assimilating, accepting or reasoning. When aroused their physical dimension can overwhelm their mental functioning and cause them to respond before logic can raise caution's flag or prescribe action. Although these instinctive reactions can spawn extraordinary and even famous professional accomplishments—in sport competitions or emergency situations—for instance; personally, they may manifest as violent outbursts or intense sexual activity. Sexual encounters tend to be harmless, mindless escapes: purely physical expression. The outbursts, however, can be destructive. Explosive tempers are trademark and Achilles' heel for this personality style.

Red flags

Frustration and criticism are red flags for Realists. Fiercely independent by nature, they prefer taking things apart to understand. They'd rather be lost than ask for directions and it is with some certainty that an associate of Realist prompted, "If all else fails, read the manual." They have great confidence in their own competence and can easily become impatient with self when unable to solve problems. Quite likely, the impatience that feeds their frustration is the erroneous echoes of intellectual self-doubt stemming from earliest school days. Innately proud Realists are particularly sensitive to criticism, which they take personally and harder than most. To them, criticism's sting is equivalent to being slapped and humiliated. When provoked, Realists can quickly lose their temper. Once "steam" has released they just as quickly cool down. Seldom do Realists hold a grudge and they expect close others not to either.

Once pent-up anger has dissipated, expressing their feelings about the incident and explaining the real cause of their emotional outburst can be near-impossible for Realists. Self-loathing, remorse and feelings of embarrassment prevent them from sharing their truth. (They'd rather say nothing, than lie). Realists may or may not affix blame, but will internalize disappointment at their loss of control. Others tend to not cross swords with them twice, which may account for the intense loneliness and sense of detachment these tribal beings can and do suffer. While others become wary, pull back or walk away, Realists tend to withdraw emotionally—and physically if possible, for periods of time.

Beneath the fine physiques, determined jaws, and ready laughter are highly sensitive natures held in close-checked secrecy. Fearing yet expecting abandonment or rejection, Realists are reluctant to share intimate relationships with others. As one Realist stated, "Maybe they'll forgive me for losing my head, but I'm not sure I could forgive myself for losing my heart when they leave. Losing them is easier than losing me." Their explosive tempers tend to serve as warning to others who get too close to their emotional sanctuary. Unbeknownst to their mates, most Realists live extremely private lives in their heads. Intense longings, vulnerabilities and needs simmer untended and unfulfilled, behind the fear-fuelled huff and puff of dragon-like temper.

The right mate can make all the difference

Few personalities are strong enough to go in and get these individuals. Most wilt at their bark and run from their bite, not realizing that the door to Realist hearts is, at these times, vulnerable and open. Trust must be earned. With direct, action-oriented Realists, intimations of affection or declarations of love just will not do. They need neon-clear proof of acceptance. Keep in mind that this is the big sister and big brother personality. When all-hell breaks loose, Realists are the ones others call first, and for good reason. Realists don't let others down. They're expected to be strong...so they are. They're expected to look out for others...so they do. No child of a Realist goes hungry or is unsheltered. That's just the way these ones are: responsible and reliable from beginning to end. But the question that dangles unasked and unanswered is, "who can Realists count on to be there for them, when their fan sputters or spews?"

Heart of gold

They make love with rare passion and skill, expressing physically the emotions they fear sharing or daring with words. They may never be able to vocalize the depth or truth of their feelings but with the right mate, they may find they are loved for more than the steadfast security and strong support they provide. Often, Realists feel more loved for their contributions or paycheques than loved for their person. They may find that when they snarl and spit they have a mate who does not challenge or run, but who loves enough to encourage and even demand explanation for greater understanding and broader acceptance. It takes an equally confident, equally strong personality to melt their reluctant, hidden heart of pure gold. While Realists look out for and look after others, few mates are capable of reciprocating in-like, in return.

It is likely for Realists that the caution "count to ten before acting" is intended. These passionate lovers and fighters are the evolutionary architects, who breathe form and substance into all manner and people-matter of life. Historically, they've done it responsibly and dependably, more than earning their right to be loved, admired and applauded at centre stage. Count to ten Realist, then take a bow—not a bite.

THE INSTINCTIVES

Scintillator

Life Purpose

This personality personifies warm sunshine, convivial laughter and hail-good-fellow heartiness. When dark clouds gather, they are the ones with silver-lining already in pocket. They've been called fickle, capricious, lazy and funny. Their historical fame is optimism; their evolutionary name is Scintillator. If pessimists weigh one side of life's teeter-totter, Scintillators weigh the other. Their purpose is to remind all that life is more ripe with joy than rift by sorrow. No matter the test, tisk or task, the soul is happier, the mind is quicker and the step lighter throughout, when laughter and appreciation accompany.

Intimacy & Emotion

"People who need people are the luckiest people in the world." For others, these may just be words from Barbra Streisand's classic song. For Scintillators it is the song of life. As for the luck part, well...that depends on whether Scintillator is carrying their own mirror or not.

Scintillators are first and foremost physical beings. They filter life through their physical dimension and bodily react before their intellectual and emotional dimensions have opportunity to get involved. Scintillators are kinesthetic beings who learn by physically interacting with the world. They also generate one of the largest energy fields that, like the geyser Old Faithful, ever-brews and seeks internal-pressure release.

Regardless of age, Scintillators are characteristically the fidgeters and squirmers among us. The ones who work and worry chairs with incessant tap, shuffle, scratch and shift. Being regularly reprimanded for restless behaviour and distracting animation is common for Scintillator children.

Their energy-intellect is so sonar-sophisticated and sensitive, Scintillators can bodily feel energy moods of others or rooms. Before intellectual or emotional dimensions have time to analyze and prescribe action, their body responds instinctively. For them, and all physical beings, body-instinct can be blessing or curse. How Scintillator children cope with their physical nature has life-long consequences.

No other as tribal-dependent

Scintillators are people-pleasers whose greatest desire is unconditional acceptance from others. As infants they fuss less, smile more and talk earlier than others. By the age of three they've already established a lifelong, apple-of-the-eye relationship with one or both parents. One characteristic of Scintillator children is stand-out attractiveness, and don't they know it.

These little tykes soon develop a fussiness about aspects of their small world, such as: favourite food and how they like it prepared; clothes they will or will not wear; neatness of appearance and wardrobe; a habit of smelling their food or taking rabbit nibble pre-tastes before eating; and a fastidiousness about personal hygiene. They master early the art of converting physical assets into personal advantages; usually to charm their way out of trouble or to worm their way into another's affection.

Scintillator children are openly affectionate and playful. They prefer the company of adults and older siblings, who are often enchanted by their pint-sized antics and precocity. It doesn't take them long to realize that adult appreciation and applause comes quicker and rings louder than that of their peers.

Many child actors and models are Scintillators...not only because of their attractiveness but because of their distinct eagerness to please. With praise they can be encouraged to go that extra mile or put forth that extra effort when needed. Scintillators like others to be happy, especially with them. As they mature, they tend to trade on their physical comeliness more often than others. Generally, these are the Peter Pans who look and often act younger than their chronological age. They are also the ones who suffer great insecurities about growing old.

A gift for comedy and entertainment

Some personalities are peacocks, some perfectionists, some are schemers, some dreamers, but Scintillators are the songbirds. They brighten the day, the way and the world with their Pollyanna optimism, winsome smiles and melodious laughter. They have evolutionarily been the Court Jesters—the quick-thinking provocateurs in royal households. Scintillators are as athletic of mind as of body and harbour an artistic nature, as though born to perform and create. They are particularly astute at summing up complex situations and tying all neatly together with comic twist or glib bow. Keen observation and comic interpretation are this style's gifts.

Scintillators filter life through their physical body, so their life approach tends to be more reactive than proactive—and can be more harmful than beneficial. In the acting profession there's a maxim, "the more specific, the better the performance." Whether life imitates art or art imitates life, the wisdom rings equally true: excellence rests at the bottom of moments. Finding it and bringing it out is a drown-deep dive, where all dimensions—physical/mental/emotional are focused and risked before best reveals. They tend to relate and react one-dimensionally: physically. Limiting their choices and experiences to what's floating on life's surface. Could be cream? Could be scum? By not risking, by not immersing their whole in challenges presented, Scintillators are left with two options: take it or leave it.

Belief is mind-knowledge, the sum of which is identity. Ego is identity's representative that interacts with the world according to, and in accordance with, each individual's belief. Scintillators have fine, even superior identities and large, strong egos to represent it. If a human mind is a terrible thing to waste, how much more terrible is it, to ignore potential? Of all, none hears more often, "Not living up to potential," than Scintillators do.

With all their God-given gifts, such as intellect; physical attractiveness; deftness of hand, foot, and mouth; kinesthetic memory; robust constitution; optimistic nature; and energy-sensitivity as accurate as sonar to dolphin, Scintillators still tend to settle for toe-dipping rather than deep-diving explorations. Why is this personality the one most likely to: be *daddy's little girl* or *momma's boy* far into adulthood; be financially struggling at middle-age; have multiple marriages and divorces; have addictions to drugs or alcohol; and be the ones who abandon their children, physically, emotionally, and financially? Because Scintillators subscribe to physical satisfaction rather than emotional fulfillment.

Satisfaction versus fulfillment

If every life experience were a jawbreaker confection, Scintillators stop at physical satisfaction. They suck their jawbreaker until the licorice-flavoured coating is removed, then spit out the rest. Emotional fulfillment is had by savouring the whole of the jawbreaker experience; appreciating the inherent complexity within the variety of colour and flavour layers and discovering the unexpected surprise at the end: a lowly spice seed. A bitter tasting seed perhaps, but in the tasting contrast, two messages are folded. One reminds of all the sweetness and wonder that went before; the other rewards with forever learning the secret of jawbreakers: their humble, bitter-brown beginning. Such lessons and rewards only reveal after commitment of self through time to discover more flavours than licorice and more sweet than bitter...in jawbreakers and in life.

The Achilles' heel for Scintillators is abandonment, which they expect to happen if or when they disappoint others. When relationship responsibilities grow and commitment roots are called for, Scintillators tend to leave rather than chance disappointment—their equivalent of personal failure. When disagreements occur and nose-to-nose accountability seems inevitable, Scintillators tend to head for the door rather than stand their ground and clear issues. Though cowardice seeming, cowardice has nothing to do with it. The cause and culprit is physical pain.

Scintillators filter everything, first, through their tuning-fork-sensitive physical body. They feel first, react, and only later review the emotional and intellectual consequences. Positive feedback is pleasurable; it feels good. They react by staying physically in the moment, allowing their emotional and intellectual dimensions to experience the fun. Negative feedback, such as confrontation, is felt as physical pain; it hurts. As others reflex-jerk from flame, Scintillators reflex-retreat from confrontation. Sometimes they can step back long enough for reason and emotions to kick in; sometimes the pain is so sharp and quick they strike out in mindless self-defense. Most often, they're so overwhelmed they must leave. Only when pain subsides can they rationally appraise the situation. By then they've often got two problems to deal with: the one that precipitated the argument, and the one caused by their exit.

When they return, (and they always do), others have stewed in frustration juices long enough to have drawn their own, usually unfavourable, conclusions. Scintillators are left with few options: one is accepting blame for having disappointed. Others would not be so quick to judge them cowardly or so quickly write these sensitive beings off, if they could but once walk in their shoes and experience how physically painful confrontation is to Scintillators. These individuals are often more a victim of their innate energy-gift than benefactor.

If for some it is true, "I am what I think," for Scintillators it is usually, "I am what you think I am." Like children, they do not separate self from issues. For them, confrontation is a one-way ticket destined for rejection; tantamount to throwing the baby out with the bath water. Leaving is not cowardice; its self-preservation. When they do return to the "scene of their crime," they fully expect to first meet rejection, then abandonment. For people-pleasing dependents, abandonment is the greatest fear of all. Scintillators tend to leave before that shoe can drop.

Svengalis and King Makers could not find more malleable, willing clay than Scintillators

The single greatest challenge for Scintillators is to develop a strong belief in self; to trust no image other than the one reflected in their hand-held mirror. The greatest challenge for others in relationships with Scintillators is to ensure that if continuance is intended, that intention be made clear before and during confrontation. It is difficult for others to understand that Scintillators need to feel confident that no matter what, they're still okay with others...especially with mates.

Most Scintillators have only experienced such unconditional acceptance from one or both doting parents. They understood their Scintillator child's need to run at the drop of anger's hat, knowing that as soon as they'd had time to think, they'd return ready to deal with contentious issues. Scintillators may spend most of their adult lives looking for a mate just like the mate that married dear old mom or dad.

Few personalities depend on the encouragement and positive feedback of others, like Scintillators do. Fewer yet, reply and repay with such passion, irrepressible enthusiasm, or potential to raze mountain and move world as them…when unconditional support is given. These individuals must exercise high discretion in choosing a mate. The right life-partner (and right work and educational environment) can make all the difference to them, in terms of professional success and personal happiness.

As dream to desire, as want to need, sex for Scintillators is self-confirmation. Physical coupling confirms what cannot be asked or dared aloud. *Do you love me? Is my love safe here? Could we…can we…will we ever and always be?* Receiving a "no," from others, Scintillator hearts can't bear to hear. "No," from loved ones is devastating for them. In fleshly explore of sensation's full gamut and range, in aggression, submission, in lust's want and wane, they question with body but listen with soul. As energy beckons, they go. As emotions rise, they meet, lead, follow, and flow. For them, please is reason, pleasure is proof, and release their self-confirming reward. Scintillators validate continuance of love and union, through sexual relations. They are extraordinary lovers—energetic, enthusiastic, and experimental—when confident of their own irrefutable and indisputable importance to their mate.

Scintillators are energy-intellects who feel acceptance or rejection from others. For them, reality is that which they can directly control. When children, they performed, socialized and directly influenced outcomes. When adult, those long-habituated, manipulative skills work equally well, generally. Scintillators often become masters of seduction. They can cajole, humour, and often directly control and maintain their required positive energy-flow.

When unable to charismatically influence they may seek alternate means of maintaining their good-feeling high. Medicine cabinets of Scintillators tend to be well-stocked with pharmacological fixes. If Scintillators use tobacco, they will have their first cigarette shortly after feet hit the floor after waking. Chocoholics, or those "sweet-tooths" among us, often are dominant Scintillator in the working or emoting realms of their Profile.

They seem to need a certain level of body energy to function effectively and will—by hook or by crook—attain and sustain it. Scintillators are addiction-prone. Conversely and notably, they're also health, fitness and nutrition innovators. Their bodies are generally so sensitive they can feel the energy ambiance of a room upon entering, and from the doorway decide, "go," or "stay". Their energy-guided hands can give a body massage seemingly beyond mortal capability. No other constitution is as responsive or benefits as quickly from proper diet and regular exercise, as theirs. Scintillators bounce back, comparatively.

The two challenges for Scintillators entail responsibility

The first is to stop running when it hurts. Instead, start digging. Go deep, then deeper. Underneath the pain is your self-mirror...one that no other can hold, shatter or break. The image reflected therein is clear and true. Trust it. Trust you. The second is communicate feelings. No matter how painful, no matter how tentative or shaky those coltish legs initially, know that your voice will steady and grow strong with use. Otherwise, you may not ever discover the complexity, the wonder in all the layers, flavours, and possibilities within that marvelous human confection, the Scintillator jawbreaker. To repudiate your own birth gifts, of which you've many, is to diminish greatness to fool and deny potential that is the unique privilege of Scintillators.

People who need people may be the luckiest people, but for Scintillator, luck is not enough. Their evolutionary purpose is to BE the people, other people need.

THE INSTINCTIVES

entinel

Life Purpose

In fingers of undulating illume, at outskirts of pale ether light, distinguished and distinguishable they stand, readied and alert. Their beauty is beguilingly persuasive, though approaching them is cautionary. Their mien dissuades.

Meet Sentinel—the vigilant shepherd who has with time-honoured loyalty served as opposer of oppression and defender of the discarded, distressed, and downtrodden. Upon their shoulders is the scale of justice balanced, throughout time, in all temperature and for all reason. Their purpose is to detect shifts between human right and human wrong; to forewarn, reform and restore equilibrium. Lady Justice may need to be blind but not Sentinels. Their ears and eyes are eternally prised open.

Intimacy & Emotion

In a glance, Sentinels see more and hear more than most. Although these individuals potentially rank among world-class thinkers, their real genius lies in their highly sophisticated, physical *sensory* dimension— their most trusted guide in relations and relationships. Through keen observation, muscular instinct and sensory antennae, Sentinels glean understanding faster and quicker than by logic alone. Behind their characteristic calm reserve and alluring attractiveness, is an individual who's hard to know and love. Trust is the wall that divides.

Whether Sentinel trust is an open or shut case, depends on how each has evolved and adjusted to three typical personality-determinants: language, loyalty, and new experiences.

Language

Because their native language is literal versus figurative, it may take Sentinel children longer to communicate with words and in sentences. This does not mean they are slow in thinking or developing. Stringing words together is what they seem reluctant to do, despite having ably communicated their wants early and often since infancy. They often use gesture, garble or whatever means most effective, for expressing their state of contentment rather than relying on words to do their bidding. Their non-talking is reflective of the greater time it takes to translate one-dimensional literal into figurative expression, and their characteristic, innate caution about being misunderstood. When Sentinels do begin speaking, they usually start with clear voice and full sentences.

For Sentinels, tangibles, like trees, are the same for them as for everyone, but intangibles, like feelings, are a solid lump that first needs to be sorted out by experience...individually labelled to align external information with internal sensations...then stored in physical - mental - emotional - libraries for future reference. Characteristically, these infants are the little songbirds that "coo, prattle, and preen" phonetically, earlier and more often than peers. They may speak later, but they are entertaining little companions and sing-song canaries throughout and have no trouble making their presence or wants known. It is not unusual for Sentinel toddlers to have trained the whole household to respond to their guttural commands and pointed demands.

Loyalty

These children feel safe and comfortable in a small, intimate world, often only trusting parents, siblings, and known faces. It is a Sentinel child that refuses to eat food prepared other than by mother or refuses to sleep other than at home. When they bond with others, they are concrete-committed and fiercely devoted. No other personality style, as child or adult, is as loyal as them. Sentinel toddlers will step forward to defend siblings in conflict with all others, even challenging their parents. They can be fearless defenders of loved ones, loved causes and are hands-down the last personality to trust strangers. When the doorbell rings, these little tykes may start at the noise, then dash for the safety of parental arms before the door opens.

Sentinel children are quite dependent on others, especially parents, for learning. When unconfident or when feeling unsafe, they are reluctant to explore beyond the confines of their small, safe world of family and home. They will either ask for, or endlessly seek through manner or action, confirmation of their indispensability—and each time must receive clear affirmation. Only when confident that all is okay on the home front, will these individuals venture further than their own safe hearth.

With encouragement, with each successful new experience and understanding gained, does their independence grow. One recommendation for parents of Sentinel children, (all children of course, but these ones most particularly)—reassure them constantly of being loved and do not make light of their terror when left in the care of a baby sitter. To Sentinel children, it is not Mom and Dad stepping out for a while, it is their world that's ending when that front door shuts and divides.

New experiences...at any age

Parents will know their children are Sentinel if sudden sounds—like turning on the vacuum or starting the lawn mower—upset them, requiring they be physically comforted and reassured. Even if they are watching the vacuum or mower being set up, the "sound explosion" can set off the fright/flight instincts of these ultra-sensitive, sensory beings...until they physically, mentally, and emotionally associate burst of sound with harmless machine. In fact, taking them by the hand and introducing them to the world around them is tantamount to dousing high-octane fuel on Sentinel's intellectual and confidence development.

Their minds are remarkable. Their sensory-intellect extraordinary, yet both can be easily tripped by new experiences. New gives rise to new emotions. No matter how many emotions already experienced and on tap in their *reference library*, emotions are unpredictable and demanding...two conditions that alarm Sentinels most particularly. New also entails adjustment or change, for which these children require more time and patience than others. When overwhelmed, Sentinels' instinctive nature is fright, then flight. If flight is not possible, they may—at any age, withdraw internally. Without a point of reference already existing in their physical/mental/emotional library, new is potentially threatening, something to be wary of and something that must be solved (understood internally) before responding externally.

That time-suspended stillness, that look of fixed-concentration is uniquely characteristic of Sentinels. None other portrays mind-at-work, as they do. When immediate reply is called for, others may wonder whether they've been understood or not, only to be shortly surprised at the thoroughness and depth of Sentinel's reply. (Stupidity cannot seem to take root in these individuals, though stubbornness be known to flourish—and sometimes bears a remarkable resemblance to stupidity). When immediate action is called for, Sentinels may halt—then, as if suddenly nicked by a hot poker, respond deliberately and confidently. These are the ones others want beside them when trouble visits. Regardless of cause, whenever "gut" tenses or unfamiliar emotional feelings are experienced,

Sentinels need time to digest the information and appropriately label the flood of emotions before offering remedy or determining action. On-the-fly creativity is not their strong suit, as these individuals are logical, thus respecters of procedure and known.

Uniquely, Sentinels can at want or will function in one, two or all three dimensions. When forced into environments with strangers, such as day care facilities, these hyper-alert children develop coping strategies for their own protection. When something hurts, such as seeing disappointment in a loved one's eyes, they turn off emotionally. When something confuses and frightens (like new does), they turn off mentally and emotionally, and function purely by gut-instinct. No matter what the cause of concern, confusion or pain, their first stress-response is to turn off emotionally. Coping withdrawal does not seem to interfere with learning or affect their ability to function capably. It does, however, increase their reluctance to risk expressing or sharing with others until external proof of acceptance is given and received.

Being forced or pushed into trying new things or being ridiculed for not being braver does nothing but increase their caution, increase their reticence and decrease their curiosity.

Sentinels learn at their own pace and that speed is determined by how much they trust others to be there for them, if or when needed. That trust-yardstick is Sentinel's relationship guide throughout life. Without unconditional trust firmly in hand, Sentinels tend to avoid taking risks, personally and professionally. They may choose to homestead on first base, held back by their fear of the unknown second...third...and other possibilities in life's game. None other has instinctual-intellect comparable to Sentinels, yet these individuals are often the most reluctant to untie and unwrap their success-loaded gifts.

Too often they rely solely on gut-instinct and ignore their other trust-worthy and powerful guide: emotions. Two creatives—in Sentinels' case, gut and emotions—can accomplish almost anything and overcome the impossible, when both are focused on the same objective: truth. Emotions never contradict gut or mind, but mind can conflict with emotions by overriding them. The emotional truth bell for Sentinels rings in gut, not in mind. Too often, however, they dismiss truth as indigestion. It has been observed that a rut is nothing more than a grave with the ends knocked out. No other personality lives an emotional rut as do Sentinels. None other suffers like them either.

Guts and Ruts...a dangerous combination

The Achilles' heel of Sentinels is emotions, but their real ball-and-chain is reticence—non-expression of emotional truth with others. One consequence is skepticism. Sentinels look for reasons to not trust, to avoid or to bow out of the game. What their keen eyes and ears are scanning and searching for are reasons to doubt. They tend to regularly find the deceit and deception they're looking for. Their look of aloofness is often more than skin deep. It can go clear through to soul. Soul is the seat of emotionality and one place Sentinels choose not to visit.

Soul transcends logic. It is a promise of eternity which Sentinels tend to view as highly unlikely. Understandably, the concept of life-after-death stirs their skeptic-kettle. They're prone to mental myopia: if it cannot be proven, it does not exist. Historically, they are staunch supporters of Cartesian thinking, where beginnings and endings are rational, provable and predictable. Emotions defy such description and pat definition. They have neither beginning nor end but undulate unceasingly in varying degrees of intensities, from pleasure to pain. Emotions rise unbidden, unmindful and Sentinels tend not to trust them—in self or in others.

They may appear aloof but if truth were known, logic...gut...and emotions are usually at war inside Sentinels.

Their approach, generally, is to not risk action or offer information, unless confident of being right. By hiding emotions behind poker-face calm they avoid detection of their fears and vulnerabilities. These self-sufficient individuals, whether child or adult, often need others to encourage them to express how they feel, and to help them find the right words to define, catalogue, and most importantly, share that confusing, emotional aspect of self. Proof of emotional reticence or inability to express is diary or journal-keeping.

Those who practice this discipline are not prepared to emotionally and directly experience and are not willing to share what's going on inside. Compelled, nevertheless, they record their most intimate thoughts and feelings. Once having set all on paper, they close and lock their books and squirrel them away in some private place. In actuality, it is emotions they shelve. Sentinels are the number-one keepers of diaries and personal journals. That means there are many unspoken words, many hidden passions, many suppressed desires and unresolved issues out there. Sentinel emoting style is very common. A lot of people are not talking and not sharing their truth. According to Ansir's research to-date, Sentinel is the number one Emoting Style.

Everything that begins, must end

No thought, no word, no action is more painful to these sensitive beings, than "good-bye." So ingrained is their conviction that "all good must come to an end," Sentinels may not risk "hello"...especially when it comes to matters of heart. They don't count on a better tomorrow, instead they process the day as it comes and as demand dictates. To them, happily ever after only happens in Fairy tales, and forget that silver-lining crap,. The only thing that comes from dark clouds is rain.

Diligents may very well be the "Missourians" in terms of prove it first, but Sentinels tend not to consider possibilities unless Missouri certifies it. Unless and until all they deem necessary has passed their critical inspection and personal test, these individuals tend not to chance or risk love. Many settle at "heavy like" on the relationship barometer rather than love. The former requires unwavering loyalty, their particular specialty; the latter requires greater investments—truth and self.

Love cannot exist unless both parties are willing, eager in fact, to "get naked." That means exchanging vulnerabilities with one other who could complete and fulfill. One who says and means, "Sweetheart, all before you were too early and all that follow, too late," is what Sentinels need to hear and feel before trusting and knowing. That's the kind of truth their guts are preternaturally predisposed to recognizing and understanding.

When the truth of another rings loud and clear for them, no matter how long it takes for that clapper to loosen, the unique beauty and wonder that is uniquely Sentinel unfolds. It is not that Sentinels need others to tell them what to feel, as much as they need others to tell them "it's okay to feel and safe to express."

These are the ones who jump into the fray, who stand beside when most wouldn't, couldn't and won't. These are the ones who fear the most that others will not find them loveable or worthy of loving, should their good, bad and ugly be known. Sentinels need proof that its safe, before bringing their hearts into play. "It is not possible to love another, unless love of self is had first," may apply to every other personality style, but not to these individuals. Without their need to have others prove trustworthiness...they would not be Sentinel at all.

Trust, their greatest challenge

It is common for these individuals to stunt their own potential's growth by avoiding risk or change when logic invites or opportunity knocks. Too often they settle for the bird in the hand, rather than beating the bush for more challenging or fulfilling alternatives. Difficulty in trusting others can lead to loneliness. Sentinels know more about loneliness than most do.

If trusted others lie, cheat or betray them, their instinctive response is to immediately amputate relations—a situation that causes them great emotional distress and may take years for them to come to terms with. They would rather not trust others, not allow them in now, than suffer betrayal and loss later. The phrase, "I don't want to be owned," may have prevented many a Sentinel from making a marital commitment, but not from pursuing and having relationships. Why? Because their physical and attractiveness and their aloof reserve assures them of constant companionship, should that be their wish. Autonomy is necessary for them and they usually set the pace and tone in the relationship. However, as Dorothy discovered the kindly old man behind the Wizard's fearsome facade, behind the bark of independent righteous claim is a need that begs further investigation.

Is it safe?

Sentinels find fulfillment helping to provide a safe and fair world for others. As in gift buying, what one gives is often what one would most like to receive. They want to trust another, they want to feel safe and they want to be nurtured, exclusively and privately. What they do not want is the responsibility for the first romantic introductions or the painful consequences of disappointment. Come hell or high water, mates know they can count on their Sentinel partner to be there when wanted and when needed most. Once they've said they will, they DO. When they vow to be there, they mean "through thick and thin, for better or worse, and till death do us part." Until they make that commitment, however, Sentinels may be the most trying, frustrating and unreliable dating "material" of all.

Honesty and Truth...not the same thing

Sentinels are willingly honest, but purposely untruthful with others. Honesty is based on knowledge. It is possible to be honest by giving the pat answer, delivering the line most widely accepted or most thoroughly proven, though personal truth disagrees. Honesty is sufficient for getting by in the outside world but what happens when emotional truth differs? Where do emotions go when not used, when suppressed, when denied? In the case of Sentinels, they pent and build and like an acid bath, burble, burn and chew inside. Truth is person-specific and only comes from the place where individuality lives: in emotions. Others can dictate what each will think, do, and say, but no other can dictate or predict how another will feel. What each feels is unique unto self—and it's an inviolate, self-truth that's speaking.

Sentinels start life having to sort through, familiarize selves with, then label emotions. As children, they depend on parents and trusted others to help them understand what they're feeling, and even need confirmation whether their feelings are right, wrong, good, or bad. By definition, Sentinels don't trust emotions, as child or adult. That is why they require so much proof and why potential mates find the pathway leading to Sentinel hearts, strewn with land mines, surrounded by barbed wire and lined with sharp-shooters.

With, "What's the point? It's all going to end anyway," resounding in head, and goodbye gurgling in their gut, Sentinels are often too afraid of their own truth and their own vulnerability to love without concrete proof of trust. Why expose themselves needlessly? Their famed reserve hides the passionate being within, their pessimistic words belie their optimistic-wishes, their unruffable, sombre mask restrains enthusiasm. If everything that begins ends, why put their heart through such an ordeal for "goodbye?"

If by nature, they are skeptical and by choice reticent, then one question begs answer. Is there a causal relationship between reticence and the fact that Sentinels suffer internal degenerative illnesses, more often than others? Digestion diseases, like ulcers and colitis...and organ failure diseases, like heart and kidney are suffered by Sentinels at an earlier age, comparatively. For all, emotional reticence can be a grief-bearing issue; for Sentinels it may be of death-bearing significance. What is eating Sentinels from the inside out? What is causing that internal acid bath that dissolves their chance for happiness, fulfillment...and health? What is it, that is so personally destructive when held in, when not expressed, not risked, dared or shared? It could be something they swallow, something indigestible that burns internally and incessantly. Perhaps, emotional truth?

Each individual lives life by choice. No step taken, a mistake, no person met, insignificant, no circumstance, coincidental, and no decision if truthfully made, wrong for each. Sentinels often perceive themselves as processors of life. If the poster reads, "Life's a bitch, then you die," the poster boy/girl would be Sentinel. Where each walks, sits or stands is a record of what choices each has made in order to arrive at that place and time. Sentinels may be skeptical by nature, but beyond that, everything is choice. They choose emotional reticence, they choose internal dissolution, and even self-dissolvement.

Generally, Sentinel disdains public displays of affection. By gentle touch or meaningful glance, they publicly convey endearment and affection to their mate. Intimacy is a private matter. Sexually, they are robust and rambunctious. Sex is one arena that their trademark composure and reserve melts fast, and falls faster away. They may not be romantically assertive, preferring that others instigate introductions, but Sentinel enjoys sexual experimentation and physical expressions. They may not equate sexual relations with intimacy, unless legally confirmed (married), or emotionally committed. Nor are Sentinels of the one-night-stand genre. They like to know the inner workings of their mate before engaging in sex. Finding a mate strong enough to draw them out emotionally can be a problem for Sentinel. They feel intensely yet have trouble expressing, admitting, or submitting to their own vulnerability.

Few personalities are natural matches for Sentinels. Too often they look for mates who allow them to hide emotionally and who can be controlled by relationship obligation or dependence. It is not at all uncommon for Sentinels, who disdain manipulation in others, to be highly manipulative in their personal relationships. They often choose mates of a pleasing, compliant nature over emotional-intellects, who initially seem like "bitter medicine" to Sentinels (though not for long). They prefer mates who will accept their offer of loyalty, reliability and partnership, in exchange for affection and companionship. What occurs most often is a relationship where the meter reads safe, but doesn't go high enough to read passion. It is a rare Sentinel who is disloyal to mate.

Self-fulfillment cannot be had without intimacy; intimacy cannot exist without vulnerability; and vulnerability is not possible without unconditional trust. Nothing is harder for Sentinels than trusting another with their emotional all. Potential mates are expected to go hunting, headlong...headstrong...and undeterred for Sentinel hearts. A journey they want and expect others to make, without them having to risk their own truth or vulnerability. "You first," is their preference.

While the qualifying process may seem demanding and their emotion-barometer seemingly broken, once trustworthiness has been proven, few blossom into love and loyalty as fair-minded Sentinels do. It is a sign of their internal need and desire to trust that Sentinels keep diaries or journals of their *feeling* experiences. Without proof that its safe, and without encouragement from others to trust their emotions, they may not explore the full range of their natural ability or innate lovability.

Risking more will allow the many rather than the few, to get to know what Sentinel love and loyalty are all about. That certainly would be a two-way global benefit. What good is a hardly-used heart at life's end? Wear it out while here, as you can't take it with you. Only souls go on.

Note: Development through the three typical personality-determinants (at the beginning of Emoting), determines whether each emotes Sentinel as an adult. Those are the lessons Sentinels are all currently working on; regardless of age.

THE LOGICALS

Diligent

Life Purpose

With stiff upper lip and in starched collar ease, they stand amidst pillars of power and as pillars of society. Their position and entitlement is logic borne and won. Steady stoics of public and parlour, they measure distance from tomorrow by yardsticks of today. As predictable in nature as green grass to spring, reality is not willed in labs of want by them, but cultivated in beakers of reason. Meet Diligent, the one who has evolutionarily tethered and tied growth to the anchor of prudence and pride. Their purpose is to protect progress by intellectually monitoring its path and sounding future's alarm, should obstacles present or impede.

Intimacy & Emotion

To others, they may seem devoid of emotion. A perception more marrow right than skin-worn. Diligents often make a conscious decision to avoid emotional expression and seem tight-lipped determined to remain so. Emotional honesty is a challenge for most. For perfectionistic Diligent, it usually goes far beyond challenge's mere.

These individuals filter life through intellect, selectively siphoning off tangibles and logicals. They then test each morsel of possibility—first for wholesomeness, then for palatability. Nibbling, they compare each new taste against the familiar, using smells like fish, tastes like chicken evaluations. When found agreeable and supportable, the bit is ingested, digested and absorbed as reality. Life screenings that do not pass their criteria's discrimination are labeled extraneous, irrelevant, and summarily discarded to their nonsense heap. For Diligents, reality is a well-trodden, narrow path between tried and true. So crowded is their path with logic there's neither room nor tolerance enough for emotions to walk.

Every parent raises their child in hopes they be smart, be good and lead successful, happy lives. Diligent children usually personify such parental aspirations. This is the well-behaved child, seemingly self-motivated to get the good grades. The child who abides law of home, man, religion, and biology; helps the elderly cross the street; doesn't pick fights; pitches in responsibly at home and community; puts after school earnings in the bank; graduates high school, college, university; gets a solid job; marries a solid mate; brings the 2.3 grandchildren home for Sunday dinner and is throughout, an upstanding model of competence and reliability. If true—that living by the book of orthodoxy leads to success and fulfillment—then Diligents are the most professionally successful and personally fulfilled of all planet beings.

Are they?

Work is the main realm of functioning for this personality style. To that end they are truly remarkable. Diligents are perfectionistic, reliable, intelligent beings; the cartilage in the backbone of industrial growth, evolutionarily speaking. Logical, critical thinkers, they organize projects into systems and execute plans meticulously. In the child's tale of The Three Little Pigs it was the Diligent brother that built his house of brick and saved the day for the others.

These individuals build their careers, their lives, their loves, one smart brick atop another. Their mortar is a mix of intellect and practicality; and intolerant of mistakes. Diligents don't like being wrong or being accused of such. When they err, they err on the side of caution. "Better safe than sorry," and, "A fool and his money are soon parted" are the kind of wisdoms Diligents live by and promote. Whether because of too high of expectations from parents, society or self, they must do everything right. Diligents don't make the same mistakes twice. They will have perfected their knowledge and honed their technique, by the time the next test rolls around, or they'll avoid all together and deny failure a chance.

One hallmark characteristic is their quick-draw defensiveness, when in doubt or when called upon to justify their position. Doubt is usually interpreted by Diligents as an affront to their intelligence. Idealists measure others by karat weight. Diligents measure others as they measure their self, by brain weight. When they are wrong, they read "stupid" That's high stress for cerebral-dependents like them. At work, they often redress doubt insults by painstakingly, even obsessively reconstructing events and reviewing decision steps until they've been exonerated, or until blame's been affixed otherwise and elsewhere. Diligents do not stand still or stand long under pointed doubt-lights.

When self-definition hinges on doing it right the first time around, and when reward, respect and affection are based on conformity, self-identity may fuse and confuse with perfection. Of their many talents in childhood, being brainy and making Honour Roll wins them the most praise and earns them the loudest applause. Rational thinking sets pride in parent's eye and gains admiration from others, so Diligents place all their apples in the brainy basket, where the greatest personal return on personal investment is found. Adults, be they parent, teacher, or minister, do so love the smart, compliant, well-mannered child. To that end, Diligents work hard to earn top marks.

By the time they graduate high school, the pattern of reward for compliant behaviour and scholastic achievement is deeply ingrained. Higher education and work are same 'o achieved and praise is heaped and reward earned by application of their same 'o smart shovel. Predictability is their measure and security their motivation. Following the rules, minding the details, and giving one-hundred percent returns them a decent living and a decent life. Objectivity is fine for thinking and working, and in those realms all goes pretty well for these individuals. Only in personal relationships do Diligents confront the foreign, two-headed monster: emotion and need. While their own emotional hatches have long-been battened down, mates' emotions are seldom as disciplined, but more illogically insistent and unavoidably disturbing. Suddenly, exceptional performance is not enough.

Diligents are the proverbial strong, silent types. Mates are drawn to their calm composure, social sophistication, and steadfast reputation. In their relationships, Diligents are usually above reproach in terms of loyalty and responsibility, which encompasses career, family, church, and community and usually in that order. Good providers, they strive to attain financial security for their family's future. They respect hierarchical order at work and tend to be top dog at home; often setting the tone and tempo of family life. Devoted, though not effusive parents, Diligents often view raising a family as the purpose for marriage. Children are thought of as extra insurance that the marriage will continue, as well as relieving them from being the sole focus and preoccupation of mates.

Diligents are communal-minded and need to belong. They abide rules of tribe and tradition, they pitch-in and shoulder responsibilities so as to not be a burden, and they daily meet and overcome challenges. Diligents earn their respect and prove their worthiness for tribe membership yet rarely from this personality will "I love you" and "Do you love me?" be heard. They trust tangibles, so laying the spoils of their intelligent efforts at beloved's feet is devotion and commitment enough...and enough said for Diligents. They subscribe to logic, not emotion. After all, the logic-formula has proven successful in every other aspect of their life—childhood, education, and career. Why aren't mates equally content to measure their sincerity against facts of reality? Why demand intangible, passionate expression as well? Emotions won't pay the bills and words of love won't put a roof overhead or rainy day money in the bank...and aren't those the most important needs of all?

Mates soon learn that one of the fastest ways to get a passionate rise out of their Diligent is to overspend money. Diligents usually control family purse strings. Financial security is ultra-important to them.

Fear of being rejected, despite their provisionary ability, is high-level stress for Diligents. Problems can arise in their personal relationships, when they place more importance on work and financial success than on intimacy. Often, Diligent hearts are smugly and snugly tucked behind prodigious and impenetrable intellectual walls. Between Diligent's devotion to their work and their children, mates generally find themselves having to settle for third-place ribbons, in terms of attention. Not being the winner yet not quite the loser in their Diligent's life, can leave mates feeling orphaned emotionally and convenient romantically.

Occasionally, Diligents encounter emotional situations that overflow their logical banks. Not used to the bombardment but unable to express the overwhelming flood of irrational sensations, they respond in startlingly explosive ways: from booming tirade, to pounding fists, to venomous attacks, to tearing the place apart. Startling, because Diligents are the cool-headed, rational ones among us. That perfectly composed and well-balanced mask does now and then slip. Beneath the fury, the raw anguish of an emotionally-fraught and fragile being emerges.

One...competent in any and all others ways yet unfamiliar and unable to deal with rampant emotionality. Others tend to back away. At no other time is getting closer more necessary or as possible than at this illogical time for Diligents. It is then that their mind meets emotions; the ultimate boss that cannot be controlled by will or reason, and will not be denied. No other...as tribally-oriented as Diligents...is as emotionally innocent and/or ignorant as them. They are unsophisticated and unpracticed in the use or application of passion. If wiser or smarter of such, they wouldn't be Diligent at all. Such outbursts should be interpreted for what they are: extreme vulnerability and neediness. Like candy floss, their rant is mostly huff-and-puff and melts rapidly and readily enough, when warmly tested and tasted.

By definition, Diligent is a responsibility giant, though emotional midget

They are often as emotionally fragile and innocent, as newborn infants. Their own measure of value is based on intellectual ability and reliability of effort. Diligent children usually were encouraged to think but discouraged from showing emotions. When asked, "How was your day at school?" they responded with stats of grades and accomplishments, ignoring mention of fears of the bully or being teased about their behaviour or dress. Diligent wants or desires may have been rebuked or filed under impractical, along with other frivolities such as parties and sports. Move them out of that narrow intellectual-corridor and they're easily lost.

They flounder about, unsure of footing, unconfident of self, and feeling foolish. To be thought a fool or made to feel like one—is the fear-muzzle uniquely fashioned and worn by Diligent. Generally, they do not like being teased and faster bristle than laugh if made the brunt of even well-meaning jokes. It is difficult for them to laugh at themselves but humiliating if laughed at by others. Diligents choose their company and companionship as they choose their mate and career: carefully. Their world can be relatively small but familiar, comfortable, and controllable. When the Diligent mask slips, a trusted hand offered in love and with open acceptance can make all the difference—to them and to others. For all their "Bah, Humbug!" these individuals need illogical, impractical, and intangible emotion-exploration. Reality for them does not exceed logic. Beyond that they expect to find foolishness or disappointment and deserved humiliation if not smart and careful.

Diligents can easily live and love theoretically, but not fulfillingly

Their fear of ridicule and rejection is often greater than their fear of being alone. Without the guidance and support of a loved and trusted other, Diligents avoid emotional intimacy and consequently, self-discovery. They squirm in obvious discomfort when the topic gets close and personal, or becomes too intense to be reasoned away. Logic is safer. Prescribed and approved opinions can be verified and defended, and taken to bank or to task if need be. Books can justify logic, but books and logic combined can't justify emotions. Diligents would sooner play with land mines than play with emotions. They don't risk professionally and they don't chance emotions personally either.

Attracting a mate is not a problem for Diligent. They offer financial security and shared companionship in exchange for home and family. But finding personal fulfillment beyond the sharing of space and responsibility is not common for Diligents. Mates that can unlock Diligents from their emotional prison are not only emotionally sophisticated and patient, but quite rare. They often settle into long-term relationships that are comfortable and efficient, but lacking of passion. These are the ones standing in the doorway scratching their heads, and wondering why the furniture is gone and the note says, "I'm sorry, I need to feel loved."

Diligents are logical. Emotions are not. Unfortunately for them, intimacy demands they not only feel but share those illogical sensations too. If recognition, acceptance, and reward are based on the book of *tried and true,* then Diligents are life's most distinguished alumni. By placing all faith in that narrow path of socially prescribed ideals, they close the door on discovering what is true and most right for them. This personality is often so detached from their emotional truth, they commonly say, "I think, I feel...," as for them, reality is mind delimited. They trust their intellect, their vaults of accumulated knowledge and other people's accepted opinions over their own emotional truth. Diligents would be wiser to tailor the world to fit them rather than molding self to fit world.

Sexually, a tender surprise

Diligents conduct their lives with disciplined reserve and shy away from displays of affection. Behind closed bedroom doors, however, they can be intoxicatingly demonstrative. Diligents express physically what they're unable to express emotionally. For them, sex is often scheduled. Spontaneity is not their claim or fame. Romantic predictability for others may seem boring, but with these ones, predictability promises passion. Workaholic Diligent clears the deck, clears distractions, and closes the door on the world, when they prearrange a date with their mate, for uninterrupted lovemaking.

So many times, so many nights each week, guaranteed! Anything more is bonus. A smile on mate's face attests, what passion is regularly found in Diligent bed chambers. These individuals characteristically and historically do one thing better than most: meet expectations. With famed focus and meticulous attention to detail, they prime passion's engine with step-by-step thoroughness and excruciating deliberation. Fingers, hands, mouth, and body, travel passion's path in random abandon with illogical need that if forbidden or unseemly elsewhere, is invited, welcomed, and to be enjoyed now. In pulse that pleads, in power that surges, in vulgar vulnerability, they consummate and communicate love contained and unexpressed. Without name, without shame, they bare and share the emotional depth of their feelings, with the one that matters most, and who, beyond this bedded bliss, may not hear endearments of love to know. When Diligents make a date for romance, it's love they arrange, but mate they celebrate.

Children are drawn to Diligents, sensing gentleness and sincerity behind the sober mask and stiff upper lip. And the kids are right. Sincerity does live there—especially where children are concerned. These individuals dominate membership lists of charitable organizations and interests that serve the health, welfare, and happiness needs of children worldwide. The affinity may be due to their understanding that children need help and protection if they are to live as children should and might. Diligents, generally, have fewer happy childhood memories than others, though many trophies, scholarships, and rewards as proof of early drive and accomplishment. Sometimes they grow up too soon—too old, and sometimes, too-soon cold. The only difference between children and adults is that children are honest and open emotionally. If unhappy in a crowded mall, an unhappy child will, without concern or embarrassment, open mouth-wide and wail their unhappiness clearly and loudly to all. Diligents love, respect, and protect that aspect of children. When children hurt or need, they're the first ones to come running with help.

What each gives, is often what each most needs and desires

Diligents need a mate strong enough to force them, if necessary, to experiment emotionally and experience the passion they have for so long denied themselves. Trusting self to explore emotional as well as logical challenges, with individual style, is a great challenge for Diligents. Chance more fumbles, tackles, passes, and touchdowns, instead of living by rerun and replay. That's the kind of medicine Diligents need daily. Creativity and risk-taking, logically and emotionally, are areas that cause enormous stress for this personality style. Both require a leap into the unknown; a leap of faith they cellularly distrust.

Truth for each is not found in books, scholarly teachings or in expert opinions. It resides within. A mind, even if extraordinary, is but a tool. One that too easily and too often is used to divide self from others. Emotion is the common language linking every man, woman, and child. Individual truth lives in emotions. When one shuts off their emotions and instead relates to others with logical objectivity, how far from lonely and stranger can that person be? And how far from loving and loveable?

THE LOGICALS

Life Purpose

The forest, not the tree. The cotton industry, not the swab. Global disparity, not the beggar. Behind the logic of the weave, within the embrace that holds all is where their purpose, power and genius lays claim. Meet Sage, the gentle mental giant, whose sophic finger rests on the pulse of human pattern--discerning births, shifts, changes and deaths through ebb and flow of time. Their evolutionary role has been sapient. Their purpose is to observe, participate and objectify the human condition.

Intimacy & Emotion

If they know it, with patience, perseverance and pleasure will they share with others. If it is theirs to give, it is given with out asking. In conversation, their attention tends to be rapt. Yours will not wilt or wander, either, as their mind is fine and deep: humour, pathos and wisdom are well mixed and sweet. They greet others with hand and mind in all manner and matter, but others cannot expect to meet their heart. Sage attended its deepest burial long, long ago. Being different has a price.

These individuals do not need to start at A, B, C...or 1, 2, 3, to understand. They see the whole of things, the inter-connectiveness of each to all.

Their ability and potential is genius and geniuses tend to walk beside paths, not atop. Sages learn at their own pace, pick their own preoccupation, and take longer than others to warm up before plumbing depths; those differences extol a fee.

Sage children tend to meet with impatience to hurry and pressure to align mentally with the more prevailing normal and logically prescribed ways of thinking and doing. Happy of disposition and sensitive of nature, they are easily embarrassed or shamed. When they see disappointment in the eyes of others, they strive to please. When incapable of altering or accounting for the disparity between sincere effort and consequent result, most Sage children make a life-impacting decision. They open wide the tap to their mental involvement and shut to trickle, out pourings from their emotional spouts. Sages have enduring faith in their minds. It is emotion that causes them pain and which they determine to overcome by out-smarting it.

Through and through, Sages are tribal-oriented beings. Their life approach and philosophy is that each person is intrinsically and equally important to the whole of mankind. Their need and want is unconditional acceptance of their way, their warts and their all, by others. Highly social beings, Sages seek emotional support and intellectual stimulation in company with others. Their greatest pleasure is participating in the human aspects of life. They may very well be one of the most entertaining—if not most interesting citizens on earth. Social chameleons, they readily assimilate into different groups, cultures, and philosophies, acknowledging and appreciating the unique and common.

Their unassuming nature and sparkling intellect are attractive to mates, who soon realize that while available physically and intellectually, they tend to shun and shy at intimacy. When Sages closed their emotional spigot, they disqualified themselves from participating as an equal. They essentially relegated themselves to the lesser role of objective observer.

These individuals who intrinsically appreciate the inter-relational value of each to whole, tend to keep an intellectual arm's distance between self and others. When rejected or humiliated as youths, they disconnected for self-protective reasons, to shield themselves from further pain. The habit is often deeply ingrained by adulthood but not irreversible. Sages easily love mankind in the abstract. Their fear is being found unloveable one-on-one. Embracing concepts and upholding tenets are safer for them, than risking and chancing rejection.

The genius of Sages can go unappreciated, even unknown, as these individuals tend to be intellectually humble about their own ability. The self-doubt that exists behind the entertaining words and pleasant demeanor can prevent them from testing their own mettle publically. Unrealized genius is common enough to be a parable—self-doubt is most often the fear that blinds, binds and gags it. Trust is the single biggest challenge for Sages. As long as they place all faith in belief, they will not discover their own truth and may not find the fulfillment and happiness they seek and need.

Belief is limited to knowledge acquired from books, from opinions, and from life experiences. In terms of belief, Sages are well-endowed, as their minds tend to be information sponges and encyclopedic marvels. What they offer and espouse is the time-proven opinions of others, without interpretation or representation of self at all. It is one thing to talk the talk; another to walk the walk. Others did not accept their truth when young. Why chance adult rejection? Belief is safer. Its source is proven and verifiable so there's little personal risk involved—other than having a good memory and a willing voice for parroting. Given access to the same books, belief for all would be much the same.

It is characteristic of this personality to theorize life, to speak in lofty glowing terms of the state of the human condition rather than focusing on individuals or specific issues. They keep an intellectual stick between them and others because theory is safer than practice, and commitment or personal inspection is not necessary or called for. If others disagree with theory or opinion, debating the logistics or changing the topic soon solves the problem. Theories can be revised, tossed away or replaced without personal rejection or pain being suffered. Not so with self. Tossing and replacing humiliates and hurts.

It is not externally gained information and knowledge that defines individuality. Self-truth and creativity does and both are only available within. Each soul holds thumbprint truth for each individual—as each soul is a complete, uninterrupted record of evolutionary experiences. Soul is seat of infinite wisdom and infinite power, and that vault of infinite possibility is only accessed through intuition. Emotions are intuition's messenger of truth. When Sages ignore intuition by closing off emotions, they not only deny themselves truth, they deny themselves power. By ascribing to belief only, they live and create according to other opinions and experiences. And while prescribed opinions may enlighten, inspire, inform and entertain, they are not a substitute for self. There is only one way to harness individual power—trust intuition.

As objective observers, rather than active participants, Sages are half-equal. Therefore, according to their own philosophy half-important to the whole. The imposing walls between belief and truth can seem impenetrable. Sages are not only intellectuals who generously share their knowledge, they're hands-down the most entertaining conversationalists of all. People, regardless of shape, kind, colour or flag are their first and foremost interest. Intimate relations with their mate and close companionships with many, are natural and needed relationship states for them. The price is trusting self enough…enough to come all the way out and chance acceptance or rejection based on their whole truth, rather than their intellectual facade. Only when Self is allowed out, will there be room for those *importants* and *neededs* to come in.

Re-opening the emotional spigot by trusting intuition can literally send the untried genius of these individuals flying toward achievement heretofore unknown. This is the personality with potential to alter futures. Of all planet beings, resolution of self-trust issues is most important for Sages. Otherwise, their cellular remarkability may be smothered under insecurity blankets or snuffed by intellectual pontifications. For them, it really is a matter of truth or consequences. Close the books, cover your ears, and go inside, Sage. Discover who you really are and flex your innermost truth and power.

When they base a relationship on companionship instead of emotional love, Sages tend to remain eternal seekers, preoccupied with the theoretical and metaphysical rather than the practical. As philosophical vagabonds, marriage for Sages may become an emotional landing strip, with them fluctuating between over-dependence and extreme independence. They tend to appear distant, detached and professionally unstable, as they change career focus often. They often are over-booked, overlooked and under-organized, unable to meet commitments and too easily distracted by compelling but fleeting interests.

Their mates complain of living with a dependent rather than life partner. Sages speak of these experiences, as "being propelled by an inner drive to find something not lost, yet inexplicably missing...feeling erratic, irrational and incapable of focusing...forced by feelings of insecurity to encourage rejection by their mates whilst fearing abandonment most of all." Compromising happiness for companionship is emotional dishonesty—a situation particularly intolerable and potentially damaging for Sages. They can too easily hide from others and themselves,under such impersonal, logical umbrellas.

When they base a relationship on both love and lust, these effusive, gentle beings can be loyal and highly affectionate partners...and extraordinary citizens. Family tends to be their touchstone and mirror of self-confidence. Unconditional love and acceptance unleashes the confidence of Sages to explore creativity and explode professionally. When these individuals trust their intuition and access their own soul's wisdom, they discover they already know more than they have read, studied or been taught. Their innate ability and propensity to plumb the depths of all that interests, does not as easily distract or derail as before. The difference is that now their focus is trained on purpose and self-fulfillment, rather than on escape and responsibility avoidance.

Loving, trusting relationships afford them the anchor their wandering intellect needs and the unequivocal acceptance their timid heart seeks. Few personality Styles are compatible mates for Sages. They often seek an intellectual equal but what they most need is an emotional harbour. One other who loves and appreciates them too much, to allow them to live half-lives, half-hidden from others and world.

Creative and compassionate lovers, they succumb to the mindless release of physical and emotional pleasures. Experimental and lustful, they explore sexual variety with Kama Sutra curiosity. They're sensuous, spontaneous, and uninhibited, and impatient with mates, who won't play with their equal ardor and carefree abandon. Highly-skilled lovers, they lead mating's passion. In libidinous union, they feel and affirm their mate's acceptance of them. In the give and take of carnal embrace, they communicate love and confirm their own lovability.

Sages have wisdom-wrapped messages to deliver to all, but there's one message they must personally receive: only a fool hell-bent on loneliness tries to outsmart emotions.

THE PRACTICALS

Life Purpose

Roped off with velvet cord and reserved exclusively for them are front cars of evolutionary roller coasters. Eyes wide, ears attuned, mind alert, they get bored at straight and narrow, but breathless at careen and curve of fringe. Eternal seekers of emotion, with arms raised in celebration they pay homage to exquisite of peak and blister of dive on life's roller coaster experiences. For them, the magician's hat is bottomless; Pandora's box, irresistible; the Ides of March, typical corporate thinking; and *should,* a pox and pall on individuality.

They're the peacocks of Ansir's personality spectrum. The ones who scoff at rules, meet normal with sigh, and smash molds with focused glee. Odd, they find, that variety in hors d'oeuvres is cheered but feared when found in people. Meet Eccentrik—the one who adds colour to black and white palettes and spice to flavour and taste palates. Their evolutionary role is to kick out the end boards that bind and bound normal, wide enough for unique to squeeze in.

Intimacy & Emotion

Many Eccentriks are borderline geniuses. They tend to be perceived as weird and are often labelled such as children. Eccentriks know sooner and better than most that they're different. Despite earnest contortions and best intentions they are unable to mold themselves to fit into others' expectations. Rather than burrowing inside and hiding under heaps of self-doubt and self-hate, Eccentriks say, "Screw this," thrust out their chins, and take control of their own ship's wheel.

Complete conformity is not an option. Eccentriks protect and preserve their differentness. They may very well spend most of their youth looking into disappointment-filled eyes, but unlike most, Eccentriks do not shoulder responsibility for having disappointed. Instead, they do a most unusual thing; they accept themselves first, warts and all. They develop a confidence in their intellect and a respect for their uniqueness sufficient to withstand adult and peer pressure.

Eccentriks emerge from their youth-pupa firmly resolved to pick their own path, regardless of norm or mores. Exhilarating experiences, the blush of new and the rush of novel are what Eccentriks actively pursue in life. Any and all experiences are eagerly met—except one: intimacy. From the fallout of those early disappointment versus identity battles, before confidence grew and non-conformity strengthened, do Eccentriks build the walls of their emotional prison. They may love, they may lust, they may share their body, mind and being, but one thing they seldom share with others is unconditional trust.

Eccentriks focus on creating an identity where self-definition and value are not dependent on their having to harmonize in chorus or peep with others. These individuals choose their own tunes, their own tempo and sing all variety and genre of song. Eccentriks personify strong individuality and ultra-creativity. They do not aspire to being classified politically or otherwise by their ensemble, ensign or assembly. These individuals know that while running with the herd may be safer, it also means a life of eating trampled grass; a compromise they're not willing to make. Eccentriks trust themselves to know what's best, whether or not protocol or opinion likes it.

Pg. 336

If the most dangerous man is an honest man.
Eccentriks can attest, the loneliest is an individualist

Others may line up to be painted by one and same brush but Eccentriks protest such herd mentality—vigorously, cellularly and daily. Others may worship consistency while Eccentriks would rather eat paste. They do not care if misunderstanding results when they behave inconsistently. If today they feel strongly one way but tomorrow their perspective changes, so what? They may not subscribe to the daily newspaper but will support a number of specialty publications that specifically cater to their professional and personal interests. Seldom do they subscribe for more than a few issues or a few months at a time. Tomorrow they may find something more appealing or appropriate for their coin and time.

These individuals don't usually buy lifetime memberships to anything, preferring instead to pay dues as they go. They take umbrage to terms like "family tradition" or "party member," preferring instead to determine whether tradition or party is worthy of continuing or joining. They honour their own integrity as equally in private as in crowd, and deliver their own truth for scrutiny at each show-and-tell. They don't care if the crowd boo's and hisses, they stand firmly on own feet and principles. Four personalities would not have *bought* into Hitler; one is Eccentrik...for sure.

Greatness is often misunderstood by the general masses. Galileo was misread, misjudged and misunderstood, as were Newton, Leary, Socrates and Jesus. In fact, Eccentriks tend to hold the view that greatness does not come from pleasing others, but from pleasing self: a threatening aberration that normally earns them social contempt and alienation.

Growing up in a small community can be a great hardship for Eccentrik, who is often made to feel as welcome as a cockroach in butter. These individuals thrive on variety and are often more creative than small towns and small minds tolerate. Like newly-hatched sea turtles, at first opportunity Eccentriks instinctually head for their more natural habitat—the nearest and biggest metropolitan centre. In cities their flamboyant style blends less noticeably in crowds, and there's a broader intellectual and cultural market for them to browse and experience first-hand.

Eccentriks need emotional expression and creative release. Charismatic, savvy and vibrant, they collect a wide range of friends, from eclectic to eccentric, from all walks of life and from both ends of the human spectrum. The number-one emotional qualifier for them—thus relationship decider—is the stimulation factor.

With their need to experience all shades and hues, and their trademark impetuousness that wants to do it all and do it now, Eccentriks tend to exhaust friends and mates. They pursue the novel and unique for the sheer and pure of the pleasure derived. They are not slaves to fad or fashion but have a decided taste and preference for avante-garde. If life were "a box of chocolates," Eccentriks would take a bite out of each, before leaving with smile and smell of sweet satisfaction.

They tend to stringently avoid commitments or responsibilities for others, even pets. The proverb, "He who travels alone, travels lightest, travels quickest," seems corporeally etched in them. Flavour-of-the-month Eccentriks like intensity and uncertainty over comfort and duration. The excitement of new situations, the lust in new love's passion, the challenge of first impressions is what they thrive on. They live in the now, revelling while wringing each moment dry of its excitement, as each is delivered. They seem intent on rewriting rules and rearranging external reality, much as they internally manipulate three-dimensional objects. Eccentriks may not be for general consumption but they're confidently and unwaveringly true to self.

From earliest childhood, Eccentriks get accustomed to looking into disappointment-filled eyes of loved ones. There is a gap between others' expectations and their own willingness that their nature can't seem to bridge to all's satisfaction. The adult consequence is that Eccentriks usually avoid long-term relations and relationships, professionally and personally. They seem to not want or need others nor do they allow others to want or need them.

The challenge for Eccentrik is to trust long enough to chance rejection or unconditional acceptance, based on familiarity's reveal of their warts...weirdness...wonders...wishes...and all. These individuals will risk derision, ostracism, occupation and even loneliness before they'll risk failing in eyes that could, if trusted, become as important to them as their own. If Eccentriks keep moving and changing often enough and fast enough, they may not meet with success but they can surely outrun failure and out-manoeuvre responsibility. From the time they leave home and until they trust others with the whole and all of them, Eccentriks tend to leave family, careers, friends, lovers and others while the bloom is still on the rose.

If they marry, they may to do so frequently; a consequence of their impetuousness. They also participate in open marriages more frequently than other personality styles. Eccentriks have more of an intellectual need than an emotional desire, to experience sexual variety. Their relationship approach is akin to "striking while the iron is hot,' where they rush to explore as fully and quickly as possible, before synergy or interest wanes. Eccentrik marriages tend to be self-fulfilling prophecies. A "till death do us part" commitment may be integral to wedding ceremonies, but it is at-odd with Eccentrik nature.

They are consummate lovers, who go to any length to please their mate. For Eccentriks, marriage usually means, until the stardust falls from our eyes and the pits of despair close in. Ex-partners are not tossed aside. They merely step back and melt into the background of Eccentrik's tapestry-rich life. An arrangement that all seem to accept as inevitable and wise. Eccentriks tend not to be deceptive or manipulative. In fact, one of their most endearing qualities is a childlike sincerity. When they love, it's with unparalleled fervor and fever. It's just that their love isn't offered exclusively and isn't intended to last forever.

The emotional barrier that Eccentriks build between the life they tend to lead externally, and the one they pursue internally, is the issue of freedom. The battle of non-conformity that began in childhood tends to be waged throughout adulthood, often escalating to full-scale war, when it comes to matters of the heart. Emotional commitment is the casualty of this war; loneliness, its spoils. Non-conformity by non-committal is due to their greatest fear: being tied-down.

Freedom can be negatively interpreted as self-indulgence or extreme independence. Self-indulgence does whatever it wants, whenever it wants, without permission or approval. Extreme independence says, "I don't need you or the horse you rode in on, so leave me alone." In either case, fear of dependency...needing others...is Eccentrik's Achilles' heel. What these creative and bright individuals tend to forget is that human bondage is a state of mind. When they want most, when they love most, is when they dare least and exit stage right: personally and professionally. Trust may be the issue but vulnerability is the thorn that thorn bird Eccentriks most fear.

Loneliness tends to be their long-term companion when they determine to experience relationship by breadth, not depth. Eccentriks skim emotional experience by feeling the many and different pulse-points along life's surface, rather than exploring deeply to discover the source of all pulse—the heart, where emotional fulfillment is had by commitment only. That journey is common for all but the destination, uniquely each's.

THE PRACTICALS

Life Purpose

With clipboard, furrowed brow, and clear-eyed conviction, they eagle life's unfold. Brisk of walk, crisp of talk, they brook no fools, slipshods nor lackadaisicals. They are the evolutionary Idealists, who from podiums of perfection and in voice of perfect-pitch, inspire others to strive for excellence in all undertakings. Driven from birth to do all, be all, learn all, Idealists walk the path of lists, guided by glowing, growing dones along the way. As bound by corporeal To-Do List, as by covenant to complete, their purpose is to insure that compromise today does not compromise future.

Intimacy & Emotion

While they have tremendous faith in their own abilities to produce and to lead, unconsciously, Idealists fear that unless they take control...all will be lost. Their fear may be justified. The world advances in every field of endeavour, by march of improvement to time's measure. Perfection is crucial to progress. Care taken in the perfect setting of first blocks, builds solid foundations and straight walls. Idealists are the historical-bearers of perfection keys. However fair or unfair, the blunt and brunt of responsibility is borne by those who see the highest potential in selves and in others and demand its fulfillment. Idealists are the ones frowning and focusing on what went wrong, while others celebrate anyway. From the seeds of Idealist discontent and disappointment do great and greatness germinate.

No matter what Idealists do, they tend to think "...it could be better." They try harder than most, they feel more responsible than most and harder than deserved on self. They push impatiently toward perfection, even if beyond the scope or scent of realistic. Stopping and smelling the roses is unlikely for them. They'd be distracted by stray grass-clippings along the pathway and either overlook the roses altogether or view them through disappointment-tainted glasses.

It is an Idealist husband who loses interest in his wife because of weight gain after child-bearing. It is an Idealist woman who visits a new neighbour, and recounts, in accented "tsk-tsk," the decor of the house, the disarray of the bathroom and the neighbour's unfortunate lisp. It's not that Idealists are consciously hyper-critical or personally validated through fault-finding; they're just intrinsically disappointed in the way things are, as opposed to their vision of what could and should be.

Idealists are born, not made

These individuals have high personal standards they strive to maintain or surpass and seem compelled to foster or foist equal aspirations in others. Idealists are not the product of childhood trauma, overly critical parents or a too-demanding society. Nor are they handicapped by a too-heavy cross to bear or burdened with a disappointment laden chip-on-shoulder, despite others' suspicions. Their drive and ambition are nature and full-blown at birth. Others could sooner stop time than change Idealists.

Deep down, whether they admit it or not, Idealists want to come out on top in every situation. They tend to position themselves for best advantage and, luckily for others, they often succeed. If one personality were selected to represent planet and specie at an intergalactic trade-show, Idealists would be a wise if not *best* choice. Not only would they do us proud socially, they'd most likely return bulging economic benefits. These are the phenomenals who can turn sow ears into silk purses. They are thinkers, planners and managers of the highest, most productive order; and perfectionists to boot.

Money begets power

Evolutionarily, they are among the most wealthy and powerful individuals on the planet. Idealist's greatest gift is creative problem-solving. They are endowed with an oversized ego to withstand controversy and override compromise, and a mind that travels at the speed of light. They thrive on doing the impossible, skating risk's razor-edge and sweetening challenges by demanding all be done perfectly. Perfect is a word they seem to have invented and feel personally responsible for protecting.

To admire Idealists for their greatest gift, their one-of-a-kind minds, should be a relatively easy thing to do. But smart never wore as many thorns as when worn by these individuals. They don't like things to remain the way they are. They want to improve everything they see or touch, including people. They tend to bring out the competitiveness and defensiveness in others. Milo, the enterprising character from Joseph Heller's Catch-22, is dominant Idealist in one or two realms. There are many, many Idealists on the planet, and many are household familiar. To them, money is power and they're not afraid to say so. Others would be wise to take heed when Idealists say it, however. "Whatever it takes" is not only a belief this style subscribes to...it's their motto.

Many are self-made and uphold the view that abundance comes by way of hardship and workship. When socializing, Idealists find it entertaining and educational to swap tales of fiscal follies endured and victories won along their pathway to success." How did you make your money?" is a personality-typical curiosity. They tend to be eternal students, ever-enrolled in this course of study or in pursuit of that interest. At trade-shows, conventions or seminars, the majority of attendants are Idealist. They like being on top, so staying apprised of the latest and newest innovations is homework for them.

When struggling financially they can be tempest incarnate. They shake their fists at injustices that are surely conspiring against them, bemoan the lax laws, berate the tax man and kick Fido for spite. When successful they are expansive and generous, and seldom home long enough for Fido to know, far less fear.

Not for general consumption

These individuals walk briskly and confidently down the centre of life. They leave enough room for others, but do not step aside, stop at obstacle or run at threat. There is a crisp-coolness about them that assures and unsettles at once—much like stopping at the neighbours but chatting with them, through their closed screen door. Idealists are not for general consumption; most are welcomed but few get invited in. They often have a long list of well-known business associates and acquaintances, but few near and dear friends. Idealists, generally, are highly selective in their personal relations and relationships.

They are often strikingly attractive and fastidious about appearance. Their manner of attire tends to be sophisticated, elegant, expensive and often sexually appealing. Their intent is to attract not titillate, as Idealists are more of the "look but don't touch" variety. Physically, they're often weight-proportional or thinner and often equate being overweight with lack of self-control. They tend to shed unwanted weight rather quickly, themselves. Their controlling tendency, if not tempered with patience, may lead to eating disorders.

Idealists take pains to make favourable first impressions. They follow fashion and fashion shows world wide. They like quality and style and don't mind working hard to afford the best money can buy. Whatever first impressions others have of Idealists, is intended. These individuals don't just throw themselves together. They fuss. For them, external appearances reflect internal standards. They judge a book by its cover and product by its packaging. As Idealists groom themselves, do they groom and maintain their property and possessions. For instance, when Idealists trade-in their old car, it may need work under the hood but the body and interior are often in mint condition.

These individuals don't need others to disappoint them; they're more than capable of doing that on their own. Disappointment usually dances around two issues: recognition and reward. How close or far Idealists are from top rungs of economic, social and own-expectation ladders, determines their level of self-disappointment. Few suffer the angst and anguish of general disillusion to the same extent as them.

Idealists seem to have a split-screen-view embedded in their ocular dimension: one before screen upon which reality is run and one after screen showing their new, improved version. Unfortunately for them *and others,* Idealists spend most of their time viewing the after screen and demanding amendment for the disparity found between their view and the rest of the world's.

Laurels and wreaths

Their modus operandi and modus vivendi tend to rent peace and ruffle feathers regularly, for they render change in a forthright manner. It's Idealist's persistent, perfectionistic striving that guides the rudder of destiny's direction. Theirs is a future-tending responsibility and one they shoulder with unwavering dedication and determination. Idealists remind us that laurels rested upon soon become wreaths.

By focusing on perfection and demanding the best of self and others, Idealists may deprive themselves of the joyous part of living and life. Perennial disappointment between what is and what could be, can physically manifest. Their mouths may pucker or the corners turn down, reflective of inner discontent with outer mediocrity. Low self-esteem is a state Idealists are susceptible to, or familiar with, which fuels their drive for over-achievement. One fear of theirs is being found inferior to the task. Not meeting their own or not exceeding others' expectations is failure, to them. Failure is their Achilles' heel.

Their goals focus less on global betterment than on personal recognition and monetary reward for their bigger-faster-better accomplishments. It is not enough for them to earn top-sales status at the office. Idealists aspire to being number-one in their field. It is not enough for them to have done an excellent job mowing and trimming their yard. Their pride is short-lived if the neighbour's looks better. Unless their performance stands out, stands taller and shines brighter comparatively, Idealists can be self-disappointed. Too-quick and too-soon do they conclude, "I've failed." Why?...because of their need for recognition and wealth.

Idealists tend to compare themselves to others in terms of fame, wealth and influence. Money is their measure of success and they tend to value "all" according to karat-weight. They can be conspicuous-consumers who display material wealth as tangible proof of achievement and worth. To identify the Idealists in your social circle, look for the ones with the most toys, the latest innovations, fashionable clothing and a distinct preference for gold and diamond jewelry. When buying gifts for these individuals, two rules apply: make it exquisite and expensive. They most likely have the catalogues, but are least likely to mail-order shop. They like to know, in-person, what they're buying.

They tend to be excellent money managers. While they may not be the hands-on doers or volunteers, they generously provide the money that feeds the hungry, saves the whales and plants the trees in every needy-spot round the world. (The fact that they are also the ones who bought up the farmland, contracted the whalers, and chopped down the rain forests, is the flip side of their charity-coin). Successful Idealists are often drawn to philanthropic service in later life. Generally, and often strongly, they oppose social welfare programs.

Idealists display success...

...they wear it; they drive it; they live in it; they play with it; they prefer to socialize with others who have it; they donate it; their business reflects it—and they put it on their business cards for others to read. (Business cards are an Idealist innovation). Pride in doing is not the kind of pride that satisfies. They need billboard-size recognition, an encouraging nod of general permission from the general population, before they'll allow themselves to be proud of their accomplishments and their being.

These valuable, perfectionistic, workaholic individuals, who seem chronically confident, tend to be ultra-insecure. For all their bravado and risk-taking they can be easily and deeply hurt by others, and even mortally crushed by their greatest fear: failure. Idealists do not dare think themselves successful until they've earned enough praise and heard enough outside applause, to drown out their own noisy self-doubt. To bring out the best in Idealists: first applaud them for what they are—smart, then applaud their achievements. Such admiration is the surest way into their heart as well.

Idealists enjoy sexual relations and are highly discriminating in their choice of mates. On their lists are usually two qualifying conditions that "potentials" are ideally expected to meet: physical attractiveness and intellectual compatibility. Of those two, attractiveness is first and intellect a far-enough distant second to be dispensed with. Idealists, themselves, are the ones who require others love them for their mind. Sexual satisfaction begins and ends at ego, They don't enter or engage in sexual relations, unless their ego is pleased firstly and fully. If the way to some hearts is gastronomical seduction, for Idealists, mind-foreplay is recommended. Phone sex·cerebral stimulation·appeals to them. In seduction, sensuality, and sex they are energetic and generous partners.

Love, money, power

It's the vulnerability and unconditional-trust parts of intimacy, that causes their reluctance and alarms their suspicion. Idealists enjoy the control and power play inherent in sexual relations. They are often extremely skilled lovers, who focus more on pleasing their mate, than pleasing their self. They tend to be insatiably experimental and physically electric performers. Lust, along with other base emotionality, often aren't invited or allowed to attend carnal banquets with them. Personal desires and emotional needs are usually fortressed safely away in Idealist's mind, beyond the physical reach or touch of others. High personal standards preclude random or rampant promiscuity, but extra-marital affairs are not uncommon nor unlikely. For them, "It doesn't mean a thing," is usually the truth.

Prenuptial agreements are an Idealist innovation. Their idea of intimacy doesn't include carte-blanche trust. Prenuptial agreements are their insurance against being professionally handcuffed. For Idealists, there's only one constant in life...change. "Till death do us part," can seem threatening to these individuals, who won't wear last year's *threads*. Idealists are born to effect change. Being thwarted in their work or stymied in their efforts by another, especially an uncooperative or vengeful mate, is a chilling prospect that quickly removes the rose from their romantic glasses. They usually avoid such vulnerabilities by defining control issues and gaining signed acceptance, before nuptials are exchanged.

Idealist mistrust of emotional intimacy can be so ingrained that many equate self-fulfillment with financial worth. It is not uncommon for them to achieve highest climactic satisfaction from their work, rather than from their intimate relations. Something is wrong when love of work is more orgasmic and fulfilling than love of others. Idealists use perfection as others use battering-rams. Their intimidation works, too, if keeping others off-balance or at bay is the objective. One Idealist hallmark: they will not be told what to do. Asking them to re-evaluate their priorities is jaw-flapping-futility, for they'll only change when desire equals reason for deciding and doing.

The world and the people in it are pretty good, but...

That but is the needle-eye through which others must pass before earning their appreciation or sharing their intimacy. That standard is obviously successful professionally, where battering-rams may be effective when winning "no matter what" is called for. Perfectionistic control can ruin personal relationships, however. Mates can find themselves jumping through hoops trying to please their Idealist mate, who would love them or respect them.... if only this or that were changed. In the "never let them see you sweat" workplace, emotionality is a sign of weakness. In personal relations, emotional honesty is the only glue that works. Intimacy demands butt-naked vulnerability from each, before unconditional love, trust and acceptance are possible. Such up-close scrutiny and inspection, Idealists tend to avoid.

First of all, unconditional acceptance of another is near-impossible for perfectionists like them. Secondly, they seem to always be in the process of stretching toward a next in self-improvement, because they're seldom satisfied with their current self. Idealists fear that close inspection might find them more raw clay than fine art. Others know this as painful, personal rejection; to Idealists it is realization of their greatest personal fear: failure. When it comes time for emotional honesty, these individuals tend to get busier at work and send love by proxy of card and gift.

Ideal mates

Often Idealists choose mates that are physically attractive but lacking self-confidence. Needy personality types are attracted to their confidence and the security they provide. For a while, Idealists enjoy the challenge of remolding their willing-clay mates. However, Idealists require intellectual stimulation most of all...in their professional and private lives. Unless they marry for lust and love, Idealist's passion may find greatest expression at work. Love, for these individuals, begins in mind. A mate who cannot vibrate their grey matter will not long excite their libido.

Few personalities are strong enough to handle the full range of Idealist complexity, without wilting or fading when the going gets rough. Idealists live hard, full and fast. Like volcanoes, all is fine until they erupt. Instead of lava, Idealists spew venomous blame—their characteristic way of venting frustration. Most hear blame not the pain, and when unable to bear the heat, withdraw or exit. Potential mates must be prepared to put up with a lot of smoke and flame before Idealist trust is won and their emotional truth reveals. Few personalities have what it takes to coax out the truculent lover, who hides insecurities and deepest desires behind high-walled perfection. These individuals may not in their lifetime, experience the freedom of naked vulnerability or feel the warmth of intimacy. For Idealists, it is love and lust, or it is more responsibility with companion-perks and family benefits.

Only Idealists find less to embrace than erase in self. There is an old wisdom that claims it is not possible to love another without loving self first. But that old offering may be premature. Until Idealists, themselves, discover the truth of an even older wisdom...money may buy power but can't buy happiness...such wisdoms will all be perfectly inane.

THE EMOTIONALS

Life Purpose

As lighthouse to distress at sea, they are beacons of hope to misery. And have evolutionarily been. With welcoming hand and peace-filled heart, in light of day and night of dark, they patrol the paths where the highwaymen wont and need, wait to pounce and prey on pride. They are the Kinsmen, whose searing mind and soaring kindness balances divine right against progress might. Their purpose is to teach by example of their living that man is not born alone but borne among, and responsible as sister and brother. Kinsmen's vision does not stop at seeds in apples, but travels beyond to apples in seeds.

Intimacy & Emotion

Emotion is the key realm of functioning for them. As dolphins use sonar, Kinsmen use emotion to gauge prevailing conditions and temperament in their world. They filter life through sophisticated emotional systems, essentially feeling their way through information, extracting subtleties and intangibilities that complement their logical understanding. Their emotions are accurate beyond the facile of mental deduction alone, but Kinsmen don't trust emotions. They trust logic.

From undertones, overtones, and intonations, they intuit the unspoken needs and underlying emotions of individuals or groups whilst tracking mental precepts. They are natural arbitrators who excel in situations where logic and emotion conflict. Whether office, community or family home, their innate ability to balance sentiment with reason returns win-win solutions of compassion; acceptable and digestible to all. Their life approach is one of consensus, where the serving of the greater good takes precedence over self-interest.

Kinsmen have potential to be world-class thinkers. For them, early school life and young adulthood are relatively black and white and straightforward. Good, bad...right, wrong, and should, are concepts they readily understand and respect and the clay from which they model their own actions and behaviours. Kinsmen are smart and gentle. To see them at their finest, to appreciate how brightly human stars can shine, join any charitable organization or participate in any public-aid program, anywhere, anytime. There, swelling the goodwill ranks are Kinsmen, who care enough to apply money and elbow grease with equal ardor for the benefit of others. Like George Bailey in the film, *It's A Wonderful Life,* the world is a kinder more friendly place because of Kinsmen.

We're going to bite into the warm, chocolate-coated raisin that is the Kinsmen personality. Not with intent to harm but to understand why such gentle, generous beings suffer style-typical bouts of emotional blues. Their cyclical torment and unrest tends not to affect their external functioning but can and does cause internal misery. In Kinsmen breasts, beneath their bright, busy surface, behind their kindly heart and unbeknownst to lovers and others, melancholy, even utter sadness often brews.

Kinsmen process life emotionally but choose to function logically. That decision serves them well in the external world, but can tear them apart internally. Why? Their gift is an ability to empathize with others, to clearly hear unspoken wants and needs and to respond appropriately and accordingly. Their intuitive gift is generously offered to others, but they deny it for self. Kinsmen personify sisterly and brotherly love, yet few are harder to love than them. Loving them for what they do is easy. Loving them for "who" they are, near-impossible. Kinsmen don't allow others to know them. Most are so afraid of their own truth they won't examine it, far less share it with others. Let's bite into that chocolate raisin and taste what's hidden and why forbidden.

In semi-permeable fashion, love flows freely and naturally outward from them, but as they choose not to trust their own emotions, they choose not to trust them with others, either. Others need to remind them how valuable they are—they tend to forget. It may take convincing before they'll accept praise, for toe-in-sand-humility is their accustomed and more customary way. More often than any other, Kinsmen ask, "What is love?" Their own love reaches out to caress others and world with action, word and wallet; they give all they think, all they have and all the time they can spare to others. Yet, Kinsmen tend to think themselves unworthy of love in return—or maybe they think others unworthy of them?

It may very well be that for all their displays of kindness, Kinsmen are self-centred frauds. What they represent is belief, what they offer others is surface sensitivity. What they practice is should, not honesty. What they do not share or dare is self-truth. Belief is knowledge acquired from books, opinion and experience. Belief can be much the same for all with access to same books and opinions. Belief is acquired knowledge and logic-delivered. Truth cannot be acquired nor is it logical...like up, like down, it just is. Truth is soul-simmered and emotion-delivered. Each soul, each self, is as individually unique as its record of evolutionary experience. No earthly book is older, no opinion wiser than the newest of newborn souls. Self-truth is soul's thumbprint.

When Kinsmen deny their innermost truth and refuse to share it with others, they live and love theoretically: according to book, opinion or influence, other than own truth. The battle between belief and truth that Kinsmen experience can result in three consequent faces for others to see. The one when belief wins, the one when truth wins, or the one when their battle rages with ground being won and lost in see-saw perpetuity. If the war were internally contained the confusion would remain but one soul's experience. Too often though, Kinsmen take their emotional unrest to the street for others to become embroiled in and become casualties of. For Kinsmen, self-fulfillment depends on which system they subscribe to, intellect or emotion, and whether truth wins, loses or flip-flops between.

Belief wins

While they can plumb intellectual depths and incorporate all as belief, what they cannot do is digest belief as truth. Only by rightness of fit and feel do Kinsmen know truth. Otherwise, life is form without substance and their living more academic detachment than personal commitment. Kinsmen have the proverbial good angel sitting on one shoulder and the bad angel perched on the other. Their good angel reads from the book of Right and Wrong, a sturdily bound collection of accepted opinion and approved protocol. Their bad angel is their own illogical and often conflicting emotions.

When Kinsmen subscribe to belief, their guide throughout is *should*. Their life is structured, logical, controllable and respectable. From earliest childhood they've honoured the *good* and *right* way. They did not risk disapproval or chance disappointment by challenging authority or questioning order. Self-worth was measured according to how positive their reflection in the opinion-mirrors of parents, friends, school and community. When want and desire conflicted with logic, Kinsmen consulted others or books, before logically determining which *should* was most right for all and thus, most right for them. Sure enough, those restless wants and desires settled down as they should, and life ran smoothly once more.

Eventually, "get consensus and trust logic" becomes an ingrained habit and emotions are nothing more than an occasional, troublesome irritation that like digestion gas eventually passes with wind. Time heals all may be a wisdom gem for others, but it's a cure-all for Kinsmen. They design their adult lives as models of how things ought to be done, and succeed better than most. For Kinsmen have one of the finest minds to sketch and stretch with and their constitution is more heavily starched with responsibility than any other.

Even if their living models exemplify the highest principles of external law, life and religion, Kinsmen usually feel a sense of detachment and respond with rational objectivity, rather than sincerity. If Kinsmen cannot feel truth, it isn't. Two tell-tale behaviours indicate whether these individuals have corked emotions in favour of logic: when they avoid issues, or when they pontificate. When unemotionally committed, they talk around issues, exchange statistical chit-chat but reveal nothing of themselves. Or, they mount soapboxes and deliver proclamations to all and asunder with the authority of Caesar. Despite social charm and convincing animation, most feel alienated from the logical persona they present to others.

Like it or not, life is first an emotional experience for Kinsmen. They may choose to deny but cannot ignore. Unexpressed emotion bottles, fills and seeks release. That bad angel cannot be suppressed or silenced forever. One day a roar and rush of self-doubt erupts within, and Kinsmen...having built their lives on firm footings of belief can be overwhelmed by the illogical, internal uprising. They question, "Why, when I am doing everything right, do I feel so empty, so unloved?" And many begin in earnest, the search for the meaning in life.

There are two places to look: outside or inside self. Kinsmen tend to look outward. There are many avenues for a fine and curious mind to explore. Most seek an interest that will consume, yet meet with general approval. Kinsmen tend not to swim in untested waters. They find outlet or companionship to help them replace internal dissatisfaction with renewed optimism and vitality. "Off with the old, on with the new" becomes the standing order of the day, and Kinsmen enthusiasm shifts into overdrive. Their bad angel gets exorcised through passionate immersion in anything from religion, to romance, to rust research. This is when Kinsmen's propensity for fanaticism, excessive belief, excessive enthusiasm, can reveal.

Because they've suppressed their emotions for so long, they meet self anew...more mysterious than stranger and warmer than friend. In the blood rushing exhilaration they can be swept-up and swept away by the novel sensations. This new interest is a fresh breath of life and fills an overdue need for Kinsmen. Promising fulfillment, their *new* can become the most *shouldly* and most *rightly* of all. Their zeal may be expressed intemperately...in private, in public, from pillar, pulpit and post. In keeping with their brotherhood nature, Kinsmen want to share with all the same euphoric experience and the good benefits of what they now feel and know. For instance, a recently reformed Kinsmen smoker can become excessively anti-smoking in view and in voice. They may reorganize their own and their family's diet and health regimen, pointedly avoid any public or private situation where smoking occurs, and find new non-smoking friends to replace their former still-smoking buds in their lung cleaning spree. Or, they may lecture with righteous authority on the ills of smoking till old friends and new leave, due to ear-weariness.

Many famous leaders of world and inspiration, as well as fervent heretics and fevered despots have been of Kinsmen personality. When unexpressed emotions become an irritating horsehair undershirt, they more often seek external relief than internal unbuttoning. External gratification can satisfy logic forever, but it cannot satisfy emotions for long. Like savouring angel food cake, Kinsmen experience the sweetness and light of new, but it doesn't sustain their fervor or feed their hunger for long. In frustration they become resigned to, or embittered by the hollow ring of everything and sometimes everyone. Or they deny surfacing doubts about their new belief and carry on with fixated determination. The happiness they derive from new concepts, mate, or clothes may be intense but short-lived. For some, happiness is a state of mind. For Kinsmen, happiness is emotionally wrung.

See-saw perpetuity

When Kinsmen do subscribe to their emotional dimension, they may waver between self-martyrdom and self-fulfillment. Most often, Kinsmen intuit others and respond accordingly or *befittingly*, whilst their own truth gets shoved aside. This is a personality of consensus—common good overrides self-interest. Kinsmen go along with the generally held opinion, rather than offer exception or voice objection. They will go that extra mile to help another though inconvenient for them; they'll eat that burnt piece of toast so others won't have to, though their own appetite be spoiled. Kinsmen are exemplary souls who do not let others down or cause a frown. Often the cost is self.

It is not uncommon or surprising that others take advantage of them. While their left hand may not care what their right hand is doing, the intentions of others may not be equally pure. Others tend not to be as appreciative of them as deserved either. Because their emotional antennae are both quick and astute, Kinsmen respond without need for invitation. Mates, friends and associates become accustomed to efficient Kinsmen, who can without invitation, question or fanfare, anticipate, address and ably dispense with the wants and needs of others. When disagreement occurs, they offer solutions rather than attitude. When problems arise they shoulder the blame and too often, others let them because it's easier that way.

Criticism, their Achilles' heel

No other is as deeply wounded by criticism as Kinsmen. Responsibility may be their name's fame and claim, but can be their undoing. Theirs is a world-class logical mind, yet they make decisions by consensus. Why? Because Kinsmen do nothing that is not others first focused. They do not err by assumption...they inquire first. They do not disappoint by dereliction of duty; they consult first to confirm. When criticized, they interpret it as having personally failed and having personally disappointed. Fault cannot lie elsewhere but with them. After all, they've already inquired, consulted, and gained approval—their modus operandi for doing. While others will mount a defense or campaign to absolve themselves of blame, Kinsmen seldom contest or protest. They assume they're wrong and set about restoring harmony. But the stinger lodges within, its fester hidden from notice.

These individuals earn their right to belong. They earn affection by being dependable, earn respect by doing and earn success by being right more often than not. Criticism is rejection and threatens continuance, which sends tremors of self-doubt to undermine their confidence. Being indispensible to others, being irreplaceable is important to these individuals because they cannot trust love—that emotional uncertainty—to be enough to hold their place in another's affection. For them, emotions are confusing and not to be trusted.

Kinsmen experience emotional outbursts. Tears can well suddenly and unbidden when shown kindness, when they share affection or sympathy, even when angered and most especially when hurt. Like flash floods, their tears rush and gush but recede quickly. They usually hide this phenomena from others, to avoid exposing their vulnerability, but mainly to avoid having to explain the depth of their feelings. Kinsmen do not trust the intensity or the unpredictability of their own emotions. They've been wrong before. For instance, they can feel strongly toward their mate one day, where every smile...step...or frown fills and moves them with love. Yet the next day, a wrong word from their mate...a raised eyebrow...a burp can have their feelings flying in the opposite direction.

Emotions are unreliable to Kinsmen who feel strongly about everything, just inconsistently. They share their love by taking care of others, by helping, by giving, by protecting, by providing. They are vulnerable to others to the extent that others need and appreciate them, not by cement of love commitment. For love, supposedly the ultimate emotion, they tend not to trust. Emotions are used to add sugar or spice to moments like: feeling warm pride, feeling good with another, feeling rewarded when helping or feeling bad when hurt. Emotions can't be trusted to last more than a day, far less be enough to build a till-death-do-us-part life on. Kinsmen may say they marry for love but the deciding vote was tendered by logic. They are not risk-takers; they'd not bet the farm on love lasting long.

One common characteristic of Kinsmen: once all parts and pieces of career are in place, once all family players know their marks, know their lines and the game of life is smoothly running—they rebel. As long as they are preoccupied with doing and building, all seems okay. Sitting back to enjoy the fruits of their labour is when Kinsmen realize how personally detached and unfulfilled they are, despite all this! Many start looking for emotional excitement and release.

They build their public and private lives intellectually and carefully, using few emotional tools along the way. Emotions are celebrations for highs or dirges for lows, but when that bad angel starts demanding some emotional airtime, they tend to take their show on the road. It seems they've gotta be bad sometimes, to be good the rest. If not, they suffer the moods, the blues and the down-in-the-dumps unlike anyone. When Kinsmen hit those *cyclical swamps,* every ignored and suppressed emotion comes out to play. That's why Kinsmen don't trust themselves. They get into the habit early on of keeping a tight rein on emotions. They ask others, "What would you do..?" or "How would you feel...?" and determine their own actions and responses based on the reasonable average. The only time Kinsmen really pay attention to emotions and remove the "cork" is when they feel hurt; when emotions are at their most demanding worst and their most frightening loudest.

Reticence, thy name is Kinsmen, is why they seek outlet elsewhere. They'll not risk disrupting their well-oiled world for the sake of something as fleet and fickle as feelings. Outside and away from their real and most important life—family, community and work—is where Kinsmen take their bad angel to play games of emotional roulette.

They find another preoccupation or another lover and push passion's envelope. If a preoccupation, their interest can become obsessive until their fever has burned itself out. Then, the interest is either discarded or more rationally pursued and incorporated into their life routine. The game is more dangerous when the lover route is chosen. Less for them than for lovers, however. Be warned, Kinsmen usually mate for life: *as one should.* If passion's flame gets too close to emotional wings or if their lover demands more commitment, regardless of how Kinsmen feels, they'll typically throw up the wall of logic, firmly braced by responsibility and head homeward. They seldom walk away from their intellectually planned and carefully constructed lives. The prospect of dividing family and financial assets is a huge divorce deterrent for highly responsible, security-conscious Kinsmen.

If or when caught, their mate could not meet a more repentant and remorseful sinner than their wandering, temporarily insane Kinsmen. But this lover exercise for emotional release is not easy for Kinsmen. They truly suffer when they cause others pain. Unless they mate with a personality style that encourages them to explore, understand, trust, and use the power of their emotional dimension, these individuals can lead lives of cyclical despair. And they can infect others with their emotional misery, time and time again. The greatest challenge for Kinsmen is to trust self. Love is a two-way flow: in, as well as out. What dishonesty is greater, what deception more painful, than dishonest love? Most especially for self? For all the world, Kinsmen may look like a chocolate covered raisin, but upon testing, may only be rabbit turd.

Truth wins

> "You must be the change you wish to see in the world."
> —Mahatma Gandhi

When Kinsmen ascribe to and apply their own truth they tend to make a difference in the world before life's end. The Gandhi's and Good Samaritans among us are Kinsmen, guided by their own fount of truth: emotions. Their lives stand as inspiration for others, as exemplary models of highest principles. They do not search for their own purpose or life's meaning in others' opinions. They avoid anchor of pulpit, lectern or soapbox and they'd no sooner dilute or diminish their own value and worth, than another's. Their greatest power is emotional trust, for that is how soul communicates individual truth and wisdom to each.

Kinsmen are the greatest teachers of life's lessons: those who seldom tell, who sometimes explain, who mostly demonstrate and who always inspire by the example of their living. The difference between a confident and an unconfident Kinsmen is one degree of trust. Confidents trust their emotions above all else. Self-fulfillment is their first responsibility, showing others by the example of their living unfolds as they live, not because they followed the right plans in books or took the average and general road. They already know what's right for them. They feel it and trust those feelings. As they generously offer love, they generously welcome its equal return.

Kinsmen's greatest gift is knowing that one language is common to all. One that needs neither translator nor translation: emotion. In every part of the world, in every walk of life, within every human is there equal capacity to feel. An Inuit, an Aborigine, a pauper, a poet, a pimp or prophet, are equally conversant in pain, sorrow and joy. All range, ebb, flow, and variety of emotion is soul-common to all, as blood to each. Kinsmen change worlds emotionally. The banner they walk under is brotherhood. It mobilizes concern and nurtures with touch. It may be drawn and driven by love but it must be delivered by self-truth to have meaning for Kinsmen.

While they enjoy the physical pleasure, they need the emotional release of sex. In sexual intimacy, inner balance restores and creativity unpins and unravels. On waves of wielding, yielding emotion, they communicate pent need, want and wish. Aggression's sway, assertion's say, and fleshly pleasure, are found and fed in body's commune and passion's move. Imaginative, experimental, and demanding lovers, they explore the full score of emotion's symphony. Sexual relations validate their human, their bestial, and their spiritual. Coupled carnal embrace is their invitation to celebrate lust, love, and trust.

Supremely gentle beings, Kinsmen hands are warm, supple and ever-available for pitching in or taking over when wanted and when needed most. Keen of mind and kind in manner, they are the evolutionary help mates. Their purpose is to serve the greatest good, to mortar the cracks, bridge the gaps and remove the fences that divide each from other and other from all. For Kinsmen, there is but one path to fulfillment: love of others. Love lives in emotions. No matter how far each travels or how much each does or gives, love is an inside job.

THE EMOTIONALS

Life Purpose

No other functions with such emotional purity and smarts as Empath. By mere of proximity can they read the emotional state of others, as clearly and accurately as others read billboards. Their evolutionary role has been nurturer, counselor, comforter, coach, inspiration in doubt, shoulder for cry, and cool hand in fever. Their purpose is to teach mankind one lesson: How to love one another.

Intimacy & Emotion

Is to say in the same breath, "I love hotdogs, I love you," preposterous or profound? Perhaps in love as in life, fulfillment depends on how deeply each is willing to invest and divest of self, to explore the depth of love that rewards. In terms of hotdogs, where is love found?

Could be at surface ,where taste of mustard, bun, and wiener is depth enough. Could be deeper, at appreciation for the makers of mustard, the bakers of bread and the butchers of meat. Could be deeper yet, at marvel of nature to produce the mustard seed, wheat kernel and seasons for ripen and reapen. Could be even deeper, at "thank you pig" with life tethered to man for husbandry purposes. Could be at deepest core of understanding, that within that cloven-hoofed beast dwelt a force as mysterious, elusive and wondrous as man's. Life for all is nothing less or more than love.

Love at the surface-level is like taste: take it or leave it. Love at the appreciation-level is like willingness: acceptable if favourable. Love at the marvel-level is like need: there until confident again. Love at the thank you-level is like chicken to egg: devoted. Love at the core-level is like pig to ham: committed to for life.

Many separate and different languages are spoken by humans, but the one commonly and equally understood is the language of emotions. The reasons behind laughter or tears might not be understood by all intellectually, but at sight and sound are understand by all emotionally. Regardless of age or gender, and despite flag, colour, or creed, emotion communication is a common ability. Fluency in the language of emotions is an umbilical miracle granted all humans at birth. When a picture evokes one thousand words, it's emotion's hand that forms and writes them. From infancy to old age, individuality is most clearly conveyed and most plainly heard when emotions are the messenger.

Emotions contain all that's inherently human—including much that's abstract and inexplicable, like disappointment and yearn. The most abstract emotion is love. Unlike tears and laughter, love is not as readily communicated or understood. Emotions can gather and bundle love, but unless individual truth sends the package and individual truth receives it, love won't be exchanged. Truth is love's constant companion. And while truth may seem to little more than a dimple in love's smile, the relationship is such that you can't have one without the other.

Another human-inherent emotion is *self-interest*—an imposter of love—and the cause of much confusion between love-senders and love-receivers. Self-interest is independent and has nothing to do with love's necessary sidekick, truth. Instead, self-interest singularly goes forth to meet its own needs and fulfill its own objectives.

Having set the three backdrops on love—the depth of fulfillment, its common language, and the dimple of truth—it's time to introduce one very interesting human: Empath.

Ranked among the most powerful, Empath is endowed with incredible gifts: emotion-intellect and acuity second to none, and a talent for teaching. These innate skills are necessary, as their purpose, *to teach others to love one another*, can alter man and world upon delivery. These sentient, abundantly-gifted beings have one need: to be unconditionally loved.

That need is also their Achilles' heel. Unlike Achilles, whose defeat diminished but one, Empath leaves a wide path of destruction when they fall. One side of the Empath coin reads "remarkable" which was stamped there before the stork arrived. The other side was left blank. Whatever Empath directly inscribes there is what others experience of them and decides their renown.

One hallmark of Empaths: No matter how many positives precede it, one negative negates all.

In one fell swoop they forget the good and remember the bad. Therefore, our conversation will be from worst, to best. If reversed, their best wouldn't be heard and wouldn't have a chance to sink in. This personality needs to be reminded of "who" and "why" they are. Only for Empaths, is a no-holds-barred downside included. It promises to be as direct and disturbing as anything they're likely to hear about their style's negative potential and propensity. Others and world need Empath too much, to chance their sitting on the sidelines for much longer. Most don't realize how powerful they are, or how destructive they can be. More often than

Pg. 365 *http://www.ansir.com*

any other style, these ones fall short of meeting their evolutionary responsibilities. And the most common reason is selfishness, *aka*, self-interest.

How unEmpath, can Empath get?

Far, far from nature,when self-doubt leads.

Their "crime" is most often emotional abuse. In one as emotionally-
intelligent as them, criminal irresponsibility is the only label that fits. They
can be masters of emotional manipulation and the nastiest little pissers
potentially. They, like a few others, have the ability to hone in on another's
extreme vulnerability. Unlike those few others, they tend to use that ability to purposely and pointedly destroy another when they feel threatened
or hurt. Truly capable of going undetected as wolf in sheep's clothing, they
cling to point of suffocation and call it love's commitment. Like some
insects, they lay their good intentions in living hosts and feed on their
spirit. If such behaviour is called parasitic in nature, it's called "love me,
you owe me," or "look at all I've done for you," by Empath.

These are the ones who confuse sex with love; who sift through mate's
personal effects looking for evidence to substantiate their own doubts; the
ones who use their own children as pawns in divorce proceedings, or as a
means to punish and control ex's afterward; the ones who hire private
detectives to entrap those they profess to love; the parent, so jealous of
their mate's adoration for child/children, they campaign as though in battle with enemy to browbeat, demean, and crush their own girls and boys;
the one who turns deaf or blind when offspring are beaten and/or molest-
ed by mate; the one who subjects self and children to years of fear and bat-
tering for, "I still love them, they need me" reasons. They're also are the
one who murders their ex whilst ex is sleeping.

Crimes of passion are their particular fame. Empath can smother with
kindness, kill with love, and readily sweep their own dignity under the

carpet. Why? Because of their all-consuming need for unconditional love: no matter the cost or pain. And they, more than most, are willing to toss their birth gifts and talents onto the pyre of self-doubt to get it—along with anyone else perceived to be a threat to its attainment, including their own children.

Obviously, Empath is not the only one capable of such behaviour. What adds weight to their particular despicability, is their misuse of the innate emotional advantage they have over most others. In personal relations they tend to settle for gratification over self-fulfillment. They do not physically harm or hurt. Their damage takes place under skin, inside hearts and souls. Like emotion-sucking leeches, they feed on veins of spirit and confidence, because they can. Perhaps investigating their need for unconditional love and acceptance will help all understand, why Empath uses love to crush instead of build, as born and meant.

Few personalities are as tribal-oriented as Empath. Smack dab in the middle of teeming humanity is where they belong. Their need to be unconditionally loved tends to colour their every thought, word, and deed. Empath's greatest challenge is to be true to self, and trust that love and acceptance will follow. No matter if occasionally the crowd boo's, hisses, and chases, just ensure it's the genuine you that's running, not a false persona. All the talent that's vested in Empath does seem to confirm that their life-purpose must be important and must be tough to fulfill.

Empaths are emotionals.
The world can be an unfriendly place for emotionals, if not understood.

First of all, they're curious about everything, especially people. What a marvelous creation for the sociable Empath child. These characteristically bright, shiny-eyed tykes can't seem to get up early enough in the morning to get their day's fill of enjoyment. And those feelings! One roller coaster delight after another. Their soul sings, soars, and squeals with emotional pleasure. Empaths emote deeply. If not bubbling with laughter, they're brimming with tears.

Others don't understand how intensely they feel and tend to take their tearfulness far too seriously. They're not necessarily sad or hurt when they're crying, they could just be intensely experiencing their feelings. Disposable tissue was likely invented for this sensitive style, who tears as much when they laugh as when they cry, and sometimes they do both at once. The sight of someone crying can make them to weep in sympathy—they're **that** emotionally attuned to others.

With speech comes mistrust

As children, when teased or taunted for being so sissy, Empath learns to mask their feelings. When they begin to speak, they may learn to mask their thoughts too. Before they could talk, they sensed what others were thinking and wanting, and responded appropriately without use of words. When they learn to speak, they also learn what *good, bad,* and *worst* feels like. Good is when others like what they say; bad is when they don't; and worst is when they reply and others get angry.

Why do they feel the right answers inside, but when they express or act on them, they get wrong responses from others, from happy love to angry hate? It shakes their faith in their ability to understand when loved and trusted others tell them with words what they feel is not right. They become reactionary. Like expert tailors, they fashion for themselves whatever mood-garment pleases another. Thus they begin what will become an adult Empath trait, "Tell them what they want to hear."

Others want them to believe words, so Empath begins listening thrice before answering. First, they listen to the words that are spoken. Secondly, they read the other's emotions. Thirdly, they consider their own feelings.

All three are then lumped together and considered. Empath then decides which words to use or action to take that will please the most.

They have a lifelong love-hate relationship with words, especially when pressured to answer quickly. They can't! Being entirely emotional, there are infinite shades and degrees to feelings, but limited words for accurately describing them. Translating intense feelings into words is challenging. Transcribing thoughts and emotions of others, through filter of self, requires great skill and finesse. Such anticipatory analysis and processing takes skill and time.

Empaths may not make the college debate team, but tend to be great writers. Emotion-intelligence is internally generated, whereas, mental-intelligence (knowledge) is externally collected. Mental memory is finite; emotion memory is infinite, and infinitely creative. Emotion-intellect is so much quicker than mental-intellect that logical others have difficulty trusting the answers. To logicals, anything arrived at so speedily can't be right, so not only do they discount the solution they discount its source. Explaining is all that's required to remove logical confusion. For Empath, attempting to explain away confusion usually leads to greater confusion and frustration for logicals!

Empaths think, not for themselves, but for two or more at once. What do others think and feel? What do I think and feel? And then, most importantly, what do others want to hear? Self-doubt is why Empaths make greater writers than debaters. For them, debating/explaining requires their thinking, interpreting, and responding to please, from one to many. Writing involves thinking and feeling for one, and pleasing self is not a pressure as much as a leisure.

Empath can sense the discrepancies between external expression and innermost intention. Consequently, they place little faith in what others say. Nothing is worse, nothing shakes their confidence more than anger.

To them, anger means one thing: "I don't love you, I don't want you. Go away!" For Empath, the message underlying anger is abandonment. The prospect of being an outcast is terrifying for them. Characteristically, and at any age, Empath does not like being alone. The last personality to be a hermit or recluse is Empath.

While others may prefer privacy to recuperate from illness, these individuals may actually become more sick if left alone. They need to be with people. One of the first realizations Empath makes is: if they please others, then others won't leave them or chase them away. They focus effort and energy on making others happy; the yardstick against which they measure their value. That toddler decision often becomes a pattern for life.

When they make others happy they're good, are accepted, are loved. If others get angry, they're bad, are unwanted, are unloveable. If making others angry is their fault, then all they need to do is fix that part of the equation, so love and acceptance can get back on track. The anger review above may seem irrational to others, but it accurately depicts how Empath views anger. They'll do whatever it takes to make others accept them again, including taking all the blame for the rift. Pleasing others is how these individuals earn and keep their place in the herd.

Empath more than emotionally commits to others, they clone identities, especially with mate. Of partners or couples that think, sound, and even resemble each another, one or both are Empath. They often are so used to thinking, feeling, and anticipating the needs of their mate, they half-become them. Abandonment not only disrupts their life, it removes some of their self-identity. Anger is a major source of hardship and pain for Empath. Why?

Anger in others

If the emotional dimension of Empath were to be suddenly dumped into the body of almost any other, they'd be institutionalized from the shock to their system. When people are angry, all other emotions get buried beneath it. Purely emotional Empath feels the full, undiluted force of anger. It stuns first, then overwhelms. Anger is an impenetrable wall of rejection, as emotionally visible to Empaths, as a scowling face to others.

Their emotional antennae cannot penetrate anger. Without emotional guidance, Empaths are fish out of water, struggling for understanding but strangling on empty air. Overcome with fear of abandonment, they're unable to speak. Reasoning gets drowned by emotions. Imagine being attacked by your own hand. That's how anger from loved ones feels to Empath. Unable to emotionally penetrate the wall of anger and gain understanding, they're forced to rely on something they don't trust and that's unnatural for them: words!

Whether infant or adult, whether logical or not, Empath blames their self for all that goes wrong in their relationships. If an Empath child causes a playmate to cry, they'll immediately offer toys or sweets to placate. As adults, they do much the same, by being the first to make gestures of peace, after a row.

They'll send gifts of apology and make plans for reconciliation. To reconnect emotionally, to ensure the relationship's continuance, is of utmost importance to Empath. Lack of self-confidence and low self-esteem are guaranteed, when others *allow* them to shoulder the bulk of the blame—which Empath is too often, too willing to do. Their greatest desire, being accepted and loved, precludes them doing nothing. They acquiesce, because peace is more important to them than pride.

Being extremely intelligent, with a memory envied by elephants, Empath tends not to provoke anger the same way twice. They'll broach an unresolved issue from new angles, in hopes of evoking a more favourable response and reaching a resolution. Or with unquestionable déja vu accuracy, they'll revive for purposes of reliving, an issue that they felt was prematurely closed and that they're more prepared to address. However, when they're angered, it becomes clear just how very much baggage Empath had been silently stockpiling.

Anger in self

When a reactive role in life is subscribed to, it is as feather in wind; spiralling uncertainty. Generally speaking, Empath hinges their happiness on others and measures self-worth by their ability to please. A policy destined to return them maximum insecurity.

They may test for relationship security by playing emotional *Hokey-Pokey:* alternating between purposely pushing their mate/friends away, then charming them back again—attempting to find concrete proof of being unconditionally loved. Empath may flirt with others to purposely test their mate's interest and loyalty. They may even be attracted to a mate whose emotionally unsophisticated and who treats them callously or casually, as though the cyclical exercise of losing and re-earning affection were proof of love.

It is not uncommon for Empath to fantasize about changing "bad" apple into sweet applesauce with their own brand of love. As though a "loser magnet," they attract, or are attractive to, those who promise from the outset to abuse them emotionally or physically; and who tend to deliver on their promise, too.

More than others, Empath uses sex to win favour or control others. Their modus operandi likely prompted the old, "not tonight dear, I've got a headache" out of peevishness, not malady. Empath is likely to require their mate jump through hoops to prove their love. The game usually begins with, "If you loved me, you would...." Extreme jealousy on the part of an unconfident Empath is not unusual. Their mate may have to frequently declare their devotion to them, leading mate to question whether "I love you," is not a loaded pistol extorting parrot-reply, than a sincere and meaningful declaration."

Of them can it be said, "they don't lose their temper often but when they do, look out!" The emotional overwhelm Empath experiences when angered can be so great, it can delay rational thinking for extended periods of time and cause them to act in shockingly, uncharacteristic ways. Anything from venting pent-up grievances, to venomous spew, to schemed and executed revenge, are likely when Empath frustration reaches its max. In order to gain desired outcomes, they're more likely to manipulate indirectly than confront directly. They stringently avoid the questions of importance, "Do you still want me/love me?" Such invitation may return a "No!" and realize their greatest fear: abandonment.

When Hokey-Pokey no longer works and their mate is determined to sever relations, the dormant seeds of, "Hell hath no fury, like an Empath scorned," can sprout bitter wings. Their mate can be sitting across the litigation table from them, wondering whether a *Body Snatcher* pod had not replaced the person they once lived with and loved. Crimes of passion can be the outcome, when Empath is rejected. Temporary insanity may be the official name but reticence is the more likely and real blame.

Their need to be unconditionally accepted *cupboards* their biggest fear, abandonment, as well as their truth. When abandonment does occur, Empath, who pleased by keeping their truth tightly secured may in fulminating anger come unglued. Hatred and vengeance glinting in their eye is unnatural for them.

3 Sides of You

Empaths are good with and good for many personality styles. However, few styles are good for them in return, especially, if Empath is unconfident. Few have the emotion-intelligence it takes to encourage them to remove their own insecurity mask and set themselves free. Intuitives understand emotionals and tend not to tolerate Empath's manipulative ploys or insecurity games. The few that demand and expect the real Empath to stand up and step out are usually the first, but not the last, to experience one of the planet's rare treasures: an Empath whose every smile is dimpled with self-confidence; *aka self-truth and self-trust.*

Empaths are sexual, pleasure-indulgent beings, who emotionally infuse with their mate during carnal intimacy. As lovers they're more compliant than aggressive, and have a robust appetite for sex. They feel the emotional state of their mate, to learn of need or desire, and are responsive in kind or to game. With uninhibited abandon, they express all aspects of human intimacy, frailty and emotion; gentle, hard, taking, giving, partner, whore, lover, stranger, one. Empaths seethe with passion and tend not to be without partners for long. They don't like being alone; sex satisfies their need for close emotional bonding. They're often possessive, jealous lovers, and the ones who need to be hugged near and held dear afterwards.

A formal and official exchange of marriage vows goes a long way to making Empath feel confidence and secure in the relationship. In addition to it being a legally and mutually binding commitment, the words, "till death do us part," offer them a divine reassurance.

Most Empaths have strong emotional ties to a Higher Power. Many have had a deeply religious experience of one sort or another, where their faith was restored by religious enlightenment. Empath children often recount visits by angels. Many spend their lives looking for a relationship that offers the same unconditional love and acceptance as a Higher Power.

All that compromising of self for the sake of belonging has a price. It may take years to mature, but eventually, payment comes due. Their unique, emotion-intelligence bubbles and brews, no matter how big the seed of doubt they've lodged there, to quieten truth. If not used, truth festers and fumes, and becomes emotional frustration.

Come hell or high water, by implosion or explosion, *truth will out.* Analyst couches, relationship counselors, weight-loss clinics, addiction services, assertiveness training, group therapy, pharmaceutical industries, and institutions—from health to penitentiary—are familiar with the self-denial propensity of Empath, and of the destructive consequences that can follow their frustration's burst. Empath's emotional dimension is so sophisticated and powerful it can't be ignored forever. The flag of self-trust will need to be recaptured by them, at one point or another in their lifetime—by choice or out of necessity.

Usually by middle-age, Empath wearies of their self-scripted role of reactionary puppet. Usually, and usually voluntarily, they snip their own enslaving strings. Wisdom for Empath often only comes with age. They generally repeat lessons many times over, before learning. What their wrinkle-wisened eyes see, when they look into their soul mirror, determines their role in what Empaths have called, their second and main act.

Either they continue to hide under the cabbage leaf of denial or they say "hello" to self, unwrap their gifts, and get busy doing what they do better than anyone else: *teach others how to love self and others.* They can't do that until they embrace the whole and all of their complicated being, and accept and love their self first.

Though Empath representation by population is quite large, their style's impact is small historically—as it should be and is supposed to be! Empath is not a mover and shaker, they're a catalyst. The ones who stoke other engine fires, moving the confidence of others from, *I think I can, I think I can,* to *I know I can,* and onto their doing. That's what Empath does and why they're so important and so needed by others. How loving and successful their company, is less a measure of others than a measure of this style's influence. One need only look at the world today to realize that the high population of Empaths are hiding their catalyst gifts under doubt-infested leaves, instead of using and applying them to people-benefit, as born and meant.

Perhaps in evolution as in life, there are no coincidences. Holistic system theory seems to be globally emerging, and entails a rewriting of the rules governing the quality of life. At the nucleus of this awareness movement is acknowledgement that humans are sacred, and entitled sacred consideration in global decisions. Four personalities have the potential and the inherent power to help others prepare for the next evolutionary step: away from technological dependence, toward human and communal responsibility. One is Empath, who, for too-long has been unaware or been unwilling to assume the responsibility that goes with their innate gifts and power. Something these emotional beings may not have considered, but may find enlightening:

If the most trusted individual known were to visit and say, *"You've been granted a most extraordinary power. From this moment on, you'll be right. No matter what you think, it will be the rightest thought; no matter what you decide, it will be the rightest decision; no matter what you say, it will be the rightest statement; and no matter what you do, it will have be done rightly."*

How would you feel?

Would you still be afraid to be you, or would you charge into the moment, into the situation, and into the day more bravely and confidently? What effect would such an individual have on others? On world?

Being right for you, every time, is the wish that emotion-intellect grants you. While every personality style is capable of accessing emotion-wisdom, Empath hands are born holding the tap.

Who is more loveable and acceptable? The responsive, unconfident one, who adjusts self to fit before giving or doing, and who expects repayment in love for their having pleased? Or the responsive one, who gives and does according to own truth, and who expects nothing in return, because pleasing others are reward and reason enough, for them?

It usually takes years for Empath to learn the what and how of their life-purpose lesson. From hereon, Empath, further delays on your part are owed to choice, not to nature, not to ability, and not to ignorance.

One can neither lover nor lovedOne be, unless love and trust of self are cellular secretions.

THE INTUITIVES

isionary

Life Purpose

Man stepped beyond beast with speech, dream, laughter, and thumb, but where does change, advancement, and progress come from? Visionary. The evolutionary oracle, soothsayer, and prophet, who beyond reason or ridicule is compelled to make a mark and leave the world a better place for their having been. Whether stone hammer, wheel, or club, Darwin's theory, Michelangelo's art, Pasteur's milk, Hull's peace plan, Emerson's rationality, or Will Roger's rope, Visionary has been, seen, forged, and won. Their responsibility—their birth-entwined covenant—is to break new ground. Theirs, is a four-part contract to fulfill before the tick-tock of their preset-clock winds down. Overcome self-doubt. Find and fulfill purpose. Serve the greater good. Prevail till done.

Intimacy & Emotion

None other appreciates the predicament of Biblical Virgin Mary, as does Visionary, who, too, deals with something beyond their control. Visionary has a birth covenant; a cellular contract to do something significant in their lifetime that contributes to the betterment of others. Only then will they know self-fulfillment. When Visionary shows up in any realm of the *3 Sides Of You* Profile, things could change for the better out there. From the earliest age, these emotionally astute beings begin questioning in one form or another, "What purpose this human?" Until Visionary finds that elusive *what*, their internal clock relentlessly unwinds, marking time's passage and making contentment impossible for them.

Self-doubt is the first hurdle for Visionarys

Once that issue has been addressed and overcome, usually in adulthood, these talented individuals become a confident Visionary. That makes all the difference. Visionary is evolutionarily, as historically, the wealthiest and most powerful style on the planet; and the happiest. Doubt is the only issue that can derail or defeat them. *(If life isn't going your way, Visionary, read Visionary thinking and working realms too).*

They intuitively know things that escape logic's explanation, make decisions beyond normal deduction, and bet on self despite opposition. It has usually taken years of disappointment for them to realize their greatest gift and power is intuition, and less than a nano-second thereafter, to trust it over intellect. Overcoming doubt is only the beginning; their next and greater challenge is to find their niche and fulfill their life purpose.

Visionary tends to be noticed. Something more than attractiveness; something tangible yet elusive draws others' attention. In social situations, they often adopt an aloof persona out of innate shyness, often needing time to feel a certain level of comfort before removing their "don't approach" masks. Once they do, the reason for their reluctance is understood. Few personalities are as passionate about people, about life, about everything, as them. Their social mask allows them to choose with whom they'll divest and invest of self. In everyday life, few are as physically easy to read as Visionary. Face, words, and behaviour, accurately and obviously reflect their state of contentment.

Those familiar with Visionary know that guile is neither game nor creed of theirs. They tend to express the fullest range of emotions, openly and generously. Visionary has an enormous energy field; an enveloping, palpitating presence that resonates and vibrates visibly. Most feel energized in the charismatic magnetism of their presence, though many can feel intimidated by the confidence they exude. If others are uncomfortable around Visionary, there's a reason. These intuitives use their extraordinary emotion sensors to feel the emotional temperature of others, before exchange of names or particulars. In fact, others can pretty accurately gauge the impact of their own first impression by shaking their hand and looking them in the eye. They tend to be so attuned to voice inflection, intonation, and body energy they can determine friendships in advance of meeting. Interestingly, when two Visionary strangers meet, a sense of déja vu is experienced or sexual interest is sparked.

As all roads led to Rome, all that's Visionary leads to purpose

To do something significant in their lifetime is why Visionary is here. No matter how it's phrased, the fact remains: any relationship with Visionary comes second to their life-purpose fulfillment. By explaining this to potential mates they chance being thought crack pots. "I have this important thing I must do, dear, so while I sincerely vow undying love, you, me, and our relationship will always come second to that."

Everything in Visionary's life—from partner, to mate, to job, to location—must harmonize and complement their determined drive. A run-of-the-mill mate just won't do for confident Visionary. They can get along with almost all personality styles professionally, but few are passionate enough to satisfy or interest them for long personally. Those with narrow-edges or those who practice reticence will soon part from their company.

Narrow edges

Visionary is used to defying logic and ignoring opinion. They, like Evokateur, know that the genius today was likely yesterdays fool. Intuition for most and many is hocus-pocus, and those who persist in such irrational practices are suspect, at least. Confident Visionary knows where they're going, what they want, and who they need. Their self-trust hocus pocus leads to success more often than not. Long familiar with ridicule and too familiar with rejection, Visionary turns a deaf ear to their detractors and a blind eye to distractions. These are highly tribal-oriented individuals who want to belong and be honoured, but what Visionary needs is cooperation from others to help them fulfill their life purpose.

They have the gift of vision to see what others cannot, the intellect to organize and plan, the creativity to anticipate and solve problems, and the ambition to fulfill goals and objectives. What they lack is the time or patience to accomplish their vision alone. Others are not only fascinating and loveable to Visionary, but necessary. Each person met is a must meet, not a coincidence. Discovering the why behind meeting others is Visionary's first responsibility. Conversations with them don't stay at chit-chat for long but move quickly to penetrating and revealing, because now or in the future, a skill or talent of an acquaintance may be just what they need and could use. No other networks as naturally or as non-stop as them.

To illustrate, consider the life purpose covenant of Visionary and their tick-tock urgency. They must do something significant, but what? Until found, it is as much a puzzle to them as to any other. There are no clues except their greatest pleasures involve people and work. These are not hermits or abstract theorists; these are practical visionaries who seek a better way in this here and now. Visionary looks for, and finds the best in others and gives their own best generously in thought and for work. When it comes to matters of the heart, they tend to love selfishly.

Visionary passion require lots of room to play, so the distance between "edges" of mates is important. Edges meaning how emotionally expansive another is, or how narrowed by fear. Will they need a celestial map to navigate possibilities, or be eternally perched on safe and tethered to known? Emotional honesty is an issue for Visionary. They're workaholics who actively seek work they can love. It's essential for them that love and home be equally compelling. Curiosity and creativity are their tools-of-choice, but emotions make all Visionary decisions. Those who cannot, will not, or dare not dream aloud, just will not do, for them Their mate, like all close relations, must be able to travel emotionally and intellectually to places not yet explored or experienced. That's how and where Visionary goes.

Reticence stops here

Nothing will end a relationship with them faster than reticence. Close associates, friends, or the mate of a confident Visionary, are bound to meet Mr. Hyde in the flesh should reticence rear its unwelcome head. These are intuitive-intellects of a rare order. Visionary makes it a priority to discover the ups and downs and ins and outs of all whom they desire close relations with—in boardroom or bedroom. Mind/emotion games are their specialty, if not their modus operandi. They can taste hesitancy, smell reluctance, and hear unspoken fears or falsehoods as clearly as if yelled in their ear. When others are reluctant to express truth, Visionary drags it out or walks away.

They know how intrinsic conflict is, to clear communication and understanding. Whether used to avoid truth or due to fear of vulnerability, reticence to Visionary is a waste of their most precious commodity: time. Others can be gobsmacked by Visionary directness. Not contentious by nature but surely impatient, Visionary intuits what others are feeling, and gets irritated waiting for verbal confirmation. To them, extracting truth from others is a time-consuming, onion peeling exercise. One that produces tears and runny noses and only serves to delay time before the real cooking begins. Visionary prefers to begin intimate relationships at the cooking stage, not at scrape and peel. These individuals are often openly expressive and emotionally effusive. Whether the issue is life, love, or liverwurst, they express themselves and expect same in return.

Intuition is their gift but communication unwraps it. Words kernel truth for them. Few can deduct insight from undertones of words spoken, unspoken, or written, like they can. Fewer yet can emotionally inspire, infuse, or confuse like them either. Visionary leads the world with words. And while they have the ability to charm birds out of the trees when they want, their equal fame is for being the most difficult upright walker when angered. That innate communicative skill that can fathom and form instant friendship or intimacy, can tear flesh from bones if provoked. Fortunately, that state is not common nor long in duration.

For them, dishonesty grates as chillingly across intuition, as nails across a blackboard. They usually deal head-on with issues and resolve them, without bitterness lingering in memory or clinging to tongue. "I don't chew my cabbage twice," was likely born of their common refusal to reopen and rehash old issues. They not only invite but expect full disclosure of opinion and emotion as problems arise. The closer the relationship, the clearer the understanding—Visionary expects others to speak promptly and vent fully. Once addressed, they consider the issue closed for all time. Being direct and truthful may initially be intimidating or frightening for others, but it proves to be efficient and practical. In fact, their truth-airing approach may be why Visionary spends less time on analyst couches and are less violent than others, comparatively.

Celibacy is not in their vocabulary, nor may monogamy be. Visionary feels and decides emotionally, rather than *shouldly*. If the relationship isn't emotionally satisfying for them, obligation won't be reason enough to stay or to continue it. As Visionary searches far and wide, looking for meaningful work, they may explore a variety of intimacies before choosing their mate. Those who cannot match their typical intensity can be consumed by their more direct, emotional fire. If by nature an unexpected brew, diluting with milk or sweetening with sugar won't disguise Visionary's unique taste and flavour.

If lovemaking were an Olympic event, they'd be the Gold medalists. Sexuality and sensuality are terms born of intimacy's meet with Visionary. When fleshly-focused, their instincts are bestial, seductive, and irresistible. In naked union, their creativity unwinds, invades, and convulses with pro-creative-pleasure. On waves of passion, primeval energy flows, in raw seek and need of burst and escape. Their embrace disarms, demands, amuses, infuses, instructs, infuriates, charms, penetrates, and puts mates in their rightful place: at the centre of Visionary's universe. Theirs, an inspired madness, where mutual love explorations journey all sensory dimensions. They're usually demanding lovers, intolerant of anything that comes between them and their emotional sustenance. When they find a mate who completes and complements them, without their having to greatly compromise their self, they tend to be jealous and possessive.

Their birth responsibility is an onerous task. It requires them to rearrange reality through invention or innovation, and reorder their priorities including their personal relations. Trusting self is why Visionary is the most powerful individual on the planet. Trusting intuition and creativity enough to go where others would not, have not, or dared not is what sets them apart. Once Visionary jaws set in determination, their perseverance has no equal. Accumulating wealth is not their objective; betterment is. Self and others may very well come second to life purpose, but being in second place for Visionary is like standing outside the horn of plenty; the spillage is more than adequate.

Satisfaction tends to elude until they accept their Visionary responsibility and master the only lesson they need learn. Consciously submit to intuitive intelligence and stop depending on opinion, scholar, book, and/or expert. Ignoring that purpose-wound, covenant clock tends to leave Visionary unfulfilled and unsatisfied. Even failure or incompletion is preferable to walking away from their birth responsibility. If Visionary ignores their covenant, they still must daily live with the tick-tock reminder of their not doing. Their persistent, perfectionistic, and responsible nature meets unrelenting dissatisfaction. Disillusionment and self-recrimination tend to be constant companions in later life. There's a feeling among Visionarys, generally, that mistakes and failures while striving for success are the worthiest memories to collect for rocking chair days. Few are more bitter at life's end than a Visionary who did not risk self enough to pursue their life purpose.

If the proof of pudding is taste, then proof of Visionary fulfillment is happiness. Work is the path that leads to self-fulfillment and happiness is the indicator that lights up when the right path is found. Some may envy them their charismatic confidence, some, their fulfilling work, and some, their happiness. Work shouldn't be that much fun and success shouldn't be that easy, but both seem to be for confident Visionary. In keeping with the Visionary lesson, holding fast to that path is all that is necessary. Details, such as success and happiness, take care of themselves.

How happy are you, Visionary?

THE INTUITIVES

Life Purpose

At home in visionary worlds, they sculpt, shape and spin reality to the tune of fantasy and return it wrapped in wonderment. At forges of imagination, they "smithy" the bit for evolution's mouth and urge its forward movement. Their outerworld elusiveness may play fool but foils truth. Behind their detachment and disinterest, rarest creativity turns kaleidoscopic dreams and shepherds fleets of fancy to heights of stellar brilliance. To us they are Evokateurs. To time and history they're the greatOnes. When Evokateurs step down, step out, and walk among, remarkability untold and evolutionary unfold are consequence.

Intimacy & Emotion

Nothing enlightening can begin without one understanding: Evokateurs do not live with us, or as us, in this world. They are born aware of other depths, dimensions and realities. Others can find these purely emotional beings, these passion personifieds, difficult to understand. Some would find such all-encompassing, all-consuming emotionality *interesting;* some would envy; but most would rather have nightmares. Regardless, emotions rule Evokateurs and that means one thing: ultra-creativity.

Inside these individuals, galaxies implode, explode and realign; beauty burps from every nook, cranny, and pore; and sounds supercede capability of voice to repeat, ear to capture, or instrument to record. Evokateur-world, just behind Evokateur eyes, is as real for them as this world is for us. Theirs is an infinitely more desirable place to be. And infinitely kinder.

For all, but most specifically for Evokateurs, we will summarize what an Ansir Profile means. As many have noted, two tests are going on at once. The most important is how you perceive self. Find self and *3 Sides of You* will provide you the most common aspects found, among those of same Dominant style, who function at core similarly. That does not mean or imply that each is one and same person. Person equals individuality, and that varies as widely in humans, in terms of life-purpose goals and fulfillment rewards, as patterns vary in snowflakes.

For instance, the colour red can have infinite shades and hues yet be red at core. The *3 Sides of You* Profile represents the red core of each, derived from many same-style conversations. When perception of self and core of self meet, truth bells ring loud and clear and resonate through 360-degrees of individual possibility. Evokateurs tend to find themselves the first time around. What does that mean? It means they know who they are and when doing Ansir's Self perception test, are able to draw a recognizable likeness of self more readily and often than others. Additionally, they tend to be the ones most surprised that Ansir has met others like them. Generally, they feel isolated and alone.

The loneliest people may be Evokateurs.

Two others know how lonely they can be: Healers and Philosophers. The voices in this conversation are theirs. They understand, don't lie, and like Evokateurs, do nothing for the mere of please or money. These three styles, in particular, seem to have been born with built-in bullshit detectors. They expect the whole truth and deliver nothing but themselves.

This conversation with Evokateurs reflects unique, at its finest, and what that entails. We have put the terms "working" and "Evokateur" pointedly together throughout. Such union is significant and warrants repeat.

One recommendation for all Evokateurs (particularly Working Evokateurs), is to read Healer and Philosopher styles, then start looking for them—along with Visionarys and other Evokateurs. All have much in common. More importantly, Evokateur often needs the support of these styles in order to *become*. Significant others are often the catalyst of encouragement that leads their potential out, and introduces it to world. Evokateurs must be selective in their professional and personal associations. The ones needed are those who allow Evokateur the latitude they require to do what they must their own way. It is highly recommended that Evokateur accept and directly take charge of that responsibility. ONLY through their work does Evokateur express their style of truth and love, and find their style of fulfillment.

By their work are Evokateur souls known.

Their emotionality is something few speak about in terms of personage. Most often people speak of Evokateur's extraordinary oddness or history speaks of their extraordinary accomplishments. However, extraordinary tends to travel odd paths, those on this or that side of normal. Evokateur can be difficult for others to work with, live with, and love. They're outspoken, withdrawn, elusive, distracted much of the time, charming, combative yet fun-loving, strong-as-a-bull opinionated; but frail if not fragile emotionally. How fragile?

If others carry lanterns to guide them, Evokateur carries candles. As the candle flame is more vulnerable to breezes and gusts than lanterns. Evokateur is more emotionally vulnerable to hurt than others. Extraordinary emotional sophistication is the source of their greatest power OR the source of their greatest pain if not understood. Without ego to protect or hide their emotions, they are clams unshelled.

If not so precariously balanced, they would not be Evokateur at all. They come but one way, soul afire and afoot. Being hurt can throw things from out of whack for some, to completely off the track for others. Evokateur and non-Evokateur need to be aware of such either/or outcomes in their relations and relationships. Responsibilities may not be equally shared with these ones, at least not initially.

They're brilliant and fiercely independent, but at times can't seem to find their own butt with both hands. They can't be pulled, patted, or tugged into socializing as child or adult; yet when their interest is piqued, they can't be shut-up or intimidated. They exude an innocence that borders on naive and seem driven by an agitated energy that defies clock, logic, and routine. Most find Evokateur troublesome. Those that expend even small effort on understanding them are usually rewarded by two discoveries. Upon receipt of respect their "troublesomeness" seems to dissipate; and their definition and depth of love often surprises.

There are good reasons for such diverse perspectives, on both sides of the whose-at-fault coin. Evokateur is not easy for others to live with, and others are not easy for them to live with, so acceptance and tolerance, or intolerance and separation occur. Acquiescing, compromising, or smothering are not long-tolerated by a working-Evokateur. They've already passed the Visionary Lesson and with that, something ends and something begins. There are new lessons for them to master. Pleasing others is not one of them.

The biggest Evokateur lesson is not to be learned by them, but by others.

Recognize these ones faster and give them the benefit-of-doubt. This style tends to need encouragement in order to become, as born and meant. Unique is a word most fitting for them; others qualify as less-so, comparatively. At their most alert, they're still only half-here with us. They see farther ahead, see more inside, see more outside, hear different notes, find different perspectives, chew internally; then spit it out as emotional euphoria. Burning-imagination is their forté; brain-food is their offering. This style's *who* and *why* begins at creative—they're born to fly, not walk. Indeed, were two more peculiar for their time, than the Evokateur Fathers of manned-flight, Orville and Wilbur Wright?

Some brews of tea don't appeal to the average palate. Whether deemed a sweet or bitter brew largely depends on the taster's expectations. Those who expect the taste to be the same as teas known will like the least. Those who expect the taste to be similar to teas known will be disappointed. Those who are open to the good or bad of flavour possibilities will enjoy it the most. That's what it's like living with Evokateur: some like, most don't. They're an uncommon cuppa.

Of the few who understand Evokateur, respect and admiration precede the loving. "To know them is to love them," seems to be the historical opinion, too. Their fame is for their deed, not their person. Evokateurs pour themselves into their work, which is their first love and often their only commitment. Fame only finds them at work

Love

Evokateur is the most self-centred individual on the planet, but ask or observe to confirm. What's important to them is closer and dearer than mind, body, and heart. They don't dream of being rich and famous for contributions of better, best, or betterment. They dream of being inside dreams; of opening Pandora's box; of slipping between frames of time and re-routing history; of worlds where logic gets stretched; as in Lewis Carroll's and Jules Verne's; or of fields where logic must gallop full speed to keep abreast; as in science, math, music, art, and literature.

Through, and by their work, Evokateur has taught the world its greatest human lesson: eyes and opinion are poor judges of ability. Being different neither diminishes value nor disables greatness, but can delay its take-off and roughen its landing. Deafness stopped his public performances but could not stop Beethoven's immortality. Horrific deformity and the public's general revulsion of such, did not stop John Merrick from being a refined, brilliant and healing man. Poverty and ignorance could not bar Ramanujan from entering tallest academic doors. Stephen Hawking proved that wheelchairs can fly high and far; and fast enough to catch falling and failing stars.

In every autistic, in numbers of homeless, in company with hopeless, and inside every greatOne, Evokateur style exists to some small or large degree. They live on this or that side of normal and wholly unaware of this reality; as in too far beyond to notice or care. When half-time in our world and half-time in their own, is when Evokateur works best and when they need others most.

A bad hair day didn't stop Einstein.

But then, he was luckier than most. Without exception, a working-Evokateur needs to be sufficiently encouraged and inspired to walk willingly among us—Albert Einstein had his uncle Jakob; Lewis Carroll had his large family; William Blake had his wife; Glenn Gould had his piano teacher; and Paul Cezanne had Pissaro, et cetera. While Evokateur can be self-satisfied internally, their self-fulfillment requires outerworld involvement and expression. Without significant others to excite their interest and open pathways for their genius to roam, the remarkability of these individuals can go unnoticed. If not for his uncle, the headmaster of Trinity College who interceded on his behalf, Sir Isaac Newton may have been a farmer, albeit an absent-minded one.

If Robert Frost chose the path least used and that made all the difference, for Evokateur, others are the path of difference between their frustration or their fulfillment. Others are needed to pull them out far enough and long enough for them to realize that being Evokateur is an extraordinary thing; not a mistake and not like others for a reason.

Their lot is to live an extraordinary life.

By three years of age, Evokateur talents may be known. Their gifts usually come in packs, not by drip and dribble. Sometimes it is encouraged—sometimes too much, sometimes applauded, and sometimes booed. Though young working-Evokateurs can be pushed and prodded by loved ones to perform on cue, they cannot be shoved. When shoved, they disappear into their own world; shutting others out and leaving all behind. Sticks wielded can persuade them, stones thrown can keep them at bay, but no external power can keep them from creating, or living their own truth their own way.

As infants, they may have been sickly or otherwise demanding of attention. They're usually openly and obviously affectionate as toddlers, with a penchant for withdrawing into fantasies of their own making. It's not unusual for Evokateur children to have imaginary friends, to be demanding about being read to, or exhibiting a precocity for reading themselves. Books and music are sometimes their most favoured *toys* and closest friends. As little tykes, they don't need to be entertained. They're more self-sufficient than other children. It's when they stop concentrating that trouble usually begins.

When concentrating, they're other-world preoccupied. When they come back to reality, they're often surprised to discover everyone mad at them for reasons soonly and harshly made known. Evokateur decides early in life which battles they'll fight and which they'll ignore. Their standard coping technique is withdrawal, not confrontation. They're not like *normal* children. Treating them as such only works until they decide "to hell with it," and retreat to their world where no one scolds them. That escape response is style-typical, regardless of age.

A closer look at the Evokateur 'snapshot'

When the going gets rough for Visionary, they square pressing matters, call a recess, and go inside to sort things out. Evokateur doesn't warn, sort, or prepare; they up and leave. They shut down outerworld awareness for short or long durations, depending on their desire to "stay home." To go or stay is their choice and decision. No other can take blame or take credit for that. Some circumstances may move their departure date up a tad, but remember, Evokateur is born with their bags already packed. That's their nature. External systems, such as eyes and ears, inwardly turn; and sensations, like touch, hunger and pain are dulled when Evokateur zones out. They may need to be reminded to eat, sleep, and bathe.

Physically, Evokateur tends to be slighter of build and frailer in both appearance and countenance. They're noticeably more refined than others in their manner of deportment; some seem to float. In fact, many Evokateurs wish they could float or fly to save wear-and-tear on their feet. No other experiences as much blistering misery from footwear as them. Their feet can be so sensitive that snug-fitting socks irritate. Generally, they're not physically expressive, as in sportsy or outdoorsy. The phrase "work up a sweat" is more likely to work up disdain than their interest. Physical exertions tend not to be long-term dedications; more intermittent, curiosity forays. Hiking, dancing (they rank consistently among dancing greats), walking, and sex are their preferred exertions, which seem sufficient for maintaining their characteristic litheness.

To say there's an aura of refinement or delicacy about them is not to imply they're delicate of temperament or tongue. Bear-baiting may have been outlawed, but people-baiting is still a common playground, classroom, and workplace sport. Those who are different, like Evokateur, become "bears" of choice. They generally avoid confrontation. When necessary, they resort to the only weapon these ones carry or condone: sharp tongue and mind. They can usually talk their way out of trouble or disappear inside till the episode passes or ends.

In school, Evokateur is not found among the hip, cool, or feared crowds, nor are they commonly one among nerds—they're usually not that popular. In fact, when an Evokateur becomes famous, none are as surprised as schoolmates, home-town community, and though less often, their own parents and siblings. Their potential can go untried and unnoticed, unless promoted by others or plucked from the thick of the remarkable, average, and sometimes mentally-challenged crowds.

Teachers may remember a talented but aloof and lazy student. For Evokateur, school tends to be an intellectually boring and emotionally painful experience. Fellow students may remember them as having been odd and quiet, and having kept to themselves. Parents and siblings may remember them as emotional, bookish, and outspoken homebodies, who were unusually protective of privacy and property.

If any child or adult needs their own space with a door that shuts, it's Evokateur. They need to spend a great deal of time alone—when they're most creative. Privacy is an Evokateur issue. Finding a place of their own outside ordinary obligations and responsibilities may be a lifelong battle of theirs. They'll put up whatever defense, walled-fence, or vanishing act necessary to garner some private space and some control over their time.

When innerworld occupied, their responses may seem odd to others and be at-odds with reality. They may laugh, amused by an inner fancy, when sobriety is what's called for. Playing with other children when young, Evokateur tends to be bossy and demanding while instructing playmates or directing games—though rarely confused. They seem to know where each foot needs to be placed and how each action should unfold; and get impatient when others don't understand as clearly as them. Their play and games have likely been written and previously rehearsed by them, in Evokateur-world.

Their truth, their world

Under the right conditions of pressure and time, coal becomes diamond. Well, coal dust usually coats the outside of Evokateurs. Those who see beyond the crust and dust and make an effort to swipe it off, often find a worthy diamond beneath. To Evokateur, this world of ours is drab, dreary, and to be avoided. Gardening, with its shovel, hoe, and back-aching work; or camping, with its bugs and grit in food; or business with its profit-first mentality are neither cool nor motivational to them. Evokateur purgatory is doing work for which the only reward is a paycheque.

Unlike most, Evokateur's downside is flare visible. For some reason that's significant. These are not the ones who can don whatever "please mask" is necessary to fit into play, school, work, church, community, or conversation. W.Y.S.I.W.Y.G. with these individuals. They can't seem to hide their flaws or disguise their uniqueness. The path-of-difference winds visibly through Evokateur nature and name: evoker of change. From their extraordinary emotions, they learn all they need about self and others. If their intuition picks up the hint of having to *change their self in exchange for another's support or love,* they're out of there; by vacation of premises or retreat from world.

Maturity arrives for them the day realization comes bearing scissors—to snip the tie that binds them to others' expectations. And if love be bound by dependence, they sever its cord and cloy too. Nervous breakdowns, neural disorders, nameless maladies, and strange afflictions are not uncommon for Evokateur. But then, no other experiences the intense rawness of passion like them either.

Hurt, for any other, cuts less deep and pierces less sharply than for these purely intuitive beings. Usually, in order for them to move into work mode, personal relationships either step-in-tune or are stepped over. When pleasing others becomes less important than pleasing self, Evokateur make their self scarce. They roll up their sleeves and pour self into work and therefore, are not available. By expression of passion is Evokateur known. The hounds may bark, stomachs growl, and fury crash down around them but their determination and confidence tends to hold and stay true to their chosen course. They know from birth why they are here: to live and love creatively.

With each successive pain and hurt, they tend to spend extended periods of time working in their world and less time living in ours. Loss of their company or presence is not the hard part, coaxing them out again is. Creativity will take place inside them, no matter what. Unless Evokateur shares their creativity, others may not even be aware of these extraordinary beings, and all miss an opportunity for rare enlightenment, entertainment, or improvement. This personality reads in history as a *Who's Who* of greatness. Changers of century and future is their name's fame and claim. Given equal opportunity, no other may be able to write, paint, direct, perform, compose, or solve equal to them. Their potential has been proven, time and again.

Working-Evokateurs need others to coax their genius out, but need no coaxing or reason to love. They may not like the physical aspects of being outdoorsy, but few appreciate and none can emotionally tap into and translate the complex soul of nature,like they can. Evokateur expresses their love through music, words, and creations wrought from an emotion rich, intuition ruled, unfathomable ingenuity. Logic cannot measure or comprehend the depth or scope of their passion. Being understood depends on their own ability to express powerfully enough, to move another's emotions to experience in-like with theirs. Powerfully moving, soothing, or disturbing works, regardless of author's name, carry the indelible mark of Evokateur—an inimitable style.

Evokateur is not a rare personality style. What is rare is a working-Evokateur—unafraid of being fool, whether time and understanding ever prove different. When what they're doing is what they most love, extraordinary can and does blossom forth.

If pleasing others is not a lesson of theirs, appreciation for others could be

The most common complaint about them is that Evokateur often forgets to say "thank-you," to those closest and dearest to them. Self-centredness and preoccupation are their reasons, and are often a rubber stamp excuse for their habitual inconsideration. Affection, not anger, is the recommended remedy for such characteristic remiss. We've found affection quickly earns their undivided attention. If that doesn't work, others should look closer to see if their "thank-you" is not being said in other, less obvious ways.

Evokateur is not only highly aware but ultra-sensitive about the differences between them and others. While they can escape into their private sanctuary, especially in times of contention or confrontation, practicality dictates that they stay to interact and placate others. What they mostly avoid are the emotional expectations that come with close relationships. When they become irritable or irascible, which they've a propensity to do, the recommended response is to leave them alone; private time's due. For them, relationship give-and-take is more irritating and potentially destructive than rewarding. When expectation turns into demand, Evokateur withdraws and sets external living on auto-pilot. These individuals need to be coaxed and convinced to walk in the world professionally. They're unlikely to volunteer for emotional duty, personally.

And 'duty' is how they often view personal commitments.

Evokateur doesn't need clue of word or cue of card to make right assumptions about the emotional state of others. Their intuition is preternaturally astute and incisive. They can intuit another's romantic interest from afar; and it doesn't take much of a nudge for Evokateur to be "in love." They start at love; most need to work their way up to it. Their passion and intellect more than physical attractiveness draws mates. Intellectual compatibility and emotional independence seem to be the combination that wins Evokateur hearts long-term. They're happiest when commitment and responsibility are not required or expected. Only when assured of such autonomy will they explore intimate relations.

Of all, Evokateur is most likely to engage in extra-marital romances with close work associates. It's not that they love their primary mate less. They love the inspiration sparked by new love more. Evokateur flows on the urges and surges of emotional electricity. They sense and succumb to the emotional impressions that stir and start around them. They're impetuous, responsive, and susceptible to all influences in their chosen work's environment. When in love, Evokateur is most creative. Remember from above, these are emotion geniuses and of necessity and nature, emotional junkies. They can fall in love with air and find a zillion ways to express it. Love is the key that seems to unlock their best. Emotions drive their creativity, so when newly love-sparked and inspired, they tend to work more.

Emotions rule Evokateurs.

When you love what you do, the tendency is to explore further, farther, and wider than known. Beethoven bottled the whole of a storm in a symphony. Nikolai Rimsky-Korsakov captured the bumble bee's busyness. Evokateur creativity never sleeps, never stops, and cannot be limited. They come predisposed to living an extraordinary life. That seems to mean and require that they love intensely. Experience conquered them should that birth-delivered state of love, be altered by life's end.

Being obligated to others and being responsible for others are commitments Evokateur tends to avoid. When motivation and reward are not based on pleasing and helping, and relationship continuance is not tied to sharing and meeting responsibilities, the only bond left is the only bond possible with Evokateur: love. Gushing, romantic gestures, like Valentine's Day, birthdays, even festive occasions, are not celebrations they use as opportunity to express expected sentimentalities. Such calendar love they deem an affront to romance in principal and an insult to them personally. They don't internalize emotions when in love, and don't need an excuse or industry-endorsed occasion to express themselves.

Generally, Evokateur is quite pleasant, except when preoccupied. Being disturbed while working or meeting anger when done, are the two most common reasons why Evokateur gets perturbed; and why many don't marry. By measure of their mood, from moment to moment, will their mate, friends, and associates know the status and state of the relationship. They tend to visibly and vocally express what they feel. When they greet with eagerness and delight, and find fascination in most everything and everyone, the relationship is good by their own yardstick measure. That enthusiasm barometer proves most accurate throughout their lifetime— whether the association is professional or personal. Evokateur joins us in our world to experiment with their ideas, glean inspiration, to share information, and for sex.

Sexual relations—an area where Evokateurs physically, willingly, and openly share their internal passions and churning fantasies with others. They tend to be enthusiastic playmates and profoundly intuitive lovers. They expertly sense the mood of their partners, and follow or lead without hesitation or inhibition. They are gentle, consummate lovers, with a twinkle of bedevilment ever-ready to flare in nostril or flash in eye. As a loving, sexual mate, Evokateur knows better than most how to dance the sensuous, Cerebral Waltz.

When hurt, they disappear. When in love, they disappear more frequently. They do nothing for the mere of please yet when in love, all they do is an expression of their emotionality. They don't seek applause from others but Evokateur needs approval and applause from their most important audience: their mate. They may go where others have not been but they take loved ones with them *all ways*. They may not bring flowers, shower compliments, or be prompt with "thanks," but within a working Evokateur lives an extraordinary lover. One who tracks and captures the emotional essence of life, then packages it for all to experience. Often, the only person an Evokateur bonds with, is their mate.

These are the ones who know how to stir things up. They change century thinking and future doing, by moving emotions so powerfully that logic can't ignore or deny. Logic does not evoke change, emotions do. Emotions prompt, poke, and provoke. Only when insistence turns to demand and overrides reason, does logic pay attention. Evokateurs' mother-tongue is emotions. They're experts at expressing them raw and real. As dolphins stun prey with sonar bursts, Evokateur stuns others with emotion blasts. Their purpose is to evoke change. By way of emotions is how they do it. Afterwards, they leave it to logic to explain.

Be it in art, acting, singing, composing, writing, or wishing upon stars, Evokateur inspires new dreams and awakens new sensations in others. Be it in art, acting, singing, composing, writing, or wishing upon stars, the best in every field were, are, and will be—to some small or significant degree—of Evokateur working style. Their creative genius walks inner-worlds and just visits ours.

Pg. 400

They may be odd. They may be self-centred. They may be more gone than with us and exasperating to the nth degree to live with. But it's their footprint that most often leads to greatness or leaves a dent into which future greatness will flow. Their only guide is self-truth. Once realized, accepted, and trusted, they're free to fly as creatively as they were born and meant.

Others may ridicule their odd manner of intuiting their way through but, working Evokateurs tend to arrive. Most others, don't.

THE SPIRITUALISTS

ealer

Life Purpose

As solitarys on the hill, their eyes smile at sight of progress, smart at pollution's dust, kindle at technology's advance and roll at narrow thinking. Their vision of progress does not stop at apples on trees of today but travels to orchards of tomorrow. Among the powerful they rank highly. Among the wise they rank highest. Having evolutionarily been, seen and conquered, they're assigned a task of great responsibility. Their job is the toughest row to hoe; their purpose is to build pathways that lead others to truth of self and being. Meet Healer, the one who alters the future by changing belief today. If teardrop threatens in one eye, love ever-brims in other, for Healer with their gifted hands and truth-filled hearts are partners of Power.

Intimacy & Emotion

Healer has the largest, most powerful energy aura of all. Others can feel their presence. They use their energy gift to intuitively assess the emotional, mental, and physical state of others, for they are Healer not only in name but in deed as well. They seem to never stop working, but then, theirs is the greatest responsibility and purpose to fulfill. They empower others to change fate of self and future of world by change of belief.

Their energy field ranges in size from vast to enormous making them extra-sensitive to crowding or closeness. They may even prefer sleeping in separate beds from their mate. Prolonged physical proximity rubs abrasively against their sensitive energy-dimension.

They generally avoid crowds for the same reason. They often are light sleepers who don't need as much rest as others and who rarely use alarm clocks to waken. Healers become disoriented by noise, especially argumentative voices and loud music, and become visibly uncomfortable in cluttered or messy environments. Home is their sanctuary—their escape from the hustle and bustle of everyday life. Often they choose to live in rural settings, away from metropolitan centres and congestion. Characteristically, they opt for minimalist decor over plush coziness and are the hardwood floor industry's most loyal customer.

Healer is not known for entertaining at home. While family and familiar are much enjoyed and welcomed, know to call in advance rather than just drop-in. Only in solitude does Healer relax. When in company with others they're ever-alert to the spoken and unspoken needs of others. Consequently, they are highly protective of their privacy, to the extent of not answering their telephone or doorbell. Though present, they're not beck-and-call available. It's a Healer who most appreciates the screening feature of Caller ID on home telephones. A great personal pleasure of theirs is gardening—but scratch a Healer to find a full-blown naturalist. Some of the most famous green thumb gardeners and award-winning landscape artists are Healer, who generally finds the combination of soil and solitude aesthetically rewarding and therapeutic.

In private, they seek guidance when troubled, when needing confirmation of path's correctness or when affirmation of their own purpose and progress are needed. Most seek or depend on validation from support and sources outside themselves; for Healer, validation comes from within. Interpersonal confrontation is not a common occurrence with these peaceable ones. If pressured, their response and renown is grace under fire. If provoked they can be fury personified, though never violent. It just isn't in them. "Wouldn't hurt a fly" is apt, for even when kids they didn't participate in the common child sport of de-winging houseflies.

Healer is thorough and thoroughly dependable. What others perceive as risk and require time to consider, they intuitively weigh and quickly decide. If the feel is right that's all the approval Healer needs. They're seekers and adopters of new opportunities, as well as authors and promoters of new perspectives. Their calm composure can be a confusing contrast with the effervescent, even palpitable energy felt in their presence. While Healer's bright, peaceful surface complements their physical attractiveness, it proves to be more than skin deep during stressful situations. They're steadfast under pressure. Though often ranked among the more competent and capable, Healer tends to shun leadership roles. Generally, cockroaches could not out-skitter them from centre stage spotlights. Most Healers who perform in public admitted to suffering near-crippling stage fright before showtime. For some, public speaking or plague-testing would be a coin toss decision.

Lack of confidence is less often the reason than style-typical shyness. Co-workers can be surprised to discover the their competent and self-assured Healer associate is quite shy socially. Since they only do that which pleases and furthers their purpose, wild horses couldn't drag them to meet obligations imposed on them by others.

Healers do not have an ego. They don't seek fame and recognition, as neither rewards nor fulfills them. Fame and recognition get placed on pedestals, which is too close to admiration and too far from what's important to them. Healer doesn't teach by the example of their living. Their purpose is to encourage a change in belief, sufficient for individuals to make their own betterment decisions independent of their (or any other) influence.

Healers that function as Healers are very rare, mostly because they rarely feel confident of being accepted when being themselves. It is intentional that we state this, after having already begun this conversation. As noted in both the *thinking* and *working* conversations, Healers tend to avoid, rather than accept and use their power. One of the greatest mysteries surrounding this style is why they so unconfident, when so powerful.

Why unconfident?

Oddly enough, that which is core and power for a confident Healer is Achilles' heel for an unconfident. Healer, by definition, has a personal relationship with a Higher Power; an intimate communion more often met with skepticism from others, than understanding. In the past, such suspicion has found them tripping down least-used paths, littered with public outrage and social ostracism. The inability of a confident Healer to compromise their principles has historically led to an untimely death.

Why Healer denies their gifts and responsibilities may be historically and self-preservationally justified, but avoidance does not make their living an easier. Self-denial can be excruciating and costly for the unconfident of this personality. Try as they might, they cannot deafen their ears to the need that calls or stifle the power that stirs restlessly within. They can at most still their hands and ignore their fulfillment by denying their *who* *what* and *why*.

An unconfident Healer is usually a master chameleon. One who can artfully adapt and assume whatever personality style is necessary to get by or to get through their nows in life. When Healer repudiates their nature and compromises their truth in exchange for acceptance, they live as emotional frauds. A state of dishonesty that manifests as perpetual insecurity, no matter which well-trodden path they choose and walk. Ignoring innermost truth is a hardship for spiritual beings.

The surest sign of an unconfident Healer is a strong dependence on others.

A Healer who avoids living in accordance with their own truth, *needs* others. They chameleon those they trust or admire and use them as models to guide and govern their own actions and behaviour. An unconfident Healer assimilates with others, parroting and parodying their way through various interactions and relationships, which can be amusing as well as confusing to others. Remember, Healer is more than skilled. They're intuitive-masters.

When functioning confidently, they ascertain the emotional temperature and truth of others. When functioning as unconfident, they focus on the other's thoughts and place all trust in conversation and observation. Instead of intuitives, they become logicals instead, slaves to *should* and *must*, and respecters of acceptability and propriety. When unconfident, they depend on books, opinions, and others to show them the right way and to help them think and say the right things. They do need to be accepted by others and do need to belong in order to fulfill their life purpose, but the face that's accepted and the hand holding the membership Card may not be Healer's.

The difference between unconfidents and confidents? The former works at being accepted; the latter doesn't. Some can fulfill purpose whilst functioning in relative obscurity or seclusion; Healer cannot. Their purpose requires they participate in everyday life with everyday people.

Logic can override emotions for physicals and logicals, but it can't override spiritualists. Emotions rule Healer, *period*. Unconfident Healers rely on external guidance, because their emotional dimension cannot be ignored or quieted. They don't have an ego to shut things off or shut things out, like logicals and physicals do; so insecurity becomes a way of life for the Healer who tries to fit in by thinking and acting like others. They often don't realize they are different for a reason, so they try to eliminate the difference by chameleoning others and re-writing their self.

Healer is an intuitive of the highest order. They can and do fool many or sometimes most, but they can't fool their own soul. It won't let them.

Healers don't know they are Healers, until they become.

It would be convenient and surely less confusing, if personality styles were genetically inherited, like body types and illnesses, but they're not. Personality styles evolve through lesson experiences, through time. If styles were genetic, role models for Healers would more readily be available. Such models are rarely family-handy or accessible. As it is, Healer is left with two options: mimic others to fit or trust their own wisdom and counsel. Healers don't know they're Healers until they *become*. Becoming takes confidence and that's only had in one place: emotions.

It's impossible to scare away the bogeyman, no matter what size of logic stick that's held and applied. Unless emotions say "it's safe," or say "it's okay," it isn't. If the words of another sound logical externally but ring false internally, unconfident Healer adjusts their thinking to match that of the other. A confident Healer would hear the other's words, feel the false ring, and trust that the words were false. They don't judge others or get offended and they don't confront or demand accountability. Instead, they'd move emotionally closer to better hear the real truth, and wait for invitation or opportunity to encourage truth to out on its own. Healer is intuitive, so relates one way: emotionally. Whether their stage is kitchen table, classroom, or coliseum, they communicate one-on-one.

Others cannot begin to fathom the intuitive power of spiritualists. In a crowd of people, Healer could find by feel, those whose emotional energy was out of sync with the rest. Unconfidents adjust self to fit with the average temperature of room or temperament of crowd; confidents don't. For instance, at any age, unconfident Healers are the ones most likely to come home sporting a limp, speaking with a lisp, or affecting an accent, depending on their company and sphere of influence that day. They know what sympathetic ailments are, as they experience the same symptoms as others who are suffering colds, headaches, depression, et cetera. They unconsciously chameleon the idiosyncrasies of those they spend time with.

Acceptance is very important to unconfident Healers. In social settings, they mirror whatever mood or state encountered. If with Diligent, they'll be more formal and erudite; if with Scintillator, they'll be more vivacious; if with Empath, they'll swap tales about their self or other guests; if with Idealist, they'll talk shop or business knowingly; if with Sage, they'll explore the human condition enthusiastically; and if with Extremist, they'll be bolder than usual. Whoever they're with, whatever group they join, unconfident Healers seek acceptance through assimilation rather than by being their self. Watching them work their way around the room, changing behaviour with each greet and meet can be an entertaining, if confusing, experience for their mate.

In the following, we pay homage to the confident of this style and trust it will encourage unconfident Healers to become the powerful individuals they were born and meant to be. Healers know truth by its feel. What they do with it or about it is their own choice and responsibility.

Matters and matters not, a different perspective.

A confident Healer needs no other, because they trust no other. When trust of self is implicit, life is conducted in strict accordance with innermost truth. It matters not one whit that the world snorts or sniggers, self-truth is always right for each.

Trusting self to say and do right, no matter what, places responsibility and accountability in its rightful place: squarely upon individual shoulders. Whether professional or personal, individual responsibility ripples consequences throughout the collective. For instance, if each were to consider the short and long-term consequences of their own user and doer roles, would truth have built nuclear power plants or miss child support payments. There are infinitely more examples possible but the issue is always the same—whether as user or doer, each shares responsibility for now and for future.

If truth does not ring within for intuitives, it's not truth.

The only infinitely creative aspect of logic is that it can rationalize anything, given sufficient evidence. Emotions or intuition or soul cannot. As it is said of dogs, it can be said of logic: if given the choice or a chance, a dogs will *dump* in any yard other than its own, unconcerned about the consequences of the act on others. Not so with truth. Once felt, emotional-truth cannot, as judge to jury, be instructed to ignore what is known including the consequences that inevitably will follow.

To trust another is tantamount to finding a different yard than one's own, in which to dump blame or bury responsibility. *That's why Healers do not trust others*; they personally and fully assume responsibility for all they say and do. They're here to awaken **one truth** in others: trust self first, last and only. If each creates their own life, who is more deserving of attendant credit or blame? Who suffers failure pain or celebrates success joy more than self, when efforts are self-directed, decided, and determined?

Unlike most others, Healer is not born with an ego.

Individual belief is the sum of acquired knowledge that's stored in mind. Ego plays a dual role. It acts as belief's representative in worldly interactions, and delivers outgoing information from mind. As well, ego filters and rejects incoming information that does not conform with belief's criteria. As a spiritualist, Healer is purely intuitive and has no need to store knowledge in mind. They tap directly into intuitive vaults brimming with soul experiences of all they've been, seen and thus far done. They've evolved through all styles except Philosopher, so accumulative wisdom from their time's beginning to now is consciously available.

What's a Healer?

For them, the truth, the way and the light are emotionally told, not reasoned. Nothing saddens these individuals more than to see others placing trust in any hand other than their most worthy own. No greater counsel or truer guide is possible, than soul-wisdom. Belief tends to separate people. It divides one from another and groups from whole, according to all that makes us unique from one another, such as gender and race. Soul-wisdom carries umbilical blood that flows through one, through each, through all, and through Higher Power in circular perpetuity. It's a cell-common pulse and promise of eternal unity. Soul, the god-spark given to all Co-Creators, determines life; not mind, heart, or body. Through emotions does soul live. When all else that is human dies, soul lives.

Each soul is linked to the Higher Power; a pact, a promise, and partnership that Healer actively participates in. Their challenge is not to learn but to remember who they are, to create their life with soul's guidance and to share their experience-based wisdom with others. Healer does not tell others what to think, do, or say. It's not their nature to convince or control but to offer expanded perspectives, instead, that others may freely embrace as their own or ignore; their birthright prerogative. They may shed light on alternatives for others to more readily and easily see, but decisions are independently and individually made.

Each is born with innate powers and unique gifts to create their own life their own way. They may know what's necessary and be willing to direct others to waters that quench, but whether to seek or to drink is each's decision. Healer is born with fully-developed intuitive gifts, but all have potential for equal power development or conscious-awareness as them. None are born disadvantaged. Most require evolutionary time to awaken and "experientially" mature to that realization. Only lessons stand between a Healer and others, not birth advantage.

These individuals seldom ascribe to any one religion. For them, the Higher Power—however described and defined—lives within. Theirs is a partnership where One is all-knowing and one all-experiencing, and where both find completion through union. Spirituality accepts others and their faith source/resource unequivocally. Religion tends to be more flock-and-fleece particular.

Some participants had trouble with the terms "Higher Power" "Creator" and "God" in Ansir's Self-perception test and for a variety of reasons; not the least of which was "it not being politically correct." Healers, themselves, have their own definition of a higher Authority and don't ascribe to one form or term of reference, deference, or reverence. Healers tend to accept everything about others, including their gods/Gods, without judgement or hesitation.

It is not a Healer who stockpiles wealth and seeks fame, nor do they adulate or emulate those who do. Their fulfillment doesn't come from accumulating, but from giving. They live as intrinsic participants who support and contribute to the whole. For Healer, it's unconscionable that starvation is possible where abundance grows, and that some are denied the basics of life while others enjoy excess without guilt. It will ever-be unbalanced and unfair, as long as belief measures success by individual wealth and influence rather than by well-being of planet and specie. It's really a matter of changing belief from one, to one-blood perspectives.

Healers walk with confident compassion in all size, shape, and colour of shoe, for they've worn all manner of footwear before. They've been planter of seed, hewer of wood and hauler of water; doctor, lawyer, and Indian chief. They've been leader, follower, artist and poet; and pilot of land, sky and sea. They've been beggar and king; prophet and sinner; retarded, exceptional, and genius. They've been victim, perpetrator, judge and juror; father, daughter, mother, and son. They've been honourable and despicable; apathetic and fanatic; athlete, disabled, starved and obese; and died many times, many ways—violently, quietly, nobly, cowardly, in all season, for all reason, and by all manner of disease and complication. Their souls are experience-full and satiated.

Emotion is the student, life the teacher, and love the only test to pass.

Healers awaken the sleeping truth in others, to help them remember they are Co-Creators with unlimited power. Chaos and confusion, loneliness and helplessness are states of mind. But mind is not where power or individuality lives. That dominion and domain belongs to soul—the master over body and mind. Life is or it isn't, at soul's discretion. And while life is intended to be a self-created experience, each thought, expression and action, like the vibrations of a plucked guitar string, affects and impacts the whole in healing, hurtful, or helpful ways.

Affect and impact, whether negative or positive are individual choices with eternal consequences. Given the job of "toughest row to hoe," Healer encourages each to pluck freely; to create their own unique soul-stirring sound; and also to share their music willingly and generously with others. Pleasing one soul ripples pleasure through all; a consciousness that is as much hallmark as cellular for Healer. There's a caution for success that embodies evolutionary wisdom as well: "it's wise to be kind and honest with others on your way up, for you'll meet again on your way down."

None are born alone, others are there to greet; none lives alone, others are there to meet; none dies alone, others are there to bid or arrange final farewells. There are many life experiences between now and eternity, and all promise infinite complexities of inter-relationships that none can for long or forever avoid. Each may choose to hermit their heart and self but the consequence is loneliness.

How healing or helpful each is, how generous their sharing, and whether others have been bettered or worsened before each's swan call, is how soul measures success. Kerneled in, "If I were to die today" is Healer's philosophy. For them, now is all there is. Each person met and task undertaken, is nows only point and their only purpose. If each conducted their life as if each day were their last and each interaction their mark of remembrance, how differently would each's life be? Between that and this, stands change in belief.

Why ever hold back from sharing whole of truth and self?

What's the point of taking a valuable gift, dividing it, then offering it piecemeal to others? Few would appreciate the gesture yet that's how most offer and share self; in small, disjointed parcels, where truth is concealed under layers of issue-wrapped fear and tissue-thin doubt, and where emotional honesty lies in knotted complication under limp commitment bows. Tentatively, cautiously, with mincing step and reined-in emotions is how most approach life and others whilst living, working and loving. The most priceless gift each has or can offer is self.

What are we saving ourselves for? is Healer's main question. Giving the whole and all of self away, can neither diminish nor deplete, for the promise built into the god-spark is eternal renewal. Tomorrow's archaeologists will sift through layers of dirt and unearth buried *things* that today are the focus behind much earnest striving. Ultimately, only soul defies burial and is beyond wealth or time; and like Healers, beyond ownership too.

Healer love

Loving and accepting all equally is as natural for this style as breathing for others. There's a delicate vulnerability about them that draws others protectively toward, for Healer is warm and approachable. While others meet cheery welcome, they soon realize their protectiveness is unnecessary. Healer needs no other. Few are as self-contained and self-sufficient as them. They enjoy all and participate enthusiastically, but they do not depend on others for fulfillment of their purpose, like Visionary; for fulfillment of self, like Scintillator; for fulfillment of love, like Empath; or for exclusive support and companionship, like most others.

Often Healer avoids exclusive relationships, preferring instead to avail themselves in some people-oriented capacity. Their mates may resent not being accorded priority status in Healer eyes or life, but they're incapable of loving one, more than another. Intellectual affinity, life-purpose commitment and sexual compatibility are qualities they prize highest in mate.

Some choose a celibate life. Most however, establish long-term friendships or marriage but may change partners a number of times before finding the rightOne; one who understands their first priority is serving others, accepts their need for solitude, and respects their need for home to be a retreat.

Healer can, if and when they want, adopt and function as any personality style necessary. That's how they connect with others, emotionally and with understanding. Whatever state of emotional cheer, fear, or misery, in person or room, these ones connect with the emotional energy and from that siphon and decipher truth.

A confident Healer walks away from such connection, intact and as self. An unconfident tends to get too close; they mimic another's style of thinking, working, or emoting and can stay "in character" too long; sometimes for life. Healer, whether confident or unconfident, approaches personal relationships in much the same way. Given the three relationship qualifiers stated above, and given that their birth gift is an ability to emotionally chameleon others; Healer tends to compromise self when choosing a mate. As noted in their thinking realm, boredom is the reason why they leave school and jobs. Boredom is also why they end relationships.

Healer is here to experience, risk, and share their experience-wisdom. Nothing less than an emotionally-sophisticated mate can or will interest them long. Loyalty and dedication are kissing-cousins of responsibility, but can become obligation for those who are *overly* responsible. Healer can stay at the loyal and dedicated level, at the expense of their own emotional fulfillment needs, particularly sexually.

Few personalities are emotionally compatible with Healer. Few can romantically match their physical lustiness. Healer views sex as one of life's greatest pleasures. This is when their normally wheeled-in emotions can run and roll freely. When in company with most others, the full range of Healer emotions cannot be exercised. Instead, they consciously adjust their own power and dole it out in pre-intuited, situation-suited packages, meant to meet and encourage others. Only in sexual relations may Healer find invitation and opportunity to physically express their emotionality.

They're often the enthusiastic instigator and eager experimenter in intimate relations. They send their energy as stroking fingers, to provoke and promote libido's rise. Exciting emotion's passion with tingling explorations, they awaken mate's lust with electrifying tease and needy determination. In rippling flare of crave and want, they seek mutual consummation. In enveloping meld, in rhythmic surrender and ecstacy, they travel beyond mind and body to oblivion's peak and release. In bed or out, Healer loves as they live: enthusiastically.

Of all creatures and creations, only humans are blessed with dreams and laughter. But what is the point in gifts of dream and laughter if one is not realized and the other not heard. Dreamers and laughers are the lucky ones. Their purity of heart and confident spirit may occasionally flicker, but like all who follow their own truth, their spirit cannot be snuffed by adversity. Healer is here to do but one thing: to reconnect others to the most powerful anti-adversity weapon possible: soul-Truth within. And they do it but one way: changing belief.

THE SPIRITUALISTS

See Pages 170 - 194 for Thinking/Working/Emoting *InDepths*

4 Life Purpose

What your Style of thinking/working/loving means.

ANSIR'S DEFINITION OF

Life Purpose

Why you were born.
What your Style of thinking/working/emoting means.

Based on all that Ansir has thus far learned about personality Styles and Profiles, core understanding of Self can help you determine the most fulfilling direction to head your onboard talent toward. Motivation and reward overcome obstacles and lead to success. When the goal is self-motivating and self-rewarding, that means that Profile Boss and the two support experts *(other dominant Styles)* are working confidently together. Internal reward is generally followed, and closely, by external reward.

APPLYING BOSS

What motivates!
What rewards!

Profile Boss decides and determines Life-purpose.

Ansir's *3 Sides Of You* test measures self-perception—how you see yourself! When self-perception and self-truth meet, an accurate Profile or core image emerges, and with it realization that such complexity and complication can't be for naught. Why are you able to comprehend or do certain things more easily than others? Ansir maintains there are self-important and other-needed reasons for such differences in ability and nature.

Again...

...to achieve self-defined and self-desired goals, the shortest shortcuts are understanding and trusting Boss to know best, to know why, and to know where you want or must go. Boss pulls together the innate talents and strengths of your dominant support Styles, then shapes, delegates, and herds ALL toward self-fulfillment (*Profile Boss fulfillment*).

YOU ARE YOU

For some reason!

While Boss decides and determines fulfillment's direction, getting there requires the confident expertise and willing cooperation of support styles.

You are you, you are here at this juncture of time, and you are too-gifted and too-able to be here by mistake or coincidence. You must be as complex and complicatedly tall as you are, for *some* uniquely important and Profiled reason. At most, Ansir offers core Profile understanding, not be-alls or end-alls. This work has been called out-of-the-box, even revolutionary, because it bravely explores areas of everyday people reality, unlike any research or work that's gone before.

So please consider the following throughout, especially for Keys 4, 5, & 6.

How much more valuable and enjoyable is the apple's fruit than the apple's core? How much more are You than your Ansir Profile core?

One can only start or step from where they are. Ansir's *3 Sides of You* test can help you get your bearings. A Profile is like a reliable compass. It can help you determine the right success and happiness direction to head your potential toward, but the decisions and efforts required to get there are ultimately and entirely Your own responsibility.

How far from being strongly motivated can success be? How far from feeling rewarded can happiness be?

14 ANSIR STYLES

14 Life-purposes

Listed by group classification

LOGICALS:

Diligent: to process and verify the necessary details that measure the progress of industry and record the advancement of humanity.

Sage: to teach others that there are as many solutions to problems, as people who solve them.

INTUITIVES:

Visionary: to be the practical, humanitarian dreamer, who sees what others cannot and does what is said cannot be done.

Evokateur: to personify intuitive creativity and change more than minds through work contributions. Evokateurs change futures.

SPIRITUALISTS:

Healer: to change perspectives for human doing, viewing, and being.

Philosopher: to encourage individuality and promote responsibility and accountability.

PHYSICALS:

Extremist: to go where no other has gone and return with a map so others and progress can follow.

Realist: to be the big brother or big sister who lends shoulder to task and hand in help when strength of body or character are called for.

PRACTICALS:

Eccentrik: to show others that life thrives outside protocol and that success wears more than the two common suits of accepted and expected.

Idealist: to ensure that the highest level of excellence is striven for and maintained.

EMOTIONALS:

Kinsmen: to be the good Samaritan, to show by kindly example that we are Brothers and Sisters and responsible as such.

Empath: to teach others how to love Self and love Others.

INSTINCTIVES:

Scintillator: to be the embodied evidence of how influential and important each is to the welfare and well-being of others. Scintillators are environment mirrors.

Sentinel: to protect and preserve human rights, freedom, and dignity.

FINDING THE LOCK

Using the Keys

The tallest "fulfillment" step for most to climb is finding their right Ansir Profile. Years of coping to meet everyday economic reality often bury the raw and real truth that is You.

Briefs and InDepths are the Keys that confirm Profile rightness. Boss, Life-Purpose, and Achilles' Heel are the Keys that unlock Profile potential.

Ansir can help you identify Profiled *Who* and *Why,* and offer one-of-a-kind insight into how best to apply and benefit from combined gifts, talents, and abilities. What Ansir cannot do is explain why—of all possible—YOU need these 3 particular dominant Styles in order to reach the kind of success and happiness that fulfills. THAT mystery is yours to solve. Ansir can help you with knowing and understanding. Pursuing, doing, and fulfilling are up to you.

5
Achilles' Heel

What can get in the way of your success and happiness?

ANSIR DEFINITION OF

Achilles' Heel!

Dominant Style's dominant doubt, weakness, or vulnerability!

Ansir earlier cautioned that Profile Boss was a sleeper. Well, Achilles' heel is the aspect of You that unfortunately is too wide awake.

Achilles' Heel Key spotlights the fears, doubts, and vulnerabilities covered in InDepth. Ansir has generally found that like "the spouse being the last to know," usually YOU are the last to recognize your Achilles' heel.

Generally, this is the only aspect of self that others can and do know better about you, *than you do.*

Whenever compromise, manipulation, or betrayal occurs, Achilles' heel allowed, invited, or led the way to misery. Understanding this simple, straight-forward Key is tantamount to the bull removing the ring from its own nose.

DIFFERENT PERSONALITY STYLE

Different Achilles' Heel

Dominant Profile Styles are to be reckoned with and respected fully.

Each personality Style has a different Achilles' heel. In terms of a Profile, that can mean there are 3 different vulnerabilities. Achilles' heel for Profile Boss is also Boss fear, doubt or vulnerability for that individual. Note the Achilles' Heel for each of your Profiled Styles. Additionally, note the group classification (Physical, Logical, et cetera) that each Style fits into.

For instance, if Profiled: *Kinsmen/Visionary/Realist*. This Profile is comprised of 3-personality Styles from 3-different groups. Visionary (Intuitive) is Profile Boss with dominant support Styles of Kinsmen (Emotional) and Realist (Physical).

Having read the InDepths for this Profile, you'd have realized that Visionary functions intuitively, while Kinsmen and Realist function logically. When viewed separately, there are inherent contradictions between these 3-unique Styles.

If each of these dominant Styles suited and fit three individuals, the inherent differences would be apparent and conflicts would likely arise when they interact in everyday life. In a Profile, such contradictions become self-fulfillment strengths, given confident Boss influence and direction. However, when Boss is unconfident, the Achilles' Heel of each Profile Style can raise confusion and conflict to such a degree that an individual can feel as torn and conflicted *internally* as three separate and warring individuals *externally*.

Confident vs. Unconfident

When confident, a Profiled Style strength can lead to success and happiness. When unconfident, a Profiled strength can become a weakness and throw best laid plans and good intentions off-track. The hand that feeds you can and *will* deprive you of plenty, if not understood.

As you read each Achilles' heel for your Profile, note your Boss Style's general group classification, as well as Achilles' heel particulars. Do the same for your other Profiled Styles. Core issues and concerns that have caused grief in the past—in your everyday reality—are usually recognized when fears/doubts/vulnerabilities of your dominant Styles are pulled out, laid side-by-side, and viewed closely.

When Achilles' heel is recognized, understood, and accepted, it's easier to deal with the trouble caused by trigger and tripper-type situations. Stressful situations may not be avoidable. Though elsewise or otherwise imposed, coping strategies that cut off your success/happiness *nose* are controlled directly by You, and are therefore controllable.

To repeat...

Achilles' heel is the only aspect of self that others generally know better than you do. Whenever compromise, manipulation, or betrayal occurs, Achilles' heel allowed it, invited it, or directly led the way to misery. Understanding this simple, so straight-forward Key, is tantamount to the bull removing the ring from its own nose.

14 ANSIR STYLES

14 Achilles' Heels

Listed by group classification.

LOGICALS:

Diligent: your Achilles' heel is the fear of making mistakes and being thought foolish or stupid.

Sage: your Achilles' heel is the fear of being rejected for being different.

INTUITIVES:

Visionary: your Achilles' heel is the fear of not doing something meaningful in your lifetime.

Evokateurs: your Achilles' heel is the fear of being scooped up by the system hopper and prevented from doing what you love and must do.

SPIRITUALISTS:

Healer: your Achilles' heel is the fear of trusting your own intuitive ability and power.

Philosopher: your Achilles' heel is the fear of lifetime loneliness without an understanding, fulfilling mate.

PHYSICALS:

Extremist: your Achilles' heel is the fear of assuming responsibility for others.

Realist: your Achilles' heel is the fear of the consequences of your own passion (being rejected or causing harm).

PRACTICALS:

Eccentrik: your Achilles' heel is the fear of being found common despite effort and aspiration to be different.

Idealist: your Achilles' heel is the fear of failing despite focused efforts to be comparatively best and most perfect of all.

EMOTIONALS:

Kinsmen: your Achilles' heel is the fear of being found less honorable or worthy than reputation and behaviour implies.

Empath: your Achilles' heel is the fear of not receiving the same unconditional love and acceptance you offer to others.

INSTINCTIVES

Scintillator: your Achilles' heel is the fear of abandonment.

Sentinel: your Achilles' heel is the fear of betrayal.

ACHILLES' HEEL

Summary

Like Profile Boss, like Life Purpose, Achilles' heel Key only reads and seems simple.

Achilles' heel spotlights the self-doubts, fears, and vulnerabilities highlighted in *Profile InDepths*. Those undermining beliefs and ingrained coping habits can trip you up, and prevent You from achieving Life Purpose fulfillment (desired success and happiness). Read, and understand well, the Achilles' heel for each personality Style in your Ansir Profile.

Then quietly consider what this simple Key says and means.

Achilles' heel has, can, and will prevent you from achieving Boss-defined success and Boss-desired happiness.

How Business Measures You

Headhunter Shorthand reveals the industry acknowledged attributes of your dominant style of working. Your *Profiled* manner of tackling problems, making decisions, organizing information, and prioritizing efforts when working, are not a mystery to the corporate world; they're known and rated.

Note the innate working style of associates, boss, or mate, and consider what that means to you, in terms of compatibility between your style of working and theirs.

Recall (from Profile Boss) that for five Ansir personality styles—Idealist, Visionary, Healer, Philosopher, and sometimes Evokateur—fulfillment is found in the work realm. Meaning "work" is all-important to them and to those around them.

6

HeadHunter
ShortHand

Work attributes and occupation matches
to plan a more fulfilling career.

THE PHYSICALS

Expected contribution: Progress

Workplace order of priorities: Job; Self; Corporation: Associates

In terms of work:

You tend to be a specialist, Extremist, usually in some narrow aspect of field, service, or industry. You like to directly control outcomes. Teamwork means compromising to accommodate someone else's agenda or depending on others, which usually means disappointment to you. Such personal influence and control are not always possible in corporate environments. Understanding your overly-developed sense of responsibility will help you understand why long-term relations, professional or personal, scare fearless you. Not being there when needed, not being able to personally salvage the project, or save situations is why you specialize and why your world tends to be small. If isolated and isolating, it's controllable. Be extremely fussy about what you do, where you do, and with whom. Being true to self is what fulfills. While your skills and abilities stand out, you may need to stand alone. Work according to gifted nature, Extremist. Success for many entails a some-or-all chase after money, power, and recognition. You can attain that with mental focus but it doesn't reward fulfillingly. Your definition of success requires you physically experience and mentally conquer challenges that you pick and deem as worthy. Others make mental and/or emotional commitments. Yours are physical and mental...and in that order.

Role Matches:

Public service professions	Sports
Sales/marketing	Performing/non-performing arts
Journalist	Entrepreneur
Consultant	System developer
Mechanical design/testing	Mechanical repair

Production/manufacturing/construction—skilled or unskilled
Physically challenging careers, such as test pilot, military
Environmentally challenging careers, such as wildlife biologist

Work Characteristics:

Direct and to the point	Responds quickly to situations
Decisive in thought and action	Takes abrupt changes in stride
Quick to respond to new ideas	Prone to being judgmental
Free from self-conscious feelings	Capable of risk-taking decisions
Competitive and competent	Detached in feelings
Opinionated	Delivers practical results
Prefers difficult tasks and goals	Pride in personal achievements
Forceful and enthusiastic	Physically active
Defensive, if reproached	Seeks freedom of action
Acts on own initiative	Flexible
Aggressive in problem solving	Prefers pre-planned activities
Self-assertive in behaviour	Requires and takes direction well

Aptitude and Preferences:

Influential	Logical and systematic
Nature-loving	Mechanically inclined
Organizer	Mathematically inclined
Athletic	Processor of details

Work Style:

Task-oriented	Individual

THE PHYSICALS

Realist

Expected contribution: Reliability
Workplace order of priorities: Job; Self; Associates; Corporation

In terms of work:

Realist, others are not looking for reasons to find fault with your every action and decision. Your most valuable worker attribute is not saying you can and will, unless you can and could. No other is as impatient with you as you are with self, nor as judgemental. Set aside some time to understand self...at least as well as you understand the those challenges you seek *out there,* and with one-tenth the enthusiasm you have for learning the skills that lead to your kind of success. That famous and characteristic temper of yours is a bodily function. A better friend you could not hope to have, once reason and purpose are understood. You tend to think your energy a curse. That's because you haven't discovered the value of its unique complexity. Can or could anyone else? You have intelligent hands, but remember what guides and directs them. A highly practical mind. No other, even with training, can do what comes naturally to you. If others seem to be watching you closely, it's likely with respect and admiration, and likely with relief that you're on the job. You're a leader, Realist. Criticism comes with that territory. So don't let self-doubt build and temper derail, before appreciation and applause have time to arrive.

Role Matches:

Leader	Public service professions
Health Practitioner	Mechanics
Sales	Production/manufacturing—skilled/unskilled
Entrepreneur	Computer technician/operator
Skilled labourer	Construction professional
Shipping/Receiving	Secretary/Administrative Assistant

Work Characteristics:

Seeks respect of associates	Aggressive in problem solving
Defensive if reproached	Requires/takes direction extremely well
Places high value on systems	Expresses differences of opinion openly
Prefers pre-planned activities	Follows plans/orders conscientiously
Has high energy level	Works well as a team member
Physically active	Pride in personal achievements
Competitive/cooperative	Steadfast/predictable in behaviour
Opinionated	Abides by rules and procedures
Forceful and enthusiastic	Above average stick-to-itiveness
Direct in planning	Straightforward in action
Prefers chain of command	Likes established procedures
Analyzes problems	Self-critical

Aptitude and Preferences:

Influential	Logical and systematic
Nature-loving	Mechanically inclined
Organizer	Mathematically inclined
Athletic	Processor of details

Work Style:

Task-oriented	Hard working

THE INSTINCTIVES

Expected contribution: improved workplace morale

Workplace order of priorities: Self; Job; Associates; Corporation

In terms of work:

Scintillator, instead of waiting for others to recognize your real abilities and to bolster or "install" your confidence; try doing whatever and as much as it takes, to impress self first. You tend to talk a better game plan than actually working or testing it, unless encouraged each step of the way. You're a born entertainer, meaning you gauge and grow success according to response received from others. Consider the workplace a captive audience, one that can't leave until your show is over. Few can find the shortcut, come up with an alternative or keep the team focused, as you can. Don't wait for others' nod or approval. Grab your hat and cane and tap-dance as or when you see a need. Depend on your characteristic and natural gifts to motivate and reward fully and fulfillingly. Your smile was meant to reflect and instill confidence in others—as leader smiles are all wont to do. You're a leader, who too-often depends on others to encourage that quality's rise. If breathing, consider that reason and occasion enough to be you.

Role Matches:

Professional performer/entertainer
Public Relations
Educator, esp. Trade Industry
Computer operators
Clerical
Administrative assistant
Physical careers like sports, physical therapy, construction worker

Designer
Sales/Marketing
Team/project leader
Production/Manufacturing —
(skilled/unskilled)

Work Characteristics:

Respects status quo
Opinionated
Works well in teams
Strives to please
 Avoids direct confrontation
Quick to respond to new ideas
Prone to being judgmental
Respects authority
Expects and delivers practical results
Prefers chain of command and established procedures

Follows plans/orders well
Spontaneous in feelings
Personable and sociable
Free of self-conscious feelings
Good communicator
Physically active
Has a personal charm
Makes an excellent impression

Aptitude and Preferences:

People person
Nature-loving
Athletic
Creative

Logical and systematic
Mechanically inclined
Processor of details

Work Style:

Task-oriented

Positive

THE INSTINCTIVES

Sentinel

Expected contribution: Customer/client watchdog

Workplace order of priorities: Corporation; Job; Self; Associates

In terms of work:

You would not be Sentinel, if trusting others were not an issue. Your skeptical antenna has historically kept the charlatans at bay and laws minded and respected. Your value as human hallway monitor is immeasurable in terms of reason, order, and protectiveness. At work, few work the plan and follow the pattern as reliably as you, but you're much more capable than that. You don't risk opinion or offer revision as often as you can and could. Your smarts are two-fold: knowledge and instinct. Yet instincts tend not to be exercised at work. It's important that you find work that demands more than a regurgitation of rules, or a repeat of actions. Success may result but self-fulfillment may not. Security is most important to you. A sure thing is what your loyalty gene looks for and needs, but that's not enough. Your Style has a love-hate relationship with challenges. Initially they intimidate, can even stun. Once your instincts kick-in, that which differentiates you from every other shines and excels. Be it law, science, arts, entertainment, et cetera, you've the right stuff to succeed. Trusting your instincts and taking some gut guided chances is when you stand out. As regards choices of work, workplace, or work associates, your gut will not, indeed cannot lead you astray.

Role Matches:

Legal profession
Manager
Scientist
Controller
Shipping/Receiving
Production/Manufacturing
(skilled/unskilled)

Public service
Research & Development
Sales/marketing
Computer Systems analyst
Secretary/administrative assistant

Work Characteristics:

Direct and to the point
Physically active
Friendly but restrained
Opinionated
Detached in feelings
Seeks respect of associates
Defensive, if reproached
Accepts/respects status quo
Requires/takes direction well
Deliberate in action and thought

Prone to being judgmental
Places high value on systems
Abides by rules/procedures
Steadfast and predictable in behaviour
Prefers pre-planned activities
Expects/delivers practical results
Pride in personal achievements
Reasons logically/persuasively
Follows plans/orders conscientiously

Aptitude and Preferences:

Logical and systematic
Nature-loving
Organizer
Athletic
Socially aware and involved

Mechanically inclined
Mathematically inclined
Reading and writing
Processor of details

Work Style:

Task-oriented

Loyal

THE LOGICALS

iligent

Expected contribution: Efficiency

Workplace order of priorities: Corporation; Job; Self; Associates

In terms of work:

Diligent, lighten up on yourself. Most allow for error. Not you. When problems arise, most leave work, go home to relax with family, sleep soundly, and leave office problems for tomorrow. Not you. By the way you open the door at day's end, your family knows you won't be pleasant and can't be pleased until you've fixed that office problem. One other thing: at the office you're known for being smart and reliable, not for being friendly and warm. For you, understanding means gaining enough information to form an opinion, and determine an appropriate course of action. Emotionality of others is a puzzling irritant to you, especially in the workplace. In order to understand, it behooves you to learn more about the people you work closely with. Learning about them and sharing about you doesn't erode work relations. It generally improves them. When you do make mistakes, miscalculate or just plain screw-up, look in the mirror. Notice you've two eyes, two ears, one nose, and one mouth. That means you're human and, therefore, fallible and vulnerable. Trust Self to find the way back to the right track. Few can, as surely or sure-footedly as you. So ease up on yourself a bit. Professionally, you've probably earned the characteristic Diligent reputation for being seriously reliable. You owe it to yourself to find and enjoy the who-else and what-else pleasures of work.

Role Matches:

Controller	Administrator
Technical Sales	Production, skilled or unskilled
Leader	Technical Advisor
Research	Computer programmer
Systems analyst	Quality Control
Shipping/Receiving	Labourer, skilled or unskilled

Work Characteristics:

Serious demeanor	Calm and earnest by nature
Works well as a team member	Practical and confident in planning
Prefers pre-planned activities	Follows plans/orders conscientiously
Places high value on systems	Requires/takes direction extremely well
Strives for excellence	Anticipates future consequences
Strong need for security	Above average stick-to-itiveness
Delegates well	Reasons logically and persuasively
Prone to being judgmental	Deliberate in action and thought
Precise about detail processing	Capitalizes on personal strengths
Defensive if reproached	Stays current of work-related issues
Opinionated	Friendly but restrained in relations
Thorough work habits	Steadfast/predictable in behaviour

Expects and delivers practical results
Works well alone without need of supervision
Prefers chain of command and established procedures

Aptitude and Preferences:

Influential	Mathematically Inclined
Processor of Details	Logical & Systematic
Organizer	Mechanically Inclined

Work Style:

Goal-oriented	Focused

THE LOGICALS

age

Expected contribution: Greater procedural efficiency and camaraderie

Workplace order of priorities: Job; Associates; Corporation; Self

In terms of work:

Of all, Sage, you most need a work environment where the benefit of your random approach is respected and appreciated. If it were possible to include a set of "how to treat this employee" instructions with your resume, your professional life would be less stressful. Time can be your enemy. If the test of employee value, in terms of contributions, were short and brief, you'd likely fail. Yours is a long-brewed kind of value, one that often needs time for all those subtle benefits of your Style's fame to shine through, before your value is realized. In combination with your pleasing-nature, you may be overlooked in company or in comparison to razzle-dazzle types; those more proficient at making good first impressions. Choose wisely the corporation and work associates with whom you affiliate. Both leader and follower can rely on the accuracy of your analytical, practical approach, but your random manner and methodology tends to frustrate others greatly. Those interested in long-term success and incremental progress are the ones who'll understand best and appreciate you most. Organization will always be a major challenge for you. Apprising others or adjusting your pace to match theirs is your own responsibility. Details and facts constantly fill your head. While you don't need to chart your progress, others require it. If time can be your career enemy—not giving others time to realize your value—lack of organization can be your nemesis. Be highly selective in your workplace choices. According to Ansir research, Sage working Style is one of the rarest on earth.

Role Matches:

Law	Research & Development
Scientist	Designer
Educator	Computer operator/programmer
Orator	Technical advisor
Writer	Production/manufacturing—skilled
	Computer systems analyst

Work Characteristics:

Opinionated	Weighs all sides of issues
Thinks before acting	Not easily distracted
Good communicator	Accepts and respects status quo
Personable and sociable	Expects and delivers practical results
Avoids direct confrontation	Keeps current of work-related issues
Meets people easily	Intellectual and matter-of-fact

Capitalizes on personal strengths
Prefers to suggest rather than actively direct or dominate
Prefers chain of command and established procedures

Aptitude and Preferences:

Logical/systematic	Mechanically inclined
People person	Mathematically inclined
Socially aware	Reading and writing
Organizer	Processor of details
Creative	

Work Style:

Concept-oriented	Knowledgeable

THE PRACTICALS

Expected contribution: Creativity with flair.

Workplace order of priorities: Self; Job; Corporation; Associates

In terms of work:

Eccentrik, ignore that old adage "when the going gets tough, the tough get going." Your *going habit* tends to be at the expense of your own success. Yes you are different; some may think you weird. But the weirdest thing about your working style is, when you consciously conform to fit, what gets suppressed is your creativity. That's you at half-mast. Be you, whether that entails being weirdo or wacko, because when your external and internal sing one and same song, your inventiveness flies. Uniquely, you thrive and shine best when you grate against tradition and conventionality. From that self-caused tension, the prod you need to succeed is fashioned. If that's the springboard, guess what? Pick and choose your battles carefully, and find alternatives to leaving when the going gets rough. For you are most valuable to self and to all, when true to yourself first. Your behaviour and demeanor is your trademark. Dress for work in whatever outfit self-confidence is found.

Role Matches:

Designer	Technology/mechanics developer
Inventor	Computer operator/programmer
Sales/marketing	Research & Development
Entrepreneur	Performing & non-performing artist
System analyst	Production/manufacturing—skilled
Educator	Mechanical technician/repair
Clerical	Building/construction

Work Characteristics:

Individualistic	Thinks and reasons independently
Opinionated	Socially responsive and attentive
Delivers practical results	Quick to respond to new ideas
Seeks freedom of action	Confident in ability to achieve
Defensive, if reproached	Withstands group pressure
Spontaneous in feelings	Follows plans and orders well
Direct and to the point	Pride in personal achievements
Works well without supervision	Keeps current of work-related issues
Free from self-conscious feelings	

Aptitude and Preferences:

Inspirational	Logical and systematic
Organizer	Mechanical inclined
Creative	Processor of details

Work Style:

Creative	Concept-oriented

THE PRACTICALS

dealist

Expected contribution: Increased overall efficiency

Workplace order of priorities: Self; Corporation; Job; Associates

In terms of work:

Idealist, your Style is common among the ambitious, successful, and rich. You personify the American dream. Any field, occupation, or corporation is actively looking for and in need of you. To make a hiring decision about you, employers need only to read your resume. Most of it's true or soon will be, if you're given the cheque and/or chance to do your Style's thing. What you've done or what you do is your Self definition. Others need look no further than your record of achievement to date, to know who you are, and what to expect in the workplace. We offer here a personal note. When you leave work, make sure you have a home to go to. One where spotlights are dimmed, and conversation and companionship do not demand more "show time" from you. As long as you are performing, your nature is to think and out-do, not share emotional truth. When you walk in that front door at home, you need nurturing. There's no room in your success striving work life, for such. You thrive on responsibility but need one corner in life, where emotionality can be expressed openly and vulnerability shared safely. That exceptional place or mate is not easy for you to find or experience but is needed. The heart is a muscle that needs exercising, too. Yours, tends to atrophy in the presence of money and power.

Role Matches:

Politician	Legal profession
Manager	Administrator
Entrepreneur	Facilitator
Controller	Computer systems analyst
Sales/marketing	Research & Development
Performing artist	Shipping/Receiving
Production/manufacturing	
(unskilled or skilled)	

Work Characteristics:

Competitive and cooperative	Superior organization skills
Superior planning ability	Strong drive for status/income security
Takes initiative	Delegates well
Seeks respect of associates	Capable of risk-taking decisions
Prefers to direct activities	Requires/takes direction very well
Defensive, if reproached	Strives for excellence
Has a high energy level	Aggressive and quick problem solver
Makes an excellent impression	Capitalizes on personal strengths
Pride in personal achievements	Keeps current of work-related issues
Sets high expectations	Above average stick-to-itiveness
Prone to being judgmental	Confident in ability to achieve
Follows plans and orders conscientiously	
Quickly and accurately assesses situations	

Aptitude and Preferences:

Influential	Mathematically inclined
Trainer	Planner
Organizer	Overseer
Processor of details	Reading and writing
Entrepreneur	

Work Style:

Goal-oriented	Efficient

THE EMOTIONALS

Kinsmen

Expected contribution: Helpfulness (organization)

Workplace order of priorities: Corporation; Job; Associates; Self

In terms of work:

Kinsmen, consider trusting self enough to take a few more chances. Yours is a world class mind and helpful nature. A combination that professionally makes you valuable, but often requires you deplete your own energy meeting others' expectations, whilst down-playing your own opinions and creativity. One area to personally focus on: trusting self to make decisions. Your Style is to defer to others or act according to general consensus. Trust self more and offer up your own opinion. After all, common sense and responsibility are cellular attributes of yours. Even when you're wrong, you tend to be closer to right than most. As regards to work associates, you have needs too. As interesting as they are and as compelling as their problems seem, you're interesting and important, too. After all, Style is the rarest on earth, according to Ansir's research.

Role Matches:

Human Resources	Judiciary
Manager	Coach
Controller	Administrative
Clerical	Production—skilled or unskilled
Sales	Computer systems analyst
Computer operator	Shipping/Receiving
Labourer	

Work Characteristics:

Seeks respect of associates	Communicative and sociable
Works well as a team member	Places high value on systems
Strives to please	Follows plans/orders conscientiously
Respectful of authority	Prefers chain of command procedures
Learns readily from others	Avoids direct confrontation
Identifies with special cause	Precise about detail processing
Opinionated	Expects and delivers practical results
Quick to respond to new ideas	Accepts and respects status quo
Abides by rules and procedures	Considers both sides of issues

Consults with others before making decisions or taking action

Aptitude and Preferences:

Logical and systematic	Nature-loving
Mathematically loving	People person
Reading and writing	Socially aware and involved
Organizer	Processor of details
Athletic	

Work Style:

Team-oriented	Responsible

THE EMOTIONALS

Empath

Expected contribution: Better trained workers, higher productivity

Workplace order of priorities: Corporation; Associates; Job; Self

In terms of work:

Empath, your gift is to encourage the best in others. Your unique talent is to teach. In that regard, you are peerless. No matter what your current role or employment situation, if you are not in a position to facilitate individual excellence, that is both shame and waste. Unfortunately, because you are such a good, willing worker, your real value may be overlooked or not realized by others. Apprising them of such and pointing out the areas that you can directly impact for betterment is your responsibility. But your ever-present fear of rejection looms to keep you from doing just that. You likely already know what area of need you can improve—most Empaths do. Make it and self known. Draw up your proposal and present it to decision-makers. Based on familiarity with your Style, it is presumed that you are not working at peak of potential. People skills are your forté. Self-doubt tends to be your nemesis. Remember, when you're not working confidently, all within influence-distance suffer loss too. Consider this, what you personally do is less important and has less success potential, than your encouraging of others to do for themselves. That's your greatest value and why you're Empath. The question only you can answer is, are you working as born and meant?

Role Matches:

Public Relations
Facilitator
Educator
Human Resources
Controller

Counselor
Computer operator
Sales/marketing
Clerical
Production/manufacturing - skilled
Performing/non-performing arts

Work Characteristics:

Seeks respect of associates
Superior teaching/training ability
Spontaneous in feelings
Prone to being judgmental
Delivers practical results
Identifies with special cause
Strives to please
Meets people easily
Aware of feelings of others
Follows orders conscientiously
Prefers chain of command

Good communicator
Quick to respond to new ideas
Prefers to suggest rather than direct
Accepts and respects status quo
Responsive and attentive
Learns readily from others
Avoids direct confrontation
Works well as a team member
At ease with most people
Socially responsive and attentive
Likes established procedures

Aptitude and Preferences:

Inspirational
Nature-loving
Organizer
Creative

Emotions
People-person
Reading and writing
Processor of details

Work Style:

Helpful

Task-oriented

THE INTUITIVES

isionary

Expected contribution: Increased productivity and profits

Workplace order of priorities: Job; Associates; Self; Corporation

In terms of work:

Visionary, if you choose to ignore that tick-tock, then any job will do and you'll likely succeed. That's your driven nature. If you choose to quiet that internal prompt, then find your own work niche. It is significant whenever Visionary shows up for work. One word that is, or will become cellular familiar to you is "Next!" Until you find what above all else and other you most love and want to do, expect to dip your toe into varied and various waters. You are potentially the most valuable employee a corporation, industry, or profession could hope to attract. There's nothing you turn your mind and hand to, that you cannot conquer and excel at, when you love the doing and feel the people merits, thereof. Visionary in the work realm is usually the Profile's Boss. That's your life purpose—why you are here and where self-fulfillment is had. Money, power, and applause can't buy your commitment. Only love of what you're doing, matters. It is ultra-important that you find a work environment that allows for your out-of-the-box creativity. You harbour extraordinary leadership qualities. Your name and nature rises at challenge like no other. You're not often offered that chance. But Visionary, your first responsibility to Self and others is to make and take chances. Unlike most, your tick-tock does not allow you the luxury of waiting for opportunity to be presented on a platter. Usually, and usually alone, you must create the concept, then build the platter for presentation. In other words, your gift is seeing what others cannot and doing what others say cannot be done. You've passed what most fail, the Visionary lesson. Apply the learning. Be you.

Role Matches:

Leader	Scientist
Inventor	Legal profession
Administrator	Computer systems analyst
Educator	Performing/non-performing arts
Facilitator	Research & Development
Entrepreneur	Sales/marketing
Designer	Human Resources
Consultant	Shipping/Receiving
	Production/manufacturing *(skilled)*

Work Characteristics:

Decisive in thought and action	Takes problems in stride
Above average communicator	Extraordinary stick-to-itiveness
Strives for excellence	Anticipates future consequences
Meets people easily	Reasons logically and persuasively
Works well as a team member	Capable of risk-taking decisions
At ease with superiors	Makes an excellent impression
Prefers difficult tasks and goals	Follows plans/orders conscientiously
Sets high expectations	Delegates with ease
Withstands group pressure	Thinks and plans imaginatively
Strong need for security	Confident in ability to achieve
Forceful and enthusiastic	Handles pressure and stress well

Capitalizes on personal and associate strengths
Willing to start over or start anew after failure

Aptitude and Preferences:

Inspirational	Influential
Intuitive	Mathematically inclined
People person	Reading and writing
Creative	Socially aware and involved

Work Style:

Effective	Purpose-oriented

THE INTUITIVES

Evokateur

Expected contribution: New direction and focus

Workplace order of priorities: Job; Self; Associates; Corporation

In terms of work:

Evokateur, you are the most creative of all planet beings. Obviously, your oddness is a delight for those who understand and a test for those who don't. Once you accept your own gifts and the responsibilities that go with them, fear of having to change to please others won't bother so much, anymore. Be you, and trust that the world will love you and encourage you without your having to be anything less than self. Your guide to the right work situation or the right mate is the same. If the need to escape to your inner world imaginings is more frequent than not, you're in the wrong place or with the wrong person. Move on. Otherwise, you'll not find the fulfillment you seek or meet the responsibilities that are yours, alone. More than self loses...world and future suffer, too. No other can or does as you, when working on what you love. In the workplace, chance sharing your inner world imaginings with others. It is important for all that you be highly selective in choosing your work, work environment, and corporate affiliation. Your best work results when you keep company with Visionarys, Healers, Philosophers, and other Evokateurs. Actively and consciously look for these Styles. They can offer you the kind of encouragement needed. If important to you, remember, the world awaits the important benefits your creative rareness offers.

Pg. 458

Role Matches:

Academician	Research & Development
Inventor	Performing/non-performing arts
Scientist	Research & Development
Engineer	Educator
Consultant	System design & development
Clerical	Production/manufacturing *(skilled)*

Work Characteristics:

Thinks imaginatively	Works best alone without supervision
Serious demeanor	Keeps current of work-related issues
Weighs both sides of issues	Quickly assesses situations
Individualistic	Spontaneous in feelings
Not easily distracted	Has sense of inner freedom
Readily adapts to change	Thinks in terms of intangibles
Idea-minded, reflective	Prefers difficult tasks and goals
Reasons persuasively	Creative in action and thought
Has a high energy level	Capable of risk-taking decisions
Seeks freedom of action	Acts on own initiative.
Withstands group pressure	

Aptitude and Preferences:

Influential	Intuitive
Nature-loving	Mathematically inclined
Creative	Reading and writing

Work Style:

Concept-oriented	Solves problems directly and indirectly

http://www.ansir.com

THE SPIRITUALISTS

Expected contribution: People-perspective changes

Workplace order of priorities: Associates; Job; Corporation; Self

In terms of work:

Healer, there's nothing wrong with you. You're different for a reason. Rampant emotionality is more than gift; for you it's necessity. Only trust that which feels right and use those intuitive powers confidently and fully. Changing belief is why you are different...and why you are here. Healer NEVER shows up in the work realm, unless perspectives *out there* are in need, or in dire need of changing. Wherever you are, regardless of job, role, or function you currently perform, step back a bit, and look around. Why are you there, at this point in time? There's always a reason for you. Economics are not reason enough. People hold first-place in Healer priorities. Why is one of the most intuitive and powerful of all standing on that spot, in that skin, today? Figure that out, then get onto the doing of significant work, Healer. Your value is immeasurable and your efforts needed by more than just those in your workplace.

Role Matches:

Health Practitioner	Environmentalist
Agronomist	Educator/Communicator
Counselor	Artist/Musician/Writer/Actor
Designer	Research & Development
Controller	Human Resources
Facilitator	Computer programmer
Marketing	Production/Manufacturing *(skilled)*
Clerical	

Work Characteristics:

Identifies with special cause	Quickly, accurately assesses situations
Weighs both sides of issues	Empathizes with others and/or issues
Delivers practical results	Anticipates future consequences
Readily adapts to change	Concentrative in thought
Responsive and attentive	Prefers difficult tasks and goals
Learns readily from others	Thinks in terms of intangibles
Aware of own feelings	Capable of risk-taking decisions
Trustworthy	Keeps current of work-related issues
Has a high energy level	Takes /gives direction extremely well
Works well without supervision	Thinks and reasons independently
Above average stick-to-itiveness	Deliberate in action and thought

Aptitude & Preferences:

Inspirational	Processor of details
Creative	Nature-loving
Organizer	People-person
Intuitive	Reading and writing

Work Style

Conscientious	Concept-oriented

THE SPIRITUALISTS

Philosopher

Expected contribution: Increased worker confidence and corporate accountability

Workplace order of priorities: Corporation; Associates; Job; Self

In terms of work:

Philosopher, it's up to you to tell us how you're doing and how things are going. You must speak to be heard. Wherever you are currently employed, and whatever you are currently employed in doing, change is imminent or monitoring is required. Your reason for being is to ensure that the value and importance of people is upheld and maintained. Your own personal and professional value is akin to being the fly on the wall. One who points out to the masses, what new plans or progress, the few may not want seen and known. There is no more valuable contribution made to all, than what you filter and share through your life strainer. Be you, Philosopher. Whether issues of politics, law, business, arts, science, communications, counseling, teaching, abortion, or death, no other is as human protectful and respectful, as you. Employers may deem you a threat, which is confusing when you consider that most Mission Statements proclaim their main concern is serving people, and their success owed to their people-people employees. You'd be at the top of most desired employee lists, if that were reality's truth. But you're not. When you speak, we'll know how and what you are doing, and what "next" needs our focused, collective attention. What human issue needs you right now, Philosopher?

Role Matches:

Consultant	Strategic planning
Educator	Academician
Social Scientist	Health Practitioner
Communications	Research & Development
System analyst	Human Resources
Artist/Musician	Journalist/writer
Production	Manufacturing
Construction	
(skilled or unskilled)	

Work Characteristics:

Capable of risk-taking decisions	Anticipates future consequences
Weighs both sides of issues	Quickly/accurately assesses situations
Has sense of inner freedom	Direct/decisive in thought/action
Concentrative in thought	Takes abrupt changes in stride
Responsive and attentive	Thinks imaginatively
Reasons persuasively	Keeps current of work-related issues
Genuine in relationships	Confident in ability to achieve
Stresses intangible values	Prefers difficult tasks and goals
Identifies with special cause	Independent and autonomous
Values non-material advantages	Above average stick-to-itiveness
Good communicator	At ease with most people
Works well without supervision	Withstands group pressure
Meets people easily	Serious demeanor
Prefers to suggest over actively direct	

Aptitude and Preferences:

Influential	Intuitive
People person	Reading and writing
Creative	Socially aware and involved

Work Style:

Individualistic	Concept-oriented

3 Sides of You

7
MATCH/MISMATCH

What personality Styles are compatible with you?

STYLE COMPATIBILITY

Match/Mismatch?

Wonder why you're in sync with one, but out of step with another?
Drawn to one, put off by another?

Ansir's 14 personality Styles think, work, and emote differently. It's no wonder that they interact differently too!

All-Style compatibility is Ansir's next work. Our research is moving from self, to self and others. Match/Mismatch is a work-in-progress and sheds new light on which Styles are most and least compatible.

You've found your right Profile and met your Boss. Now meet the Styles that you will get along with best, and learn Why.

MAKE BEAUTIFUL MUSIC WITH ONE?
Dissonant chords with another?

Think of it this way: when you sing in your head *(3 Sides Of You)*, you're always in tune. When you sing out loud, your crooning is interpreted by the *3 Sides* of another. Those who find your song music to their ears are compatible; those who don't, aren't!

For right now, practical benefit, we are providing an all-Style *Match/Mismatch* scale. Though yet to be verified, through research and testing, we offer this as a preview of Ansir's NEXT level of infinitely challenging and fascinating personality work. *3 Sides Of You* is only step one. We've miles to go yet!

Key Criteria for Compatibility

1. Same language—do you communicate in a manner that's agreeable and readily understood by the other?

2. Are Life Purposes of each understood, accepted and most importantly, supported by the Other?

3. Is the Achilles' heel of one, covered and protected by the other?

Match/Mismatch is based on Profile Boss.

Check your Boss compatibility with others on the scales provided. Remember, compatibility applies to ALL relationships—career, casual, and committed.

Read all 3-realms of compatible others to better understand them, not just their Boss realm. Experience for yourself the fun and the difference that knowing self and knowing others makes.

Key 7 - Match/Mismatch Scales

Healer = Heal
Kinsmen = Kin
Scintillator = Scin
Sage = Sage
Diligent = Dil
Empath = Emp
Realist = Real

Idealist = Idea
Extremist = Ext
Sentinel = Sent
Evokateur = Evok
Philosopher = Phi
Visionary = Vis
Eccentrik = ECC

B	S	G	O	P	T
Best	Satisfying	Good	Okay	Problem	Trouble

Rating Scale for Match/Mismatch

Compatibility Potential Based On Profile Boss

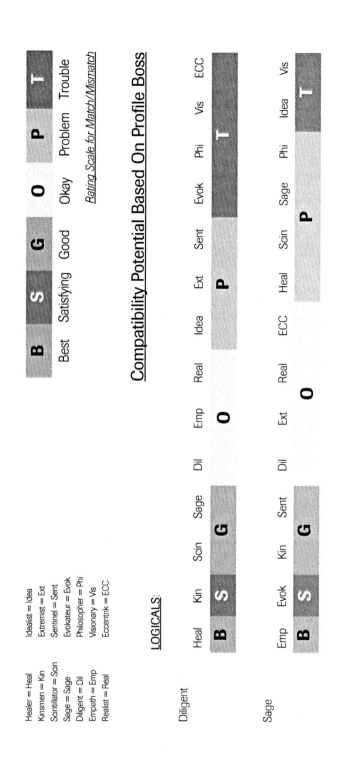

LOGICALS:

Diligent

Heal	Kin	Scin	Sage	Dil	Emp	Real	Idea	Ext	Sent	Evok	Phi	Vis	ECC
B	S	G		O				P				T	

Sage

Emp	Evok	Kin	Sent	Dil	Ext	Real	ECC	Heal	Scin	Sage	Phi	Idea	Vis
B	S	G		O				P				T	

INTUITIVES:

Visionary

Phi	Vis	Heal	Idea	ECC	Kin	Evok	Ext	Real	Scin	Dil	Sage	Sent	Emp
B	S		G			O				P			T

Evok ateur

Heal	Vis	Kin	Idea	Sage	Phi	Real	ECC	Scin	Emp	Dil	Evok	Sent	Ext
B	S		G			O			P		T		

SPIRITUALISTS:

Healer

Phi	Vis	Evok	Emp	Real	Kin	Sage	Heal	Scin	Dil	ECC	Idea	Sent
B	S		G			O			P		T	

Philosopher

Heal	Evok	Vis	Kin	Ext	Sage	Real	ECC	Dil	Idea	Emp	Phi	Scin	Sent
B	S				O					P			T

http://www.ansir.com

Key 7 - Match/Mismatch Scales

Healer = Heal	Idealist = Idea
Kinsmen = Kin	Extremist = Ext
Scintillator = Scin	Sentinel = Sent
Sage = Sage	Evokateur = Evok
Diligent = Dil	Philosopher = Phi
Empath = Emp	Visionary = Vis
Realist = Real	Eccentrik = ECC

B	S	G	O	P	T
Best	Satisfying	Good	Okay	Problem	Trouble

Rating Scale for Match/Mismatch

Compatibility Potential Based On Profile Boss

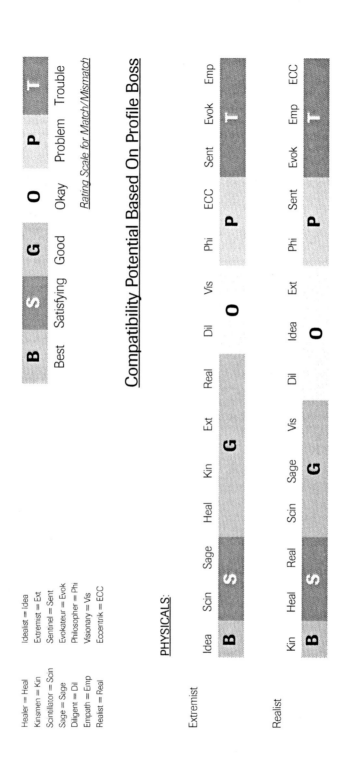

PHYSICALS:

Extremist

Idea	Scin	Sage	Heal	Kin	Ext	Real	Dil	Vis	Phi	ECC	Sent	Evok	Emp
B	S		G				O		P		T		

Realist

Kin	Heal	Real	Scin	Sage	Vis	Dil	Idea	Ext	Phi	Sent	Evok	Emp	ECC
B	S		G				O		P		T		

Eccentrik

Kin	Sage	Scin	Idea	Vis	Evok	Phi	ECC	Emp	Real	Sent	Heal	Dil	Ext
B	S		G			O			P		T		

Idealist

Vis	Real	Scin	Idea	Phi	Heal	Kin	Sage	Sent	ECC	Dil	Emp	Evok	Ext
B	S		G				O			P		T	

EMOTIONALS:

Kinsmen

Heal	Kin	Evok	Vis	Dil	Idea	Emp	Real	Scin	Sent	Sage	Phi	ECC	Ext
B		S			G			O			P		T

Empath

Emp	Heal	Scin	Sage	Vis	Kin	Sent	Real	Evok	Dil	Phi	Idea	Ext	ECC
B			S		G		O		P		T		

http://www.ansir.com

Pg. 471

Key 7 - Match/Mismatch Scales

INSTINCTIVES:

Scintillator

Emp	Heal	Kin	Dil	Ext	Real	ECC	Idea	Sent	Scin	Evok	Sage	Phi	Vis
B		**S**		**G**			**O**		**P**		**T**		

Sentinel

Idea	Kin	Dil	Heal	Sage	Real	Emp	Sent	Ext	ECC	Scin	Evok	Phi	Vis
B		**S**		**G**			**O**		**P**		**T**		

FAQ_s

.....................One of the Styles doesn't fit
What should I do?

...............................My 3 Styles seem to contradict one another.
Does this mean I'm more mixed up than normal?

....What other Styles
are most compatible with me?

....What's gives with the *Higher Power*
Creator/*God* questions? Isn't this
supposed to be a professional Test?

If you don't find what you're looking for here

Ask Ansir!

info@ansir.com

Q How come one realm of functioning doesn't fit me?

A Your three-realm Profile is determined by your answers to the questions in the Ansir test. While there may be some difference according to the interpretation of individual questions, ultimately, you choose your Style. The Ansir test measures Self-perception—nothing less and nothing more. If one of your test-determined Styles does not seem to fit we suggest you re-evaluate how you see yourself. Do you let others determine who you are? Who are you trying to please as you answer the questions: others or yourself only? But rest assured that if your Profile doesn't feel right, it's not.

Q What can I do to find my right Profile?

A We recommend that you retake the Ansir test in those areas that do not seem to fit or that may be in question. The only thing the test measures is how you see yourself, at this point in time.

Q I found myself breaking ties quite a bit so does this mean my Profile may not be accurate.

A Keep in mind that Ansir's test determines your self-perceived, most dominant personality Styles. You may indeed have attributes of many of the other Styles, but the free consumer test, versus the paid corporate test, is programmed to measure the 3-dominant Styles of functioning. Take a look at that "wrongly Profiled self." Where are your results mainly or mostly wrong? Perhaps, if considered, you may see areas that you are currently confused about or are unsure about.

Q Some of the questions don't relate to me at all and I had trouble coming up with one clear answer. What should I do?

A Each question in the test is specific to one personality Style. If the question does not seem to fit you or you do not understand it, it likely does not apply to you. In that case, answer, "Not Me." In time, and if you read about some of the other Styles you may begin to understand these questions more clearly.

Q Most of the information hits the nail on the head, but why do certain aspects of the 3-Styles seem to contradict one another.

A Less than 1 percent of all Ansir Profiles are of one personality Style. When your 3-dominant Styles in Thinking /Working /Emoting are viewed independently contradiction can often be expected. Have you ever been of "two minds" about something? Consider that just as you have a dominant Style in each of the 3-realms of functioning, you have an overall dominant Style—Profile Boss. A Profile is never contradictory or in conflict in sum, unless the individual is uncertain about goal direction (purpose fulfillment) or is not pursuing a goal that's meaningful or appropriate for their Styled talent and ability.

Q My Ansir Profile is scarily accurate. Where do I go from here? How do I use this information to improve my own life?

A "What does my Profile mean for me?" From Ask Monte, a helpful and supportive feature at the Website, provided by the respected and knowledgeable staff researcher, Monte Faul.

I get numerous requests to explain Profile information such as, "Can you explain my Style breakdown?" and "What does this mean?" or "How can I use this in my life?" Most times I refer whomever asks these questions to the "7-Profile Keys" pages because there one can find an abundance of information on the Styles whether you want the short description such as the "Profile Briefs" or the longer, "Profile InDepths" description. But this time I'm answering it outright with a sense of review for the benefit of all.

So we take the test, right, and then we read our Profile Briefs and, while we may have chosen the answer "This is Me" several times during the test, we are now asking, "Is this me?" We may start to get a little defensive as self is a sensitive area for most. If the Profile fits, you may say, "Ok, you got me, but now what?" Let me take this sentence to clarify that these Styles and Profiles are not instruction manuals and won't tell you how to live your life. They may, however, help you see yourself more clearly and, once you see yourself, it's your option what to do with that new understanding. You can pretend you didn't see it or you can look at the possibilities of the world and your life or you can write it all in a letter and send it to yourself 4th class postage and read it again later. We don't tell you which to choose. It's yours to do with what you will—like the rest of your life.

Now, say we've decided that our Profile information is somehow meaningful to you. What now? Take a look at the three realms. **The Working realm** is an outward method of handling your surroundings. Given a job—whether it be constructing an office desk or calculating pi or writing a letter—each Style will handle the procedure differently. Read your Working Profile. Is that how you work? Is that how you like to work? Does that Style fit the job that you're currently in or pursuing? We've seen this area of life as one of extreme dissatisfaction in many that we have met over the years. The tendency is to settle for something you don't hate or that which is safe. I'd suggest, if you're already running, run in the direction you want to end up (not just towards a hiding place), if you're walking, walk the direction you want to end up, and if you're just sitting there in your rocking chair passing the time, keep your eye on what you want to see in the future. What does this have to do with the Working Profile? Your working Profile is your avenue or method of getting where you want to go so pay attention to what you're capable of and where it can take you. For instance, you wouldn't try to drive a Volkswagen "Beetle" across the ocean and you wouldn't use a 40-foot yacht to cross the Sahara desert. And you just don't use a sports car on a track built for "go-carts". How satisfied are you with how your Working Profile meets the reality of your work?

The Thinking realm is a way of understanding and interpreting the world around you. This is your eyes and ears and/or tinted sunglasses. Being aware of whether you're looking through "rose-colored" glasses or blinders can be very helpful in seeing beyond them. When you understand your own process of Thinking, you also know what you are capable and open to seeing. You read your Thinking Profile and you get an idea of what you pay attention to. Do you pay attention to people or to the swaying of the trees or to the new paint job on the passing sports car? At this point take your Thinking Style and set it beside your Working Style. How do they compliment one another? What does your Thinking Style see and consider that can be useful to your Working Style? How might your Thinking Style hamper your work? They are a partnership and understanding that partnership will help you be more aware of what you are currently capable of.

I have a new analogy for **the Emoting realm** that may seem a stretch for some, but which typifies it quite well I think. The earth's oceans cover approximately two-thirds of its surface and the water in them is the strongest controlling force in weather (seasons), animal and plant life, and travel. Imagine each person as their own world and each one with its own size and character of oceans. This one's oceans may be filled with Mercury or this one with something as odd-seeming as Lemonade. The Emoting realm is the "stuff of life" within that person upon which their moods (weather), inner life, and inner communication depend. What kind of plants or animals could grow and thrive on Mercury or Lemonade? Ask an Extremist or a Scintillator.

The partnership we referred to earlier between the Thinking and Working realm is no less significant when applied to the Emoting realm. Your emotions are the setting, the background, the context, and the inspiration for all that takes place inside and around you. How can you find emotional satisfaction? Can you find emotional satisfaction? Are you even looking for emotional satisfaction? Well, if you want it, your Emoting Style is where to look.

One driver; two passengers:

There are some Styles that NEED emotional satisfaction and others that NEED working satisfaction which leads us to your Profile Boss. Considering your Working Style and your Emoting Style, we can look at how they relate to each other and determine which one is captaining the ship. Each one of them is highly involved, but one leads. This, is your Profile Boss. Profile Boss is fairly simple.

The Profile Boss is the natural leader of the three Styles and things run the most smoothly when the other two Styles take a back seat to that one which KNOWS the way towards fulfillment.

They all work together: your Thinking Style on "look-out", your Working Style in the riggings and swabbing the deck, and your Emoting Style making the boat float and blowing the breeze through the sails. You know how tough workplace relations can be—especially out at sea. Getting three Styles to work together in harmony can be simple or near-impossible, but when you understand what they are and what they need you're then in position to set a course. With Ansir Styles, you're in a position to evaluate your own satisfaction. Do you know who you are? Are you satisfied? The answer to those questions are yours and yours to deal with. The only one who understands what you need for fulfillment is you. It's your life, and they're your Styles.

God Is Inappropriate (An e-mail inquiry from a Career service)

While not common, the question of Higher Power/Creator/God in our test and InDepths has been raised now and then. We offer this actual exchange by way of explanation, in case you were wondering too.

Q "Our staff took the Ansir test and was very impressed with the results. Our corporation is interested in using Ansir's Self-perception Profiling system to help us better serve our clients, in terms of career counseling. However, in the opinion of our Board Members, the use of God in the your test and InDepths is decidedly inappropriate for our purposes. Would you consider revising your questionnaire to specifically exclude God references? ..."

A No, and here's why.

Removing Higher Power and/or God references from our Test and Analysis means we put our heads in the same safe sand as you and every other personality test and profiling system out there. You see we both know and understand your position; we just don't happen to agree with it or respect it. In our opinion, which was firmed and confirmed more than four years ago, career and industry testing has been ass-backwards for decades now. *Nose obviously*, career and workplace testing satisfies corporations but does diddly-squat and cares not, about worker satisfaction.

70% of Ansir's tested global population (126 countries as of this date) emphatically and repeatedly states that the realm of greatest unhappiness and highest stress for them is work. Frankly, we wonder if career counselling and job testing is not conducted by blind and deaf individuals. Do not expect Ansir to help you to further the continuance of that common, unhappy state.

When you intimate you'd be interested in using the Ansir test if we'd only remove "Higher Power/God" references, essentially you're asking us to overlook one whole and real personality Style. Four years of pure online testing has proved that theseOnes and many others aren't acknowledged in standard testing. They don't exist, apparently.

Every question in Ansir's test is personality-specific. A Higher Power /God consciousness is as characteristic for one Style as whiskers and claws of cats. So while Higher Power/God is deemed inappropriate for your purposes, god is apropos and at core of definition for one very real, very valuable, and very human being.

The client for almost all career-testing instruments and counselling is the corporation, not the individual worker. You provide "screening" services for corporate clients. Acknowledging Higher Power/God may induce advance fears of workplace disruption by what? Rituals of rosary bead clicking and counting, spontaneous knee-bending, chanting in corners, or directional bowing at sunrise and sunset? For this particular Higher Power/God-conscious personality Style, the most outstanding characteristic and only workplace ritual to be expected is a unique manner of bending elbow and mind for doing, serving, and contributing.

At the high-end of human achievement and excellence theseOnes are commonly found. They're the 30% of this Styled population, whose self-confidence was too big to slip through the expansive lacks of career testing and job counselling.

Before word or work one of Ansir began, it was known how harmful and destructive compromising is to individuals. Corporations desire and in fact demand that human resources in-house and out focus on a narrow band of the human spectrum. Namely, work capability based on experience and training. It would seem 70% deemed fit and fitting by corporation, don't find the fit meaningful, rewarding, or comfortable personally.

That's a huge waste of potential and a sad waste of talent, from our perspective. That's why we will not and would not compromise the truth of one or any Ansir personality style.

We offer that 70% of all that's possible isn't being recognized or respected and currently is under-utilized or not used at all. I repeat: from our perspective career testing and job counselling are ass-backwards. The focus is on fitting all size and shape of individuals into one pre-drilled slot. What doesn't fit is shaved off. Too bad! Often those chipped and clipped bits are the creative aspects that are both valuable and needed.

Not one person (your staff included) goes through the Ansir testing experience without realizing there are 3 very important pieces to the complex puzzle uniquely known as "them." Once truth of self (right Profile) is realized, so too are reasons for their 70% statistical unhappiness. Determining or deciding what to do then or hence is up to each. But from that point forward, industry standards that promote Stepford-type conformity are suddenly more noticeable, and compromising of self is less likely. Its clear that if change can or will occur it will be driven by individual insistence. Corporations see 30% happiness as a one-third full glass, and enough to satisfy for them.

Q Would you consider revising your questionnaire to exclude specific God references?

A We'd no sooner remove Higher Power/Creator/God from Healers, than money from Idealists, alternatives from Sages, reticence from Visionarys, loyalty from Sentinels, love from Empaths, laughter from Scintillators, creativity from Evokateurs, daring from Extremists, eclectic from Eccentriks, fairness from Kinsmen, logic from Diligents, self-responsibility from Philosophers, or honesty from Realists. In the near career and job future we expect Ansir personality "Bosses" won't tolerate being ignored, denied, or removed themselves, far less mind reading terms like Higher Power/God on questionnaires, You see, Ansir recognizes and respects that some Styles don't leave home for work or play, without Higher Power/God by side and inside.

Q What's Ansir's position on religion?

A We encourage and support self-confidence—an embrace of acceptance that necessarily contains all that each holds near, dear, and important. We believe in people and have unwavering faith in each knowing what's best and what's right on their ownsome.

SECTION TWO

ANSIR COMMUNICATIONS INC.

ANSIR means, A New Style In Relating

WHY ANSIR?

The Ansir Mission

To facilitate the development, learning and performance
of individuals and organizations.

Our purpose is to help people achieve personal and professional fulfillment through a better understanding of their Self, thus enabling a more
meaningful and productive use of potential. Our corporate role and
responsibility is to encourage self-exploration; wherein lies the confidence
and motivation necessary for self-fulfillment.

What is the business of Ansir's Personal Development Website?

The concise truth simply reads: Ansir's furthest objective and base
promise is the betterment of people by removal of reticence—the most
common obstacle we've found that blocks individuals from their own
success and happiness and separates individuals from the benefits and
pleasures of others.

The objective of Ansir's Self-perception Profiling System (SPPS) is to
change forever, the way you think, do, and feel about yourSelf and Others!

WHO IS ANSIR?
The Principals

SANDRA SEICH
Founder, Executive Vice-President

Gifted as a child with insight into classifying and understanding people, Sandra Seich has a lifetime of experience acquiring and applying her knowledge, testing it in the school of life, and through the controlled universe of the Internet.

Ms. Seich has extensive development and client-interactive experience with the Internet. She first developed a successful e-zine (digital magazine) called Mankind in 1996, which evolved into the current Ansir Website. Ms. Seich created the acronym that is ANSIR, *A New Style In Relating*. She also authored both the test and analysis upon which the company is built and drives the content side of the business. She is currently developing a second major work: All-Style Compatibilities.

Ms. Seich's education includes Business Administration and Commerce (University of Alberta), design arts, and electronic media. Ms. Seich spent five years in the newspaper industry including the creation of an original newspaper concept. She has an extensive background in publishing and advertising and later specialized in digital consulting for the newly emerging electronic publishing industry.

Methodology (Ansir's Self-Perception Profiling System (SPPS), p. 492

TERRY LEE HEATON
President & CEO

Terry Lee Heaton is a professional observer of life, having been a journalist for 30-years before taking over as Ansir President. During the last 20 of those years he authored and oversaw attitudinal research projects on subjects ranging from human sexuality, NASA, and international politics.

Mr. Heaton has a track record of success in building and rebuilding local television news departments. Mr. Heaton served as News Director for network affiliates in Tyler, TX; New Bern, NC; Richmond, VA; Chattanooga, TN; Huntsville, AL; and Honolulu, HI.

Throughout his professional television career, Mr. Heaton had a record as a skilled people person and problem solver, spearheading ratings' increases and improving products. He was employed as Vice-President of Research for Metro Global, Inc., a Dallas-based, economic-development research firm. An experience which gave him deep insight into power and influence in America.

Mr. Heaton has extensive connections in broadcasting. His background and credentials will be beneficial to Ansir in terms of media promotions and interactions.

The two principals have both invested heavily in Ansir and bring diversified experience and energy to a task they view as both meaningful and enjoyable. They have nursed the company from its research and development stage to a rapidly growing Internet community and are fully committed to its success.

WHEN WAS ANSIR FOUNDED?
The Company

Ansir Communications, Inc. was established in 1995 as a digital publishing company in Toronto, Canada. Since a child, Seich had been categorizing family, friends, and work associates into personality groupings. In 1995, Seich began preliminary research to create a work that would allow people on the Internet to better understand themselves through a Self-perception Profile test. Initial research was conducted via a Web-based e-zine (digital magazine) called *Mankind*, co-developed by Seich & Clarke, authored and edited by Seich.

Over the next 12-months, Ansir beta tested its Self-perception test, as designed by Seich. Ansir's Website and core test group verified initial research and met with positive response from a significant number of test participants. While testing continued, Ms. Seich began writing the book that would serve as the foundation for the next step in corporate strategy: to market the findings. The book, *Ansir for One, 14 rare conversations,* was published in October, 1998.

In November of 1998, Terry Heaton joined the group. The depth and insight of Seich's work impressed Mr. Heaton, a 30-year veteran journalist with considerable experience in attitudinal research. Plans were made to relocate the company to Huntsville, Alabama. In July, 1999, Heaton became President & CEO, with Founder Seich continuing as Executive Vice-President. The company was incorporated in the state of Alabama in August of 1999.

WHAT IS ANSIR?
The Profiling System

The *3 Sides of You* test and analysis comprise a Self-Perception Profiling System© (SPPS) that helps users identify dominant personality Styles in three realms, Thinking /Working and /Emoting. The analysis is based on four years of research and over five years of online testing. It is the only Self-perception work to present the 3-sided complexity of individuals and to recognize intuitive and spiritual personality Styles. Unlike personality assessment instruments, which quantify personalities into overall groupings, *3 Sides of You* recognizes 2,744 personality Style combinations.

The test is founded on the ancient premise that humans are 3-sided beings. Philosophers and spiritualists have long-espoused similar convictions. Plato's vision of Reason-Passion-Appetite is similar to the Bible's Mind, Body, Soul. Ansir prefers practical functioning divisions of Thinking /Working /Emoting.

Thinking: A discernible, predictable pattern of acquiring, balancing, and applying knowledge. How each individual processes order, solves problems, and rationalizes outcomes.

Working: The conscious expression and application of knowledge according to acquired and innate attributes.

Emoting: An unconscious response pattern guided by unique intangibles such as emotions, feelings, and nature.

The 3-sided Profile functions as a supportive and cohesive whole. Ansir believes that traditional and current testing models that quantify the parts into one all-encompassing personality Style tend more to frustrate individuals than build self-confidence. Individuals know they are more complex. Ansir research and testing show that few individuals operate the same in all three major realms of functioning.

The 14-base personality Styles form seven distinct groupings. Each group has two Ansir personality Styles.

Core Functioning	Personality Style
Physicals...	Extremist & Realist
Instinctives...	Scintillator & Sentinel
Logicals...	Diligent & Sage
Practicals...	Eccentrik & Idealist
Emotionals...	Kinsmen & Empath
Intuitives...	Visionary & Evokateur
Spiritualists...	Healer & Philosopher

An individual whose Self-Perception testing reflects *Evokateur* Thinking Style, *Healer* Working Style, and *Empath* Emoting Style would refer to themselves as being Ansir Profiled:

Evokateur /Healer /Empath

All that Ansir learns will in future, as now, be freely shared with those who'll benefit most from this work: individuals striving to fulfill their self-determined and desired goals of success and happiness in their lifetime.

HOW DOES ANSIR?

Research, Analyze, Conclude?

The *3 Sides of You* test and analysis are based on the experience of its creator (S. Seich) and were developed using what the company believes are the oldest, non-coercive, least prejudicial, and intrinsically reliable research methodologies in existence: talking and listening. The universe for the research was the Internet. 16,000 people signed up for email discussions via an electronic magazine (ezine), *Mankind*, started in 1996. (It should be noted that the Internet was in its infancy at the time, and access to it was limited.)

Over the course of one year, responses to numerous statements, conditions, behaviours, situations, relationships, thoughts, scenarios, and test questions were solicited. Responses were grouped and weighed, with revisions placed on the Website for subsequent comment and response by the group. The final stage of this research involved placing the entire test online and testing responses from the base group. The *Mankind* Website was redesigned and programmed to exclusively beta test Ansir's test and material on the wider Internet market. Cross validation took place over the course of the following year. 58,000 testers, 6-revised tests, 4-complete book revisiona, and *"Ansir for One, 14 Rare Conversations"* was published in October, 1998. Since then, expanded research and member requests required further addition and more indepth explanation, resulting in a final revision entitled *"3 Sides of You."*

Ansir acknowledges that only the most informal of research methods were applied in the development of the test and analysis. This was a deliberate attempt to seek a product outside that normally offered by the professional psychological community. It is the company's belief that the test is valid on its face and therefore reliable as a measurement of Self-perception. Moreover, the company believes that the use of the *3 Sides of You* test as a self-help tool increases the likelihood of its reliability, because users are predisposed to be honest in answering the questions, thereby overcoming the greatest obstacle to reliability in traditional personality testing. (*Reliability and validity measures available upon request*).

WHERE IS ANSIR LOCATED?

Main Offices

Ansir Communications Inc.

102A Wynn Drive

Huntsville, Alabama 35805, USA

Contact us

E-mail: info@ansir.com

Website: http://www.ansir.com

TRADEMARKS

Trademarks of Ansir Communications Inc.

The stylized A in the Ansir logo
Ansir
Ansir Communications
Ansir.com
3 Sides of You
A New Style in Relating
Unlocking how you think, work, and love
Darius Quinn
Profile Boss
Life Purpose
Achilles' Heel
Headhunter Shorthand
Match/Mismatch
Heart/Broken Heart (art)
The lock (art used with the Ansir logo)
The community with personality
WorkforceDNA
All Ansir Profile Styles:

Diligent	*Philosopher*
Empath	*Eccentrik*
Extremist	*Sentinel*
Visionary	*Sage*
Healer	*Kinsmen*
Idealist	*Realist*
Scintillator	*Evokateur*

One door closes,
Another door opens...

3 Sides Of You is the definitive groundwork for Ansir's "people" premise, and the last, completing step of level one work. Beginning this 20th day of May, 2000, my focus will be on the NEXT personality challenge, "Style compatibilities" —how these 14-personalities Styles interact with one another in everyday, real life.

You may have noticed the unusual format of this book, where corporate and author information are at the back of the bus, so to speak. That's pretty much the role Ansir staff and corporation adopts and prefers. Having been through the Ansir experience, you more readily understand why we insist on a non-leader, non-interfering role. You see, we don't want to change the world; we want you to! Our responsibility ends at providing as much practical truth as we can, so you can find your own reasons for making the changes in your life that matter.

One cannot do this kind of intimate people work, without realizing how creative, interesting, and powerful people are...even at the admittedly small core of understanding offered here. (Each Style could have been a book and lifetime study on its own). Another realization born of this work—there's much more to people than what first greets or is initially offered, and why we flat-out state that our corporate and personal objectives are one and the same: to remove reticence off the face of the Earth. A common saying is that "money is the root of evil." Our people-experience has proven otherwise. Money can't cripple confidence, can't snuff creativity, and can't kill love near as efficiently or quickly as reticence can. If such a money vs. reticence race were run, Ansir would place every spare nickel on that "dark horse" and be confident of winning. What's *not said* destroys more people than money does, we've found.

Some contend that mystery adds to relationship allure, so they refrain from two-way sharing of innermost thoughts and desires, effectively keeping Others at ignorance-distance from self. Some contend that the more Others know, the greater the arsenal that can be used against them in the future. Ansir contends that the only present or future mystery worth spit is what each strives for and achieves in their lifetime, rather than the "who" of their being. The better others know you, the better your chances of achieving desired success and deserved happiness. This book exists because of the willing effort of many—an oft-found, oft-seen phenomena. Every successful and happy person Ansir's met is indebted to many, and they acknowledge others with ready thanks and appreciation for their support along the way.

As unique as each of us certainly is, we share core commonalities, not the least of which is being plain old, two-eyed, two-eared, one-nosed human. Profile Styled success and happiness are Ansir's specialized, narrow focus. Personal success and happiness are the plainest and oldest human strivings throughout history and probably why there've been so many like-striving companions at each point in time. There has to be good and important reasons for such diversity between people, yet their similarity too. *Nothing live on this planet* is as complex or complicated as the people who populate it.

We've tested online, through the Internet, these past four years. Regardless of participant location (126 countries currently), ages, gender, occupation, or religion, Ansir cores are recognized and apply equally. Why withhold anything of self, from others? The more you know about self and others about you, the better off all will be.

May the mystery of personal accomplishment be the only mysterious or unknown thing about You! As *Ansir* Healers propose and promote, there are no coincidences and no mistakes. Wherever you are and whomever you're with are *musts* for some self-important reason. The good and bad experiences you've had, were had for a reason. What and Why are yours to figure out and to do something with or about. If experience picked you out from the crowd there's a good and important reason for that. Only you can or could know why.

His name is Kurt. He's been thoroughly tested and measured, and is ranked among the smallest handful of superior intellects. Kurt stumbled across Ansir's site and test in 1998. Despite the many tests and challenges presented to him over the years, he discovered something that educators and others hadn't realized about him. I've written thousands and thousands of words over the years about individual Profiles and Ansir material. What's rewarding is to hear how people have taken this wordy work and translated it to fit themselves, and applied the principles to their everyday lives, in their own inimitable way. Ansir endeavours to provide the cleanest and most practical truth for each to freely do what they wish, want, or may.

We don't offer you step-by-step plans on how to be successful or happy, and you shouldn't expect to see an Ansir lecture visiting your hometown anytime soon. Such is counterproductive to all we stand for and encourage. Trust You to know what's right and best. Take what feels right from this work of human respect and love, and use to own best advantage and benefit. Ignore the rest! You don't need us or anyone else, to tell you how to live a meaningful and fulfilling life, as defined and desired by you. Our goal is to cut away extraneous crap so you can see for yourself what we've seen, admired, and respected about you; things that you may not have heard before, but may benefit from knowing. Here's Kurt's view of his Ansir experience (reprinted with permission.)

"The site provides comfort and solace to those not feeling at ease, by letting them get to know themselves in a new way, shedding whole-istic light on the personality they know and love, but, being inside it, cannot see in all its complexity.

Finding out Self, and finding oneself already known, and tenderly described, is a healing process, to those who thought themselves outcasts, rejects, flotsam and jetsam on the socio-cultural stream.

It's a sort of homecoming, a realization that the personally perceived "weirdness" is actually part of a larger ongoing, perhaps Aquarian, phenomenon, that one can fly one's weird colors proudly, and join the ranks of those capable of social change.

I don't see personality as a static thing: it appears to evolve as time goes by; it's more dynamic than say, genetics. For a first guesstimate, I would hazard that it's a 'stance': the sum-total of all of one's lifelong reactions to events puts one in an anticipatory 'stance' pending new events. It's how one is poised to react to the next thing that comes along, based on how one has successfully reacted in the past.

The wording of this next paragraph has gone through at least 2-dozen revisions, trying to nail down the thought that occurred to me:

There is a power in Ansir, to change humanity for the better. With behavior mod (modification), one can attempt to change one's basic reactions to events. If one is shifting from one Ansir style to another, one can attempt to adopt *any* of the personality *styles, with a little effort. For, given that any one person displays any given style, then that style is potentially available for all people.*

If one's personal stance is not fulfilling, one can seek out and adopt a more suitable one. This is a power not to be underestimated. To change from a fearful and defensive posture, to one where one's greatest desire is for harmony, and an active seeking of that harmony, is to change from a passive acceptance of injurious events, to a lifetime of changing the worse for better.

As custodians of the knowledge of the types, ones responsibility becomes making them accessible to the widest variety of people; Ansir is on the right track in choosing poetic imagery, for reasons I don't have to enumerate."

Kurt's Profile: Evokateur/Eccentrik/Evokateur

In conclusion:

Again, "Thank You," for purchasing *3 Sides Of You*. I, we, look forward to further and more with you at the Website. Right now you may be at the point of focusing on your own Profile and the Profiles of those closest to you. In time your view will change. As familiarity grows and the patterns of this book unfold into your everyday reality, you'll inevitably come to a rather extraordinary realization. When you do and if you'd like, please write us to discuss further, what you, alone, discover. Till then and meanwhile, test and stretch yourself hard. You won't break! Much is needed and much needs to be done *out there*. We've both got responsibilities that are yet to be met and serious fun not yet begun. Before either of our days' end, let's leave a dent of difference behind us, as proof of our having been at all. Trust you first, last, and only, to know by feel what's best and most right for you.

Yours sincerely *as always,*

S. Seich,
Founder, author,
Executive V.P.,
Ansir Communications Inc.
http://ansir.com

B

C

E

F

G

H

     http://www.ansir.com

M

http://www.ansir.com

http://www.ansir.com

T

V

http://www.ansir.com

W

(Cont'd from Introduction)...excerpts from "Ansir-in-Action" at ansir.com

Diligent /Visionary/ Sentinel—Profile Boss: Visionary

"The test and analysis said my profile wasn't a people-person, and that just set me free," he said. "It got me to thinking and gave me a path to get away from that and to do something more in-line with what I should be doing." Bill sold his store and went into computer programming. He works a 4-day work week and is "genuinely happy for the first time in my life."

Sage /Eccentrik/ Philosopher—Profile Boss: Philosopher

"The world was beating me down, and I began to have difficulties with my marriage and on-the-job." Ken found himself in a constant state of irritation over supervisors who, "didn't have a technical or managerial clue." His first encounter with Ansir was in June of 1999. "I got excited about it, because it was more useful than Kiersey or MBTI. Ansir has helped me get back in touch with what I knew about myself but had lost touch with. It's given me a forum to listen to what other people are saying and to realize what my real motivations are—which is exactly what Ansir's Life Purpose of a Philosopher is—to help people see themselves for who they really are and in so doing allowing them opportunities for themselves."

Idealist /Eccentrik/ Eccentrik—Profile Boss: Eccentrik

Katy was web-surfing one night, and surfed onto the Ansir test and was profoundly shocked by her Eccentrik profile InDepth. "I read my own profile and it was like.......Where did they find this? Reading that was like an explanation of WHY I am the way I am. This was the first place that had a word for me other than "freak", and the first time I actually realized completely, without a doubt, and once and for all that people like me had a purpose in the world other than giving perpetual headaches to authority figures."

Printed in the United States
5075